COOKIES, COLESLAW, AND STOOPS

Nicoline van der Sijs

Cookies, Coleslaw, and Stoops

The Influence of Dutch on the North American Languages

Amsterdam University Press

The publication of this book has been made possible by the support of The Nederlandse Taalunie (Dutch Language Union).

A Dutch version of this book is also available, titled *Yankees, cookies en dollars. De invloed van het Nederlands op de Noord-Amerikaanse talen*, ISBN 978 90 8964 130 4.

Translation: Piet Verhoeff and Language Unlimited.
Cover Design: Kok Korpershoek and Jonatan van der Horst
Book Design: Kok Korpershoek and Femke Lust

ISBN 978 90 8964 124 3
E-ISBN 978 90 4851 042 9
NUR 624/632

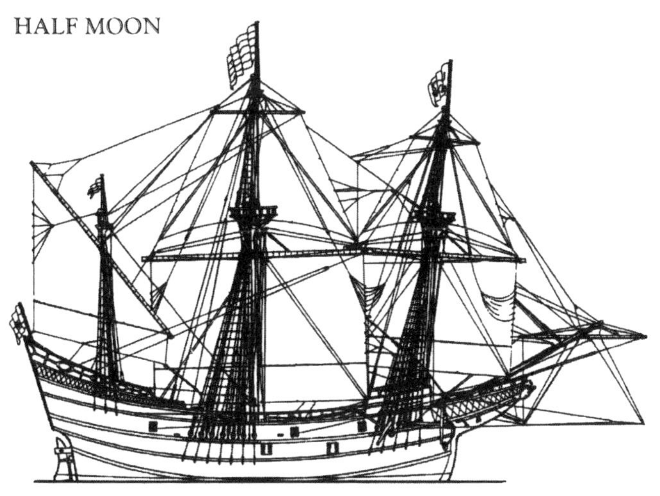
HALF MOON

Contents

Preface

In 1609 the first Dutchmen, Flemings, and Frisians landed on the American East Coast; they brought with them their culture, customs, and religion, and, of course, their language, too. The Dutch language was to remain the official language of the East Coast for half a century. Although the Dutch colony was taken over by the English in 1664, Dutch managed to hold its own surprisingly long in the United States. Four centuries have passed in the meantime – which is what we celebrate in this "Hudson year" – and up to this day, the Dutch traces in the North American languages have not been wiped out. This book describes why that is and what those traces are. It will become abundantly clear that there have been special linguistic and cultural ties between the Low Countries and the United States for a very long time.

At first, Dutch immigrants came to the East Coast of America to trade with the Native Americans. They brought furs back with them to Europe, and in exchange they took all kinds of Dutch products with them to the New World. Much of that was new to the Native Americans, who adopted the Dutch terms for these items, adding them in their languages. In chapter 3, 69 Dutch loanwords that were borrowed by one or more North American Indian languages will be discussed.

When New Netherland was annexed to New England in 1664, English began to compete heavily with Dutch as the primary language in the area. Dutch remained in use for quite a while, however; this was true in (originally) Dutch circles, as well as outside of them. Despite this, Dutch eventually lost more and more ground to English. Just when most Dutch descendants had exchanged Dutch for English, halfway through the nineteenth century, a second wave of Dutch, Flemish, and Frisian immigrants arrived and settled in several American states, bringing Dutch and Frisian to the American continent once more. Some of them quickly exchanged their native language for English, others stuck to Dutch or Frisian. Chapter 1 describes the fates of the Dutch, Flemish, and Frisian languages in relation to both the first and the second wave of immigrants. There are significant similarities between the ways in which the Dutch of the two waves has developed, and the domains where it has held out the longest. Possibly the most spectacular aspect of this process is that many speakers were so devoted to their native language that they passed it on from generation to generation. Even now, it seems that many Americans are very proud of their Dutch roots, despite the fact that so few of them can speak Dutch nowadays: "If you ain't Dutch, you ain't mu(t)ch" has become a stock phrase, often found printed on cards, T-shirts, and plaques.

Both the English and the Dutch languages have developed in America, independently of European English and Dutch. On the American continent, new words were made or borrowed for specific geographical circumstances, indigenous animal and plant species, individual social and cultural developments, and technical innovations. New phrases were developed, and the language went its own way in spelling and grammar.

Language became an issue when the US declared its independence from Great Britain in 1776. The newly independent country tried to forge its own identity and its own form of government to differentiate itself from its former mother country. In order to distance itself as much as possible from Great Britain and everything connected with it, the Americans came to stress the differences between the English and the American culture and language. This is probably also a reason why English has never been accepted as the official language of the US. Despite this, in actuality, English had become the principal colloquial language in the young US. In order to distinguish themselves linguistically, too, from the erstwhile mother country, the Americans decided not to regard the peculiarities of the American language as mistakes any longer but as characteristics of their own national language. For these expressions, words, and phrases that were typical of America, John Witherspoon, head of Princeton University and one of the signatories of the Declaration of Independence, invented the term *Americanisms* in 1781.

Now it was official: American English was different from British English, and that was something of which to be proud. To make the difference between the two languages even greater, the lexicographer Noah Webster proposed to introduce a special American spelling in 1789, making it clear directly from the form of the words whether a text was written in American English or in British English. In this way, the spelling deviations that had been used in the US for a long time – and that had been regarded as spelling mistakes up until then – could now be used as evidence of America's own national identity.

And that is what happened – from the nineteenth century onward, articles and monographs, and especially dictionaries, were published in which the unique character of American English and the Americanisms were described. Among the special items was the introduction of loanwords from languages of groups of immigrants, for example, from the Low Countries. These loanwords did not occur in British English, or did so only later, sometimes through American English. Chapter 2 describes which words American English borrowed from Dutch. There are about 246 words which, for the most part, are still in use: some of these are used very generally, others only regionally, and a small group of words are used only as historical terms.

This collection of loanwords gives a fascinating picture of the contacts between Dutch and English speakers on the American continent. It testifies to the long-lasting cultural influence exerted by the Dutch. It will not come as a surprise that words used by the colonists to describe the new landscape and hitherto-unknown plants and animals, have lived on in American English. The Dutch language has left its mark on everyday American life, too, with words for food, beverages, household goods, clothing, and other similar articles. A number of social customs and social institutions have been defined in part by notions that have their roots in Dutch culture and politics. The trade contacts resulted in a number of terms related to trade, units of money, and measure, as well as transportation by both sea and land. Surprisingly, there are also a few loanwords originating from children's language and slang.

The use of Dutch loanwords will be illustrated with quotations; from the quotations it will become clear how long these words have played a role in American English: the first quotation provided in the texts is always the earliest-known instance of usage. From the dates of the quotations it can be gathered whether the word was borrowed from the first or the second wave of Dutch immigrants.

The collection in chapter 2 contains only those loanwords mentioned in multiple sources. Obscure Dutch loanwords mentioned in only one or two American English sources without elucidation have not been included. There are a number of lists of Dutch loanwords in circulation that have been copied endlessly – most of them derived from Mencken's three-volume *The American Language* or from an article by W.H. Carpenter (1908-1909). Thus, the Dutch loanwords *connalyer* "crowd" (from Dutch *canaille* "mob"), *coss* "chest (of drawers)" (from Dutch *kast*), and *klainzaric* "untidy" (from Dutch *kleinzerig* "over-sensitive") are said to have been used in American English; these words have not, however, been included in any of the dictionaries of Americanisms, nor are they mentioned in the *Dictionary of American Regional English* – we do not know anything about their function, or by whom, when, or how they were used. It's possible that these are ghost words; for this reason, these words have been excluded from this work.

It might seem impossible that 246 Dutch loanwords could have a particularly significant impact on American English – but don't be deceived. The situation of the Dutch language in the US can be called unique: right from the start, the Dutch formed a very small minority among the inhabitants of America – even in New Netherland there were people with many other nationalities and mother tongues in addition to the Hollanders. Nevertheless, this small group of Dutchmen managed to exert a lasting influence on the American language and culture. The scope of the linguistic inheritance of the Dutchmen is not in proportion to the number of speakers. The American linguist Charlton Laird claimed in 1972: "More words per capita have been borrowed into American English from [the] early Hollanders than from any other sort of non-English speakers."

The size of the Dutch share in American English becomes clear when the Dutch influence on American English is compared with that on British English. In the *Oxford Dictionary of English Etymology*, about 500 British English words have been included that derive directly from Dutch, of which the earliest, such as *dam*, date from the twelfth century. The contacts with British English, then, lasted for nine centuries. Because of the small distance, the contacts between England and the Low Countries were frequent and occurred under all sorts of circumstances: trade, wars, travels, immigration, literature. The contacts with American English, on the other hand, span "only" a mere four centuries, the number of Dutchmen involved was small, and the situations were limited. Despite these factors, the figures show that Dutch's influence on American English was proportionally – let's say yearly – greater than its impact on British English. This is because the Dutch and the American languages and cultures mixed in the US, making the contacts much more intensive than the superficial contacts between Brits and Dutchmen. Incidentally, the mother tongue of the Britons coming to America contained a variety of Dutch loanwords which had been borrowed in Great Britain at an earlier stage. Such words will not be discussed in this book, for the Dutch loanwords in British English tell us nothing about the linguistic and cultural influence of the Dutch on the North American continent.

The number of German immigrants that have come to the US over the years is considerably larger than that of Dutchmen and, in turn, they have provided more loanwords for American English. Some words that Dutch and German have in common have been brought to the US both by Dutch and by German immigrants – this will be indicated, where necessary, in chapter 2. No words from Pennsylvania Dutch – a language spoken within Mennonite and Amish communities in Pennsylvania, Indiana, and Ohio – have been included. Contrary to what the name suggests, Pennsylvania Dutch is a variety of German, not Dutch, and its speakers call their language *Pennsylvania Deitsch* or *Pennsilfaanisch Deitsch*. This *Deitsch*, a variant of *Deutsch*, has been anglicized to *Dutch*, hence the confusing name *Pennsylvania Dutch*.

Finally, a word of thanks. This book has been produced at the request of the Dutch Language Union and with a subsidy from the Ministry of Education, Culture, and Science – and I would like to thank both these institutions. Several people have read the early sketches of this book and have made important suggestions. I owe a debt of gratitude to Sybe Bakker, Hans Beelen, Jan van den Berg, Joan Houston Hall, Jan Noordegraaf, and Piet van Reenen. Additionally, Van Cleaf Bachman, Peter Bakker, Willem Frijhoff, Jaap van Marle, Rob Naborn, Christine Valk, and William Vande Kopple have supplied me with useful information. Piet Verhoeff and Language Unlimited have translated the text. A Dutch version is published too, titled *Yankees, dollars en cookies. De invloed van het Nederlands op de Noord-Amerikaanse talen*. Ed Schilders chose the illustrations, which are an important contribution to the text.

PRINTING THE NAME "AMERICA" IN 1507

Engraving of a printery at the moment when the name America *appears in print for the first time, in 1507. In that year, the German-French cartographer Martin Waldseemüller (in the centre of the engraving) ordered the first map of the world that showed the whole American continent to be printed in Saint-Dié, with the title* Universalis cosmographia secundum Ptholemaei traditionem et Americi Vespuccii aliorumque lustrationes *(A drawing of the whole earth following the tradition of Ptolemy and the travels of Amerigo Vespucci and others). America was, of course, named after the explorer Amerigo Vespuccci. In May, 2003, the Library of Congress managed to acquire the only remaining copy of this map. (Source: The Printing Art, Vol. 4, # 5, Jan. 1905).*

CHAPTER 1.

The Dutch language in North America

1.0 "The last real speaker of the dialect"

Every good story has at least one villain. Fortunately for our story, but unfortunately for linguistic scholarship, the history of the Dutch language on the American East Coast also has its villain. What is more: that history ends with him. His name is Lawrence Gwyn van Loon.

Van Loon was born in New York City in 1903, and he died in the village of Gloversville, New York, in 1985. When he was a boy, his maternal grandfather, Walter Hill, taught him the *tawl*, the Dutch that at that time was still spoken in the Mohawk Valley. During his holidays, together with his father and his grandfather, the young Van Loon would visit a number of older people who still had some command of the *tawl*. That was the beginning of Van Loon's lifelong relationship with the Dutch language. But already during the days of his secondary education, as he wrote in 1980, "things got ... a bit blurry ... but at least skeletons remained." While a medical student, he spent the summers of 1930 and 1932 in the Netherlands, at the Wilhelmina Hospital in Amsterdam, "where I quickly found that what I knew from Gramp and all the others was an oddity (to say the least)." Here he also met his Dutch wife-to-be, Grietje Prins, whom he married in 1932. He set up practice as a general practitioner in Reading, Pennsylvania. At home, Dutch was the language spoken with his wife and children.

The interest in the Dutch language spoken on the American East Coast that was awakened in his youth remained with Van Loon during the rest of his life. He devoted several publications to it, starting in 1938 with the book *Crumbs from an Old Dutch Closet. The Dutch Dialect of Old New York*. It was published by Martinus Nijhoff, a prestigious publisher in The Hague. Van Loon describes Mohawk Dutch, the dialect he had heard spoken in the Mohawk Valley in his youth. Interestingly, nowhere in the book is any account given of how the material was collected, nor of who the informants involved were; what we do find are a few quotations by a certain "Mr. and Mrs. Dewitt Link" about halfway through the work. In 1939, two articles by Van Loon appeared in influential periodicals, *Onze Taaltuin* and *Eigen Volk*, both of which were published under the auspices of the Royal Dutch Academy of Sciences. The first article dealt with Jersey Dutch, a relic of Dutch in New Jersey, and the second with Dutch cultural traces on the American East Coast.

As recently as the year 2000,Van Loon's 1938 book was characterized by an American linguist as "one of the most cited sources on the structure of the Dutch dialect of upstate New York and its late survival." That is not surprising: it was the first and only description of Mohawk Dutch. In 1975, Van Loon presented himself in a letter to the Dutch-American authority on the Dutch language, W. Lagerwey, as "probably the last speaker of this type of Dutch, which he had heard and learned in his youth."

Without doubt at the instigation of Van Loon, the historian Van Cleaf Bachman repeated this in 1980 when he called Van Loon "the last real speaker of the dialect." In that year, 1980, Van Loon published a story in Mohawk Dutch, "Het Poelmeisie," which he remembered from his youth. He had heard the story, about a boy who was tempted by a beautiful woman to step into a pool and then subsequently drowned, around 1915 from "Mrs. Dewitt Lynck of Glenville Village, New York." In her introduction to the story, the historian Alice Kenney writes that the story is of great importance because "the possible contributions of Hudson Valley Dutch folklore to American literature have gone unrecognized because so little was known about them."

The jubilant mood over the description of the last phrases of spoken Dutch on the American East Coast changed to one of deep mistrust in the course of the 1980s, when it was established that other work by Van Loon, also relating to relics of Dutch settlers on the East Coast, was based on forged documents – we shall come back to this later. Retrospectively, all Van Loon's work and all the documents he had handled became suspect.

From investigations by, among others, Charles T. Gehring (which will be discussed below), it has appeared that Mrs. Dewitt Lynck, who is cited as a source both in the *Crumbs* and in "Het Poelmeisie," was of Scottish, not Dutch, descent: her maiden name was Mary Jane Lowe. Her former neighbors claimed she didn't know a word of Dutch. Moreover, the Dutch linguist Jaap van Marle says that the story "Het Poelmeisie" cannot possibly have been handed down orally for 300 years, because its style and

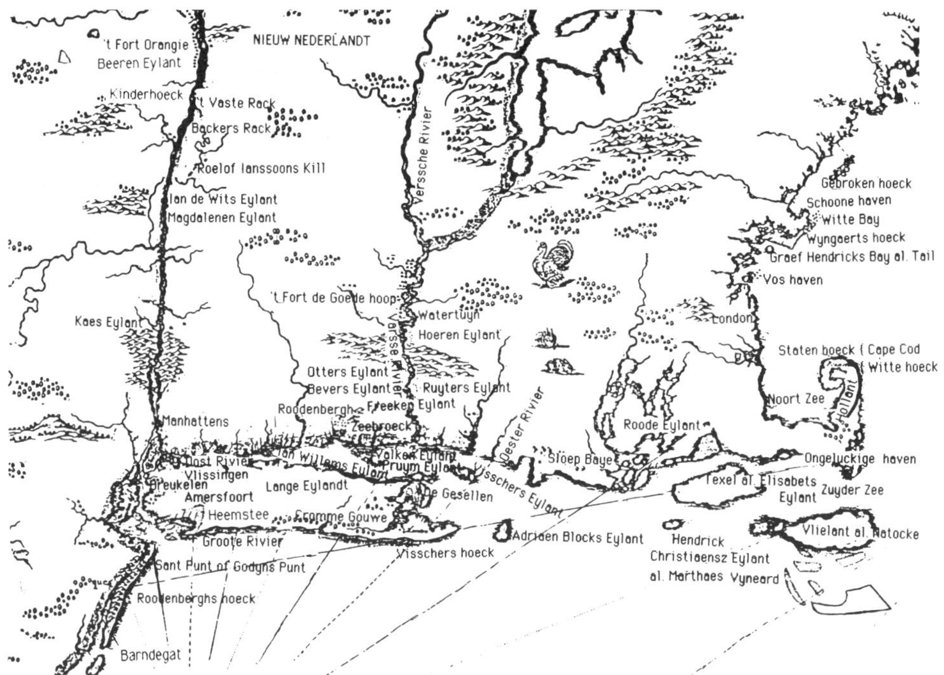

Illustration 1.1 – Based on the map of New Netherland by Nic. Joh. Visscher, published in 1655 by Justus Danckerts (source: Daan 1987: 66)

vocabulary are much too literary and artificial. He thinks the story has its roots in the romantic nineteenth-century fairy tales as collected by the Grimm brothers. What is fact and what is fiction in Van Loon's 1938 book and his articles from 1939 and 1980 is as yet difficult to establish – we shall have more to say about this later on. The fact that all these works were written at a time when "only skeletons remained" of the Dutch that Van Loon had heard in his youth, while for many years during his married life he spoke and heard contemporary twentieth-century Dutch, makes one fear the worst.

It is a fact that, as late as the early twentieth century, there were people living on the American East Coast who spoke a form of Dutch brought there by seventeenth-century Dutch settlers that had been handed down from generation to generation; this is testified by others, who unfortunately did not record the language. But let us go back to the beginning: the arrival of the Dutch language in America.

1.1 Dutch colonists and Native Americans

The Dutch language landed in North America in September 1609, when the English captain Henry Hudson sailed *De Halve Maen* up the river that was later to receive his name. By order of the United East Indian Company, he had gone to try and find a northern route to the Indies. Instead he found a densely wooded island that was eminently suitable to be a colony: Manna-hata. During this first expedition, the Dutchmen had already come into contact with groups of what they called "wild" people, the stereotypical name the Dutch used in far-away countries for the people they encountered there. But they were "amiable and well-mannered people," with whom they traded beads, knives, axes, dried currants, and beans for furs.

Dutch settlers were eager to find new suppliers of furs after the fur trade with Russia had collapsed due to the overhunting of beavers; they were very interested in North America, rich in game as it was. The Dutch also cast a greedy eye on the abundant American timberlands. After 1609, they continued to send new expeditions to further investigate the newfound territories. On a map from 1614, the explorer Adriaen Block, whose name we still find in Block Island, was the first to call the province *Nieuw-Nederland* (New Netherland), thus claiming it for the Dutch. On the map he also drew the *Lange Eylandt* (nowadays known as Long Island) and Manhattan.

At first, Dutch traders sailed to New Netherland and back with their products. For the fur trade with the Native Americans, several trading posts or factories were founded along the rivers – the first of these were Fort Nassau and, not far from there, Fort Orange (presently Albany), established in 1614 and 1624, respectively. From the deep interior, "river Indians" came in small boats to bring their products.

In 1621, Dutch traders founded the West Indian Company, which was given the monopoly of the trade with North and South America by the Dutch government. In 1624, colonists settled permanently in the area between the Zuydt River, the Noort River, and the Versche River – later called Delaware, Hudson, and Connecticut – and New Netherland became a Dutch province with Dutch as its official language.

A year later, in 1625, the Dutch settled in Manhattan, the place that would evolve into the capital New Amsterdam. That is why the year 1625 is part of New York's municipal seal and is considered to be its date of settlement, although many historians think that another year would do more justice to historical reality – 1624, for example, when the first colonists arrived. In any case, it is only since 1977 that 1625 has been considered New York's official "birthday"; before that the year 1664 was seen as such.

In 1629 the West Indian Company set up *patroonships*. These enabled new colonies to be founded under the leadership of a *patroon* (see 2.4). The first *patroon* was Kiliaen van Rensselaer who founded *Van Rensselaerswijck*. In 1645 his former *scout* (see 2.4), Adriaen Cornelissen van der Donck, founded *Colen Donck*, or "Colony Donck." Van der Donck published *Beschryvinge van Nieuw-Nederlant* ("Description of New Netherland") in 1655, one of the first books about New Netherland, written by someone who had actually lived there. Another Dutchman who published about the New World from his own experience was Jacob Steendam, who lived in New Amsterdam from 1650 to 1662. His publications consisted of two long poems: the first, from 1659, was *Klagt van Nieuw-Amsterdam* ("New Amsterdam's Complaint"), in which the Republic of the Netherlands is charged with doing too little for the new colony; the second, "'t Lof van Nuw-Nederland" ("New Netherland's Praise"), was published in 1661. The two poems make him the first American poet.

These works, as well as other later books about New Netherland, indicate that the Dutch encountered a kind of nature in America that was new to them, with many thitherto unknown animals and plants. The Dutch were the first Europeans to name certain places, plants, and animals on the East Coast of America, and these Dutch names have often been preserved until the present (see 2.2 and 2.5).

Early "evidence" of the contacts between the Dutch and Native Americans

The Dutch settlers and Native Americans carried on a busy trade with each other, but until recently, hardly anything was known about their early contacts. This seemed to change when Lawrence G. van Loon, mentioned above, published an article in *The Indian Historian* in 1968 entitled "Tawagonshi, the Beginning of the Treaty Era." In it, Van Loon gave the text of a treaty concluded between Dutch and Native American traders, written in seventeenth-century Dutch on two pieces of animal hide and dated 21 April 1613. The opening words were "Here on Tawagonshi ...," and it was signed by two Dutch traders, Jacob Eelckens and Hendrick Christiaenssen, and four Iroquois Indians, "chiefs of the Long House," called GarhatJannie, Caghneghsattakegh, Otskwiragerongh, and Teyoghswegengh.

From this early colonization period, not a single contract between European traders and Native Americans from North America was known. The discovery, therefore, was sensational, and the publication caused quite a stir. But straightaway, there were doubts, too, about its authenticity – and these were more than justified.

In the 1980s, critical linguistic and historical investigations by, among others, Charles T. Gehring, director of the New Netherland Project of the New York State

Library, brought to light so many anomalies that it has become clear by now that the document was not written in 1613, but somewhere in the middle of the twentieth century. It had already been discovered that the names of the chiefs were really Iroquois place-names that could be found in several modern handbooks. It also appeared that the seventeenth-century Dutch prose text contained compounds which did not exist in that period at all. The letters of the manuscript either suggest that they were written laboriously and unnaturally, or they show modern, non-seventeenth-century characteristics. Also, the signatures of the two Dutch traders are by one and the same hand, and that of Jacob Eelckens does not agree with an authentic signature preserved in the Amsterdam City Archives. Finally, it would appear that the text was not written with a quill and not on pieces of hide but on paper – but that is difficult to prove. As it is, the original treaty cannot be found and has not been seen by anyone but Van Loon. Van Loon claimed that he had left it with two chiefs of the Onondaga in 1978, but on inquiry it turned out that this cannot be the original treaty, for it was written on paper and not on pieces of hide. A photocopy of the treaty, which Van Loon in his article claims to be in the archives of the American Indian Historical Society, has never been found.

Research done by Gehring and others also revealed that Van Loon had been trying to peddle his manuscript since 1959; however, prospective publishers were hesitant or sceptical, and the manuscript remained unpublished. In 1960, Van Loon even offered the treaty to the state of New York, for an amount of five figures, but the purchase again fell through because of doubts as to its authenticity. Eventually, Van Loon managed to get his manuscript published in 1968.

That the Tawagonshi Treaty is a fake is by now an irrefutable fact. Unfortunately, various sites on the Internet still refer to it as "the First Treaty In Land and Resources Records." Two things still remain unclear: first, where did the treaty come from? Van Loon did not commit himself, maintaining only that he got it from someone "who was the agent on the Missisaqua Reservation in Canada many years ago." The second question, much more interesting, is: who was the forger? For the time being, it cannot be proved that that was Van Loon himself, but this seems to be an educated guess, especially so in view of later discoveries.

Van Loon's interferences with the history of the Dutch in North America have not been confined to the "earliest" treaty. Nearly twenty years earlier, in the *Dutch Settlers Society of Albany Yearbook* of 1939-1940, he had published a letter and a map purported to have been drawn by Jeronimus dela Croix, one of the three Dutch expedition members who explored the Mohawk Valley in the winter of 1634-1635 under the leadership of Harmen Meyndertsz van den Bogaert. This was a historical event, and Van den Bogaert kept an important journal at the time in which he registered, among other things, the earliest Mohawk word list – about 200 words. The letter and map by Dela Croix produced by Van Loon, however, were much more detailed than Van den Bogaert's journal, giving additional important historical information. After what we have described above, no one will be surprised to learn that these documents, too, were fakes. Another investigation by Gehring and others showed that they had been written with modern ink and a modern pen – albeit on old, perhaps seventeenth-century, paper. The handwriting of Dela Croix's fake letter and map resembles that of the Tawagonshi treaty, which in turn shows similarities to Van Loon's own handwriting. Other "discoveries" by Van Loon that proved to be false before publication were an early deed to Manhattan, a map of Albany from 1701, and a map of the Hudson River – with the latter, though, Van Loon denied any involvement.

We will meet Van Loon once more below, because the story of the Dutch language on the American East Coast is pervaded by his name.

A historic purchase

The West Indian Company had instructed the Dutch settlers to treat the Native Americans fairly and honestly, forbidding them expressly to meddle in interior matters. The fact was that the Native Americans with whom the Dutch settlers carried on trade, belonged to various tribes who regularly waged war with each other. On a narrow strip of land on the coast of what is now Connecticut lived the Pequot. The Delaware (Munsee and Unami), who called themselves Lenape, lived along the Delaware. The Mahican lived along the upper reaches of the Hudson River. The Mohawk or Iroquois lived around Lake Mohawk. The largest Iroquois tribe consisted of Seneca, who lived around what currently is called Seneca Lake.

There was much rivalry between the Mohawk and the Mahican in particular. In 1626, against all instructions, the Dutch settlers joined up with the Mahican, possibly in the hope of forming a useful alliance with them for the future, thus taking sides in the struggle among the Native American tribes. In the skirmishes, a few Dutchmen were killed. Additionally, as a result of this, the colonists deposed the then-leader of the colony, Willem Verhulst, and elected a new leader, Peter Minuit. For four years, Peter Minuit was governor of New Netherland. His name would long have been forgotten but for the fact that he played a major role in what proved, with hindsight, to be a historic event.

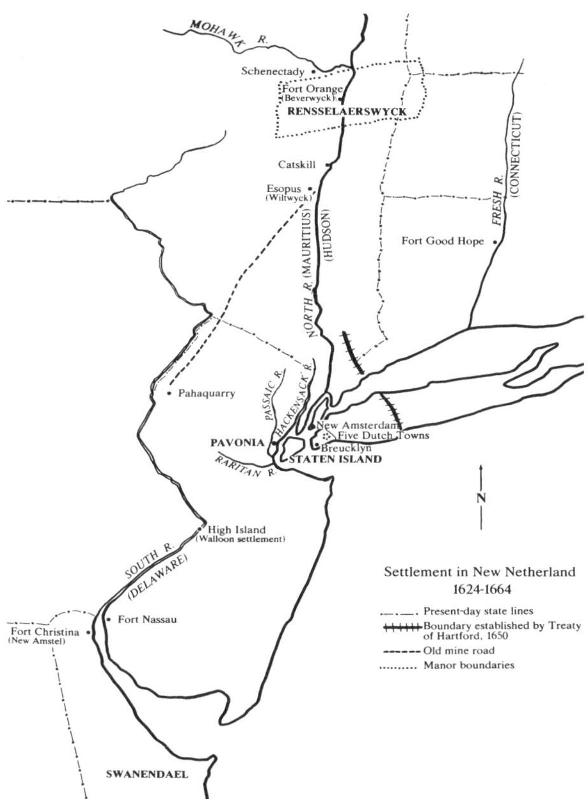

Illustration 1.2 – Settlement in New Netherland (source: Kenney 1975: 21)

Minuit judged that the small group of Dutch colonists should settle in a strategically situated, easily defendable spot, thus to be the better protected against possible attacks by other European colonial powers or by Native Americans.

He chose Fort Amsterdam, founded a year before on the southern part of the island of Manhattan. To be able to extend this, he bought the whole island in 1626 from the local American Indians, who were probably members of the tribe of the Lenape, in exchange for goods valued at 60 guilders. "Hebben t'Eylant Manhattes van de wilde gekoght voor de waerde van 60 gulden, is groot 11000 morgens" ("Have bought *t'Eylant Manhattes* from the natives at the value of 60 guilders; is 11,000 *morgens* large") was the laconic message to the States General. This purchase has become known as the most famous, cheapest, and most lucrative real estate transaction in history. It worked as a precedent as well: from that time on, European colonists regularly bought larger and smaller pieces of land from the Native Americans.

This purchase is often referred to as a sly move by the greedy Dutch, who fooled the guileless Native Americans with it. However, the story has by now been qualified, among others by Russell Shorto in his magnificent work from 2004, *The Island at the Center of the World. The Epic Story of Dutch Manhattan and the Forgotten Colony That Shaped America.* The Native Americans, who did not even live on the island, did not have the notion of legal ownership of land – they probably thought that they were leasing the land temporarily or that they were giving the Dutch the right to temporarily share the land with them. The amount in goods that was paid was, moreover, in agreement with the land price current at the time. In hindsight, however, now that the "priceless" metropolis of New York has been built on that site, the amount of 60 guilders may seem to be modest.

Fort Amsterdam became the center of the town of New Amsterdam, which rapidly developed into a busy seaport. Its population was not pleased, however, to see the neighboring colony of New England growing much faster: around 1650 there were about 50,000 colonists there, as compared with barely 7,000 in New Amsterdam. In addition, the colony suffered financial losses because of bad management as well as quarrels between inhabitants and governors, and between governors themselves. The States General in The Hague discussed the matter and decided to reorganize the colony. New Amsterdam was granted town privileges on 2 February 1653. A municipality was established, and all inhabitants received official citizenship: they became citizens of the Netherlands with all rights and duties, thereby attaining a direct interest in the community. They retained this status after the English took over, whereas in the home country England, only a small part of the cities' population had such rights. On 2 February 2003, "Charter Day" was celebrated, commemorating the 350th anniversary of the "birth" of New York City. New Amsterdam was significant in many aspects that have impacted American culture and politics. General citizenship, still an important vested right in North America, is thus one of the legacies of the Dutch. The American Dream – the opportunity for every American to rise

Illustration 1.3 – Chief Cornplanter – chief of the Seneca, with pipe (source: Wikimedia Commons, after a painting by F. Bartoli, 1796)

Illustration 1.4 – Native Americans of New Netherland (source: engraving from David Pietersz. de Vries, Korte historiael, 1655: 175)

from paper boy to millionaire, as the saying goes – can also be seen as having its origins in Dutch politics. The West Indian Company prohibited the formation of guilds in New Netherland, to avoid their becoming too influential, as was the case in the Low Countries, where workers were obliged to be members of the guilds. The direct consequence of this prohibition was that all trades and professions were open to everyone, and that everyone thus had the opportunity to climb the social ladder.

Conflicts with Native Americans

After the conflict of 1626, the Dutch made peace with the Mohawk. Later, however, new conflicts arose between Dutch colonists and groups of Native Americans, usually instigated by lack of understanding or suspicion. Thus, the then-governor Willem Kieft, after an incident in 1641 in which a colonist was killed, decided, against all good counsel, to start a war with the Wappinger or Wappani Indians. The Wappani were a Native American tribe that spoke a language closely related to that of the Lenape and the Mahican. Kieft's hidden agenda was to drive away the Native Americans, hoping to further extend the colony. Several tribes now joined forces and united against the Dutch. "Kieft's War," also called the "Wappinger War," lasted from 1643 to 1645. After both sides had suffered great losses, an armistice was reached in August 1645.

David Pietersz. de Vries was an eyewitness to this war. He was a *patroon* who, together with some other people, had founded two colonies in 1631 and 1638, first Swaanendael and later Vriessendael, that were both overrun by the Native Americans. De Vries tried to mediate between the Dutch and the Native Americans, and was very critical about the way in which the Native Americans were treated and about Kieft's methods. In 1643 he returned to the Netherlands, where in 1655 he published *Korte historiael ende journaels aenteyckeninge van verscheyden voyagiens* ("Short Historical Notes and Journal Notes of Various Voyages"). This is the first book that gives detailed information about the life of native North Americans (see 3.2). Among other things, he mentions that the Native Americans called the Dutch *Swannekens*, which in their language meant "people of the sea" or "people of the salt water."

In 1659 and again in 1663, the Dutch confronted the Esopus, a tribe of the Unami Delaware who lived in the neighborhood of the Dutch settlement Wiltwyck, halfway between New Amsterdam and Fort Orange. Those skirmishes went down in history as the First and Second Esopus Wars. In 1663, the Dutch called in the help of the Mohawk. Eventually, the war was ended, after the leader of the Esopus had been killed.

Conflicts with European competitors

The Dutch had much more to fear from other European powers in North America than from the indigenous population. This became apparent in 1664, when the English sailed into New Amsterdam, and director-general Peter Stuyvesant had to surrender the province to them. This incident was one of the causes of the Second English-Dutch War. During the peace negotiations in 1667, it was agreed that the English and the Dutch could keep the American colonies they had taken from each other. *In concreto*, this meant that the Netherlands could keep Suriname and surrounding territories in South America, and that New Netherland remained English. The shareholders of the West Indian Company welcomed this situation – they were more interested in the profitable slave trade from Africa to South America than in the fur trade, which was on the decline because of overhunting and farming by the North American colonists: Suriname for New Amsterdam – that was a profitable exchange for the Dutch.

It took another decade before the command of New Amsterdam was definitively transferred to the English. The English then gave New Amsterdam the new name of New York, after the English town and province, but especially after the new owner, the Duke of York, under whose leadership the colony resided. The English use of "New" in the place-name can be traced to Dutch influence, by the way, according to Stewart in his *Concise Dictionary of American Place Names*. Before that, the English hardly ever formed place-names with *New*, but after taking over New Amsterdam they embraced this Dutch practice. The English renamed Fort Orange and the nearby settlement Beverwyck to Albany, after the Duke of York's Scottish title: the Duke of Albany. Wiltwyck's new name became Kingston. The English made treaties with the Native American tribes and established the borders of the territories.

Illustration 1.5 – "Peter Stuyvesant's Army entering New Amsterdam", drawing by William Heath (1795-1840) for Diedrich Knickerbocker (Washington Irving), A History of New York *(source: Collection University Library Leiden (UBL HOTZ 3844))*

The period of Dutch supremacy in North America thus did not last long: from 1624 to 1664, the American East Coast was a province of the Netherlands, with Dutch as its official language. After that, English became the most important language on the East Coast, with the Dutch and the Native Americans adopting English as at least their second language. After some time for some of them, it even became their first language. The forty-year period of Dutch rule left its mark on the Amerindian languages spoken in the area of New Netherland, however, as can be seen from the number of loanwords in these languages (see chapter 3 for a survey of Dutch loanwords in Amerindian languages).

1.2 The Dutch language on the American East Coast: Low Dutch

New Netherland roughly comprised the present-day states of Connecticut, New York, New Jersey, Pennsylvania, and Delaware – a territory many times bigger than present-day Holland and Belgium combined. The population, however, was concentrated in several small regions, especially around New Amsterdam and Fort Orange. It could hardly be otherwise: the group of colonists was small. At the time when New Netherland fell into the hands of the English, the colony counted an estimated 9,000 to 10,000 inhabitants, of whom about 1,500 lived in New Amsterdam.

From the start, the small colony of New Netherland was home to people from all parts of the world with a host of mother languages – besides Dutch, among others High and Low German, Frisian, French, English, Norwegian, Swedish, Danish, and various Amerindian languages. In addition, there were a small number of slaves from Africa speaking various African languages as their mother tongue. The Dutch and the Dutch language formed the largest minority, and in New Amsterdam they were a significant majority. Those Dutch settlers spoke several Dutch dialects. At that time, there was as yet no uniform standard language. A written standard language was being developed in the seventeenth century in the Low Countries, but the spoken Dutch language continued to show many differences throughout the linguistic territory for centuries. A majority of the new colonists hailed from the provinces of North Holland and Utrecht and spoke their own dialect.

The spoken Dutch language of the American East Coast came to diverge from European Dutch, just as American English has come to be different from British English. One of the reasons for this was that the contact with European Dutch was largely severed after 1664; another reason was the influence of English. The overseas variant of Dutch in the course of time acquired the name *Leeg Duits*, *Laeg Duits*, *Laag Duits*, or *Low Dutch*. *Leeg* is a dialect variant of *Laag*. The origin of the term *Leeg Duits* is not certain. The historian Van Cleaf Bachman, who, as we hope to show, has played an important role in the research into this variety, suspects that the Dutch settlers had already begun to call their language *Leeg* or *Laag Duits* during their colonial days, to distinguish it from the civilized Dutch that was spoken in the church (*Nederduits* "Netherdutch" was at that time the usual term for the language later to be called *Nederlands*). The English term Low Dutch, he says, is a translation of *Leeg Duits*. I think, however, that it was the other way round – *Leeg Duits* was not found before the end of the nineteenth century, whereas the term *Low Dutch*, used to indicate the spoken Dutch language in the US, is much older. In the *Boston Gazette* of 8 October 1795, there is a reference to "A white Girl ... who talks good English, high and low Dutch." The term *Low Dutch* already existed in British English to refer to Dutch in Europe – *Low Dutch* was the English translation of *Nederduits* (in Dutch, *neder* means "low"). The definition of *Low Dutch* in American English probably was narrowed to mean "Dutch spoken language in the US," as opposed to the *High Dutch* (*Hoogduits*) of the Germans, the *Pennsylvania Dutch* for the spoken German of Pennsylvania, and the *Dutch* or *Holland Dutch* for Dutch in Europe. The speakers of *Leeg Duits* themselves usually called their language simply *de tawl*. In the course of the nineteenth century, they learned the English term *Low Dutch* for their language and translated it back into Dutch as *Leeg Duits* or *Laag Duits*. This is a good illustration of the English influence on Dutch on the American East Coast: people no longer knew that the Dutch equivalent of *Low Dutch* was in fact *Nederduits*, and so made a new translation.

The foundation for Low Dutch was laid in the period between 1640 and 1690, as was shown by linguist Anthony Buccini in 1995, in a study that was as beautiful as it was extensive. From 1640 onwards, the number of Dutch settlers on the American East Coast was substantial; after the English took over, hardly any Dutch colonists came there, and after 1690 many Dutchmen moved to regions in New Jersey and Albany. The linguistic differences within the whole area where Low Dutch was spoken were only minimal, which means that the language must have been formed before people moved away to the various regions, since speakers from the various regions had little contact with each other later on.

Within European Dutch there were substantial dialect differences, but wherever speakers of different dialects met, they adapted their speech for better communication. From Buccini's study it appears that on the American East Coast, and perhaps already in the northern Dutch towns where the colonists had lived, a strong dialect levelling took place in the seventeenth century that favored the dialect spoken in the cities of Holland and Utrecht, especially *Amsterdams*, and that the levelling continued in the new colony. The sound *a* in Low Dutch had a somewhat *o*-like pronunciation, which explains why a number of Dutch loanwords that are written with *-a-* in Standard Dutch were borrowed in American English with *-o-* or *-aw-*and *-au-* (cf. *boss*, *coleslaw*, and *crawl*. For more on these words, see chapter 2; for more examples of the sound change, see 2.16). The sound development of *a* had probably already occurred in *Amsterdams* and had then been brought to America by the colonists. In Standard Dutch, the *o*-like pronunciation came to be regarded as uneducated in later centuries, but because the contact between Low Dutch and Standard Dutch was broken, this pronunciation could become the normal one in Low Dutch. The diphthong in, for example, *taid* ("time") also comes from *Hollands* (most of the other dialects use *ie: tied* here). Finally, the pronoun of the second person singular *jij*, *je* (you) and of the third person plural *hullie* (they) also come from this dialect.

Buccini found no traces of an influence of Southern Dutch on Low Dutch – which earlier scholars such as dialectologist Jac. van Ginneken had assumed. This is confirmed by the form of the American-English loanwords from Dutch that are mentioned in

Illustration 1.6 – Drawing of a school class by Joel Altshuler (source: Storms 1964)

chapter 2 of this book: for example, they never have the southern diminutive ending *-(e)ke* (see **Yankee** in 2.4 and see 2.16).

Even though the Dutch were not in the majority in the Dutch colony, the Dutch language was predominant. According to Buccini this was due to a number of reasons: several non-Dutch colonists would have lived in Holland first for some time and would have learned Dutch there; Dutch was the official language in the colony both for the government and for the church, which stimulated people to learn the language; Dutch and non-Dutch persons married; and, finally, non-Dutch speakers had regular contacts with the dominant Dutch group because the population was concentrated in a few small areas. The result was that the non-Dutch majority adapted themselves to the Dutch and learned the Dutch language. This is also apparent from the fact that in the later vestiges of Dutch on the American East Coast, no influence from other languages such as German (High or Low) or French could be detected.

The Nederduits *of the Church*

In addition to the Low Dutch spoken language, the erstwhile Dutch colony knew another variety of Dutch: the *Nederduits* of the *Nederduits* Reformed Church – the congregation to which most Dutchmen belonged (see 2.7 for some other, smaller Protestant groups). As early as 1628, the first full-time dominie, Jonas Michaëlius, arrived on the East Coast and he was followed before long by the first schoolteacher, for the Dutch custom of having a "school with the Bible" was transported to America: all schools were linked with the Church. Services were conducted in Dutch, but the language used was the *Nederduits* of the Dutch Authorized Version, an archaic, highly formal language that deviated considerably from the daily spoken language (also from that in the Low Countries, for that matter). This *Nederduits* was taught in the Dutch schools. All dominies came from the Netherlands or had received their training there. In the Dutch services, Frenchmen and Walloons took part as well, as Michaëlius reported to Amsterdam in 1628, for there were few among them who did not understand the Dutch language.

When the Dutch transferred the control of their colony to the English, the Articles of Capitulation that were drawn up gave the Dutch a great many rights, among them the freedom of religion (see the introductions to sections 2.4 and 2.7). From 1696, therefore, the *Nederduits* Reformed Church of New York officially came under the classis of Amsterdam and not under the Anglican Established Church.

During the whole of the eighteenth century, the Reformed Church in the US tried to secure an independent position with regard to the mother church in the Netherlands. The first request to be allowed to found an independent classis or provincial church council was firmly rejected by the Amsterdam classis in 1709. As from 1754, however, an American branch was created, and it held regular meetings. Not everyone was happy about this development. In order to avoid a schism, the Articles of Union were passed in 1772, which established an independent position of the Dutch Reformed Church in North America with respect to the Amsterdam classis, while at the same time it was agreed officially that the policy of the Dutch Church was to be adhered to, and that there was to be regular close contact with Holland. This also implied that the rules of the Church were to be followed that were drawn up during the National Synod of Dordrecht in 1618/19, as well as the three articles of confession of the Reformed churches in the Low Countries, namely the Dutch Articles of Faith, the Heidelberg Catechism, and the dogmas of Dordrecht (the three Formularies of Unity).

In 1792, after the American Declaration of Independence, what was then called the Reformed Dutch Church in the United States of America drew up its own statutes. In 1819, the church changed its name to Reformed Protestant Dutch Church in North America. The "Dutch" was abandoned as late as 1867 and the name officially became "Reformed Church in America." That "Dutch" should have been retained all that time proves how much the church in America remained conscious of its Dutch roots.

The fact that the Dutch language and the Church remained so closely linked together for more than a century supported the preservation of Dutch in the US for a long time: Dutchmen who switched to English still had to learn Dutch to be able to follow the church services, if they remained members of the Dutch church – which is what most of them did. But everywhere, Dutch was pressured by English, even in the church. Still, things looked good at first for Low Dutch; one could even discern ground gained and new speakers.

Growth of Low Dutch

After New Netherland had been annexed to the English colony New England in 1664, hardly any new Dutch settlers came to the American East Coast. Many Englishmen came to the region, both from other areas of America and from England, and from other countries, too, people settled in and around New York. The Dutch segment in this city, where the Dutch used to form the majority, decreased to about 50 percent in 1703.

Under the pressure of the English, many Dutch people went from Manhattan and 't Lange Eylandt (Long Island) to new territories: to Albany, at the upper reaches of the Hudson River and the lower reaches of the Mohawk River, and to territories in New Jersey, such as the region around Bergen, and to Somerset County. What George Washington called "the Dutch Belt" reached from the north along the Hudson through New York to the Raritan River in the south, in New Jersey. Here, homogeneous communities developed, where people stuck to the Dutch language and church and to Dutch traditions and customs. It is estimated that in 1735, 90 percent of the 4,505 inhabitants of Somerset County and 25 percent of the 4,764 inhabitants of Middlesex

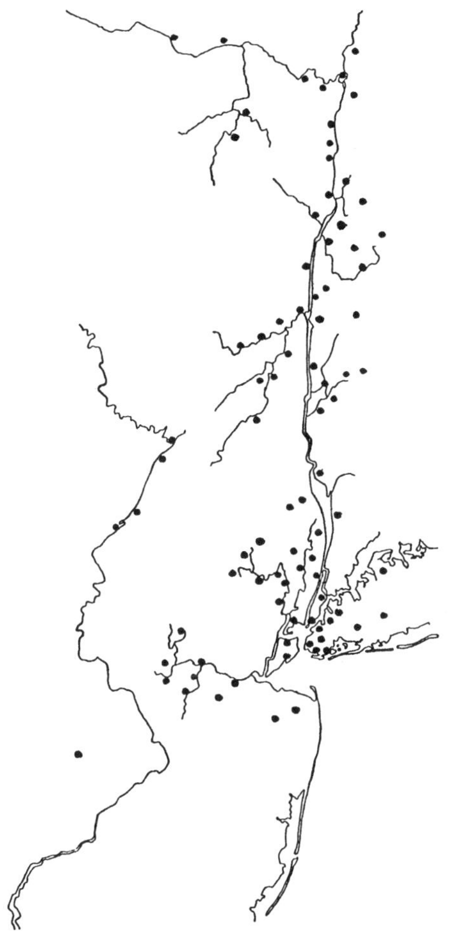

Illustration 1.7 – Distribution of Reformed Dutch Churches in 1775 (source: Bachman 1982: 3)

County consisted of Dutch people. The total population of eastern New Jersey, 26,500, consisted of about 50 percent Dutch people, as research by Vermeule has shown. As late as 1776, the sheriff found it difficult to find a sufficient number of English speakers in this area to compose a jury, as William Smith records in his *History of the Province of New York from the First Discovery*. In the second half of the eighteenth century, the Dutch inhabitants of big cities like Albany and Kingston formed a large majority, and they controlled the local administration.

And new Dutch speakers kept arriving as well. The families had more children than nowadays. Other colonists in areas where the Dutch had the upper hand, such as Englishmen, Frenchmen and Germans, often learned Dutch and often married into Dutch families. In the eighteenth century, many slaves, too, learned Dutch from their masters. This can be seen by the fact that advertisements regularly appeared in papers offering blacks as slaves with the recommendation that they knew Dutch. The Reformed Church also stimulated people to learn Dutch, for, since this church did not discriminate on the basis of race, many black people will have tried to better their standard of living by joining the church, journalist Lucas Ligtenberg says in his *De Nieuwe Wereld van Peter Stuyvesant* ("The New World of Peter Stuyvesant").

Loss of territory

Although at first the number of Low Dutch speakers was on the increase, the language came to be more and more crowded out by English in official circles. After the transfer of power to the English, the position of Dutch in official matters was taken over by English. In the justice system, Dutch was replaced by English. Richard Nicolls, the first English governor, successor to Peter Stuyvesant, immediately appropriated the Dutch archives. In 1683, it was decreed that from then on, all official documents in New York must be drawn up in English. In municipal documents, however, Dutch continued to be used in some regions for a long time: in Long Island, municipal archives were kept up in Dutch until the American War of Independence (1776), and in other townships, too, archives kept being written up in Dutch for some time, and people still reckoned by Dutch guilders and stivers (see 2.10).

But English became the general colloquial language, and the language for legislation and education – even to this day, the US has no official language. Dutch settlers, too, had to express themselves in English in their written contacts with the authorities, and for that purpose they had to learn passable English. And so, as an expedient for Dutch settlers, a unique linguistic guide appeared in 1730, *The English and Low-Dutch School-Master / De Engelsche en Nederduytsche School-Meester* by Francis Harrison, a schoolteacher in Somerset County, New Jersey. The book was published by William Bradford in New York and it is the only Dutch-English language guide printed in the US before 1800. Although Harrison claims that the book is written for both English and Dutch speakers, it is clear from the contents that the book is intended especially for speakers of Dutch in North America wanting to learn English, since the book contains only a grammar of English, not of Dutch, and the glossary and most of the sample sentences are English-Dutch. The book appears to offer a unique opportunity to acquaint oneself with the Dutch language as spoken on the American East Coast in 1730, but linguist Rob Naborn has shown that unfortunately the book was compiled from language guides that had already been published in Holland in the seventeenth century.

In the churches, too, the influence of English was felt, most in New York City. As early as 1726, the council of the New York Church sounded the alarm over the level of knowledge of Dutch among its members. In 1763, the council wrote to the Amsterdam mother church to report that hardly anyone understood Dutch anymore, and to ask for permission to appoint a dominie who could also preach in English. That permission was granted in 1764 and, although some of the members walked out, the tide could not be stemmed: in 1769, a second dominie was appointed who also preached in English. In 1773, the church council of New York resolved to appoint a teacher at the state school who was able to teach both in English and in Dutch. In 1785, the last teacher to do his teaching exclusively in Dutch resigned.

Elsewhere, too, churches switched to English. In Kingston, New York, an English-speaking dominie was appointed – while a majority of the congregation still conversed in Dutch. Churches often quickly changed their official language to English to retain their younger members. What also mattered in this change was that, although congregation members spoke Dutch, the gap between spoken Low Dutch and the *Nederduits* of the sermons was becoming too wide. The last Dutch sermon was preached in 1833. Most Dutch churchgoers were *realpolitiker*. In 1826, there was a story in the *Magazine of the Reformed Dutch Church* about a farmer who had prayed in church in Dutch for fifty years, resisting at first the introduction of English. But after some time he realized: "We are all Americans – happy Americans. The language of the majority must prevail. Our sons must learn the English, if ever they would aspire after honors and important stations in life." Nevertheless, just before the start of World War I, there still were churchgoers in Bergen County, New Jersey, who spoke Dutch with

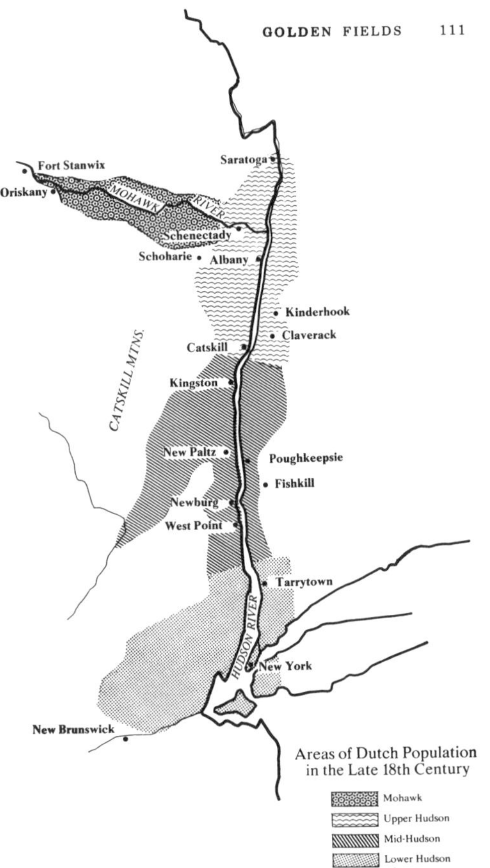

Illustration 1.8 – Areas of Dutch population in the late eighteenth century (source: Kenney 1975: 111)

each other, despite the fact that there had been no sermons preached in Dutch there for 80 or 90 years.

In the second half of the eighteenth century, people began to translate the major Protestant tenets into English, from which we may deduce that the church members had problems with the Dutch text. In 1763, some psalms were set in English to Dutch melodies. Dominie Lambertus de Ronde, one of the two Dutch dominies in New York City and advocate of the use of Dutch, published a book in 1763 in English on the Heidelberg catechism, thereby becoming the first representative of the Reformed Church in America to publish a theological work in English. In 1782, the Heidelberg catechism was translated into English for children. The year 1793 saw the English translation of the Church's creed, its prayer book, and the church order. In 1794, the first general synod was convened of the Reformed Dutch Church, which by then had become independent. The statutes of this meeting were kept in English, not in Dutch, which means that at that moment, English had replaced Dutch as the official language of the church in the US.

This did not prevent the church from growing – perhaps it even owed its growth to the change to English. In 1792, there were 116 congregations, in 1821 there were 187, and in 1845, 274. Still, in the early part of the nineteenth century there were about 250,000 Americans who still read the gospel in Dutch, as we can read in Jacob van Hinte's impressive survey, *Netherlanders in America*, written in 1928 (English translation 1985, this figure can be found on page 58).

The consequences of American Independence

In the last quarter of the eighteenth century, the number of Dutch speakers on the American East Coast was probably at its highest, according to Bachman's calculations: he estimates that in the states of New York and New Jersey, about 100,000 people spoke Dutch in 1790. Illustration 1.8 shows the area where towards the end of the eighteenth

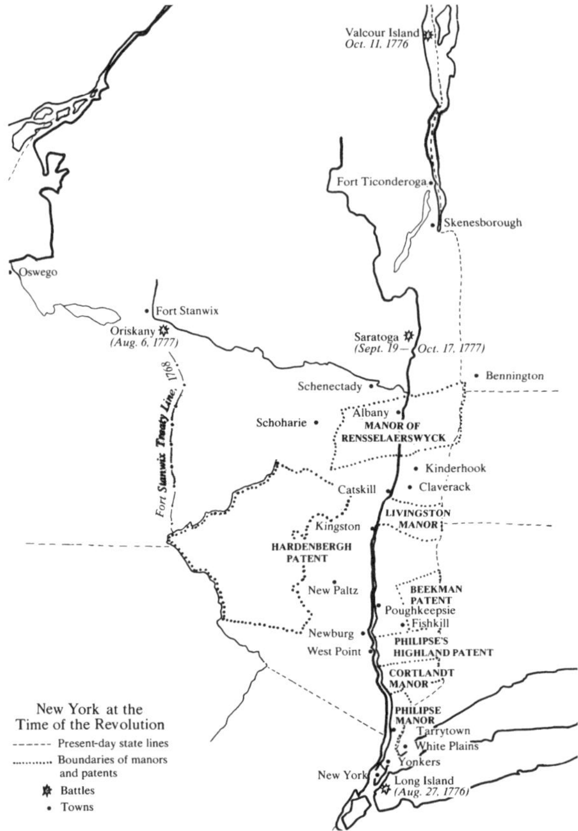

Illustration 1.9 – New York at the time of the American Revolution (source: Kenney 1975: 156)

century, the Dutch population had settled. Not all people of Dutch extraction, incidentally, spoke Dutch (or exclusively Dutch). This region, however, was different from other regions – not only regarding religion (see 2.7), but also regarding all kinds of Dutch customs and cultural phenomena: special foodstuffs, household goods, tools, means of transport, architectural style, and clothing (see 2.1, 2.3, 2.8, 2.12 and 2.13).

After this period, the area of the "Dutch Belt" – the region where Dutch was spoken – diminished severely, and American Independence was an important factor in this. The position of English, namely, was reinforced by that independence. New York was the first city that succumbed to English. At the time of the American Revolution (1775-1783), probably a third of the population of New York could still speak Dutch. Young people of Dutch origin had played Dutch games as children (see 2.11), and they still knew Dutch, but as they grew older they changed to English more and more. Between 1776 and 1783, the British used New York City as a basis for their sorties, and British officers were billeted with Dutch families. The Dutch areas in the state of New York suffered badly under the hostilities.

If they wanted to keep abreast of the developments, the inhabitants had to learn English. Many Dutchmen sided with the rebels. After Independence Day, the Dutch inhabitants of New York joined the other Americans to build the new nation, disregarding their private interests and their own language and culture. New secondary schools were built, none of them Dutch-language institutions. All this had unfortunate results for the Dutch language and Dutch culture.

In rural areas outside New York City, Dutch was more resilient – there were many Dutch speakers west of the Hudson, in New Jersey, around Kingston, and along the upper reaches of the Hudson and the Mohawk. The importance of Dutch in the state of New York is clear from the fact that in 1788, dominie Lambertus de Ronde translated the American Constitution, drawn up the year before, into Dutch. The Constitution had to be approved by special committees in all of the (then) 13 states of the US. De Ronde's

Dutch translation was published by the city of Albany and, thanks to this translation, the Constitution received such strong support from the older male population that the state of New York came to accept it. The Constitution came into force in 1789.

Dutch influence on the American process of becoming independent is perhaps even greater than already described. Research has shown that during the drafting of the American Declaration of Independence in 1776, Thomas Jefferson was inspired, among other things, by the Dutch "*Plakkaat van Verlatinghe*" written by the States General in 1581, in which the Dutch declared that they no longer acknowledged the Spanish king as their sovereign. Dutch ideas about individual and national freedom, expressed in 1664 by Peter Stuyvesant in the Articles of Capitulation, were for a second time clearly influential, and had an important impact on American society. Other founding fathers, including John Adams, Benjamin Franklin, and Alexander Hamilton, were also well acquainted with Holland and the prevailing ideas there, which they held up as an example to their followers. Friesland was the first province of the Dutch Republic to recognize the independence of the US; some people even speak of a world first. This recognition by the States of Friesland took place on 26 February 1782, and the States General were to follow this good example a few months later on 19 April. In 1909, Americans unveiled a plaque commemorating this happy event in the Frisian Province House in Leeuwarden. But the Dutch, in turn, were the first – or so the story goes – to fire a salute for an American vessel, thereby semi-officially acknowledging the independence of the US: this happened as early as 16 November 1776, when an American ship entered the harbor of St. Eustace, and since 1990 this has been celebrated as Dutch-American Heritage Day. While on the subject of commemorations: 19 April is known as Dutch-American Friendship Day, because on that day in 1782 the States General resolved to accept John Adams as minister plenipotentiary of the US, thereby recognizing and acknowledging the US's independence.

An interesting anecdote: George Washington, installed as first president of the US in 1789, would have liked to be addressed officially as "High Mightiness," the American translation of the Dutch title, *Hoogmogendheid*. This was because the title was also used by the Stadtholder of Holland. Congress did not agree, however, and after much deliberation, "Mister President" was chosen as the form of address.

After American Independence had been declared, a central legislative system was developed, trade and industry increased, and trains appeared on the scene, making it possible for people to travel across large distances. All this led to more intensive contacts between speakers of English and Dutch. Dutch people who were not yet bilingual learned English as their second language, except for those who were farmers in very remote areas. In the new industries, English was the lingua franca. This appears from an advertisement in the Catskill *Recorder* of 1807 for new turnpikers: "Wanted ... 10 or 15 sworn TURNPIKERS ... No Dutchman need apply unless he is pretty well Yankeyfied." This notwithstanding, the Dutch made a small contribution to the American trade vocabulary (see 2.9).

As a result of all these social changes, an increasing number of people exchanged Dutch for English in the course of the nineteenth century. When the compulsory education law was introduced in 1910, this proved to be the fatal blow to the last vestiges of rural Dutch.

Illustration 1.10 – Benjamin Franklin in his printery (a Dutch loanword) (source: collection Ed Schilders; litho probably around 1935)

Jersey Dutch and Mohawk Dutch

After the descendants of the Dutch settlers had given up Dutch in the early part of the nineteenth century, even in areas such as western Long Island in New York and the Raritan Valley in New Jersey, Low Dutch only lived on in two regions that had no contact with each other: Bergen and Passaic County in New Jersey on the one hand, and around Albany, along the upper reaches of the Hudson and the lower reaches of the Mohawk in the state of New York on the other. Dutch was spoken in these areas until well into the twentieth century, albeit gradually less frequently, and then only by older people who also always knew English. The Low Dutch spoken in these two areas is called Jersey Dutch and Mohawk Dutch, respectively. The last native speakers were probably born between 1860 and 1880, and up until the 1960s there were a few elderly people who still could speak the language. That, then, is a good three centuries after their forebears had settled in the New World! But these were the last vestiges – in the early twentieth century, an informant reported that he knew only one other person with whom he could converse in Low Dutch, and that person lived in a different village, so that they could hardly ever use their mother tongue. That picture, however, is too lopsided, because the historical geographer Jacob van Hinte reports that he regularly met people speaking "Old Dutch" in both the Mohawk Valley and New Jersey during his journey through the US in 1921.

Before the twentieth century, nothing was published in or about Low Dutch, except for a number of interesting remarks about the language that were recorded by Dutch travelers or immigrants in the nineteenth and twentieth centuries. These often remarked that they found Low Dutch difficult to understand, which shows how far apart Low Dutch and European Dutch had grown. But what is perhaps more important is the statement that, in general, they understood the language, after some initial effort. Thus, when the Dutch dominie Gerardus Balthazar Bosch visited New Jersey in the 1820s, he was amazed that Dutch had survived in America so long, but he also remarked that this Dutch had become "very bad, uncouth and coarse, and contaminated with many wrong expressions." According to him, the language was quickly going to disappear completely, something that he did not regret: "our language will, on the whole, not lose a great deal with it." And in 1866 the wife of the Dutch ambassador in New York, in a letter to her relatives, wrote that one in ten people will understand you when you speak Dutch to them, although they do not exactly speak "our civilized Dutch," but rather a farmer's dialect. When Jacob van Hinte carried out research for his book *Netherlanders in America* in 1921, he met an old farmer in Midland Park who spoke Dutch, but he could barely understand him. In his book, Van Hinte describes (1985: 59-62) a whole series of meetings between people of the "Old Dutch branch" and Dutch travelers or nineteenth-century Dutch immigrants, the latter being especially surprised by the fact that they could communicate with the others in Dutch.

Only after the language had practically become extinct did linguists start publishing about it (see box 1 for examples from those publications). New York linguist John Dyneley Prince was the first to publish a description and glossary of Jersey Dutch as it was spoken then in 1910 in Bergen County, New Jersey. Prince had learned Dutch as senator of Passaic County, a district where many thousands of Dutch people lived. In his introduction he remarked that up until 30 years prior to his writing, Jersey Dutch was spoken in rural areas by Dutch, English, German, and French colonists, but that since then it had been ousted by the arrival of state schools, and that at that time it only lived on in the memory of about 200 older people, most of them over 70. What was remarkable, he said, was that young people had preserved "the curious jerky intonation, unclear diction and the marked singsong tone of voice, which were the characteristics of the parent speech." Prince had collected his data in conversations with four elderly informants.

In 1939, our good friend Van Loon published an article about Jersey Dutch. In 1964, a word list of about 1,600 words by James Storms (1860-1949), a native speaker of Jersey Dutch who called himself "about the last surviving person in my section," appeared posthumously. As it turns out, the word list printed in Van Loon's 1939 article is largely based on the then-unpublished vocabulary list by Storms – something Van Loon does not mention in his article, although he does name Storms as one of his informants.

About Mohawk Dutch there is only one publication, Van Loon's 1938 *Crumbs from an Old Dutch Closet* mentioned above. This book includes a relatively extensive word list, based on that by Prince; Van Loon replaced Prince's Jersey Dutch words with their Mohawk Dutch equivalents. Like Prince, who, incidentally, had encouraged Van Loon to published the *Crumbs*, Van Loon identified some words in Low Dutch said to come from an Amerindian language; the Mohawk Dutch words *johnny dog* "beaver," *enookierat* "muskrat" and *suikerdas* "raccoon" were said to come from Iroquois words. Later, in 1980, he recounted how in about 1930 he had met a Native American who had addressed him with the words *Hoo come jawn?* which, Van Loon said, was pure *tawl* for "How do you do?" This too probably stems from the word list by Prince, who had recorded the greeting *hû kom je ân?* for Jersey Dutch. How reliable Van Loon's data are cannot be said with any certainty; what becomes clear in any case is that the language contacts between Dutch speakers and Native Americans continued to fascinate him throughout his life.

Box 1. The entries for the letter F in the three vocabularies of Low Dutch published in the twentieth century

The letter F from "The Jersey Dutch Dialect" by J. Dyneley Prince from 1910 is shown below. Each entry has the English word, followed by its Jersey Dutch equivalent; after that the provenance of the Jersey Dutch word is given (N. = Dutch); where the provenance is not given in the original, it has been supplied by me in square brackets. B, D, H, Hk are the initials of the four informants: Bartholf, De Freece, Hopper, and Hicks. The spelling of the Jersey Dutch words is as close an approximation of the pronunciation as could be managed.

Farm *pläk* = N. *plek* "spot"; "farm" = *boerderij.*
Farmer *bûr*; pl. *-e* = N. *boer.*
Fast (speedy) *xāu* (Hk); *kāu* (D) = N. *gaauw; je rāid hārd* "you drive fast" (Hk) [Dutch *je rijdt hard*].
Fault *sxjilt; häm āixe sxjilt* "his own fault" (Hk) [Dutch *schuld; zijn eigen schuld*]; *mäs* "error" (Hk) [Dutch *mis* or English *mess*].
February *Februāri* (Hk) [Dutch *februari* or English *February*].
Feed (infin.) *fâdere;* (imv.) *fâder* (D). = N. *voederen* [respectively *voeder*].
Fellow (person) *kääd'l* (Hk) = N. *kerel.*
Fever *kôz* = N. *koorts.*
Few *wääinix; bêtše: dā bän bêtše vān dāx dāt lêve dāt däuts sprêke* "there are few today that live who speak Jersey Dutch" = N. *weinig* "few" ; *beetje* "a little." This is a wrong use of *bêtše.*
Fifteen *vāiftîn* = N. *vijftien.*
Fifty *vāiftix* = N. *vijftig.*
Find *vände; vond; xjevonde* (Hk) = N. *vinden.*
Fine *mûi; mûi oxtent* "a fine morning" (Hk) = N. *mooi.*
Fire *vuer* (Hk); *vîr* (D) = N. *vuur.*
First *êrst* (Hk), almost *êst* = N. *eerst.*
Fish *väše* (n); *fässe* infin.; (D) = N. *visch; visschen.*
Five *vāif* = N. *vijf.*
Fly *vlîxe* (infin.): *hāi vlîxt mät se wikke* "he flies with his wings" (Hk) = N. *vliegen.*
Foot *vût* (Hk) = N. *voet; plôt* (D) = N. *poot*, "paw of an animal."
For *för;* used instead of N. *om* "in order to" : *för dāt te dûne* "in order to do that" (Hk). *För* = N. *voor.*
Forget *verxête* (infin.); "forgotten" = *vergêten* (D). = N. *vergeten.*
Fork *sxôtergāfel* (D) = N. *schotel* "plate" (?) + *gaffel* "fork."
Forty *vêrtix* = N. *veertig.*
Four *vîr* = N. *vier.*
Fourteen *vêrtîn* = N. *veertien.*

Fox *voše* (Hk). Dim. of N. *vos.*
Friday *Vrāidix* = N. *Vrijdag.*
Friend *vrînt*; pl. *vrînde* = N. *vriend.*
Frightened. See Afraid.
Fro: "to and fro" = *tû en vrô*; English. N. is *heen en weder.*
From *vān, fān* = N. *van.*
Front (adj.) *vôrder*, as *vôrderspôren* "front spurs"; corrupted from N. *voorder* "further." In N. "front" = *voorst; voor-.*
Fruit *vrœxt* (Hk) = N. *vrucht.*
Full *vol: volle mân* "full moon" (Hk) = N. *vol.*
Funny (peculiar) *wonlik; as en wonlik däng* "a f. thing" (B). Corr[uption] of N. *wonderlijk.*

***

The letter F from *Crumbs from an Old Dutch Closet* by L.G. van Loon from 1938 is shown below. Each entry has the English word, followed by its Mohawk Dutch equivalent; after that I have inserted the supposed provenance of the Mohawk Dutch word in square brackets. Van Loon has partially adapted the spelling of the Mohawk Dutch words to that of Standard Dutch. (P) means: also in Prince 1910.

farewell, - farwel. [Dutch *vaarwel*]
farm, - plek (P), farm. [Dutch *plek*, English *farm*]
farmer, - boer. [Dutch *boer*]
fat, - fet. [Dutch *vet*]
fast, - gauw; hard. [Dutch *gauw, hard*]
fasten, - binde, bond, ghebonde. [Dutch *binden, bond, gebonden*]
fault, - skilt. [Dutch *schuld*]
February, - Februari. [Dutch *februari* or English *February*]
feed, - vawdere. [Dutch *voederen*]
fellow, - keerel. [Dutch *kerel*]
fever, - karts. [Dutch *koorts*]
few, - weinugh; beetse. [Dutch *weinig, beetje*]
field, - felt; akker. [Dutch *veld, akker*]
fifteen, - fyftien. [Dutch *vijftien*]
fifty, - fyftugh. [Dutch *vijftig*]
fight, - feghte. [Dutch *vechten*]
find, - finde. [Dutch *vinden*]
fine, - mooi. [Dutch *mooi*]
fire, - fier. [Dutch *vuur*, in dialects *vier*]
first, - eerst. [Dutch *eerst*]
fish, - fesse. [Dutch *vissen*]

five, - fyf. [Dutch *vijf*]
fly, - fliegh; flieghe (verb). [Dutch *vlieg; vliegen*]
foot, - foet. [Dutch *voet*]
for, - for. [Dutch *voor* or English *for*]
forget, - verghete. [Dutch *vergeten*]
fork, - gaffel (hay); fork (table). [Dutch *gaffel; vork*]
forty, - feertugh. [Dutch *veertig*]
forwards, - forwards. [Dutch *voorwaarts* or English *forwards*]
four, - fier. [Dutch *vier*]
fourteen, - feertien. [Dutch *veertien*]
fox, - vossie. [Dutch *vosje, vossie*]
Friday, - Frydagh. [Dutch *vrijdag*]
friend, - vrint. [Dutch *vriend*]
frightened, - verskrokke; bang. [Dutch *verschrokken, bang*]
from, - fan. [Dutch *van*]
front, - voorsyd; verder. [Dutch *voorzijde; verder*]
fruit, - frught. [Dutch *vrucht*]
full, - fol. [Dutch *vol*]
funeral, - beghrafenis. [Dutch *begrafenis*]
funny, - wonnelik; wonlik (P). [Dutch *wonderlijk*]
fur, - bont. [Dutch *bont*]

***

The letter F from *A Jersey Dutch vocabulary* by James B.H. Storms from 1964 is shown below. Each entry has the Jersey Dutch word; after this I have added the supposed provenance of the Jersey Dutch word. The spelling of the Jersey Dutch words represents the pronunciation.

famele [Dutch *familie* or English *family*] - family.
faudt [Dutch *vaartje?*] - grandfather.
feest [Dutch *vies*] - stomach disgust.
feole [Dutch *viool*] - fiddle.
fet [English *fit*] - fit.
flaut [Dutch *fluiten*] - whistle.
fleckertia [Dutch *flikkertje*] - slight flurry (as of snow).
flow [Dutch *flauw*] - faint; weak.
fluder [Dutch *flodder*] - sloven woman.
fluderigh [Dutch *flodderig*] - slovenly.
fneeze [older Dutch *fniezen*] - sneeze.
fontaine [Dutch *fontein*] - spring.
fraum [English *frame*] - frame.
frons [Dutch *Frans*] - France.

"Negro Dutch"

In his description of Jersey Dutch, Prince said that this language was also spoken by a group of black people: "There is a small colony of old negroes living on the mountain back of Suffern, N.Y., who still use their own dialect of Jersey Dutch, but they are very difficult of access, owing to their shyness of strangers." Their speech has its own peculiarities. Prince's informant from this group was called William de Freece. One of his white informants called the language of this De Freece *nêxer däuts*, or "Negro Dutch."

By the "mountain back of Suffern," Prince must have meant the Ramapo Mountains. The anthropologist David Steven Cohen published an interesting study in 1974 about the Ramapo Mountain People, a group that today numbers about 5,000 people of mixed descent (blacks, whites, and Native Americans) who live in and around the Ramapo Mountains in the north of New Jersey and were said to have spoken Jersey Dutch. These people, also called Ramapough Mountain Indians, Ramapo Mountain Indians, or Ramapough Lenape Nation, live in remote areas and have few contacts with the outside world. They are said to have descended from some Dutch pioneers, released or runaway African slaves, and Native Americans, and their forebears were members of the Dutch Reformed Church. From as early as 1880, they have been called "Jackson Whites" by outsiders, which they consider to be a contemptuous term. The name is probably a corruption of "Jacks and Whites," which describes their origin: the tribe was said to be a combination of *Jacks*, a slang term for runaway slaves, and *Whites*, white people, among whom were Dutch adventurers. The provenance of the Ramapo is considered controversial – they regard themselves to be descendants from Lenape who had fled into the mountains to escape from Dutch and English colonists when the rest of their tribe evacuated the area completely.

The Ramapo claimed that the language of their ancestors was Munsee Delaware, and that they then changed to English, but also (and even recently) spoke Jersey Dutch. Unfortunately, apart from Prince's findings, nothing has ever been recorded of that phase: all present-day Ramapo speak English. Cohen did record a few Dutch loanwords in their language, which young people remembered from the language of their grandparents, such as *feest* ("I'm feest of it") from Dutch *vies* ("dirty, smelly, disgusting," see also 2.6), *hunt* from Dutch *hond* ("hound, dog"), *heit* from Dutch *heet* ("hot"), *hauzen* from Dutch *huizen* ("houses") and *gehst du hein* from Dutch *gaat u heen* ("please go"). From their family names, too, one can see that the Ramapo had Dutch ancestors – many of them are called De Groat, De Freese or Freece, Van Dunk, and Mann, deriving from Dutch names De Groot, De Vries or De Fries, Van Donck, and Emanuels.

Illustration 1.11 – Drawing by Joel Altshuler for the letter D of James B.H. Storms's dictionary from 1964

Van Loon revisited

At this point in the story of the Dutch language on the American East Coast, we once more encounter the omnipresent Van Loon. It so happened that in the 1960s the American historian Van Cleaf Bachman conceived a plan to compose a Low Dutch-English Dictionary. He realized that time was running out for Low Dutch; if no action were undertaken quickly, the language would irrevocably be lost. His aim was to describe Low Dutch as it was spoken between 1850 and the early part of the twentieth century. In 1965, he therefore called on informants in *De Halve Maen*, the organ of the Holland Society of New York, to provide him with data about the Dutch they remembered from their younger years. He received many, mostly short, reactions; among them one of someone whose name has become familiar to us by now... Lawrence G. van Loon.

At that time, Van Loon lived on Hawaii, where he was medical director between 1955 and 1967. On 10 June 1965, he wrote a letter to Bachman in a curious mixture of Dutch and Low Dutch (cited in 2009 by Jan Noordegraaf) that opened with the words:

> "Waarde Heer. Ek leesde met belang in de laatest nummer van de "Halve Maen" jou interest in de laag Duitsche taal van Nieuw York en Nieuw Jersey. Feitlijk doghten ek dat de "interest" even zoo uitgestarv was as den spraake, maor ek zien dat ek het verkeert had."
> (Dear Sir. My curiosity was aroused when I read, in the latest issue of the "Halve Maen," about your interest in the Low Dutch language of New York and New Jersey. Actually, I thought that the "interest" was just as extinct as the language, but I see that I was wrong.)

After 1967, Van Loon returned to the American East Coast, and from that moment on, he became Bachman's most important informant for the Low Dutch-English Dictionary. The two worked together for years, with Van Loon filling in numerous questionnaires, reading out sentences and recording them on tape, according to Jan Noordegraaf, who has written several times about Van Loon. Van Loon also gave Bachman a notebook with *Vertessels fram ons vlede*, "stories from our past," which he had heard about 1915, when he was 13, and which he had written down from memory for his children in 1942. One of those *Vertessels* was the story "Het Poelmeisie," which we mentioned in paragraph 1.0.

About 1980, Bachman stopped working on the dictionary, for personal reasons; in the following years he published a few articles, and some time later, scholars were able to access his typescript; one copy of it was deposited with the New York State Historical Association in

Illustration 1.12 – Photo of Lawrence G. van Loon (source: www.ancientfaces.com/research/photo/351750, reprinted with permission of the relatives)

Cooperstown, New York, and another copy is at the Meertens Institute in Amsterdam. In this typescript there is a lot of new material about Low Dutch that came from Van Loon. A rich mine for researchers, one might think. However, since it appears that Van Loon published falsified data about the earliest contacts between Dutch settlers and Native Americans, these data, too, have become suspect.

Is that reasonable? It is certain that from the beginning – and in the 1960s no one questioned the reliability of Van Loon's material – Bachman looked at the data supplied by Van Loon critically. In his introduction, Bachman remarks that Van Loon is certainly not an ideal informant, given his background. Since he was ten, he had lived in Reading, Pennsylvania, for 43 years, right in the middle of the Pennsylvania Dutch, and during that time he had heard more German than Dutch. His language also appeared to have been influenced by Afrikaans – during World War II he had had contact with several Afrikaans speakers. These must have made a deep impression on him, for in some of his *Vertessels*, Van Loon introduced the Afrikaans word *hierdie*, which does not exist in Low Dutch at all! What was most striking, perhaps, was the influence of "Holland Dutch" (to which he was exposed intensively since the early 1930s) on Van Loon's language. In short, Bachman concluded that, if it were possible "to find 'uncontaminated' speakers with reasonable fluency, they would certainly have to be chosen as informants before Van Loon."

Bachman cites several things as examples of Van Loon's "Netherlandisms": his intonation, his pronunciation of long *a* as an *a*- and not as an *o*-sound, and Dutch word forms such as *yndelik* "at last" and *werelt* "world" instead of the Low Dutch equivalents *endlik* and *wedeld*. What is interesting here is that tapes have been preserved on which Van Loon's pronunciation can be heard – Van Loon made recordings of a few *Vertessels* – among them "Het Poelmeisie" – before November 1943, and these are available in the US Library of Congress. They have been analyzed by Dutch linguist Jan Noordegraaf, who claims that Van Loon's Dutch is clearly understandable: he sounds like an American talking Dutch – naturally with a strong "dialectic" coloring: the vowels are certainly not Standard Dutch, the articles and the inflexion of the adjectives do not consistently run parallel with the Standard Dutch system, and he uses dialect forms such as *hullie* ("they") and *benne* ("are") instead of *zij* and *zijn*, respectively. His Dutch is nevertheless much closer to Standard Dutch than the Low Dutch of a century earlier, when Dutch travellers reported that they had great trouble understanding Low Dutch.

Bachman asked Van Loon all sorts of questions. For example, he asked why it was that in his *Crumbs* of 1938, Van Loon had written that quite ordinary words, such as *plantasi* and *pad*, did not occur in Mohawk Dutch, while it was known from other sources that these most certainly were used. Van Loon's explanation was that, at the time, he was very busy running his medical practice and therefore had less time for the book than he would have liked. Meanwhile, however, we know that Van Loon, in spite of his busy practice, did find the time to publish an article in the *Dutch Settlers Society of Albany Yearbook* of 1939-1940. This article, on a letter and a map by Jeronimus dela Croix, subsequently turned out to be based on falsifications.

What can we conclude about the reliability of the published and unpublished data supplied by Van Loon about Low Dutch over the course of the years? The conclusion seems inevitable: nothing can be regarded as a reliable specimen of Low Dutch.

It looks as if Van Loon, on the basis of vague childhood recollections of Low Dutch and the published data on Jersey Dutch by Prince and Storms, as well as of his knowledge of Standard Dutch, German, and – later – Afrikaans, created an idiosyncratic version of Low Dutch. To what extent this was done consciously or unconsciously will probably never be discovered. It was, however, a conscious step for him to volunteer as an informant and to introduce himself time and again as (perhaps) the last speaker of Low Dutch – in the introduction to Bachmann's dictionary, for instance, we read: "L.G. van Loon, who is today perhaps the last fluent speaker of the dialect." It is true that Van Loon sometimes said he was unsure as to whether he had remembered an expression well enough: "*voor de zuiver waarhyd te vertelle ben ik dikkels onzeker of ik en uitdrukking goed hae oft niet*" ("to tell the pure truth I am often unsure whether I have got an expression correct or not"). But that did not stop him from filling in numerous questionnaires, recording audio material on tape, and supplying a whole lot of information. Remember also that the contacts with his grandfather will have been greatly reduced after his move to Reading on his tenth birthday, for a journey to the Mohawk Valley in those days was a tremendous undertaking. From research into second language acquisition, we know that young children pick up a second language quite easily, but that they lose it just as quickly when they have lost contact with that second language. Yet, Van Loon would remember the Low Dutch from his youth and be able to distinguish it from the Standard Dutch that he was later to hear and speak for decades: "his speech did not suffer seriously from the atrophy of disuse which often characterizes the speech of older persons who have not spoken their childhood language in forty or fifty years," Bachman says. This seems curious.

We can only guess at the motives driving Van Loon. Perhaps his fascination for the Dutch past of the American East Coast came from the fact that he was a direct descendant of Jan van Loon, who had emigrated from Liege in Belgium to New Netherland in the seventeenth century. In any case, for years he was a member of the Holland Society and of the Dutch Settlers Society of Albany, and he was keeper of the records and translator of the Association of Blauvelt Descendants – whose members were all descendants of Gerrit Hendrickszen (Blauvelt), who travelled from Deventer to America in 1638. He most likely enjoyed the attention he received from many scholars; perhaps he felt encouraged by that attention to supply more and more data about a language that had grown rusty in his memory. Hopefully, someone will someday write the biography of this fascinating but unreliable man.

Walter Hill's Notebook

Van Loon's adventures have not yet come to an end, however. For not only was he the most important informant for Bachman, he also provided what Bachman calls "the most valuable source for the study of Low Dutch." That source is a notebook by Van Loon's grandfather, Walter Hill (1856-1925). This was the man who had taught Van Loon Low Dutch in his youth. Walter Hill's *Notebook*, which has meanwhile become famous among insiders, was given to Van Loon in 1968 by one of Hill's granddaughters.

Box 2. A fragment from the *Notebook* of Walter Hill, derived from Bachman's *Introduction to Low Dutch Dictionary*. In this fragment, Barend Myndertssen tells about the difference between *Nederduits* church language and Low Dutch from his youth (the spelling is more or less phonetic).

> Toen ek nen jonger waz - dat waz präps agtien handert därtig want ek waz gebore vlak agter de twiede vegtery met Groot Bretänie - hadde hullie nau end dan Zondaag särvis war hullie Läg Duits gebruikt. Ha - dat waz de tyd toe de kyere allehar zatte kinniegape, end som van de audes toe. Ja. Dat ez somdeng dat hullie hebbe opgegeve jare gelede want ek ben nau aal vurby de zeuventig end ek kan niet meer erendere hoe lang het ez zents hullie nen Läg Duits särvis hadde in de kark. Mar, joe vroeg aan de dominie end hem lezinge uit de Bybel. Ja. Zie. Hullie hadde nen voorlezer, mar hy waz aal errie aud end moet oogglaze hebbe end bovedit, neneder west dat niemelt meer kon die aud Holland Bybels leze, want dat gepränt waz värd bove de aledaags veok die op de banke in dat kark zatte. Zoo, netierlik de dominie moet dat aaltegader by hemzelf doene. Wäl, ek kan zeer goed erendere dat toe hy uit de Bybel geng leze hy geng niet uitspreke dezelf gelykt hy deen by de prekery. End ek hev myn vader hore zäge aan myn onkel dat het waz aaltegader maarjarn schere want niemelt in de heel kark verstong wat hy leezd end maar nen kleen hälft wat hy preekt. Ik weet niet oft dat ez het gelykt wat joe zee mar het kon. Agter veel jare ek ben errie zeker dat die dominie leezd van de Bybel end spraak van de preekstoel aaltegader anders dan hem spreke waz toe die kwaam by ons nen vizzet make. Ek hev dekkels gewonderd, mar ja, toen ek kleen waz leernd ek errie vroeg dat nen groeiend jonger waz mar nen snatneus end diend best de mond haude.

Walter Hill translated this as follows:

> "When I was a boy – that was perhaps eighteen hundred and thirty for I was born right after the second battling with Great Britain – they had now and then Sunday services where they used Low Dutch. Hah! That was the time when all the children sat staring at nothing, and some of the parents too. Yes that is something that they gave up years ago for I am already past seventy and I can't remember any more how long it is since they had a Low Dutch service in the church. But you asked about the minister and reading from the Bible. Yes. You see. They had a reader, but he was already very old and should have had spectacles and moreover everyone knew that no one anymore can read those old Holland Bibles for the printing was way beyond the common people who sat in the pews in that church. So, naturally the minister had to do all that by himself. Well, I can remember very well that when he read from the Bible he did not pronounce the same as he did when

he preached (with the preaching). And I've heard my father say to my uncle that it was all a waste of time since no one in the whole church understood what he read and only a small half of what he preached. I do not know if that is like what you said, but it could be. After many years I am quite certain that that minister read from the Bible and spoke from the pulpit altogether different from (than) his speaking was when he came and made us a visit. I have often wondered, but yes, when I was small I learned very early that a growing boy was only a snotnose and had best keep his mouth shut."

Hill was a schoolteacher by profession and, just like his grandson, he probably learned Low Dutch at an early age. He collected the data for his *Notebook* between 1870 and 1890 in conversations with native speakers of Low Dutch. The *Notebook* comprises about 100 pages and is the most comprehensive surviving document of Low Dutch. It contains a grammatical description of Mohawk Dutch, with a comprehensive word list with examples of its usage, and a few longer stories by Mohawk Dutch speakers, including Barend Myndertssen (see the text in Box 2).

Since it has become clear that Van Loon doctored data, people have come to doubt the reliability of the *Notebook*. The Dutch linguist Jaap van Marle is quite sure: the *Notebook*, too, is a forgery. But he also has doubts about the existence of Walter Hill. This, however, is unjustified: Jan Noordegraaf has shown that Walter Hill did exist and Bachman thinks he can prove that Hill knew Low Dutch. Van Marle's conclusion about the *Notebook* seems to be a little rash. As Noordegraaf says, first the paper and ink of the *Notebook* will have to be examined more closely – which is possible, for Van Loon donated the original *Notebook* to the New York State Historical Association in 1979. Further linguistic research will also be necessary. That will be trickier, for with what would the material be compared? It is older than the material published by Prince and much more extensive. Precisely for that reason, it would be good news for linguistic scholarship if the authenticity of the *Notebook* was determined. Meanwhile Bachman, Noordegraaf says, is busy setting up an authenticity check – the data available so far seem to indicate that the *Notebook* is indeed by the hand of Walter Hill. For any further discussion, it would be useful if the data from the *Notebook* were to become generally accessible. Would we then really hear the last speakers of Mohawk Dutch talking?

Characteristics of Low Dutch

Although early literature on Low Dutch is scarce, and part of the data cannot be used because it is unreliable, we do have some information about it. Charles Gehring, for instance, wrote a dissertation in 1973 on the Dutch that was used in seventeenth- and eighteenth-century documents along the upper reaches of the Hudson and the lower reaches of the Mohawk. From Gehring's dissertation, it becomes clear in how far the Dutch used on the East Coast of America began to diverge from the Dutch in the Low Countries. Low Dutch, which was based on *Hollands* city dialects, particularly *Amsterdams*, went through its own development after the contact between Low Dutch and European Dutch was by and large broken. English had its influence on Low Dutch, also in part because an increasing number of people were more or less bilingual.

Gehring found that while there was a good deal of variety in the pronunciation of Low Dutch, there was less variety in word forms. English influence on Low Dutch was apparent, for example, from the fact that of the two second-person personal pronouns of Dutch, a polite form (*gij*, later also *u*) and a more familiar form (*je*), only one survived in the nineteenth century: *je*. This was probably caused by the influence of English, which only has *you*.

In Low Dutch sentences, Gehring found, of course, several English loanwords, but the problem is that it is difficult to establish the extent to which these were in general use or just simply reflections of a particular writer's idiom. As is well known, one speaker uses more loanwords than another – this depends, among other things, on the individual background of the speakers. A few examples: *hy sal al de* ***justice*** *aen myn doen* "he will do me full justice," *volgens onze waare* ***intent*** *en meeninge* "in accordance with our true intention and meaning," *die* ***by mistake*** *gelevert was* "which had been delivered by mistake," and *fyftig pond* ***in cash*** "fifty pounds in cash." He also encountered loan translations, such as *in ordere te stellen* for English "to put in order," *meest van die teyd* for English "most of the time," and *en besye dat* for English "and besides that."

The influence of English could be traced, according to Gehring, in the syntax in particular. One example of this was the word order in subclauses: in Standard Dutch the finite verb has its place at the end of the sentence, whereas in English it is found in second position. Gehring came across several cases where the position of the verb in Low Dutch agreed with the English word order, for example: *dat sy besit die eeuwige salighyt* ("that she has eternal salvation"), which in Standard Dutch is *dat zij eeuwige zaligheid bezit*. The conclusion is that Low Dutch was being influenced by English as early as the seventeenth and eighteenth centuries. It is difficult, however, to find out to what extent and how structural that influence was: this must have varied from speaker to speaker.

We know even less about Low Dutch in the nineteenth and early twentieth centuries than about the Low Dutch of the seventeenth and eighteenth centuries. It is a fact that Mohawk Dutch and Jersey Dutch, the two varieties that we know best, showed many similarities. Two researchers have tried to make a linguistic analysis of Low Dutch on the basis of Gehring's data about seventeenth- and eighteenth-century Mohawk Dutch and Prince's data on Jersey Dutch from around 1900: the American linguist Anthony Buccini in 1995 and the Dutch linguist Jaap van Marle in 2001. In their analyses, they emphasize different highlights and reach partly different conclusions.

Van Marle's conclusion is that English has greatly influenced Low Dutch. He points out the fact that in Jersey Dutch, the articles *de* and *het* have converged into one article *de*, corresponding with the English article *the*, causing the inflection of the adjective to disappear, too. In Dutch the perfect tense is formed with the auxiliary *hebben* or *zijn*, but in Jersey Dutch – in conformity with English – only *hebben (häv)* has remained: *äk häv xjewêst* (in modern spelling "ik heb geweest") – Standard Dutch is *ik ben geweest* "I have been." It should be borne in mind, however, that in older Dutch and in dialects, the verb *hebben* is often used instead of the Standard Dutch *zijn*. Van Marle found the greatest influence in the syntax, in agreement with Gehring's findings, notably in the word order. Van Marle notes that Low Dutch has a great deal of variation: many different forms occur side by side. But from that variation, no new language system has developed, he says, and from that he concludes that what we have here is a language in decay: Low Dutch was used in very limited areas, children no longer adopted it, or if they did, it was only as a second language next to their first language, English; all of this explains why no new standards were created for the language. Van Marle claims that over the years, Low Dutch had almost become "English with Dutch words"; English had especially influenced the grammatical system, such as the word order and the verb declensions, but not the vocabulary.

The linguist Buccini, on the other hand, stresses the fact that Low Dutch usage is very archaic – which means that it still contains many elements of the language as it was originally spoken by the Dutch on the East Coast. He traces various aspects of Low Dutch back to older Dutch dialects, rather than to English influences. Of course, the influence of English can also be detected, but Buccini claims that there is no mixture of Dutch and English, and that the English influences are, for the greater part, restricted to the vocabulary and more superficial parts of the grammar and the sounds. According to him, the language remained, to the last, clearly recognizable as Dutch. This appears to be corroborated by Dutch travelers in the nineteenth century who came into contact with Low Dutch: they reported that the language sounded old-fashioned to their ears, but that in general, they could understand it with some effort.

Van Marle also mentions the word order of questions as an example of English influence on Low Dutch; he claims the word order did not agree with that in Standard Dutch. He bases that claim on the data collected by Prince in 1910 – but Prince includes only five questions, of which four show the normal Standard Dutch word order. In the absence of more data about Low Dutch, it is impossible to draw any definitive conclusions.

What remains of seventeenth-century Dutch

What is certain is that an increasing number of Low Dutch speakers began to speak English as well, eventually becoming bilingual. In their English they retained many Dutch words, some of which were adopted by English speakers, and eventually these became part of the American English vocabulary. These words are listed in chapter 2. Most of these words were borrowed by American English in the seventeenth or eighteenth century, when Dutch speakers were the most numerous. In the nineteenth century, the number of Low Dutch speakers declined rapidly, with the result that in that period American English was no longer influenced by the Dutch that had been imported by the first Dutch immigrants. But then a second wave of immigrants begane to come, as will be described further below.

Some people suppose that the Dutch influence was not restricted to loanwords, but that all kinds of language characteristics and specific meanings distinguishing American English from British English can be traced back to Dutch. The Dutch philologist Jan te Winkel gives the following examples in 1896 (pp. 343-344):

> Furthermore, many English words occur with a meaning different from the one they have in proper English, but which is immediately understood by a Dutchman. An American will say for "I think," *I believe*, as we Dutchmen do. When he is *sick*, he does not mean, as an Englishman does, 'sick," but "ill," as we do in Dutch. "To (carry on) trade" he calls *to handle*, preferring *hard money* (*hard geld*, we Dutchmen say) to paper money, although he will accept both *all two* (Dutch *alle twee*); but before a purchase he likes to indicate that actually *the whole boodle is worth not a red cent* (Dutch *de hele boel is geen rooie duit waard*); for if he looked too eager beforehand he would be a *muttonhead* (Dutch *schaapskop*). If he has visitors, *folks* (Dutch *volk*), it is sometimes *allmighty full* (Dutch *allemachtig vol*) in his house.

It's unlikely that Te Winkel's examples can (all) be ascribed to Dutch influence; modern American English dictionaries, at any rate, do not mention this in these cases, which is why these examples were not included in chapter 2 of this book. Nevertheless, the correspondence between American English and Dutch is striking.

Apart from Dutch loanwords, many family names of descendants of Dutch colonists were preserved. Names such as DeWitt, Gansevoort, Hardenbergh, Knickerbocker, Rensselaer, Roosevelt, Schuyler, Stuyvesant, Vanderbilt, Van Buren, Van Cortlandt, and the like keep the memories of the Dutch settlers alive. Dutch family names often are still recognizable with prefixes like *Van* or *De*. Sometimes townships were called after prominent families of Dutch provenance, for instance Schuylerville (after the Schuyler family, whose best-known member is General Philip Schuyler, army commander in the War of Independence), Hasbrouck Heights, and Voorhees in New York, or Verplanck and Voorheesville in New Jersey.

Van Hinte (1985:73) estimates that in the early twentieth century, about two million Americans were descended from the original Dutch colonists – which is a lot, seeing that there were no more than 10,000 colonists in New Netherland when the English

Illustration 1.13 – Two pipe-smoking colonials, dressed in knickerbockers. Does the physiognomie show that the left one is from Dutch and the right one from English origin? (source: an advertisement for the train connection New York - Philadelphia; in: The Printing Art, vol. 9 #3, May 1907)

took over this colony in 1664, and of those 10,000 colonists, probably only 6,000 came from the Low Countries. Three American presidents were of Dutch descent: Martin van Buren, Theodore Roosevelt, and Franklin D. Roosevelt. Martin van Buren's mother tongue was Dutch. In 1885, the Holland Society was founded in New York; one could only become a member if one could claim direct male linear descent from a Dutchman living in New York or the American colonies before 1675. Membership emphasized the ethnic backgrounds of the "Vans," as they called themselves, and it promoted interest in Holland, but the language spoken was English. They sang, in English, the "Dutch song," which was composed in 1898 and of which the refrain was:

I am a Van, of a Van, of a Van, of a Van,
Of a Van of a way back line;
On every rugged feature ancestral glories shine,
And all our band in kinship stand,
With all that's old and fine.
I'm a Van, of a Van, of a Van, of a Van,
Of a Van of a way back line.

The Society's official magazine, *De Halve Maen*, has been published since 1922 and, despite its name, is also in English. Nowadays, anyone can become a member if he can show that he is descended from a male person living in New Netherland before 1675, irrespective of his background: on the informative website (www.hollandsociety.com) a long list of possible second names is shown, among them many French, German, and English names – even someone called Nicolls can join; Stuyvesant must be turning in his grave.

The Dutch colonists formed the aristocracy of New York for a long time, and the Dutch families maintained all kinds of Dutch customs even after they had given up the Dutch language. But they also adapted themselves, and that was the reason for their success; that, at any rate, was what President Roosevelt, himself proud of his Dutch descent, claimed in a speech on 10 January 1890 before the Holland Society of New York:

> "We of the old Holland blood of New York have just cause to be proud of the men of note in American history who have come from among us ... [But] the point on which I wish to insist, is, that the Hollanders could never have played such a part, could never have won honorable renown by doing their full share in shaping the destiny of the republic, had they remained Hollanders instead of becoming Americans ... Had they remained aliens in speech and habit of thought, Schuyler would have been a mere boorish provincial squire instead of a major-general in the Revolutionary army, Van Buren would have been a country tavern-keeper instead of President of the mightiest republic the world has ever seen, and Vanderbilt would have remained an unknown boatman instead of becoming one of the most potent architects of the marvelous American industrial fabric; while the mass of our people, not having become Americans, would ... have rusted into a condition of inert, useless, and contemptuously disregarded provincialism."

A last testimony to the Dutch presence on the American East Coast is formed by the place-names that the Dutch left behind.

Illustration 1.14 – "The Clove at the Catskills", painting by Thomas Cole, 1827 (source: private collection)

1.3 Dutch place-names from the seventeenth century

A number of street names in the city of New York remind us of the presence of Dutch settlers. Some street names deriving from Dutch are, for example, *Bowery Lane* (see **Bowery** in 2.8.), *Bridge Street* (Dutch *Brugstraat*), *Broadway* (Dutch *Breede Weg*) and *Wall Street* (Dutch *Walstraat*; this was where the wall was built that protected the city against attacks from Englishmen and Native Americans).

Several originally Dutch settlements, together with their names, have in the course of time been swallowed up by New York City and have been degraded to boroughs or districts of this city. Often they retained their Dutch names in the process. Some boroughs were named after Dutch colonists, for example, *The Bronx* and *Yonkers* (see **patroon** and **yonkers** in 2.4). Others had been named by the colonists after a town or village in Holland, for instance, *Brooklyn* (named after *Breukelen*), *Flushing* (named after *Vlissingen*), *Gravesend* (probably named after *'s-Gravensande*), *Harlem* (named after *Haarlem*), and *New Utrecht* (named after *Utrecht*). The district of *Bushwick* was originally called *Boswijck* (see **bush** in 2.5).

Dutch names also lie at the roots of the islands *Block Island* (after the Dutch explorer Adriaen Block), *Coney Island* (after Dutch *Conyne Eylandt*, or "rabbits' island"), *Long Island* (translation of *Lange Eylandt*), *Staten Island* (*Staaten Eylandt*, so called in honor of the Dutch States General), and *Governors Island* (after the Dutch governor Wouter van Twiller, who bought the island – then called *Noten Eylandt* – from Native Americans). *Rhode Island* was by the first discoverers in the sixteenth century compared to the Greek island Rhodos because of its shape, but the Dutch settlers named it *Roodt Eylandt* "red island," and it kept that name in American English.

Also outside of what is now New York City, Dutch place-names dating from the seventeenth century have been preserved. What follows is an alphabetical list, based on the information supplied by *A Concise Dictionary of American Place-Names* by George R. Stewart (1970). This list consists of only those place-names of which it is certain (or practically certain) that they are of Dutch origin and are still currently in use.

(A survey of geographical names of New Netherland – from both Dutch and other languages – can be found at http://en.wikipedia.org/wiki/Toponymy_of_New_Netherland, and includes many place-names that are by now extinct.) When something is known about the reason for the naming, this will always be mentioned. There are, of course, many more Dutch names – for fields, brooks, and suchlike – that are only known locally and can only be found on detailed maps. Still, the following list of about 60 names gives a good idea about how and why the Dutch named landmarks. The list also provides additional information about the loanwords in this area that are mentioned in section 2.5. As will be evident, many names for bodies of water are formed using the Dutch loanwords **kill**, **binnacle**, **binnewater**, and **fly**, and many new geographical names contain the elements **bush**, **clove**, **cripple**, **dorp**, **gat**, and **hook**.

Alplaus NY. From Dutch *aalplas*, compound of *aal* "eel" and *plas* "pool"; perhaps a family name.
Arthur Kill NY. From Dutch *achter kill*, i.e., *kil*, or "stream" and *achter* "on the other side of Staten Island"; Dutch name changed through folk etymology.
Barkaboom NY. From Dutch *berkenboom* "birch tree"; perhaps a family name.
Barnegat NJ. On a map dating from 1656, the name was written as *barndegat*, a variant of Dutch *barnende gat* "burning, foaming passage" between the islands.
Beer Kil NY and **Beeren Island** NY. So called after the Dutch animal name *beer*, meaning "bear"; no doubt because there were bears there.
Bergen NJ. Probably from the Dutch city named Bergen-op-Zoom, or perhaps referring to *bergen* "mountains."
Boght NY. From Dutch *bocht* "bend," also "bay."
Bombay Hook DE. The Dutch name was *Bompies Hoeck*, *Bomtiens Hoeck* (1654) – a compound of *boompjes* "small trees" and *hoek*, borrowed in American English as **hook** (see 2.5). The marshland got its name from a Dutch colonist who bought it from a Native American; we even know what he paid for it: a rifle, four hands of gunpowder, three vests, an *anker* (see 2.10) of liquor, and a kettle. The Dutch name was adapted folk-etymologically by English speakers to the name of the Indian city of Bombay.
Bout DE. The name of the creek is from Dutch *bocht* "bend."
Bradvelt NJ. From Dutch *breedveld* "wide field"; perhaps a family name.
Butter Hill NY. A translation of the Dutch name *Boter Berg*, but the reason for the naming is unknown.
Callicoon NY. From the Dutch *kalkoen*, or "turkey"; perhaps this was not borrowed directly from Dutch, but instead through an Amerindian language. That the Dutch word *kalkoen* was borrowed by Amerindian languages will be shown in chapter 3.
Cape May NJ. Named after the Dutch captain Cornelius Jacobsen Mey, who sailed past this point in the seventeenth century.
Copsie Point NY. From Dutch *kaapje*, *kapie* "small cape"; English has added *Point* for clarification.
Cresskill NJ. Probably from Dutch *kerskil* "river bordered by cherry trees."
Crum Elbow NY and **Crum Creek** PA. Both from Dutch *krom* "bent, crooked."
Dunderberg NY. From Dutch *donderberg*, lit. "thunder mountain," named after the sound made by summer thundershowers

as they reverberated through the rocks.
Dwaar Kill NY. From Dutch *dwars* "transverse" and *kil* "stream," thus: "tributary."
Egg Harbor NJ. Translation of Dutch *Eyren Haven*, so called by the explorer Cornelius Jacobsen Mey, because he found many gull's and other birds' eggs there.
Foxen Kill NY. Probably from Dutch *vossenkil*, a compound of *vos* "fox" and *kil* "stream," no doubt because many foxes lived there.
Haverstraw NY. Recorded in 1640 as *Averstroo*, from Dutch *haver* "oats" and *stro* "straw"; probably a family name.
Hempstead NY. Known since 1644, named after the Dutch town of Heemstede; during the English occupation, the name was changed into that of an English town.
Henlopen, Cape DE. Recorded in 1633 in the form *Hinloopen*; a Dutch family name, perhaps that of a member of the crew on one of the first discovery voyages. Hindelopen, also Hinlopen, is a Dutch place-name.
Jogee Hill NY. Called after a Native American chief Keghgekapowell whom the Dutch had given the name Jochem (Joachim), and who sold land in that area to the Dutch in 1684.
Kikeout DE, NJ, and NY. From Dutch *kijkuit* "look-out post," a name regularly given to a strategically situated hill. Variants that were folk-etymologically adapted are **Kakeout Hill** NY and **Kickout Neck** DE.
Kyserike NY. Found in 1702 as *Keysserryck*, or "Empire," from *Keyser*, the name of the family possessing the land, and Dutch *rijk*, or "territory."
Maurice NJ. River and town are named after the ship *Prins Maurits*, which was captured and burned by Native Americans.
Middleburgh NY. Named after Middelburg, the capital of the Dutch province of Zeeland.
Moordener Kill NY. From the Dutch *moordenaarskil*; in the past the name was also sometimes translated literally into American English as *Murderers Creek*. The name refers to an incident that took place in 1643, when seven men and two women were killed there by Native Americans.
Normans Kill NY. Named after the Norwegian Albert Andriessen, who settled there around 1638 and was called "the Norman" by the Dutch settlers.
Orange MA and **Orange County** NY, NC, VA. All named after the title *Prins van Oranje* (Prince of Orange), which was introduced into the English royal family when Prince William III became King of England in 1688. **Orangeburg** SC (both county and town) thus named after Willem, *Prins van Oranje*, the son-in-law of George II. Already during the Dutch period, the three cities known as **The Oranges** NJ were named after the title *Prins van Oranje* of the Dutch stadtholders. In 1645, however, the name *Auronge* was found as an Amerindian personal or tribal name for this region; probably, this Amerindian name was changed by folk etymology under the influence of the title *Prins van Oranje*.
Peekskill NY. Literally "Peek's stream": Jan Peek was a Dutch trader who settled there around 1665.
Plattekill NY. From Dutch *platte kil* "flat stream, brook with little flow." The name **Plotter Kill** NY is the same name, but altered through folk etymology.
Primehook DE. From Dutch *pruimhoek*, so called because wild plums (*pruimen*) used to grow on this corner of land (*hook*).
Quacken Kill NY. From Dutch *quackenkil*, a compound of obsolete Dutch *kwak*

(often spelled *quack*) "heron" and *kil* "stream."
Raunt, The NY. Probably from Dutch *ruimte*, used in the nautical sense of *het ruime sop*, "the open sea."
Roseboom NY. From Dutch *rozenboom* "rose tree"; probably a family name.
Rotterdam NY. After the Dutch city of the same name; the name was used for several places at one stage, but because *rot* and *dam* had unpleasant associations, the name has disappeared almost everywhere, except in NY.
Roundout Creek NY. At first recorded as *Rondout* – probably from Dutch *rondhout* "unsplit wood, timber."
Sandsea Kill NY. The first part is a translation of the originally Dutch name *Zantzee*, to which *kill*, or "stream," likewise of Dutch origin, has been added.
Saugerties NY. Recorded in 1663 as *Zager's Kiletje*. *Kiletje* is a small *kil* – "stream." Zager was the first Dutch colonist on this river.
Schuylkill PA. The Dutch *schuylkil* is a combination of *schuilen*, "to hide," and *kil*, "stream," the compound was made based in part on the word *schuilplaats*, or "hiding place." The reference may be to an incident whereby a Swedish vessel hid on this stream.
Sparkill NY. From Dutch *spar* "spruce" and *kil* "stream" ; no doubt there were spruce firs growing by the riverside.
Spuiten Duyvil NY. The name refers to the dangerous currents – it is a compound of *spuiten* "to spout" and *duivel* "devil."
Steenykill Lake NJ. From Dutch *stenen-kil*, a combination of *stenen* "stones" and *kil* "stream."
Torn, The, NJ. From Dutch *toren* "tower," because of the shape of the rocks.
Verfkil NY. From Dutch *verf* "paint" and *kil* "stream," perhaps because of the color of the water.
Verkerde Kill, NY. From Dutch *verkeerd* "faulty" or "bad" and *kil* "stream."

This survey includes the most important Dutch place-names on the American East Coast still in use, but it is by no means a complete inventory; as far as I know this has not been made yet. While over the years many Dutch names have been replaced by English ones, traces of Dutch are still clearly present, in particular in New York and New Jersey.

Illustration 1.15 – Cripple, wood engraving 1872 (source: private collection)

1.4 Dutch and double Dutch

Another part of the legacy of Dutch is the cluster of associations around the term *Dutch* – most of which are negative. The Britons were not exactly fond of the Hollanders: in the seventeenth century, they were each other's enemies and competitors – both nations aspired to supremacy over the seas, and each wanted to control the spice trade from rich Asia. They also battled over territories in North and South America. Between 1652 and 1674 they fought three maritime wars, and it was a traumatic experience for the English when the Dutch fleet under Admiral Michiel Adriaensz. de Ruyter inflicted a crushing defeat on the English fleet during the Battle of Chatham in 1667, when the Dutch ships sailed up the Medway and broke through the English blockade.

There was not only a war at sea, there were also battles of words. The *Oxford English Dictionary* gives a number of expressions in which *Dutch* is used mockingly or insultingly, some of them not found before the seventeenth century, for even after peace was officially concluded, the past kept being remembered. These expressions stress the Dutch love of alcohol (cf. *Dutch courage* and the wine flowing at *Dutch bargains*), Dutch immorality (*Dutch widow* for a prostitute), and the gibberish they produce (*double Dutch*) or the stopgaps they use ("thank God it's no worse" is a typical form of *Dutch comfort* or *Dutch consolation*). At a *Dutch auction*, the opening bid is higher than the real value; the price is gradually lowered until a bid is made. *Dutch foil*, finally, is cheap imitation gold leaf.

This, then, is how the British thought about the Dutch. From the two dictionaries of Americanisms by Craigie and Mathews, it appears that the Americans, too, voiced their opinions and prejudices about the Dutch and that their ideas about the Dutch were definitely not more positive than those of the British. The phrases with *Dutch* that follow, mentioned by Craigie or Mathews, were all formed in American English; some of them were later borrowed by the British.

For the Americans, the most striking Dutch quality appeared to be their stinginess. Of American origin are the meaningful phrases *Dutch party*, *Dutch supper*, *Dutch treat*, and *to go Dutch*, or regionally, *to Dutch it* – all of them meaning that everyone pays his own share. See:

> **1887** "You'll come along too, won't you?" Lancelot demanded of Ormizon. "Dutch treat vous savez."
> **1891** *Dutchman's treat*, *Dutch treat*, a repast or other entertainment in which each person pays for himself.
> **1904** Young hopefuls at college ... need [money] to buy plug-cut and Dutch suppers with.
> **1914** We'll go Dutch.
> **1927** Dutch parties are rather more elaborate, in that while the hostess provides the dance floor, music, table, service, and cutlery, her friends bring along the drinks and the viands, raiding their family cellars and larders.
> **1949** [They] were part of Dutch treat crowd that took dinner at Fortnightly club.
> **1957** To suggest a free trade area to any of them in such circumstances looks rather like proposing to a teetotaller that you and he go dutch on daily rounds of drinks.

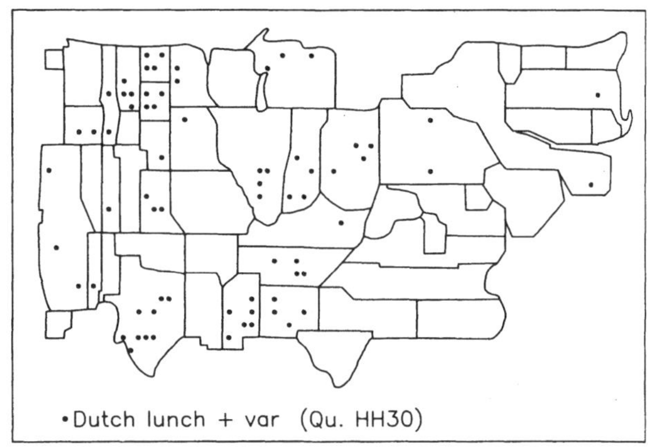

Illustration 1.16 – Map showing the distribution of Dutch lunch *(source: DARE 2: 244)*

In regional American English we have *Dutch lunch* (since 1904), by the side of *Dutch luncheon.* It has a double meaning: not only a lunch where everybody pays his own fare, but also a simple, informal lunch, usually a cold buffet. The term is chiefly used west of the Appalachian Mountains (see illustration 1.16).

Another characteristic quality of the Dutch is their bluntness: they say what's on their minds in the plainest of terms (*talk like a Dutch uncle*), and often do so in an unintelligible lingo (*that's all Dutch to me*).

1838 If you keep a cutting didoes, I must talk to you both like a Dutch uncle.

1853 In some parts of America, when a person has determined to give another a regular lecture, he will often be heard to say, "I will talk to him like a Dutch uncle"; that is, he shall not escape this time.

1872 ["Dutch Uncle" is used] in New England, in the phrase: "Talk to him like a Dutch Uncle, with tears in his eyes and his fist doubled up." (Schele de Vere)

1899 Any speech not understood is said to be "Dutch." "That's all Dutch to me."

They make a lot of noise (called a *Dutch concert* or *Dutch medley* in American slang), they talk rubbish (in slang: *to talk Dutch*), they give a scolding (in slang: *Dutch blessings*), or they go off into fits of rage (in slang: *Dutch fits*).

Additionally, cowardice and disgrace are associated with the Dutch: *to take Dutch leave* or *to do the Dutch (act)* are synonymous with desertion, while *to do the Dutch* is also used for the ultimate escape, namely, from life. *To get in Dutch* means "to fall into disgrace or disfavor," in slang also "to get into trouble."

1898 You've gone and broke the rules and articles of war ... You took Dutch leave.

1904 A week later Dal was found dead in his cell, and I believe he did the Dutch act (suicide).

1919 What the this and that do you mean gettin me in Dutch, you big space filler?

1920 Why did she ... run a chance of getting in Dutch with the very people she'd been trying to know?

1958 You can't face it ... so you're doing the Dutch and leaving a confession.

1965 The day Caper Connelly does the dutch, my guess is it'll be against somebody else.

On the other hand, the Dutch cannot easily get upset, or at least not in the Americans's eyes: *to beat the Dutch* is what they say when something is amazing, astonishing, or extreme.

1775 Our cargoes of meat, drink, and cloaths beat the Dutch.

1859 *It beats the Dutch* is an expression often applied, in New York and New England, to any thing astonishing. (Bartlett)

1906 You women do beat the Dutch.

1940 A group from New England who, slightly in the Majority, agreed on a classical name "to beat the Dutch."

Although the various dictionaries do not call *Dutch courage* an Americanism, it is noteworthy that the term was recorded earlier in American English than in British English – in which the earliest quotation is from 1826, whereas American sources already recorded the term in 1812. If not an Americanism, it came into use almost simultaneously in American English and British English.

1812 The spirit of the people is not up to it [= war] at this time; if so there would be no necessity of those provocations to excite this false spirit – this kind of Dutch courage.

1840 This ... was a company of mere militiamen got together in a hurry, and stuffed with Dutch courage for the occasion.

1852 But then came reflection in the shape of a bottle of true Dutch courage – genuine Knickerbocker Madeira.

Unpleasant things also get the epithet *Dutch*, for instance weeds (*Dutch curse*) and disease (*Dutch distemper*). See:

1830 It had often happened [in 1755] that the servants coming from Germany and Holland, after being purchased, cummunicated [sic] a very malignant fever to whole families and neighbourhoods, where they went. It was of such frequent occurrence as to be called in the Gazettes the "Dutch distemper." This year I find it stated, that it is now settled to be precisely the disease known as the "gaol fever."

1877 *Dutch curse.* "The white field daisy, so called from its annoyance to farmers" (Bartlett).

1895 "Dutch cuss"... I have always heard ... used, among farming people, as the specific name of the common, or ox-eyed, daisy.

In slang, the verb *to dutch* is used in the sense "to deliberately ruin somebody's business or career" or "to break the bank" in a casino.

In all, the expressions do not give a very favorable image of the Dutch, but it is some consolation that a number of those terms, such as *Dutch distemper*, have meanwhile disappeared. True, *Dutch disease* and *Hollanditis* have taken their place, see 2.15. Fortunately, there are also neutral expressions with *Dutch*, although they are a minority, such as *Dutch blanket* (since 1757) for a soft, woolen blanket made by or for Netherlanders in New York, *Dutch oven* (since 1780) for a particular type of pot or oven, and recently *Dutch house* for a specific kind of music, and *Dutch model* for a certain consultation model (see 2.15). For some cold comfort, finally: remember that *Dutch* quite often refers to German (because of the similarity in sound between *Dutch* and *Deutsch*) and sometimes even Scandinavians and other Germanic people.

Regional American English, too, has a large number of phrases with *Dutch*, as we can see in the *Dictionary of American Regional English.* The terms can be divided into two categories. First, there is a group of phrases in which *Dutch* simply has the neutral meaning "from, of, or concerning the Netherlands or Netherlanders," such as *Dutch ball* for a certain ball game, *Dutch cap* for what is also known as *hay barrack* (see **hay barrack** in 2.8) and *Dutch shelf* for a small shelf hanging on the wall with little knick-

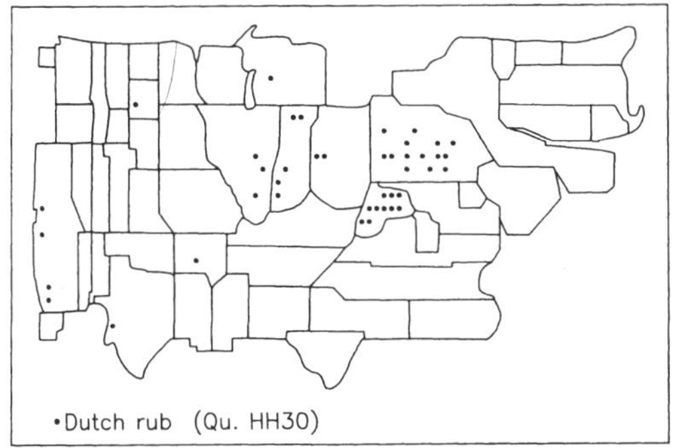

Illustration 1.17 – Map showing the distribution of Dutch rub *(source: DARE 2: 247)*

knacks on it. *Dutch* occurs in many animal names and plant names (*Dutch beech, clover, crow, fox, goose, grass, myrtle, rush*) and in names of foodstuffs (*Dutch boiled dinner, Dutch cabbage, cake, cheese, doughnut, honey*).

In the second group of terms, *Dutch* always has negative or mocking overtones – here we find the following phrases (with in brackets the date since when they have been known): a *Dutch bath* (1953) is a bath for which only very little water is needed, a *Dutch bed* (1905), in the eyes of female students, is a unmade, slovenly bed, *Dutch milk* (1905) is a funny name for beer, a *Dutch nightingale* (1942) is a frog, a *Dutch quarter* (1970) refers to a kick in the backside, and a *Dutch whistle* (1950), finally, is woodcutters' jargon for a piece of bark with the smooth side up on which it is easy to slip.

It is interesting to note that a number of phrases with *Dutch* give some insight into the social habits of the Dutch, or in any case into what the Americans thought of these. Thus, *Dutch hop* (1949) is the name for a folk dance executed after important festivities such as a wedding. A *Dutch wheelbarrow* (1890) is made by holding a boy by his ankles and keeping his legs in the air while he is walking on his hands. If you rub your knuckles on a child's head for fun or as punishment, you are giving a *Dutch rub* (1938). This expression is encountered especially in the North Midland, see illustration 1.17.

A *Dutch wedding* is the name of a game that is described (1936) as follows: "Thc gamc ... bcgins in this wisc: Λ girl sits down on thc floor and chooscs a malc partner to sit beside her. Then he chooses another girl ... and so on until all the players are seated on the floor so as to form a circle. Then the first girl holds a dime between her lips, and passes it to her partner who must receive it with *his* lips ... Then he passes it on to the next girl, and so forth. If the coin is dropped it must be returned to the original player, and started on its course anew."

The Americans turn out to have all sorts of ideas about Dutch love life. In 1950 we find an explanation of what a *Dutch kiss* is: "the ordinary variety, but one takes hold of the ears of the kissee. Very satisfactory end of a row, since it is exclusively a female's and children's kiss, and the kisser can get one last bit of revenge with a sharp pinch of the lobe." Circa 1960, a *Dutch kiss* can also be taken to mean a stolen or furtive kiss – here, *Dutch* is associated with thief. *Dutch nickel* (1949), too, has the sense "stolen kiss," and in addition, *Dutch nickel* and *Dutch squeeze* (1968) are used for "embrace."

The expression *hotter than Dutch love* or *hot as Dutch love* is used for very hot weather (1950) as well as for a very passionate relationship (1966-70) – obviously, the ordinary *Dutch love* is thought to be rather chilly. In 1982, an informant recorded: "My Aunt, who would be about 100 yrs. now, and was descended on both sides from the early Dutch settlers, would say, when walking into a hot kitchen on a summer's day:

"Whew, it's hotter'n Dutch love in here." In American slang, *to Dutch* has been used since 1990 to mean "to climax between the breasts of a woman," and a *Dutch boy* is what American homosexuals call a man having it off with lesbians – the expression is a reference to the story of Hansje Brinker who put his finger in a hole in a dike, playing with the double meaning of *dyke*.

Finally, regional American English has expressions with *Dutchman* – again, not very complimentary. Thus, *Dutchman's anchor* refers to something important that one has forgotten to bring along; in 1945, it is explained as follows: "something important that has been forgotten or left behind; from the old jest about a Dutch shipmaster who had forgotten to bring his anchor along, and so lost his ship." A *Dutchman's razor* is not sharp at all, as appears from an explanation found in 1912: "When a person treads in dung he is said to cut his foot with a Dutchman's razor." And in American slang *(Well) I'm a Dutchman!* is an exclamation of utter surprise: *if that's true, then I'm a Dutchman!*

Fortunately, we have encountered one phrase that is positive about the Dutch, and that will be our last one: a *Dutchman's measure* is the little extra added by the salesman. Unfortunately, this expression was recorded only once by an informant, so it cannot have been very popular – it can hardly be used as a counterpoise.

Most of the expressions above date from the second half of the nineteenth century or later. They fit in with the general picture of the competition that had flared up between the Dutch and the British on the American continent in the seventeenth century. It's possible that the arrival of a new wave of Dutch immigrants in the mid-nineteenth century added to this existing aversion – as far as the language was concerned, at any rate. What is striking is that, in the Dutch language, hardly anything was done to counteract this. Neither in European Dutch nor – as far as we know – in American Dutch do we find expressions in which "American" is used mockingly or negatively. Only after 1914, the Dutch Van Dale dictionary's definition for *Amerikaans* (American) did include the meanings "strange, extreme, excessive," as in "*Het ging er Amerikaans toe*" ("There were American goings-on there"). At the same time, *Amerikaans* also had a positive meaning; the word was associated with rapid growth and matter-of-fact efficiency, for example, in 1907: "The civilization material amassed after '70 with American speed" or, in 1913: ."..B. claimed, with American exactingness." Much later, in the 1970s, some Netherlanders began to use the term *Amerikaanse toestanden*, by which they actually meant "social evils and abuses as in America" – the expression probably came to be used first by Dutch liberals who criticized America's capitalism and its foreign policy. But although the phrase *Amerikaanse toestanden* ("American goings-on") is still used regularly in Dutch, it is by no means unique: in the Dutch press we also often come across Russian, Belgian, Italian, and Chinese "*toestanden*."

1.5 American Dutch, American Flemish, and American Frisian of nineteenth- and twentieth-century immigrants

"Our streets have been taken by the Dutch": emigrants in the nineteenth and twentieth centuries

After Independence, the young United States of America needed a few decades for internal reorganization and reconstruction, but in the early part of the nineteenth century, industry began to develop, roads were built and canals were dug, and large-scale westward colonization got underway, with large areas of land being cultivated for agriculture. The land was cheap, and hard workers hoped they could build up a good life and a good future. For this reason, many Europeans came to America. In the second half of the nineteenth century, colonists from the Netherlands (many of them from Friesland) and Belgium went to America as well. A strong incentive was the potato harvest failures in Europe, which caused famine among the poor. Much has been written about these migrants; what follows is based largely on the following sources: Jacob van Hinte's *Netherlanders in America* (1928, English translation 1985; especially part 2, chapter 15); Henry S. Lucas's *Netherlanders in America* (1955); *Americans from Holland* by Arnold Mulder (1947); G.F. de Jong's *The Dutch in America, 1609-1974* (1975; especially chapter 11); and Hans Krabbendam's *Vrijheid in het verschiet. Nederlandse emigratie naar Amerika 1840-1940* (2006). In addition, W. Lagerwey provides much information and many quotations in *Neen Nederland, 'k vergeet u niet* (1982).

The first emigrants travelled to a new country not only to make a living, but also in search of religious asylum. When, in 1816, the Nederduits Gereformeerde Kerk (Low Dutch Reformed Church) changed its name to Nederlands Hervormde Kerk (Dutch Reformed Church), this brought with it a new orientation: the Bible was interpreted more freely, and the government imposed regulations on the church that replaced the Dordrecht Church Order. Not everyone was happy with these innovations. The discord led to a schism in 1834: the Secession. The secessionists saw themselves as the defenders of the true reformed faith of the fathers; later, in 1892, after a merger with the so-called dissenters under Abraham Kuyper, they proceeded as the Gereformeerde Kerken van Nederland (Reformed Churches of the Netherlands). Other religious groups, too, both Protestants and Roman Catholics, were disaffected with Dutch politics. Poor people, for instance, could not provide religious education for their children in independent schools, because these did not receive state grants until 1917.

Because the secessionists were severely hindered in their religious duties by the Dutch authorities, they did not feel at home in the Netherlands and began looking for a way out. In 1845, the first group of secessionists left for Illinois. The largest groups of secessionists, together with members of the Reformed Church, came to Michigan and Iowa. In 1847, dominie Albertus Christiaan van Raalte led a group of migrants to the "Colony" in Michigan. There, Holland became the main settlement (at first simply called "the city"), surrounded by small daughter settlements like Graafschap, Overisel, Drenthe, Noordeloos, Zeeland, and Groningen. A few thousand Dutchmen joined the Colony. In the same year, dominie Hendrik Peter Scholte, together with a group of

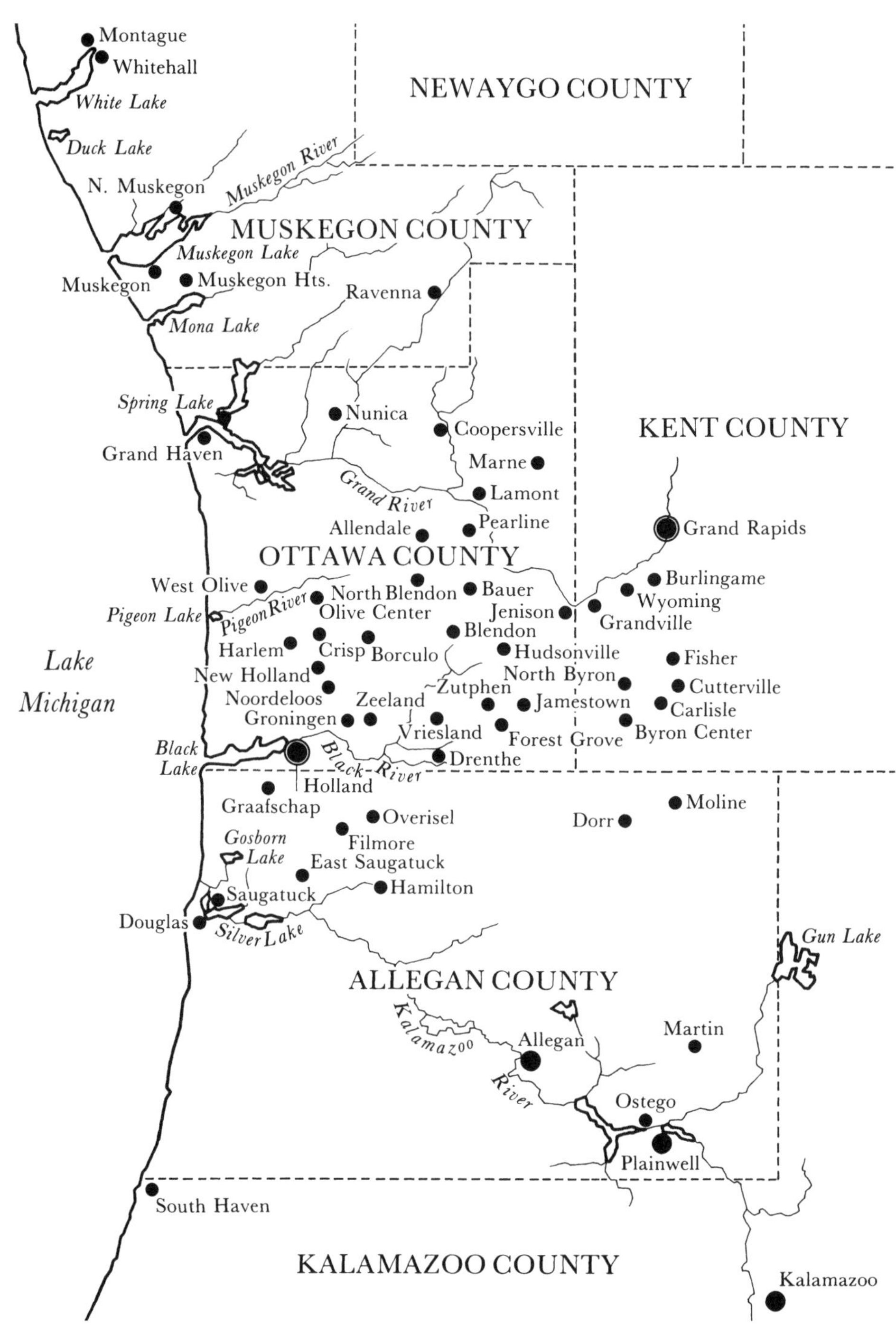

Illustration 1.18 – Map showing Dutch settlements in Michigan around 1880 (source: Lagerwey 1982: 33)

secessionists, founded the town of Pella in Iowa. Here, too, daughter settlements were founded later, of which Orange City was the most important one. Between 1846 and 1880, 2,660 immigrants came to Pella.

Groups of Catholics came to the US as well. Most of these came from the southern parts of the Netherlands and from Belgium, which had broken away from the Kingdom of the Netherlands in 1830. From 1840 on, groups of Roman Catholic Flemings settled in a number of places, including Moline and Chicago (Illinois), Kansas City and St. Louis (Missouri), South Bend (Indiana), Detroit and Rochester (Michigan), Paterson (New Jersey), and Victor (Iowa). In addition, a group of Dutch Roman Catholics, mainly from North Brabant and Limburg, emigrated under the guidance of Father Theodorus van den Broek to Little Chute, Wisconsin, in 1847.

After this first wave of immigrants, in which especially many groups of religious people came to America together, new Dutchmen crossed the Atlantic in the second half of the nineteenth century. During the American Civil War (1861-1865) the number of immigrants decreased sharply, but after that their number increased again, especially in the 1880s: more than 53,000. These were often individuals who, for economic rather than religious reasons, opted for a life in another country. Many of them went to live with relatives in Dutch settlements. Others went to places where they could find suitable employment, but they continued to settle close to one another. Thus, in the second half of the nineteenth century, Hollanders, Flemings, and Frisians went to the San Joaquin Delta in California to help drain marshes, and build dikes and polders. Towards the end of the nineteenth century, a group of Frisians came to Whitinsville in Massachusetts, where Frisian was spoken until after World War II.

Dutch settlers also began to arrive in the big cities. About 1,000 Dutch Jews settled in or around New York City. In cities such as Paterson, Passaic, Cleveland, Detroit, Chicago, Grand Rapids, and Milwaukee, Dutch Protestant enclaves were founded. In 1849, a Grand Rapids newspaper wrote: "During the past week our streets have been taken by the Dutch. The Hollanders have resorted here in uncommon numbers and their ox teams have made quite a caravan. ...They are a very stout, apparently healthy and frugal race."

After World War I, new immigration restrictions were introduced, causing the number of immigrants to decrease. During the economic crisis in the 1930s, hardly any Dutch or Belgian immigrants came to the United States. After World War II, Dutchmen and Flemings again tried to secure a better future for themselves, and between 1945 and 1990, some 130,000 of them came to the US, primarily to California and Washington State. As a rule, they quickly exchanged their Dutch for English, and for the rest of this story, they are not particularly significant.

"Dutchness"

A total of 265,539 Dutchmen and Frisians came to the US between 1820 and 1949, Lucas says in his *Netherlanders in America*. Add to this an unknown number of Flemish-speaking Belgians. The members of the "Young Dutch branch" as the Dutch migrants in the nineteenth and twentieth century were called, followed the example of the seventeenth-century Dutch colonists, the "Old Dutch branch": they settled in the

Illustration 1.19 – Map of the United States with places where Dutch settlers live (source: Lagerwey 1982: 140)

US together. In the nineteenth century, the "Young Dutch branch" was concentrated in the American Midwest. Historian Swierenga has calculated that, of the 60,000 to 70,000 Dutch immigrants who had arrived in their new country in 1870, more than 90 percent lived in only 18 counties in seven states. According to him, very few other groups of immigrants have settled so closely together. Only in the course of time did the Dutch settlers spread out over a larger area.

The reason the Dutch immigrants chose to live near each other was due to their religious convictions. The "founding fathers and mothers" of the settlements in Michigan and Iowa were, for the greater part, secessionists – they were convinced of their sacred duty to preserve the faith of their fathers. This was only possible if they stayed together: mutual solidarity would not only promote their welfare, but also make the undisturbed practice of their religion possible. In 1870, three-quarters of the Netherlanders lived in only 55 American towns. These were set up as replicas of their places of origin in the Low Countries, with the Dutch church in the middle as the main social center. In their day-to-day existence, everything revolved around Dutch religious opinions, Dutch customs, and the Dutch language. Because the Hollanders lived so closely together and stuck to their traditional Dutch culture, they were able, in spite of their relatively small numbers as compared to immigrants from other countries, to preserve their "Dutchness" for a long time – and they were clearly recognizable as Dutchmen by their surroundings. They passed on the Dutch language from generation to generation, because in that way, so they thought, the Dutch character would be preserved: "when the Dutch language is lost, one no longer finds that typical staid Dutch spirit either," someone wrote in Pella's *Weekblad* in 1923 (Van Hinte, p. 1009).

Just how long the Dutch character could be preserved in isolated circumstances was shown by the Mennonites. In the seventeenth century, Dutch Mennonites went to Germany, and later on they settled in Russia with German co-religionists. In order to escape Russian military service, they went to America in 1874. Some of them still had Dutch names: Jansen, Klaassen, Harmen. And when a Dutch Mennonite came to an American settlement in 1930, he still recognized in them all kinds of Dutch qualities (he mentioned their simplicity, their neat appearance, their clean sheds and stables and their strict morals), and some of them still had a Dutch Bible.

In spite of their tendency to stick together, the new immigrants were forced to adapt themselves more quickly than the "Old Dutch branch." In their new homeland, English was by now the general daily language as well as the language of official documents and the schools . The immigrants did not, moreover, arrive in the New World as privileged people; their weak economic position forced them to adapt quickly. They were forced to learn some English immediately on arrival, to use at work. On p. 991, Van Hinte describes a few amusing misunderstandings, including a few young workmen who got angry with their boss when they heard they were supposed to sleep "upstairs," because they thought this meant "under the stars."

However, in Dutch enclaves, especially in the Midwest, Dutch was passed on from generation to generation up until after World War II, albeit to a lesser extent. It is this type of Dutch, planted in the US in the middle of the nineteenth century and, after 150 years, still spoken to a limited degree by descendants of the original colonists, that will be discussed in the remainder of this section.

The Dutch home language of the immigrants

The Dutch of the various immigrants in the nineteenth century was far from homogeneous. The immigrants who came to the Midwest as a rule had had little education, and came from the countryside. At home they spoke a regional dialect, and often they did not know the Standard Dutch that was taught at school, or they scarcely knew it. What knowledge of it they did have was usually acquired through the church. The immigrants came from different regions of the Netherlands, so that in many cases they could hardly understand each other: *Gronings* and *Zeeuws*, for example, are not easily mutually intelligible, and Frisian is even classified as a separate language. Many of the followers of Van Raalte in Holland and its surrounding settlements came from the northeastern provinces in the Netherlands. Dominie Scholte mainly brought colonists from the region where his influence was greatest – the borderland between the Dutch provinces of South Holland and Gelderland and from the South Holland islands – when he immigrated to Pella, Iowa; this is apparent from a study by dialectologist Piet van Reenen (see illustration 1.20). The immigrants from this group all spoke country dialects, except for a small group of migrants from the city of Utrecht. What is remarkable is that so many of the immigrants came from the same townships: Swierenga has calculated that nearly three-quarters of all immigrants between 1820 and 1880 hailed from only 134 of the 1,156 Dutch townships, and what is more: half of all the immigrants came from only 55 townships – most of them in the Dutch "Bible Belt." In Pella, nearly two out of every three migrants came from an area measuring only 60 by 90 kilometers, where closely related dialects were spoken.

The fact that the Dutch immigrants spoke different dialects meant they often couldn't understand each other. Therefore, whenever possible, people preferred to settle near speakers from the same Dutch region. This is readily evident from the names of the settlements (see 1.6): Zeelanders went to live in Zeeland and Drenteners in Drenthe, and so on. Within the settlements, too, new quarters were created where people from the same region or town in the Netherlands could live together: thus, Pella had Frisian and Groningen quarters for Frisians and Groningers, respectively, and a Herwijns quarter for immigrants from Herwijnen.

Of course, it was impossible for people to remain living in isolation from other dialect speakers. Up until 1900, in any case, large numbers of newly arrived Dutchmen went to live in the existing settlements; they brought new dialects with them, and lived scattered among the others. In addition, speakers of different dialects intermarried. The result was a dialect levelling exactly like the one that had occurred two centuries before, when the first wave of Dutch colonists settled in the New World: to be able to communicate, the various immigrants adapted their speech to that of the others, so that conspicuous dialect characteristics disappeared. People did not speak Standard Dutch with one another, the way dialect speakers from different regions in the Netherlands do these days, because they were not proficient in the standard language.

The degree to which the dialects have become adapted to each other can also be seen from research on the usage of Dutch immigrants in the US done by dialectologist Jo Daan in 1966. In *Ik was te bissie...*, written in 1987, she describes her research, and concludes that the majority of her informants spoke Dutch with a more or less pronounced regional accent. Only the articulation and intonation had remained from the original dialects, but it was impossible to discover from which region an immigrant or his descendant came on the basis of the sounds, forms, and words. The Dutch dialects turned out to have changed in the US much more than Frisian had in the Frisian-American settlements; since Frisian deviated so strongly from Dutch dialects, it managed to preserve its own character.

Because the immigrants in Michigan, Iowa, and Wisconsin came from different Dutch regions, various levelled dialects, each of which was mutually slightly divergent, came into being. In the Graafschap and a few other smaller Protestant settlements around Holland, Michigan, for instance, some eastern Dutch characteristics were preserved. In the Roman Catholic settlement in Wisconsin in Little Chute (so called after a local waterfall, and called *Little Schut* by the Dutchmen), the influence of southern Dutch dialects was still clearly discernible – at any rate, this was the case in 1957, when William Shetter studied it (nowadays, Dutch is no longer spoken there). Shetter found the pronoun *gij* ("you") for the *Hollands* and Standard Dutch *jij*; he also found forms like *stökske* ("stick") en *blumke* ("flower") with the diminutive ending *-ke*, whereas Standard Dutch has *stokje* and *bloempje*, as well as the pronunciation of *g* more to the front of the mouth (known as a "soft g"), and dialect words such as *strijkholt* for "match." But here, too, dialect mixture occurred at an early stage, so this usage could not be located within one particular southern Netherlands dialect. Among the speakers in Victor, Iowa, which was founded by Flemings, southern dialect traits were also preserved.

The language of both the seventeenth-century and the nineteenth-century colonists underwent dialect levelling, but the results were not the same – for two reasons: first, the dialects in the Low Countries had changed, naturally, in those two centuries, and secondly, on arrival in the US, the two groups spoke different dialects. Whereas in the seventeenth century the city dialect spoken in Amsterdam was the most prominent, most of the immigrants who went to America two centuries later spoke a country dialect from the center and northeast of the Netherlands. When members of the "Young Dutch branch" settled in regions where descendants of the seventeenth-century Dutch colonists were living, the difference in usage was striking to both groups. In 1910 Prince remarked:

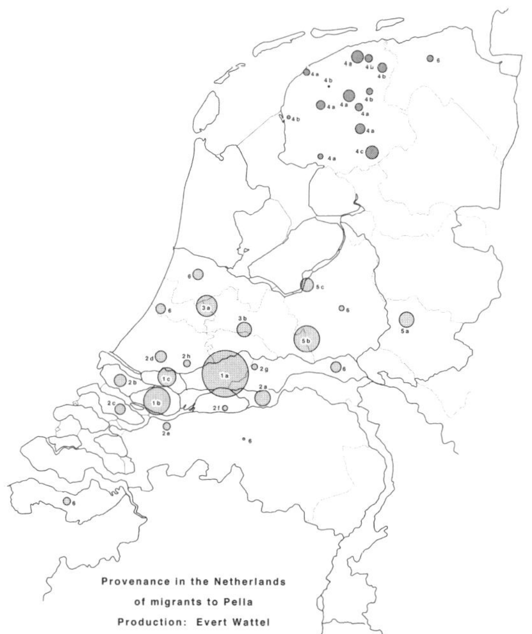

Illustration 1.20 – The Dutch places of origin of the immigrants who went to Pella (source: Van Reenen 2000: 305)

> "The old county people [in Paterson, NJ] hold themselves strictly aloof from these foreigners, and say, when they are questioned as to the difference between the idioms: *onze tâl äz lêx däuts en hoelliz äs Hôlläns; kwāit dääfrent* – "our language is low Dutch and theirs is Holland Dutch; quite different."... As old Mrs. Bartholf of Paterson remarked to the writer, when questioned as to how much she could grasp of a conversation in Netherland Dutch: *en pärti kän äk kwāit xût verstâne, mâr en pärti kän äk nît* – "part of it I can understand quite well, but a part of it I cannot."

The mutual intelligibility, of course, also depended on the dialect spoken by the new immigrants. Sometimes they understood each other well enough. Thus, when Frans van Driele came to America in 1847, he met descendants of the early colonists in Ulster County, New York, who greeted each other with *How you kom an van daag?* ("How are you today?"), and *It mankeer een beetje met you te praten* ("I want to talk with you a bit"). And although their Dutch differed from that of the new immigrants, the latter felt at home with the "Old Dutch branch."

"Zealots without love"

The first colonists in Michigan and Iowa were mainly secessionists; in the Netherlands, this denomination represented only a very small minority. Later on, more and more reformed Protestants came to the American settlements, and from 1855 on the number of reformed Protestants surpassed that of the secessionists.

The secessionists and reformed Protestants joined the church that had been brought by the Dutch to America already in the seventeenth century, the Reformed Protestant Dutch Church in North America, which from 1867 was called Reformed Church in America (RCA). Some believers, however, found this church too frivolous: there they sang too many hymns instead of psalms, they did not preach often enough from the Heidelberg catechism, and confirmation classes did not get enough attention. Also, the fact that English had by then become the language of the church caused a problem (see 1.2). In the young Dutch settlements, sermons were at first preached in Dutch. The Dutch services were therefore also attended by descendants from the seventeenth-century Dutch colonists who at last got an opportunity to hear Dutch sermons again.

Because they were dissatisfied with the association with the Reformed Church, a number of Van Raalte's followers seceded in 1857 and founded their own church. "I liked the country, but not the church," one of the secessionists said. The members of the new church then quarreled for years about the name: after Holland Reformed Church and True Dutch Reformed Church, they adopted the name True Holland Reformed Church in 1864, after which a new row started about the question of whether "true" should be kept in the name or not – a row that resulted in yet another new secession! They did not avoid hard words in the process, either: dominie De Beij reproached the members of the new organization – quite rightly, by the way – for being schismatic, accusing them, with a wealth of biblical phrases, of "harboring injured feelings of pride, diotrefism, personal feuds, of being misleading, pharisaistic, of plucking out the gnat and swallowing the camel, of harboring a spirit of seduction, of being zealots without love, and makers of sects!"

Eventually, in 1880, it was decided to delete the pretentious "true" and to call the church the Dutch Christian Reformed Church. In 1890, *Dutch* was also given up, because English and German congregations, too, had joined the church. Besides, a union had taken place with the True Reformed Dutch Church – another temporary secession. From that moment on, the name was the Christian Reformed Church in North America, making the name similar to that of the Christian Reformed Church in the Netherlands. This did not mean the end of the secessions, however: in 1924, the Protestant Reformed churches went their own separate ways.

Of all the churches with roots in the Netherlands, the Christian Reformed Church (CRC) has the most followers today, even more than the Reformed Church: in the US and Canada there are approximately 300,000, according to their website, as opposed to 270,000 members of the Reformed Church. In the Netherlands, on the other hand, the Christian Reformed Churches (as they have been called since 1892) have many fewer followers. Smaller churches in the US founded by Dutchmen include the Netherlands Reformed Congregations (since 1877, about 9,500 members), the Protestant Reformed Churches (since 1924, 7,000 members), the Free Reformed Churches (begun in the 1950s and, under this name since 1974, over 4,000 members), the Heritage (Netherlands) Reformed Congregations (since 1993, 2,000 members), and the Reformed Congregations in North America (since 1963, 1,500 members). Half of the Netherlands Reformed Congregations held part of their services in Dutch as late as 1972, but nowadays they have all made the move to English. The Protestant Reformed churches had already made that move towards the end of the 1950s.

The religious schisms were in general caused by differences in the interpretations of the faith, but in the nineteenth century the language issue – Dutch versus English – also played a role, as the members of the Christian Reformed Church found this more important than those of the Reformed Church.

Illustration 1.21 – The disembarking and arrival of the Dutch emigrants; print, 1864, ridiculing emigration (source: Lagerwey 1982: 21)

The Standard Dutch of church, school, and press

After the foundation of Dutch settlements in 1847, the Dutch language established itself – again – on the American continent. The first three generations of children that were born there had a Dutch dialect as their mother tongue. In addition, Standard Dutch "held its own" until the twentieth century.

Every Dutch immigrant in the US was a member of a church congregation – and pretty soon he had, as we saw above, a choice of several possibilities. The denominations had their intrinsic differences, but the similarities were what struck outsiders most: in daily life, the faith had pride of place. Every Dutch settlement had one or more churches, sometimes with a school attached. In the Protestant churches, the services were held in Dutch, and at home, prayers were said before meals in Dutch, and passages were read from the *Statenbijbel* (the Dutch Authorized Version of the Bible). The language of the church was not the dialect that was spoken at home but the old-fashioned, formal Dutch of the *Statenbijbel*, of the metrical psalms from the eighteenth century, and of the Heidelberg catechism. In the church, every Protestant immigrant came into contact with Standard Dutch, although this is not what was spoken at home. Nineteenth-century Dutch immigrants experienced the same gap between spoken language and church language as did their seventeenth-century predecessors. The Roman Catholics did not have this problem, because Dutch did not play a role in their church.

In the schools, the Standard Dutch that was taught was the same as that sung and preached in the church. Many children, however, saw no point in learning Dutch, for in everyday life it could not be used: their families spoke dialect at home, and in the rest of their surroundings, only English was used.

From the beginning, the press played an important part in immigrant life. The press, too, used Standard Dutch. From the Netherlands a large number of newspapers and periodicals was sent to America: between 1876 and 1885 the number increased from 25,000 to 57,000, averaging 47,000 consignments a year. But in America itself, too, Dutch papers were printed. As early as 1849, the first newspaper, the *Sheboygan Nieuwsbode*, appeared. It had been eagerly anticipated, as someone from Grand Rapids asserted in a letter to the editor in 1852:

> "There now are a good many Netherlanders in this place, at least so one would conclude when he sees the large crowd of Hollanders storming into the postoffice on Wednesday evening eagerly asking for *De Sheboygan Nieuwsbode*. Should Charley happen to say 'No,' you should see the disappointed expression on their faces, and hear the plaintive wail of the children."

"Plaintive wail" sounds a little exaggerated, but the large numbers of Dutch papers and magazines that were published in the US show that there was a large enough market for them. The Dutch-American linguist Lagerwey, in his *Neen Nederland, 'k vergeet u niet*, provides a list of over 25 Dutch periodicals, confining himself to the most important ones and those that had appeared for a longer period. In the nineteenth century, to be sure, all these publications bore a religious stamp, and another important objective was the passing on of the "gossip" that because of the distance could not be passed on by word of mouth. In the papers, the advertisements were an important component, for instance:

"IMPROVED FARMS
Ziet u uit voor een eigen farm, hier is dan de plaats. Best land, goedkoop.
Met weinig kunt gij klaarkomen. Wij hebben 2 Holl. gemeenten, een Ger. en Chr. Ger. Schrijft aan Wm. Santjer, Bejou – Min."
("IMPROVED FARMS
Looking for a farm of your own, this is the place. Good land, cheap. With little you can be done. We have 2 Dutch congregations, one Ref. and Chr. Ref. Write to Wm. Santjer, Bejou – Min.")

From the English loanwords and constructions, we may deduce that Willem Santjer had been living in the US for some time.

For the rest, the papers contained occasional poems, short stories, and news columns, both about America and the Netherlands. The American news was, of course, covered by American newspapers – and often in an even better way. The Dutch papers were very popular because they cemented together the scattered compatriots: they emphasized the links between the Dutchmen, who shared religion, language, and customs. They glorified Dutch home life and sang the praises of the Dutch language. Thus, as early as 1852, the *Sheboygan Nieuwsbode* printed a rhyming summons to read only Dutch: "Reeds snoeren ons de hechtste banden,/Leest slechts de taal der Nederlanden" ("We are getting hemmed in on all sides,/ Let Dutch words be your only guides"). Apparently, such a summons was needed even at that time. For, while the position of Dutch at home was strong enough, it was losing ever more ground to English in school, church, and press.

Loss of Dutch in the schools

Dutch first lost ground in the schools, and that began immediately on arrival in the US. On his way to Pella in 1846, Hendrik Barendregt wrote in a letter to Scholte: "Those who know good English, possess a rich gift when they come here from Holland, so I cannot advise everyone strongly enough to learn the English language." In the settlements, English lessons for adults were set up, so that they could begin to learn the language straightaway.

Children were sent to independent schools, financed by the American government, where they were taught in English. At school, the children in the Dutch settlements also learned to read the Dutch bible, they sang Dutch psalms and hymns, and they took confirmation classes in Dutch, sometimes after the mandatory classes – for it was important for them to learn Standard Dutch so that they could follow the church services.

Right from the start, there were discussions about the question of whether "Christian schools" or "Dutch schools" should be set up where the children could receive special instruction in the Dutch confessional writings and in the Dutch language, which was after all the language in which God's word was written. In the Reformed Church there was, however, a majority favoring independent schools, because members realized the importance of integration into American society: "we should not ... create a transplanted Netherlands, but a real part of the American people," to quote Van Raalte.

It is true that Christian schools were set up in 1857 in the Colony and in 1861 in Pella, but these existed for only a few years. It turned out to be far from easy to find teachers, and additionally, the institutions cost a lot of money.

The Christian Reformed Church, on the other hand, was all for Christian schools, and was prepared to supply the necessary funds. This church founded a number of schools. Until 1900, lessons were taught in Dutch, next to English of course, which was compulsory. This church attached great importance to English as well, as can be seen by the fact that in Graafschap around 1870, a teacher was turned away because his English pronunciation was so bad! In the 1880s, when parents began to notice that their children knew less and less Dutch, members of the Reformed Church, too, sent their children to the Christian schools, causing these schools to prosper in that period. During and after the 1890s, the emphasis shifted more to the conveyance of religious ideas and focused less on teaching Dutch. Over time, many townships with a substantial following of the Christian Reformed Church had a Christian school; in 1973, for example, there were more than 200 – but they had long since ceased to teach Dutch: from about 1914 Dutch had been degraded to an optional subject.

The secondary and higher education of the Dutch youngsters was also taken care of, but in English only. Dominie Van Raalte founded the "Holland Academy" for secondary education in the Colony in 1851, with financial support from the Reformed Church. On behalf of a number of parents, dominie Marten Ypma protested against the fact that English was the teaching language. He called for a teacher

> "who would be qualified to instruct students of this school with good knowledge but also to teach the basic use of the Dutch language, the pure use of which is sadly being lost. And this is occurring in spite of everyone's conviction that in the interest of religion it is absolutely necessary that the language, which is yet indispensable for many years, must be upheld so that the preaching will not become ridiculous due to the mixing of the languages. People should also, when needed, be able to wield the pen well in their native tongue." (Van Hinte 1985, p. 257)

This plea, incidentally, is noteworthy, as Ypma had founded the settlement of Vriesland in the Colony along with a group of Frisians, yet he calls for education not in Frisian but in Dutch. The protest was nevertheless in vain. The "Holland Academy" prepared students for English-language higher education at Rutgers College in New Brunswick, New Jersey, which had been set up in 1766 by the Reformed Church.

The "Holland Academy" was the first of a number of institutions for higher education founded by the Dutch. In 1853, the Baptists, at the request of dominie Scholte, established Central University in Pella, nowadays called Central College. In 1866, Hope College was set up in Holland, Michigan, for the training of clergymen. Here, too, classes were taught in English, although, because of the great importance of the Dutch Bible translation and theological works, the Dutch language was taught as well, from 1866 until 1890, from 1903 until 1925 and from 1939 until 1947. In 1882, the Reformed Church founded the Northwestern Academy, now Northwestern College, in Orange City, Iowa.

In 1876, members of the Christian Reformed Church established Calvin College in Grand Rapids. Dutch was an obligatory subject at this College, which it continued to be until the 1960s; after that it became an optional subject, the choice of which is still being encouraged, at first so that students could read the works of famous Dutch theologians in the original, and nowadays, according to the website, because "studying the Dutch language and culture will open you to a people who have long been making remarkable contributions to both the European community and the greater international scene." In 1955, the Christian Reformed Church established Dordt College in Sioux Center, Iowa, so called – for Dutch people this is remarkable – after the Synod of Dordrecht in 1618/19. This Synod is important for the history of the church because of the doctrines established there, and because of the initiative taken there for the first complete translation of the Bible from the original languages. Teaching at Dordt College, however, is done in English; the Dutch language can be chosen as a minor.

In the Dutch-speaking Roman Catholic settlements in America, parish schools were set up, too. Their aim was to give tuition in the Roman Catholic faith, rather than the Dutch language: parents preferred not to send their children to a state school, because American schools were Protestant in their set-up. The Catholic parish schools were very international, and besides Dutchmen also included Irishmen, Frenchmen, and Germans living in the settlements. In the Catholic townships with parish schools, however, Dutch had a longer life than in the places without them. Little Chute and Hollandtown (both in Wisconsin) and Victor (Iowa) had Dutch speakers until the 1960s. For higher education, especially for the training of priests, St. Norbert College was established in De Pere, Wisconsin, in 1898; the school still exists, but the curriculum has been expanded.

Loss of Dutch in the church

The Dutch immigrant churches within the Reformed Church at first held on to Dutch as their church language, but here, too, room was gradually being created for services in English, just as in the American churches. In the course of the nineteenth century, history once more repeated itself: the new immigrant churches slowly but surely became anglicized. The Christian Reformed Church stuck to Dutch longer than the Reformed Church, and the same applied to other secessionist churches. The rule was: the more orthodox the denomination, the longer its sermons were preached in Dutch.

The loss of Dutch in the church was fraught with intense emotions for many people. Many immigrants found Dutch more suitable for their religious experience than English. Some were even convinced that God only spoke Dutch, and that He would not understand them if they prayed to Him in English. Others were more realistic – they learned English, for instance, by comparing the texts of the Dutch and the English bibles, or by using an edition that had the English and the Dutch text printed side by side. Such a bilingual edition had been published as early as 1850 by the American Bible Society; in this edition, the Dutch Authorized Statenbijbel was printed together with an American bible based on the British King James version.

In the Colony in Michigan, a small group of people held English-language services, starting in 1854. In 1862, churches in both Pella and the Colony officially began to hold English-language services in addition to those in Dutch. The first Christian Reformed Church did not start services in English until 1887. Gradually, English came to be used more often for Reformed Church sermons, and the Dutch Bible translation was replaced by the English one. At first, only the Sunday evening service was held in English, and the morning and afternoon services were in Dutch. Over the years, especially during 1890-1895, the number of English-language services increased at the expense of the Dutch-language services. In 1896, the first church associated with the Reformed Church changed from Dutch to English for all of its services. Some churches started to offer services in English for fear that young people might otherwise turn away to the English church – the same argument was used in the eighteenth century by the descendants of the first colonists – with the unintended result being that older people often joined an orthodox church with sermons in Dutch, or else started a new grouping.

That young people found it difficult to understand Dutch sermons is evident, for example, from the fact that dominie Martin Flipse would only accept an invitation to the Dutch congregation in Albany in 1893 on the condition that in the evening services he would be allowed to preach in English. Deacon A.M. Donner later wrote on this subject that the older people had great problems with this, but had to accept it. "It was high time. Many of the younger people of the settlement went to the English churches, but now they came here in the evening, bringing others with them. The evening services were attended."

Gradually, the fate of Dutch in the church was being sealed. In 1910, only three out of approximately one-hundred churches held services in English only; the others offered both Dutch and English services. In Holland, Michigan, the use of the English language for church purposes was not formally accepted by the classis until 1923. The shift to English took even longer in the Christian Reformed Church; in 1907, when this church celebrated its fiftieth anniversary, there were only seven American-speaking churches in the west, of which six were in Michigan – the others still stuck to Dutch.

During World War I, preaching in a foreign language was discouraged. The governor of Iowa even decreed that in the churches, Dutch was to be used only when provided with an English translation, and he claimed that there was no sense for anybody to pray in another language than English, for "God listens only to the English language." As a result of these measures, the number of churches that changed to English rapidly increased. Still, in the 1930s Dutch-language services were held in several churches of the Reformed Church. After the Second World War, however, English had definitively won in the church. In 1929, even in the Christian Reformed Church 1143 of the 2055 congregations conducted their services in English. Around 1950, Dutch-language services were a small minority, aimed at a senior audience. Nevertheless, in as late as 1958, a Dutch-language service was held every Sunday afternoon in Grand Rapids, and this was attended by about 500 people – a whole century after the Dutch immigrant churches had been established. Part of the audience consisted of new arrivals from the Netherlands. Towards the end of the 1980s, a meeting of the Christian Reformed Church was held every year in Peoria near Pella, where Dutch psalms were sung; and in some churches of the Netherlands Reformed Congregation in Iowa and South Dakota, the afternoon services were still regularily conducted in the Dutch language.

Apart from that, Frisian religious services had been held in Grand Rapids on special occasions since 1935; this became an annual event in 1956. The driving force behind this was Bearend Joukes Fridsma (1905-2005), a professor of German at Calvin College from 1956 until 1970. As a little boy of six he had emigrated to America with his parents. The minister was the Frisian immigrant Broer Doekeles Dykstra (called B.D. for short), who had come to the US at the age of 11 in 1882. The first Frisian service attracted about 500 interested people, and in the year of Fridsma's death there were about 100. For these services in particular and at the request of the Christian Reformed Church, Fridsma translated 130 psalms from English into Frisian. A striking detail is that at the back of the Frisian-language hymnbook *Tuskentiden. Oanfoljend lieteboek by it Lieteboek foar de Tsjerken*, published in 2006, two hymns have been included in a translation by the Frisian-American Fridsma. The Frisian *Tuskentiden* is a translation of a Dutch hymnbook that was published in 2005. The Frisian edition includes some hymns that are lacking in the Dutch text. Hymns 237 and 238 are Fridsma's: hymn 237 "Hear, wês mei ús oant in oare kear" is a translation of Jeremiah C. Rankin's "God be with you until we meet again" and hymn 238 "Yn 'e namme Jezus bûcht yn alle wrâld" is a translation of Caroline M. Noel's "At the Name of Jesus." Fridsma's text is still sung in the circa five Frisian-language services held in Friesland every Sunday.

While the Protestants were pondering the question as to which language to use in a service, this was not a problem for the Roman Catholics in, for instance, Wisconsin. The Roman Catholic church had long been internationally oriented. Father Van den Broek preached in English, French, and German, as well as in Dutch. The language of the liturgy was Latin until 1962. This made the Catholics abandon Dutch as church language very quickly, shifting to English. Moreover, around 1928 the 40,000 Dutch Roman Catholics in the US lived scattered all over the country. As a result, there were only 25 Dutch Catholic religious communities, without any interrelation, as opposed to 500 Protestant ones, according to Van Hinte (p. 856-7).

Loss of Dutch in the press

From the beginning, many Dutch-language publications inserted a few articles in English. In 1850, a periodical entitled *Hollander* was published, first half in English and half in Dutch, eventually in 1865 it became all Dutch. As early as 1855, the American-minded dominie Scholte published the first English-language newspaper in a Dutch settlement, the *Pella Gazette*. Dutch settlers, however, weren't quite ready for this yet, and in 1861, the paper was discontinued due to lack of interest. In its place came the Dutch-language *Pella's Weekblad*. In Holland, Michigan, the first English-language newspaper was published in 1872 – 25 years after its foundation. Twelve years later, in 1884, the publishers of a new periodical in South Dakota, the *Harrison Globe*, deliberately chose to print several articles in English, "for those who do not know Dutch or who have a preference for English." Dutch obviously was on its way out.

The Dutch-language press was going through a difficult phase anyway: because of the relatively small number of Dutchmen and of the heavy competition, from both other Dutch-language and English-language periodicals, most publishers suffered losses and presses quickly disappeared, after which another optimistic publisher might decide to start a new one. Very few periodicals were published successfully for a number of decades, such as *De Grondwet* (1860-1938), *De Volksvriend* (1874-1951), and *De Hope* (1865-1933), published by Hope College. In its heyday, in 1909, *De Grondwet* had more than 10,000 subscribers.

When the First World War started, 25 Dutch-language papers and periodicals still existed. During that war, the American administration discouraged the use of foreign languages; the measure was directed in the first place against German, but Dutch and German were frequently mixed up. As a result, the number of Dutch papers decreased, but in 1927 there were still nineteen. In the 1930s and 1940s, this number was reduced drastically, probably, due in part to the recession, as well as the rise of (English-language) radio, film, and television and, of course, because ever fewer people could read Dutch.

The newspapers associated with the Christian Reformed Church were published in Dutch longer than the others and remained alive the longest, but even they eventually became English-language publications. *De Heidenwereld*, first published in 1896, changed into *Missionary Monthly*, and can now be read on the Internet. *De Standaard* (1875-1943) became bilingual in 1918 and then took the name *Standard Bulletin*. *De Wachter* first appeared in 1868 and since 1968 has been the official organ of the Christian Reformed Church; however, it was renamed *The Banner* in 1985.

There were also Roman Catholic newspapers, such as *De Pere Standaard* (1878-1896), *Onze Standaard* (1896-1907), and *De Volksstem* (1886-1919). Roman Catholic Flemings published the *Gazette van Moline*, which has appeared since 1907 and is still being published, now as *Gazette of Detroit*. The paper is bilingual these days and appears both on paper and on the Internet.

There was even a modest press in or about Frisian. Broer Doekeles Dykstra and Bearend Joukes Fridsma, both of whom we have mentioned above, were responsible for this. Dykstra was a preacher and a pacifist, and for a while he functioned as editor-in-chief of *De Volksvriend*, but he left there after disagreements. He then published a few Frisian booklets, and from 1935 on, he organized an annual Frisian Day (he died in 1955). He assisted in establishing the Frisian society *Us Heitelân* in Iowa. Fridsma founded the Frisian Information Bureau, which published *Frisian News Items* from 1944 until 1984 – it was in English, but it was a strong link between Frisians in the US and in Friesland.

A fluctuation is clearly discernible in the publication of newspapers with Dutch roots. At first, the Dutch-language papers jostled with each other to serve the Dutch public and to promote Dutch culture, ethnicity, and language. Next, the Dutchmen became "Americanized" and no longer could, or wanted to, read Dutch publications. Additionally, the interest in the Netherlands and Belgium evaporated. In the First World War, a series of Dutch papers disappeared and during the bad economic years of the 1930s a second series also folded; most of the surviving papers disappeared during and immediately after the Second World War. Unlike what happened in the nineteenth century and the beginning of the twentieth century, the lost periodicals were not replaced by others. However, in the early 1990s the Internet appeared on the scene. More and more information about the Low Countries and the Dutch language became available, and the interest in Dutch heritage and Dutch roots increased in the US.

A few periodicals about the Netherlands and Flanders, usually only published digitally on the Internet, are being published again; these are sometimes even partly published in Dutch.

Loss of Dutch in the home

In a letter dating from 1846, Van Raalte predicted that it was going to be more difficult to keep the Dutch language alive among the immigrants than for them to learn English. He was wrong, however, for by the end of the nineteenth century, after two or three generations, most children still spoke Dutch at home. Some families even maintained this for four or five generations.

At first, many Dutch immigrants stimulated their children to learn both English and Dutch – the best of two worlds. They realized the importance of integration into the American society. And that was "realpolitik": even in the Dutch settlements people were never completely among their own. Although nearly 90 percent of the population in Michigan was of Dutch descent in 1870 – this would remain the case until 1900 – 13.3 percent of the population were married to non-Dutch partners. The population of Pella was even more mixed: in 1875, only 50 percent of Pella's inhabitants were of Dutch descent.

In short, everyone was forced to speak English, and all Dutchmen were more or less bilingual. This was also the case in Flemish settlements. In general, the development was as follows: the first-generation emigrants usually kept speaking their mother tongue at home. The language of the second generation also depended on whether both members of a couple spoke Dutch: if the home language of one of them was English, the switch to that language was made quickly. If the language spoken at home remained Dutch, the children learned English when they went to school. In addition to this, they learned Standard Dutch in church and sometimes at school. For the children, this situation was very confusing: the language spoken at home was different from that in church, and in society still another language was spoken. The second- or third-generation parents therefore brought their children up mainly with the English language, unless they were members of the Christian Reformed Church.

In about 1900, the use of Standard Dutch decreased in the US, as we saw earlier: more and more churches (also) offered English-language services, fewer schools taught (in) Dutch, and fewer papers were published in Dutch. As a result, Dutch was no longer supported in society as the language spoken at home, and the number of people who spoke Dutch with each other continued to decrease.

Around this time, a serious offensive was undertaken by people who wanted to preserve Dutch. In 1893, J. Hoddenbach Van Scheltema, who then lived in Chicago, but originally hailed from Arnhem, wrote an article in the Chicago periodical *De Nederlander* entitled, "Heeft de Nederlandsche Taal eene Toekomst?" ("Does the Dutch Language Have a Future?"). The Belgian *flamingant* Hippoliet Meert responded to this article by producing an outline of the distribution of speakers of Dutch across the world. In order to unite all Dutch speakers in the Netherlands, Flanders, South Africa,

Illustration 1.22 – Song of the Holland-Americans (source: Lagerwey 1982: 62)

Suriname, the Dutch Antilles, and North America, Meert founded the General Dutch League in 1895; it still exists to this day.

At the end of the nineteenth century there was a revival of Dutch nationalism in the US; around this time, Queen Wilhelmina ascended to the Dutch throne (1898), and the famous politician and theologian Abraham Kuyper visited Dutch settlements in America in 1898 and 1899. During the Boer War, which broke out in 1899 and lasted until 1902, the American Dutchmen felt solidarity with the Dutch colonists in South Africa, collecting huge sums of money for them. They called a town in South Dakota "Joubert" in honor of the famous Boer general Piet Joubert, and it is said that some farmers in the Midwest gave their horses the name Oom (Uncle) Paul, after the famous Boer leader Paul Kruger.

After that, the interest in the Dutch language collapsed again. In 1900, dominie Jan Keizer pleaded for the preservation of Dutch, if only as "language de luxe," for he had to admit that "the language of the future in this country is the American language." In the same year, his colleague Henry Beets started a speech with the dramatic exclamation: "Dear friends! There is a Language at the point of death!" Four daggers were killing Dutch, according to him: the first was the disgusting arrogance of Dutch people "to act the American, to play Yankee." The second and third were the carelessness with which they spoke and wrote Dutch, and the fourth the "ignorance regarding the beautiful, strong, pithy and delightful quality of our Dutch language." In 1906, Beets also adapted the then Dutch anthem "Wien Neerlandsch bloed in de aadren vloeit" (Those with Dutch blood in their veins) for the Hollanders in America – this subsequently became the "Song of the Holland-Americans" (see illustration 1.22), sung to the tune of the Dutch anthem.

We love the land across the sea
We glory in its past;
We pray for its prosperity,
May it forever last!
But tho we love old Holland still,
We love Columbia more,
The land our sons and brethren fill
From east to western shore.

Besherm, o God! bewaak den grond,
Waarop onz adem gaat;
De plek, waar onze wieg op stond,
Waar eens ons graf op staat,
Wij smeeken van Uw' Vaderhand,
Met diep geroerde borst,
Behoud voor't lieve Vaderland,
Voor Vaderland en Vorst.

In 1903, J. Groen delivered a speech, *Our Primary School*, in which he made a plea for the Christian school where Dutch was taught; he ended with the words: "Please remember that a school can never keep a language alive, if it is not regularly used in the homes. Let us then speak that language at home with our children; not a degenerated provincialism, not a mixture of everything, but as pure as possible." The fact that people are encouraged to speak Dutch at home is significant. But in those days, just as now, people would not be told what to do in their private homes...

Worried Dutchmen in the Netherlands collected money for the establishment of the Queen Wilhelmina Lectureship in Dutch Literature at Columbia University in New York City, where Dutch literature was taught by the Dutch-American poet Leonard Charles van Noppen. The chair still exists and has in the course of time been held by eminent scholars – but it has of course never been able to get the Dutchmen in the US to bring their children up with the Dutch language.

During the First World War, most Dutch and Flemish immigrants and their children once and for all changed to using English at home. Public opinion was against the use of a foreign language, especially German, and many Americans lumped Dutch and German together. The Dutch and Flemings did not want to be associated with the enemy and gave in to social pressure by abandoning Dutch as their language spoken at home.

When new immigration laws imposed restrictions in 1917, 1921, and 1924, the number of Dutch and Flemish immigrants, and hence new native speakers of Dutch, decreased drastically. It became easier and cheaper, moreover, to travel within the United States by public transport or by the increasingly popular automobile. It was no longer necessary to live in a Dutch-language settlement to keep in touch with other speakers of Dutch. Before the start of the Second World War, all Dutchmen and Flemings were securely entrenched in American society. Most of the children who were descended from Dutch and Flemish immigrants were from then on brought up in English instead of Dutch.

That Dutch lost ground to English in the first half of the twentieth century was also the result of more Dutchmen and Flemings acquiring higher levels of education. In 1880, more than 75 percent of the Dutchmen were farmers; later generations were increasingly better educated and rose on the social ladder. This upward movement meant the end of Dutch: you could only get on socially if you had a good command of English.

The immigrants who came after the Second World War usually left the Dutch language behind them; in general, the second generation only had a passive knowledge of Dutch, and the third generation had no knowledge at all. Only in some Protestant enclaves was Dutch preserved for a little longer. Thanks to these small groups it was possible for Dutch linguists to find descendants from nineteenth- or twentieth-century immigrants with whom they could converse in Dutch as late as 1989.

In his book *Language Loyalty in the United States*, Joshua Fishman reports that in 1940 nearly 290,000 Americans claimed to have Dutch or Flemish as their mother tongue, and in 1960 this number had risen to 322,000 thanks to a new wave of immigrants. Of these, 124,000 were first-generation speakers of Dutch, and the same number were second-generation speakers – they had learned Dutch from their parents in America. Some 74,000 speakers said they were third-generation speakers of Dutch.

Loss of Frisian as the home language

From the first, there were various settlements in the US where Frisian played an important, if not the main, part. In Pella, Iowa, there was a Frisian quarter, in Whitinsville in Massachusetts, a group of Frisians had settled at the end of the nineteenth century, and Friesland, Wisconsin, and Vriesland, Michigan, were founded by Frisians. In these settlements, Frisian was passed on to following generations for some time. On 8 and 9 August 1928, Herman Bottema, born in Gorredijk, Friesland, but a long-time inhabitant of Milwaukee, reported on a visit to Friesland, Wisconsin, in the *Leeuwarder Courant*. He wrote:

> "When a person has lived in the city for 42 years and hasn't heard a single word of Frisian, at least not in the street, it is surprising to hear Frisian spoken, even by the toddlers. The old settlers speak real Frisian to this day, without, as is the case with many other nationalities, mixing in a number of English words. The little town of Friesland is sixty years old and perhaps even a bit older. ... The second person I met was a lad who was eleven years old. I addressed him in the Frisian language and to my amazement he responded in the Frisian language and said, 'Yes, my father and my mother were born in Friesland and I also can speak the Frisian language.' "

Illustration 1.23 – Example of Yankee Dutch "Wat is dat piese roop daar behain de boot?" (What is that piece of rope there behind the boat?) (source: pen drawing by D. Lam in Nieland 1929: 133)

In 1952, M. ten Hoor wrote about Frisian in America in *Friesland. Toen, nu, straks*: "There is no thorough investigation into the duration and distribution of the language. All we have is loose reports, which tell us that no longer than ten years ago children in the streets of Vriesland, Wisconsin could be heard speaking Frisian in their games. The writer knew families in Ellsworth, Michigan, where in 1914 only Frisian was spoken at home. This language transmission was of course promoted by the arrival of new immigrants from the mother country. In spite of all these circumstances, the Americanization of the second and third generations of the colonists had the loss of the language as daily means of communication as a natural consequence."

Not only were Americanization and the dominance of English responsible for the loss of Frisian – it also suffered from the competition with Dutch. Every Frisian knew a little Standard Dutch through the church, and many Frisians had contacts with Dutchmen in their immediate surroundings. In mixed settlements where both Frisians and Hollanders lived, the Frisians switched to Dutch, in some cases soon, in the second generation, but by no means always. This also depended on the family structure: if one of the married persons was non-Frisian, then the language was abandoned sooner in the home. In mixed American-Frisian settlements the second or sometimes third generation switched to English. In predominantly Frisian settlements, the language was preserved the longest. In 1966, Jo Daan talked to several Frisian speakers in Whitinsville – it struck her that their Frisian had suffered very little from English or Dutch. The conditions for the three languages were clearly demarcated: Frisian at home, Dutch in church, and English everywhere else.

Whereas Dutch was supported not only in the church but also in the schools of the Christian Reformed Church and in the press, this was not the case with Frisian. Frisian was used strictly at home and was not written. In addition, says Jaap van Marle, it had little prestige in some areas: an ethnic Frisian in Vriesland, Michigan, told him in the 1990s that Frisian used to be regarded as a sort of second-rate language ("an inferior language") even by Frisians themselves. During the ten years (from 1989 to 1999) in which Van Marle carried his linguistic investigations in the US, he had been unable to find third- or fourth-generation Frisian immigrants who still spoke Frisian, except in Friesland, Wisconsin out.

In 1945, nearly every inhabitant of Friesland, Wisconsin, spoke Frisian. Until the 1960s Frisian was the general spoken language, also in public life. Frisian was also used here by people without a Frisian background. When Van Marle visited the place in 1999, he found that the number of Frisian speakers was still remarkably large. But these speakers were all sexagenarians or older – before long, Frisian will be extinct in Wisconsin, too. Their descendants will remain proud of their Frisian ethnicity, though – some youngsters, even those who do not speak Frisian, still pride themselves on their Frisian background.

Yankee Dutch: "Wat is de troebel?"

Soon after their arrival in America, the Dutch and Belgian immigrants adopted a number of English loanwords for which there were no Dutch terms, notably in the fields of politics, social activities, schools, sports, and suchlike. In his *Netherlanders in America* (1955), Henry S. Lucas describes in chapter 11 how people began to speak of *store* instead of *winkel*, *bark* instead of *bast*, *farm* instead of *boerderij*, *trip* instead of *reis*, *sale* instead of *uitverkoop*. Verbs were formed from English words, such as *klieren*, *klearen* or *klaren* from *to clear*, *kleemen* from *to claim* and *fixen* from *to fix*. Still, the number of English loanwords and English constructions in written and printed sources such as Dutch-language periodicals and newspapers remained relatively limited. In the immigrants' letters written to relatives in the Netherlands (collected and edited by Brinks, Lagerwey, Lucas, and Stellingwerf), the number of loanwords and loan translations is not particularly large, either – probably because the writers had ample time to think about the phrases in their own language. A study by Van Marle and Smits has shown that later, too, in the late sixties and late eighties of the twentieth century, the number of English loanwords in American Dutch was very limited. They did register a shift in the parts of speech borrowed: in the late sixties especially nouns were borrowed, in the late eighties more conjunctions (especially *and*, *but*, *because*); in both periods, moreover, the number of interjections (*well*, *see/you see*, *you know*) was very high. In all, only about 3.6 percent of all the words were English, in both periods.

On the other hand, the spoken language of especially those immigrants who switched quickly to English, underwent a strong influence by American. The Dutch vocabulary was largely replaced by English words and phrases, but word order and sounds remained Dutch, and the English loanwords were pronounced in a "dutchified" way, for example: *'t is een sjeem* for *it's a shame* or *bevoor de piepel* for *before the people*. English-Dutch compounds were made, for example, *cornstokken* for *cornstalks*, and Dutch words got new meanings after the example of homophonous American-English words – thus, *drijven* "to float" acquired the meaning "to drive." Loan translations were made such as *publieke school* (for *public school*), *Dankgevingsdag* (for *Thanksgiving Day*) and *wat is de troebel?* (for *what's the trouble?*).

This spoken variety of Dutch is mockingly called *Yankee Dutch*. In the first half of the twentieth century, a few text collections in this lingo came out: Dirk Nieland published *Yankee Dutch* in 1919, and *'n Fonnie Bisnis* in 1929 (see box 3 for a sample). In 1936, John Lieuwen published a collection of poems *Troebel en Fon (Trouble and Fun)*, followed in 1947 by *Swet en Tears (Sweat and Tears)*. In how far these books give a reliable picture of the language used by the Dutchmen cannot be ascertained: the hybrids almost certainly occurred – and are still encountered – but some of the examples look a little artificial, and the accumulation of linguistic forms inspired by English seems exaggerated.

Yankee Dutch is a transition phase between Dutch and English: the people using it want to Americanize fast and are on their way towards a complete change to English. People who speak Yankee Dutch without knowing it and against their better judgment were and are ridiculed. On the other hand, Yankee Dutch is also cultivated: as more

Box 3. A sample of Yankee Dutch

In his *Netherlanders in America* (1955: 586-587), H. Lucas gives an instance of Dirk Nieland's Yankee Dutch, followed by the English translation. The Yankee Dutch bristles with English loanwords in dutchified form.

> 'n Goed kontrie om in te leven is ook 'n impoorten ding. En beter kontrie als be Joenait Steets is er op toe nou nog niet uitgevonden, zoover als ik er met bekweented ben. Aiteljoe, het meent 'n lat, hoor, dat ieder kid hier 'n sjens heeft om Prezzedent te worden. Dat poet er pep in toe gohed. Of kos, de troebel is dat er not geen 1/100,000,000 sjens is, but 't is toch 'n lat better als in ol kontrie, waar 'n kommen feller als ik meebie nog geen prezzedent van de Men sessaaitie worden kan en er sjoer geen halve seeken over prakkezeeren hoeft om evver lekted te worden voor king. No, no, de Joenait Steets is 'n fain kontrie, hoor. Joebet!
> ("A good country to live in is also an important thing. A better country than the United States has until now not been discovered, so far as I am acquainted with the matter. I tell you it means a lot, believe me, that every kid here has a chance to become President. That puts pep into 'go ahead'. Of course, the trouble is that there is not a 1/100,000,000 chance, but it is a lot better than in the Old Country, where a common fellow like me maybe cannot even become president of the Men's Society, and where he surely does not have to think a half second about ever being elected king. No, no, the United States is a fine country, believe me. You bet!")

people became bilingual, Yankee Dutch became a source of amusement. In Pella, until well into the 1980s, at parties, weddings and festivities texts were recited in Yankee Dutch, amidst great hilarity of the guests. To understand the wordplay, one ought to be well versed in both English and Dutch. Most of the puns are based on homophonous Dutch and English words with different meanings. Thus, you will talk about *glad streets* in January (Dutch *glad* meaning "slippery"), and a man *spitting* in his garden (Dutch *spitten* meaning "to dig").

The genre of the Dutch-English hybrid language has recently become popular in the Netherlands, too, thanks to publications such as *I always get my sin* (in Dutch *mijn zin* means "what I want") and *We always get our sin too* from 2005 and 2008 by Maarten H. Rijkens. Rijkens here recorded "bizarre" English he supposedly heard from the mouth of Dutchmen, such as the famous "How do you do and how do you do your wife?"

American Dutch, American Flemish, and American Frisian

After World War II, most of the Dutch, Flemish, and Frisian immigrants had definitively switched to English, sometimes via an intermediate stage, Yankee Dutch. In some isolated colonies, where Dutch culture, customs, religion, and language held pride of place from the start, the languages of Dutch or Frisian were more or less preserved among older speakers until the second half of the twentieth century or even until the present day. In these colonies, rapid Americanization was not striven after, and the Dutch or the Frisian language was passed on from generation to generation. That language deviated from the language as spoken in Europe and is therefore called American Dutch, American Flemish, and American Frisian respectively.

The usage of these varieties by speakers has been recorded by a number of researchers – unfortunately only after World War II, when this variety was already on its way out, and the number of speakers had drastically been reduced. In 1966, Jo Daan and Henk Heikens of the Dialect Division of the Amsterdam Meertens Institute made recordings of conversations they had with Dutch and Frisian speakers in some places, such as Holland, Michigan, and Pella, Iowa. In 1972, Paul Ostyn wrote his dissertation on the language characteristics of American Flemish, based on one publication year (October 1970 – October 1971) of the *Gazette van Detroit*. In 1988, Philip Webber wrote a monograph on Dutch as spoken in Pella, known as "Pella Dutch." And in 1989, Jaap van Marle and Caroline Smits asked Dutch-speaking informants in Iowa to translate 83 English sentences and word combinations into Dutch and to do an assessment test, and recorded a number of conversations on tape; they then published some articles on this material, and in 1996 Smits used the data from the translation test as the subject for her dissertation. In all the publications referred to, except those by Van Marle and Smits, a few longer text samples are included that illustrate the informants' usage; box 4 contains a few examples.

Characteristics of American Frisian

Little is known about American Frisian. In 1928, Herman Bottema reported that Frisian in Friesland, Wisconsin, had remained fairly pure, with few English loanwords, as we saw above. This agrees with Jo Daan's experiences much later, in 1966. She interviewed several first-generation immigrants or their offspring who used Frisian as their language at home, among others in Whitinsville, Massachusetts, and in Friesland, Wisconsin. In these places they still spoke Frisian at home; most speakers also knew Dutch. From the interviews by Daan it appeared that Frisian in the US had changed much less than the Dutch dialects. Usage, of course, varied from informant to informant. Most informants used a few English loanwords. The material collected by Daan has never been investigated systematically. In 1988 T. Anema investigated, on the basis of this material, whether the sounds of Frisian from Whitinsville had been influenced by English. That turned out to be the case, both for adult first-generation immigrants and, to a larger degree, for immigrants who had come to the US as children and for second-generation immigrants. In all cases, however, the influence appeared to be

Box 4. Some text samples of American Dutch, American Frisian, and American Flemish

A sample of the American Dutch usage of Elisabeth Rus-Van Steenwijk, who was interviewed by Jo Daan in **1966**. She was born in Pella; her grandparents on her father's side had emigrated in 1847, her mother in 1891 from the western part of the Betuwe, Gelderland.

"Ja, maar zie je, mijn moeder die was maar zes jaar uit Holland, en vroeger leerden ze geen Amerikaans als ze uit Holland kwamme, want 't was hier alles Hollands. Maar da's met de wereldoorlog one is da veranderd, toe is 't Amerikaans gekomme... O ja, we leerden wel Engels op skool, maar de minuut da we uit de skool kwamme, dan vloge we naar buite en dan was 't alles Hollands."

("Yes, but you see, my mother had been from Holland only six years, and in those days you didn't learn American when you came from Holland, for it was all Dutch here. But that is with the world war one that changed, then came American ... O yes, we did learn English at school, but the minute we came from the school we rushed outside and then all was Dutch.")

A sample of the American Frisian usage of a husband and wife who were interviewed by Jo Daan in **1966**. The husband was born in Makkum, Friesland, and emigrated to the US when he was 11 years old. The wife was born in the US; both her parents spoke Frisian.

"Ik ken my net begripe hoe't dy minsken dy't yn Nederland, yn Friesland geboren binne – ken my niks skele hoe lang at se hjir west hê – at se dat dy tael nou fejitte." – "No, dat ken ik net begripe en dat leau ik ek net."

("I can't understand how the people who are born in the Netherlands, in Friesland – I don't care how long they have been here – that they now forget the language." – "No, I can't understand that and I don't believe it either.")

An example of a riddle in Pella Dutch recorded by Philip Webber in **1988**:

"Achter in de pasture staan twee palen, op die palen is een ton, op die ton is een draaiom, op die draaiom is een bal, op die bal is een bos, en in die bos [presumably, in terms of the informant's own explanation of the riddle: dat bos] lopen alle kleine kriepertjes [kruipertjes]. Wat is dat?"

(On one occasion I was told of an object out in the pasture consisting of two poles, on which sat a barrel, on which sat a pivot, on which sat a ball, on which there was a forest (or: sheaf, shock?) with all sorts of creatures running around in it. What might that be?)

The answer, of course, is a person with lice in the hair.

A sample of American Flemish published in the *Gazette of Detroit* in **1970-1971**:

> We zagen dadelijk dat we iets bijzonders zouden te smullen krijgen; we aten er een excellent diner (prime beef) met alle bijgerechten, het ontbrak er aan niets. We lieten het ons goed smaken. Daarna wenste Ray ons een aangenaam verder vervolg van onze reis en we zetten onze plezierritje voort. We reden voorbij Pelston, het koudste plekje van het noorden van Michigan en we feestten dan onze ogen aan het natuurschoon van die stille streek waardoor we bolden met de autobus. Eindelijk kwamen we aan de Machinaw brug. Die is 5 mijl lang, de langste "single expansion" brug in de wereld... de zon zat op haar best en "dipte" zoals een grote vuurbal in het water.
>
> (We saw straightaway that we were going to get something special to regale ourselves on: we had an excellent dinner of prime beef with all the trimmings, nothing lacking. We really enjoyed it. After that, Ray wished us a pleasant continuation of our journey and we proceeded on our pleasure trip. We passed Pelston, the coldest spot in the north of Michigan and we feasted our eyes on the nature beauty of that quiet region through which we rolled with the motor-bus. At last we came to the Machinaw bridge. It is 5 miles long, the longest "single expansion" bridge in the world ... the sun was at its best and "dipped" like a great ball of fire into the water.)

An example of American Flemish that was published on 5 February **2009**, in the *Gazette of Detroit*:

> Zijn kinderen gewichtheffers? Als je kinderen naar school ziet gaan dan is het opvallend welke zware boekentas ze op de rug meedragen. Wat daar allemaal in steekt? Ik heb me die vraag ook al gesteld. Hoe dan ook, onderzoek wijst uit dat veel van die boekentassen veel te zwaar wegen voor die jonge ruggen. Volgens een reglement mag het maximum gewicht van een boekentas maar 10 procent wegen van het gewicht van de drager. Voor 80% van de leerlingen is dat gewicht hoger. Een artsenvereniging heeft gewaarschuwd voor de kwalijke gevolgen van te zware boekentassen.
>
> (Are children weight lifters? When you see children going to school it is striking what heavy satchels they are carrying. What is in it? I have asked that question myself, too. Anyhow, investigation has shown that many of those satchels weigh far too much for those young backs. Regulations say that the maximum weight of a satchel may weigh only 10 percent of the weight of the carrier. For 80% of the pupils that weight is higher. A medical society has warned for the bad consequences of satchels that are too heavy.)

limited. In 1995, Jaap van Marle and Caroline Smits drew some comparisons between the American Frisian and the American Dutch verbal system. They confirm Daan's conclusion that American Frisian has seen fewer changes than American Dutch.

Characteristics of American Flemish

The Flemish dialects that immigrated Flemings took with them to the US were levelled out, just as the dialects of Dutch colonists in the US: marked dialect features that occur only in the odd Flemish dialect have disappeared, but American Flemish has retained some clearly southern characteristics. Thus, the word *teljoor* ("plate") is used instead of Standard Dutch *bord*. American Flemish, then, deviates from Standard Dutch and also from American Dutch.

Paul Ostyn studied the peculiarities of written American Flemish, but he did not look at the frequencies. As a result, we do get a good idea of the details in the language use, but we do not know how widespread they are. Nevertheless, all kinds of general data appear from his study. Ostyn concludes that many influences from English can be seen in both the vocabulary and the grammar. In the vocabulary this includes not only loanwords but also loan translations and loan meanings, and changes in the use of prepositions, for instance, or adjusted idioms. A few examples: *wij hadden een goede tijd* instead of *we vermaakten ons* (after English *we had a good time*), *met muziek bij ...* instead of *met muziek door...*(after English *with music by ...*), and *hij blijft overleven door zijn echtgenote* (after English *he is survived by his wife*).

But by no means can all changes in the vocabulary and the grammar be ascribed to English influence. There is also, in part, loss of the Flemish language. Sometimes in American Flemish a general term or a homophonous word is chosen instead of specific, infrequently used words that the speaker may not readily call to mind. For instance, we find *in Europa waren er veel oorlogen* instead of *in Europa woedden er veel oorlogen* (for *many wars raged in Europe*).

In the grammar, Ostyn found all sorts of changes, notably in the word order, which could not be traced back to English or to Flemish, but were occasioned by hypercorrection: the application of language rules also in cases where they do not apply in Belgian Flemish dialects. He mentions among others *ze hebben een bijzonder schone winter* ***hier*** *kunnen doorbrengen* – cf. English *they were able to spend an especially beautiful winter* ***here***. Standard Dutch is: *ze hebben* ***hier*** *een bijzonder mooie winter kunnen doorbrengen*.

Ostyn does point out that the influence of English should not be overrated. For every deviation from Standard Dutch, he says, we should first find out in how far the deviation is part of the mother language that the immigrants brought with them from Flanders. Thus, for instance, *hij heeft er zeven jaar gebleven*, with auxiliary *hebben*, did not derive from English *he has stayed there seven years*, as you might think. Standard Dutch is *is gebleven*, true, but in Flemish *heeft gebleven* is quite normal. Of course, in some cases English may have supported the usage of the dialect.

Since the *Gazette of Detroit* is still in business, it is possible to compare the usage from 1970-1971, studied by Ostyn, with present-day American Flemish (see box 4).

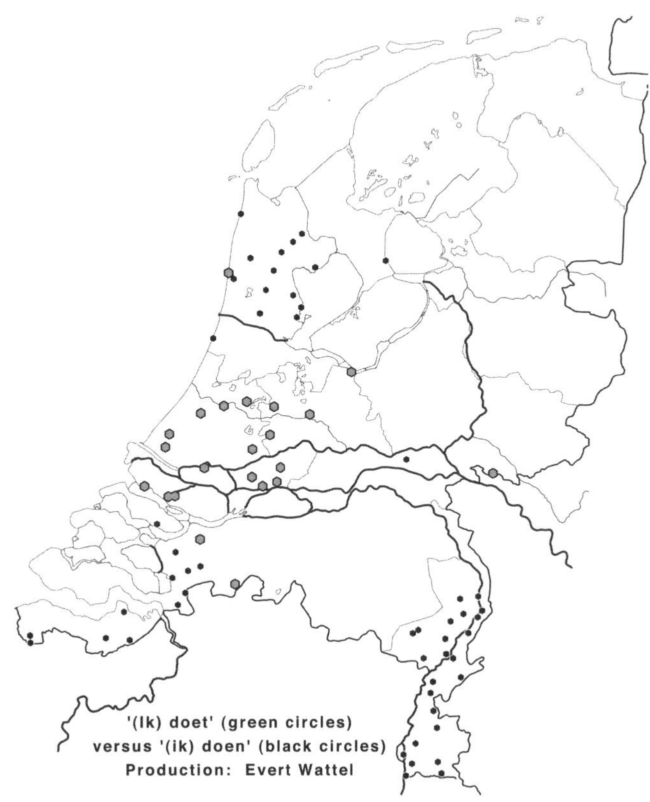

Illustration 1.24 – Map showing the distribution of ik doet *versus* ik doen *in the Dutch dialects (source: Van Reenen 1999: 72)*

It appears that this variety has in the course of time become more adapted to (southern) Standard Dutch: in 1970-1971 clearly more dialectisms (*bollen* for "rolling on") and English loanwords (*dippen*) or loan translations (*zijn ogen feesten*) are to be found than in 2009. Since we are dealing with written language, it is of course possible that today's editor checks his texts more rigorously than his colleague did 40 years ago.

Characteristics of American Dutch

Of the three, American Dutch has been studied the most. From the data collected by Jo Daan in 1966 it appeared that the usage of the informants showed large individual differences – in the number of loan translations and loanwords from English, in the number of grammatical changes with respect to Standard Dutch, and in the number of switches between Dutch and English. In the informants' Dutch, various regional dialects could be recognized, but they could not be traced back to specific Dutch dialects. The differences in usage were caused by all sorts of non-linguistic variables and by the personal histories of the informants, such as differences in religion, financial status, education, and length of stay in the US. Linguistic variables, such as the language spoken in the home and the degree of bilingualism, also played a role.
As a result of these individual differences it was practically impossible to reach

general conclusions about American Dutch: the line between general linguistic characteristics of American Dutch and individual usage was nearly impossible to draw in many cases. The relationship between English and Dutch often made it difficult to ascertain whether a word or a sound or construction was English or Dutch. Thus, the pronunciation "skool" for *school* can be traced back to the English pronunciation as well as to that of the Dutch dialects.

What did come out in Jo Daan's study was that the majority of her informants did not use the sounds that feature in English and not in Dutch, neither in their English nor in their Dutch. Most of the 1966 informants pronounced *w* and *r* as in Dutch: they pronounced *w* with the lower lip and upper teeth rather than, as in English, with both lips; *r* was pronounced more to the front of the mouth than is usual in English. Shetter, who in 1957 had studied the usage in the Roman Catholic community of Little Chute, found, however, that the pronunciation of *w* and *r* had been influenced by English there.

Van Marle and Smits compared Daan's 1966 data with the information they had gathered from informants from Iowa in 1989. According to Van Marle and Smits, American Dutch of 1966 is close to Standard Dutch, having a "non-dialectic" character, whereas the differences between American Dutch and the standard language have increased by 1989. That is because American Dutch had developed further as compared with 1966. This happened partly because of the influence of English (by way of illustration they mention the very rare form *hij schrijfs* instead of *hij schrijft* "he writes," with the English verb ending *-s*). But what is more important, they say, is that American Dutch has experienced independent changes. As a result, several irregular forms disappeared – a plural *kalven* was formed instead of standard language but irregular *kalveren* ("calves"), and *omen* instead of *ooms* ("uncles"). The independent developments appear, according to them, especially in the reduction of linguistic forms: various meaningful form distinctions disappear. Thus, *wij loop* ("we walk"), perhaps on the analogy of *ik loop* ("I walk"), takes the place of *wij lopen*. The cause of the independent developments within American Dutch is, they think, the fact that American Dutch is "disintegrating"; this disintegration is caused by language loss in speakers who at one time had learned Dutch as their first language, or by insufficient language command by speakers for whom English had always been their first language. Speakers get out of touch with the grammatical rules and the requirements of language practice: they no longer know what correct Dutch is. However, their investigation also shows that in the free conversations the deviations from standard Dutch occurred far less frequently than in the translation exercise. According to Smits, this might be accounted for by the fact that in conversations, speakers use a limited vocabulary with fixed combinations and forms that they call up from memory. It is more probable, though, that in the translation exercise the source language - English - interferes and that translation is less reliable as a measuring instrument for linguistic usage.

Criticism has been leveled at Van Marle and Smits's studies by Dutch dialectologists – notably Daan and Van Reenen. This criticism especially concerns the fact that their study did not take into account the background (linguistic, social) of the informants or the dialects on which American Dutch is based. Part of the "special developments" of American Dutch, it appears, can be retraced to the Dutch dialects brought to the

United States by the immigrants in the nineteenth century. In an extensive study, Van Reenen shows, for instance, that *hij hebt*, *wij doene(n)*, *ik doet* (instead of Standard Dutch *hij heeft* ("he has"), *wij doen* ("we do"), *ik doe* ("I do") are not developments peculiar to American Dutch, but derive from the *Gelders-Utrechts-Zuidhollands* dialect. The preterite form *leesden* instead of standard *lazen* ("read") can also be traced back to a Dutch dialect, it appears. The preference for the auxiliary *hebben* ("to have") instead of *zijn* ("to be") in, for example, *ik heb gegaan* instead of standard *ik ben gegaan* ("I have gone") can likewise be traced back to Dutch dialects rather than to the influence of English *I have gone*, although English, of course, may have stimulated the choice of *hebben* – Ostyn pointed this out earlier.

Both Daan and Van Marle and Smits find large individual differences within American Dutch. Daan accounts for these from non-linguistic variables. Van Marle and Smits add to this as explanation the gradual switch to English, which differs from speaker to speaker. They describe that change as follows. In the first phase, Dutch is the first and English is the second language, in which the speakers are less proficient, and from which they borrow words. In the second phase, the speakers are bilingual, and both languages can influence each other. In the third phase, English is dominant and the command of Dutch is diminished, with the result that Dutch can be influenced by English, not only through loanwords but also in sounds and grammar. In the fourth phase, finally, the speakers have become English speakers, knowing a few Dutch words and phrases at best. The speed with which these phases are gone through differs per individual, per group, and per region. According to Van Marle and Smits, the same differences in phases can be found in the 1966 and 1989 databases: Daan's database from 1966 represents a different phase in the development of American Dutch from that of the collection they put together in 1989 for Iowa Dutch. This might suggest, however, that the data in the two collections form a unity, although evidently this is not the case; as we saw earlier, the usage of the informants shows great variation.

Webber gives a description of Pella Dutch in about the same period as Van Marle and Smits's study, namely 1988. He claims that most of the sounds and forms in Pella Dutch agree with those of (spoken) Standard Dutch, but that dialect features and regional features have also been preserved, such as *bennen* for *zijn* ("to be") and the third person plural pronoun *hullie* for *zij* ("they"). In earlier days, the language showed even more dialect features. English has influenced the vocabulary of Pella Dutch, in the form of loanwords, loan meanings, and loan translations. Webber's conclusion is that Pella Dutch fits within the spectrum of what is regarded as acceptable and possible Dutch. Recent visitors from the Netherlands think that Pella Dutch sounds old-fashioned, Webber says. The language he describes does not give the impression of being in a process of disintegration – but perhaps that is a matter of definition.

From the various sources it appears that spoken American Dutch has come closer to Standard Dutch over the years. It is true that the first immigrants did not generally speak Standard Dutch, but the later immigrants, notably in the twentieth century, were fluent in it more often. Additionally, in the twentieth century, contacts with relatives from the mother country were made easier through improved transport and postal communications, and through the printed word, contact with Standard Dutch was much better. In 1957, Shetter found that the Dutch of the younger immigrants in the Catholic enclave of Little Chute was much closer to Standard Dutch than that of the first immigrants, with dialectisms disappearing as a result.

In 1988, Webber not only described the language of Pella, but also its speakers. He studied who spoke Dutch, and when. For that purpose, he found about 200 to 250 people who still spoke Dutch, of whom 60 filled in a questionnaire. Most of them were third- or fourth-generation speakers. He asked questions such as: To whom (parents, grandparents, husband, children, friends) do you speak in Dutch? Do you use Dutch to swear in, in sermons, in anger, at work, in telephone conversations, to talk to animals, in dreams, as a secret language? Does the use of Dutch give you status or profit? From the answers it appeared that after the First World War, they spoke less and less Dutch, although they still knew it, and that the status of Dutch decreased, while in the 1980's, when the knowledge of Dutch had been drastically reduced, the value and status of the language were on the increase – the use of Dutch emphasized their ethnicity and their sense of belonging. For the rest, older people in particular spoke Dutch, and by no means always with their children; they did not pass Dutch on to a following generation, which in the long run will mean the end of American Dutch.

The points of agreement between American Dutch and Low Dutch are, to my mind, striking. Both varieties were not described before they were on their way out and the number of speakers was small and they were old. Both varieties turned out to be conservative, having preserved several elements of the Dutch dialects originally introduced by the immigrants. Both varieties have undergone individual developments as well. They were both influenced by English, but – for Low Dutch we follow Buccini's theory here – to a limited extent: in any case limited in that the varieties – unlike Yankee Dutch – remained clearly recognizable as Dutch, albeit, according to present-day Dutchmen, as old-fashioned Dutch. One point of difference here is that, over time, American Dutch has been somewhat influenced by Standard Dutch, while that has not been the case for Low Dutch.

American Dutch will share the fate of Low Dutch: together with American Frisian and American Flemish it will gradually die out with the last speakers who raised their children with English instead of the Dutch language. At best, this dying-out process might be delayed somewhat through the few language courses offered in Pella and elsewhere.

What remains of nineteenth- and twentieth-century Dutch

Dutchmen who quickly switched to English interspersed their Dutch with English words and loan translations, as we have seen above. But their English was not immediately perfect, either: it showed a lot of Dutch influence at first. Some Dutch loanwords in the English of Dutch immigrants or their descendants were borrowed by their English neighbors, in exactly the same way as this happened with the Dutch loanwords of the seventeenth-century Dutch colonists. But there is a difference, as will become clear in chapter 2: not only has American English borrowed far fewer Dutch loanwords from the second wave of immigrants, but those words are also more narrowly distributed. Most of the words borrowed in the nineteenth or twentieth century seem

Illustration 1.25 – Example of Yankee Dutch "Ja, maar die kous willen mij niet doorlaten" (Yes, but the cows do not want to let me through) (source: pen drawing by D. Lam in Nieland 1929: 123)

to be found only regionally and to be unknown in general American English. Some have even been used only for a short period and in a small area, so they have not been included in any dictionaries. That they were used at all can be seen only from a few articles written at a time when Dutch was spoken much more generally than nowadays.

Van Hinte, in his *Nederlanders in Amerika*, was still optimistic in 1928. Although he observed that there were few, or no, words of "Young-Dutch origin" used in American English at that time, he expected that this situation would change, since at that time many different books on Dutch-American life were coming out and because many Dutch immigrants were gradually beginning to occupy important positions in American cultural life. That expectation has only partly come true: some Dutch loanwords have indeed been adopted, but their number has remained restricted. Van Hinte made only one exception (p. 1007): according to him, Dutch did have considerable influence in the field of diamond cutting in that period, owing to the leading position of Dutch and Flemish diamond cutters in New York. Thus, American diamond cutters would talk of a *skive* (after Dutch *schijf*), where their British colleagues would say *disk* or *wheel*. And a New York factory owner, Van Hinte reports, sent an order to Amsterdam or Antwerp, reading: "send immediately verstelpitten, doppen and tangen" – the last three words being Dutch names for (parts of) instruments used in diamond cutting. All these Dutch loanwords have passed into oblivion by now, in spite of Van Hinte's prediction.

In 1940 Peter Veltman recorded Dutch remnants in Holland, Michigan. He assumed that Dutch would have disappeared there in a few years, but that took considerably

Illustration 1.26 – Advertisement for erwten soup (source: newspaper cutting around 1960 for Royco soup)

more time – at the moment, there still are Dutch speakers in Holland, although their number is considerably smaller. Veltman did assume that some Dutch words and phrases would live on in the region, even after the Dutch language had died out. He seems to have been right there. He especially mentions Dutch names of foodstuffs, such as **advocaat**, **balkenbry**, **boerenjongens**, **erwten soup**, **hutspot**, **olykoek**, **pot eten**, and **snert**, all of them mentioned in 2.1, and **dingus** (see 2.14).

For other words his prediction did not come true, probably because the Dutch name was unpronounceable for Americans, such as *bruine bonen met spek* ("brown beans with bacon"), *jan in de zak* (sort of "plumduff" or "spotted dick") and *koffie kletz* ("chatter over coffee" – in the morning men go to the local restaurants to discuss business matters over cups of good Dutch "Java"). A number of literal translations of Dutch expressions, too, has become largely extinct by now, such as *here around* for *around here*. Stopgaps such as *once* (*imagine once*, *listen now once* "just imagine, now just listen") and *too yet* (*I have to go there too yet* "I have to go there as well") immediately divulge the Dutch background of the speaker, who translated *eens* and *ook nog* into English. English speakers have rarely copied this: according to DARE *too yet* is uncommon, and *once* is labeled "chiefly in German settlements areas." However, *go with* for *go along* (Dutch *ga mee*) is, according to DARE, very common in Wisconsin and in Illinois; it is used chiefly Inland North, and influenced in some areas by Dutch, in others by German or Scandinavian constructions.

In 1958, Dorothy Vander Werf described what was left by way of Dutch in Grand Rapids, Michigan. She relates how some firms in that period used Yankee Dutch to draw people's attention. One gas station used the text:

De best of der lifes dey gif te you
To service you all and rescue too
If je have trouble mit your car or truck
Phone de number below and you'll never be stuck.

This must have been understandable for both Dutch and English speakers – otherwise the text would not make any sense. She also noticed the frequent use of *once* (*let me see it once*). Students of Calvin College, including those without a Dutch background, used all sorts of Dutch words, she said. They described tasteless food as *flauw*, called a drink a *slokje* and said the car went *kapot* when their car broke down. Vander Werf claims that Dutch expressions were circulated among others thanks to the *coffee kletz*, the custom among Dutchmen to exchange the latest news items and gossip over cups of coffee. Non-Dutch speakers took over these expressions to show off their knowledge of the language or to be funny. All of the expressions mentioned by her have disappeared by now, except *vies*, said of tasteless food, and *I am benauwd*, said when a room was very stuffy (see **benaut** and **feest** in 2.6). The German counterparts of *kapot* and *(coffee) kletz*, namely *kaput* and *klatch*, are, according to DARE, very much alive and well in large parts of the US.

In 1988, Philip Webber noted that visitors to Pella made remarks about Dutch words and phrases that they had not come across elsewhere. He mentions a number of words that also feature in Veltman's and Vander Werf's studies for Michigan, such as *benauwd*, *flauw*, *slokje*, *vies*, *going with*. And a shambles, a mess, is called *rommel* in Pella and *to mess around* is *knoeien (around)*. Prepositions are used in unexpected ways, for example, **under through** (see 2.14): *the water runs under through the bridge* or *the water runs under the bridge through*. The number of Dutch-based interjections is especially large, according to Webber; he mentions both *once* and *too yet*, sometimes even combined within one sentence, which results in hilarious sentences such as *would you like to lend a hand once yet?* an almost literal translation of Dutch *wil je ook nog eens meehelpen?* ("Won't you help us out?") He also mentions the use of *say*, translating Dutch *zeg (those were pretty good results, say!)* meaning "really" (those were really pretty good results!) and the questions *oh so?*("Is that so?") and *oh not?* ("Isn't that so?") Finally, he reports that *coffeetime* (not *coffee kletz*!) has become the local term for snack time and even for the snack food itself.

From the examples just given and from chapter 2 it appears, as we have said, that the contribution of nineteenth- and twentieth-century Dutch immigrants to American English is much more limited than that of the seventeenth-century colonists. The question is why that is the case. That question is what occupied Vande Kopple in 1982. He points out that the Dutch in the nineteenth and twentieth centuries did not form a unity: one part of them rapidly adjusted to American society, another part clung to Dutch culture, language, and religion, but that part, too, was split up and sectarianized – just as in the Netherlands and Belgium: the immigrants were members of different religious communities, they spoke different dialects, and they brought with them local customs from the various regions from which they originated. Religion, more than anything else, prevented the Dutch settlers from having real contacts with the Americans; at work they had superficial contact with English speakers, but in their private lives they kept aloof, isolating themselves: in the Dutch settlements all kinds of restrictions obtained that were dictated by the fact that the church was opposed to worldly pleasures. In as late as 1947 there was not a theater or a cinema in Zeeland; in Orange City, close to a major road, all filling stations and shops were closed on Sundays. Even now, some settlements founded by Hollanders, such as South Holland, are conspicuous by their puritanic lifestyle. Moreover, at first Dutch immigrants did not fill any important posts in American society. They all learned English, and those who made mistakes were ridiculed both by younger Dutchmen and by Americans. English, especially good English, had more prestige than Dutch. All these factors prevented Dutch words to be loaned by English.

All this is radically different from the situation in the seventeenth century: then, Dutch settlers and their descendants were the elite for some time, their language had prestige and was even taken over by speakers with a different mother language. What is also important is the relatively small range of Dutch immigration. In all, 265,000 Dutch immigrants went to the US between 1820 and 1949, but many more came from other countries. Historian Robert P. Swierenga claims that in 1985, there were 3 million Americans of Dutch descent, which is less than one percent of the population. Relatively speaking, this is a much lower percentage than at the end of the eighteenth century when the independent United States were established; at that time the Dutch Americans – descendants from the seventeenth-century colonists – formed 3.5 percent of the population, with 80,000 people, and in the states of New York and New Jersey, the Dutch descendants constituted as much as 17 percent of the population. Moreover, the territory of America had become much larger since Independence. And because most of the nineteenth-century immigrants settled close together in a limited number of places, it was in only a small part of the US that they had any influence. Dutch loanwords were restricted to that territory, as a rule, whereas the earlier loanwords were first disseminated among English speakers along the entire East Coast, and from there carried on to the west and south of the United States, ultimately dispersing all over the country.

That the first wave of Dutch immigrants were more proud of their descent than the second one can also be seen from their surnames. The nineteenth- and twentieth-century immigrants wanted to integrate in American society – so they anglicized their family names, which sounded strange to English ears. In chapter 11 of his *Netherlanders in America*, Lucas gives a large number of instances. Members of the Vroegindewey family (literally "early in the meadow") changed their unpronounceable name to Early or to Dewey. The changes were often simple: Bakker called himself Baker, De Jong became De Young or simply Young, Gardenier became Gardener, Glas became Glass, Kok became Cook, Mulder became Miller, Stronk became Strong, Vriend became Friend, Wagenaar became Wagner. But especially names that were difficult to pronounce for Americans were changed: De Leeuw became Lion, Evenhuis became Evenhouse, Groeneveld became Greenfield, Jansen became Johnson, Naaktgeboren (literally "born naked") became Young (!), Oudshoren became Oussoren, Overweg became Overway, Van der Lane became Van Lane, Van der Meulen became Vandermoon, Vloedman became Flutman, Woudhuis became Woodhouse.

Owing to this anglicization, a man's Dutch descent could no longer be deduced from his surname – a different situation from that of the immigrants who came to North America in the seventeenth century, for although their names sometimes underwent a small spelling change (Van der Bilt becoming Vanderbilt, etc.), the Dutch character of their names was usually preserved; they prided themselves on their Dutch roots, while the immigrants of the second wave did not want to be conspicuous in American society; although, of course, not everybody changed their names straightaway, and some of the names could still be recognized as Dutch despite their English appearance, for instance because they began with Van.

Incidentally, Dutch names were not anglicized everywhere; notably in places with substantial Dutch populations there was less reason for that. In Pella, Iowa, round about 1980, about one-quarter of the 7,500 inhabitants had surnames beginning with Van (Vanden, Vander, etc.). Many other Dutch names were also preserved in Pella, such as Harmeling, Hiemstra, Gosselink, Kuiper, Nieuwsma, Vermeer, and even Niemantsverdriet and Naaktgeboren. The names, moreover, were pronounced as in Dutch: Vroom rhymed with English *roam* and Huizer with English *miser*. In Victor, Iowa, where Flemings had settled, Dutch names were also preserved, they could be recognized by their "Flemish" spellings: Claeys, de Meulenaere, De Coster, De Decker, Wauters.

The Dutch immigrants of the nineteenth and twentieth centuries chose English first names for their children: Annabelle, Caroline, Annette, and Joyce, or Andrew, Arthur, Earl, and Marvin, or they gave them names that were almost identical in English and Dutch: Esther, Hans, Nelly, Peter, Simon – not blatantly Dutch names: Aaltje Visser became Alice Fisher and Fennigje Blaauw was called Fannie Blue. This also happened in Dutch settlements like Pella, but especially older inhabitants there were still proud of having a Dutch name in the 1980s.

Frisian proper names, too, were adapted, sometimes even more drastically than the Dutch ones, because they differed more from American English. The family name Banninga became Banning, Dijkstra became Dexter, Kerkstra became Church, Mellema became Miller, Okkinga became King, Tjepkema became Chapman and Zijlstra became Sisco. In Dutch settlements, the Frisian names were often preserved, though. In Pella in the 1980s, the originally Frisian inhabitants were called "the maws and the straws," referring to the fact that many Frisian surnames end in *-ma* and *-stra*. Frisian first names were also anglicized: Bouke became Bert, Ferke became Fred, Jouke became Jacob or Joe, Lolle became Louis, Romke became Ralph (or Roy), Sjoerd became Stuart, Sybe became Sidney and Yme became Elmer. The same goes for girls' names: Boukje became Bessie, Fetje became Fannie, Maaike became Margaret, Minke became Minnie, Tsjitske became Jessie, and Wijtske became Winnie.

Holland Mania

While it is true that the linguistic contribution by the nineteenth- and twentieth-century immigrants was relatively small, they did play their part in the revival of the interest in Dutch culture. That interest had already started before the arrival of the first immigrants of the second wave, halfway through the nineteenth century, and at first was concentrated on the Dutch roots of New York. It started in 1809 with the American writer Washington Irving, who, under the pseudonym Diedrich Knickerbocker, published the satirical *A History of New York*, followed by the stories of *Rip van Winkle* (1819) and *The Legend of Sleepy Hollow* (1820). Irving did not have a Dutch background, but in his time, the city of New York, where he had been born in 1783, still had a clearly recognizable Dutch character, one could still hear Dutch spoken in the streets, and many of Irving's friends were of Dutch descent. In addition, Irving visited the Low Countries in 1805. The image he created of the seventeenth-century Dutch colonists has long determined the Americans' notions about the Dutch "burghers," as appears in chapter 2.

The historian John Lothrop Motley gave a scientifically better justified sketch of the Dutch Republic in his *The Rise of the Dutch Republic* from 1856, and its sequel *History of the United Netherlands.*

Nineteenth-century Dutch society was at the center of the children's book *Hans Brinker or The Silver Skates* by Mary Mapes Dodge from 1865. Whole generations of American children have grown up with this book; since 1865, it has always been in print. Dodge had not been to Holland when she wrote the book – she relied on Motley's historical works. For details about daily life in the Netherlands she received information from the Dutch family Scharff from Newark, who had emigrated to America in 1845. It is from Dodge's book that the myth of the Dutch boy who put his finger in the dike to prevent a flood originates; the story is to be found in chapter 18 of the book. It is not based on actual Dutch events, although many American and Dutch people believe it is. Most Dutch readers think, moreover, that it was Hansje Brinker who was the leading character in the story, but in Dodge's story it is an anonymous boy. In American English, *finger in the dike* has become a popular expression.

And then, between 1880 and 1920, we see the birth of a real "Holland madness" or *Holland Mania* in the US – as Annette Stott calls it in her book from 1998. The occasion was the celebration of a century of Independence in 1876. Several American writers claimed that the Republic of the United Netherlands rather than England was the "mother" of the US. But the contemporary Dutch art and culture also enjoyed warm interest from numerous Americans. All kinds of cultural and political institutions and social customs were mentioned that America was said to owe to the Netherlands. Americans travelled to the Low Countries or to Dutch settlements in the US to get into contact with "authentic" Dutch culture.
That interest was not one-sided – in the nineteenth century, the Dutch became interested in American society, too, partly thanks to news from Dutch immigrants. The Netherlands discovered America through publications by travelers, novelists, journalists, politicians, and scholars. In *Uncle Sam en Jan Salie*

Father Knickerbocker visits Washington Irving. Knickerbocker's History of New York, *was a masterpiece of learned spoofing.*

Illustration 1.27 – "Father Knickerbocker visits Washington Irving" (source: Our Literary Heritage – A Pictorial History of the Writer in America, Van Wyck Brooks & Otto Bettmann; undated reprint by Paddington Press of the 1956 edition)

("Uncle Sam and Johnny Ninny") by the historian Lammers (1989), we find a description of how, through these writings, the Dutch got to know American world, American ideas, and American institutions; they showed great admiration, on the one hand, for the economic progress and enterprise of the Yankees, while on the other hand, critical notes could be heard on the subject of, for example, the American Civil War. At the time of the celebration of the centenary of the American Independence, articles were published in which parallels were drawn between the Netherlands and America, and George Washington was called a second William of Orange. The American language, too, received attention in Dutch publications of the nineteenth century. The year 1863 saw the publication of *De Vlugge Engelschman* (The Speedy Englishman), a manual to help you learn to read, write and speak English quickly and without a tutor. The book, in which, by means of illustrative phrases, practical information is also given about, e.g., the railways ("in America there are only two classes") went through at least 15 reprints. In 1854 M. Keijzer published a translation of Bartlett's dictionary with the title *John Russell Bartlett's Woordenboek van Americanismen, bewerkt door M. Keijzer.* For the publication, the following reasons were given: the increased trade with America and the increase in American literary works, as well as the large numbers of emigrations. In 1894, J.H. van der Voort published *Hedendaagsche amerikanismen*, an adaptation of T. Baron Bussel's *Current Americanisms* – the only argument this time was the increased number of Americanisms in English-language novels and newspapers – no further mention was made of emigrants.

The interest in everything Dutch and Flemish receded in the US after 1920. Dutch and Flemish immigrants became invisible in American society after their names had been adapted, and the number of loanwords the Americans borrowed from the nineteenth- and twentieth-century immigrants was relatively limited. But there is one domain in which the Dutch and the Flemish have left their traces in this period: American topography.

1.6 Dutch place-names from the nineteenth and twentieth century

Many of the new Dutch place-names that were put on the map of America, have been preserved up to today. Below we will list the most important of these – some of them occur in more than one state. Most of the place-names from the nineteenth and twentieth century have been given by groups of Dutch Protestants who named a newly founded place after the Dutch town or province they originated from. Some of these have disappeared by now: at one stage there were the towns of Hellendoorn and Staphorst in Michigan, both of them called after their Dutch counterparts. Not all Dutch or Flemish place-names were founded by immigrants, either: Harlingen, Texas, got its name from its resemblance to the Frisian town, and the name of Watervliet, Michigan, is probably identical to that of a Belgian town by accident.

There are far fewer Catholic place-names referring to Dutch place-names, but they do exist, such as New Netherland, Minnesota (by now obsolete), and Hollandtown, Wisconsin. Catholics also named Wilhelmina, Missouri. A number of places have been called after towns in Belgium – sometimes by Flemish immigrants, but sometimes by Walloon immigrants as well, but it cannot always be determined by whom. This is the case with Antwerp, Michigan and Ohio, Brussels, Illinois and Wisconsin, Charleroy, Pennsylvania, and Ghent, Minnesota. Belgian families from Luxembourg and the Walloon provinces were responsible for the names of Belgium, Bonduel, Luxemburg, Namur, Rosiere, and Walhain – all of which are in Wisconsin.

Another group of names was used to honor important Dutch financiers and land buyers. The New York towns of Barneveld, Batavia, Boonville, Cazenovia, DeRuyter, Leyden, and Licklaen owe their existence and names to the Holland Land Company which bought land at the end of the eighteenth century. The construction of railroads, along which new stops were founded, was partly financed by Dutchmen, after whom the towns of Amsterdam, Missouri; De Queen, Arkansas; DeRidder, Louisiana; Hospers, Iowa; Mena, Arkansas; Nederland, Texas; Vandervoort, Arkansas; Vanoss, Oklahoma; and Zwolle, Iowa are named. Nederland, Colorado, owes its name to a Dutch mining company and Enka, North Carolina, to a cotton producing firm.

A number of places have taken their name from famous Dutchmen (often members of the royal family) or important historical events: Barneveld, Wisconsin; Ghent in Ohio, West Virginia and Kentucky; Leyden, Massachussetts; Liege, Missouri; Nassau, New York; Orange City, Iowa; Waterloo in New York, Oklahoma and Oregon; Westerlo, New York; and Wilhelmina, Missouri. Most of these names were not given by Dutch or Flemish immigrants.

But not everything is what it seems to be ... Deventer, Missouri, for instance, is not called after the similarly named Dutch town, but after a certain Deventer Miller: when a post office was opened in this place in 1910, land owner Frank May suggested a number of appropriate names on the basis of names of family members and friends, among them that of Deventer Miller. The government selected the name Deventer.

Amsterdam, ID. This name was given by Dutch colonists in 1909, after the largest Dutch city. **Amsterdam**, MT, also owes its name to Dutch colonists. **Amsterdam**, NY, is older: this place got its name in 1804 in a period in which exotic names were used and people were aware of the Dutch tradition in New York – which originated from the first wave of settlers. **Amsterdam**, MO, is so called because the firm of the most important financier of the local railway company had its seat in Dutch Amsterdam. That financier was Jan de Goeijen, a Dutch coffee trader and banker, to whom Arthur Stilwell, the founder of the Kansas City Southern Railway, turned when he ran out of money. De Goeijen started to sell shares in the American railways in 1890. As a token of appreciation, Stilwell called several places after De Goeijen or members of his family or after Dutch places with which De Goeijen had a link.

Antwerp, MI and OH. So called by Flemish immigrants after the city of Antwerp in Belgium.

Barneveld, WI. Founded in 1881 and named after the seventeenth-century Dutch statesman Johan van Oldenbarnevelt, especially known from J.L. Motley's *Life and Death of John Barneveld* (1874). **Barneveld**, NY, is older by a century, but is also named after the Dutch statesman: at the end of the eighteenth century the Holland Land Company was founded by thirteen investors from Amsterdam; they bought land in the west and middle of the state of New York and in the west of Pennsylvania. One of their agents, Gerrit Boon, founded the town of Oldenbarneveld(t) in 1793, which became Olden Barneveld in 1819, and – after an intermezzo in which it was called Trenton – it has officially been called Barneveld since 1903.

Batavia, NY. The place and its surroundings were bought by the Holland Land Company in 1792 and Batavia became its headquarters in 1802. Among the investors of the Holland Land Company were some Dutch patriots who had seized power in 1795 in the Batavian Republic, which replaced the Dutch Republic; they named the New York town for Batavia, which is the Latin name for the Netherlands.

Belgium, WI. The town of Belgium was founded between 1845 and 1860 by Luxembourgian families who named it after the country Belgium; at the beginning of the nineteenth century, Luxembourg and Belgium were part of the United Kingdom of the Netherlands. In 1830, Belgium broke away from the Netherlands, and in 1839 Luxembourg was divided between the two: the greater part of Luxembourg became a province of Belgium, the smaller part remained united with the Netherlands until 1890 and then became independent. In Belgium, WI, the Luxembourg Fest is still celebrated once a year.

Bonduel, WI. Named after the Jesuit missionary Florimund Bonduel by Belgian immigrants.

Boonville, NY. Named after Gerrit Boon at the end of the eighteenth century. Boon was an agent of the Holland Land Company and founder of this town which he had christened Kortenaer, after the seventeenth-century Dutch admiral Egbert Bartholomeusz Kortenaer.

Borculo, MI. So called in the middle of the nineteenth century by Dutch colonists from the Dutch town of Borculo.

Brussels, IL and WI. In the middle of the nineteenth century named by Belgian immigrants after the Belgian capital which the Flemish call *Brussel* and the Walloon call *Bruxelles*.

Cazenovia, NY. At the end of the eighteenth century, Jan Linklaen, an agent of the Holland Land Company, named this town after Théophile Cazenove, another agent of the Holland Land Company.
Charleroy, PA. This town was founded by Belgian immigrants in 1890; they established a glass factory there, just as in the Belgian town of Charleroi.
De Queen, AR. Named after the Dutch financier Jan de Goeijen by the founder of the local railway company, Arthur Stilwell. Because people could not pronounce the name De Goeijen, he was called Jack or John De Queen, which was also the name the town received. De Goeijen was not pleased: "How would you like it when I told you that I named my son after you and you found out that he was called William?" he is supposed to have asked Arthur. However, the name also offered opportunities: the local newspaper, which has been published since 1987, has adopted the remarkable name of *The DeQueen Bee*.
DeRidder, LA. Arthur Stilwell named this town after the maiden name of the Belgian sister-in-law of his most important financier, Jan de Goeijen, Ella De Ridder-De Goeijen.
DeRuyter, NY. At the end of the eighteenth century, Jan Linklaen, an agent of the Holland Land Company, named this town after the seventeenth-century Dutch admiral Michiel Adriaensz. de Ruyter.
Drenthe, MI. So called in the middle of the nineteenth century by Dutch colonists originating from the Dutch province of Drenthe. In the town of Drenthe were immigrants who were also from Staphorst and surroundings, and, at first, these people did not agree with the name Drenthe; Staphorst is located in the Dutch province of Overijssel. Provoked by this, an angry farmer nailed a notice to a tree with the text "Staphorst begins here!"
Enka, NC. This town was founded in 1928 for the employees of the American branch of the Dutch Enka Company, the largest cotton producer at that time. At first the company was called the *Nederlandsche Kunstzijdefabriek* (Dutch Artificial Silk Factory). This long name was shortened to the two initials N and K in the spoken language and pronounced as *en-ka*; this subsequently became the official company name.
Friesland, WI. So called in the middle of the nineteenth century by Dutch colonists originating from the Dutch province of Friesland. **Vriesland**, MI, was founded by dominie Marten Ypma. Other towns in Wisconsin that were founded by Frisians are **East Friesland** and **New Amsterdam**, the latter of which was founded as Frisia in 1853.
Ghent, MN. Named after the Belgian town of Ghent by Flemish immigrants.
Ghent, OH, WV, and KY, are named after the Treaty of Ghent, which ended the war of 1812 between the US and the United Kingdom; one of the reasons for this war was that both parties claimed possession of Canada. Henry Clay, one of the American negotiators, was the one to suggest the name Ghent, KY.
Graafschap, MI. So called in the middle of the nineteenth century by colonists originating from the German *graafschap* (county) of Bentheim, which is situated to the east of the Dutch province of Overijssel. The dialect spoken in Bentheim closely resembles that of *Twents*, the dialect spoken in Overijssel. In the nineteenth century, an Old Reformed Church was set up in Bentheim which had connections with the secessionists in the Netherlands.

Groningen, MN. So called by Dutch colonists after the Dutch province or town of Groningen. In the nineteenth century, **New Groningen**, MI, was also named after this province or town. This town is now part of Zeeland, MI, and the name New Groningen has only been retained in proper names such as New Groningen School and New Groningen Cemetery.
Hague, ND. Founded by Dutch colonists in 1902 and named after the Dutch city of The Hague.
Harderwyk, MI. So called in the nineteenth century by Dutch colonists originating from the Dutch town of Harderwijk. Harderwyk is now part of Holland, MI, and its name has only been retained in proper names such as Harderwyk Christian Reformed Church.
Harlem, MI. So called in the nineteenth century by Dutch colonists originating from the Dutch town of Haarlem.
Harlingen, TX. Developer Lon C. Hill founded this town in 1904 on the northern bank of the Arroyo Colorado river. He wanted to make it into an important trade hub, easily accessible by road as well as by water. That is why he called the town after the Frisian town of Harlingen, which was just as strategically located. This is notable, since as far as we know he did not have any connection with the Netherlands or the Dutch province of Friesland.
Hoboken, NJ. This place-name already existed in the seventeenth century, but the similarity to the former Belgian town of Hoboken near Antwerp (a district of Antwerp since 1983) is due to a folk-etymological transformation taking place in the nineteenth century. In the seventeenth century the Dutch originally called the place Hobocan Hackingh or Hopoghan Hackingh; *hobocan* was derived from an Algonquian word meaning "tobacco pipe," and *hackingh* was a derivation of the Dutch verb *hacken*, *hakken* "to chop," because the Native Americans used the site as a quarry for stone from which pipes could be made. The Dutch occasionally called the place Hoebuck or Hoboquin as well, but never Hoboken (which would not be obvious either, because there were hardly any Flemish people among the Dutch colonists). During the English period, Hoebuck or Hoboquin was used in official documents. In the nineteenth century, when the Antwerp place-name became more known due to Belgian immigrants, the name was changed and linked to the Belgian place-name, especially in the two-volume *History of New Netherland* by E.B. O'Callaghan (1846-1849). **Hoboken**, GA, does not have a direct link with Belgium, either: it is called after Hoboken, NJ; thus, neither of these towns got its name from Flemish immigrants.
Holland, MI. Named after Holland, the name of a Dutch province (nowadays divided into North Holland and South Holland) and as *pars pro toto* used as a synonym for the Netherlands. There used to be two settlements there, South Holland and North Holland, but these have blended into Holland. Holland, MI, has as its nickname "The Tulip City" because of its annual Tulip Time Festival, which has been celebrated there since 1930. There are 28 places in the US that are called Holland; these places were described in the Dutch book *Holland USA*, written by the journalists Bram Donker and Anne Wesseling and published in 1997. Three-quarters of these towns have no link with the Netherlands or with Dutch colonists, incidentally, but have been named after a land owner or investor called Mr. Holland. In South Dakota there is **New Holland**, which actually was founded by

Dutch immigrants, just as **New Holland**, MI, and **Hollandale**, MN, were. **Hollandtown**, WI, was founded by Catholic Dutchmen in 1851; the village was first called Franciskus Bosch, but was renamed Hollandtown two years later.
Hospers, IA. Called after the Dutchman Henry Hospers by the railway company that built a station there. Henry Hospers was the mayor of Pella and the founder of Orange City, near which the town of Hospers is situated.
Leyden, MA. This place-name does not originate from Dutch immigrants. Leyden was founded in 1737 and became an autonomous municipality in 1784; thereafter it was named for the Dutch town of Leiden because the Pilgrim Fathers, the English Puritans who left for North America in 1620 to found a colony in Massachusetts, had lived for some time in the Dutch town of Leyden before they went to America. According to Stewart's *Concise Dictionary of American Place-Names*, the choice of this place-name is important, for it shows that people were looking for new, non-English names after American Independence because English names had become unpopular. **Leyden**, NY, owes its name, since 1797, to the Holland Land Company.
Liege, MO. The defense of the Belgian city of Liège against the German attackers in 1914 made such a deep impression in the US that the American town was named after the Belgian one in 1918, whereby the French name Liège was adopted instead of the Dutch name Luik. The name did not originate with immigrants.
Lincklaen, NY. At the end of the eighteenth century, this town was named after Jan Linklaen, an agent of the Holland Land Company.
Luxemburg, WI. This town was founded between 1845 en 1860 by Luxembourgian families.
Mena, AR. This town was founded in 1896, when a local railway was built, financed by, among others, the Dutchman Jan de Goeijen. Mena was named after his wife, Mina de Goeijen-Janssen. *Mina* in Dutch sounds like Mena in American English. Therefore, the name is not, as has often been suggested, a shortening of the name of the Dutch queen Wilhelmina, who, by the way, did not mount the throne until 1898.
Middleburg, IL. So called by Dutch colonists originating from the town of Middelburg in the province of Zeeland.
Namur, WI. The town was founded by Walloons around 1850 (the Flemish call this Belgian town Namen).
Nassau, NY. Prince of Oranje-Nassau is a Dutch title – in chapter 1.3 we already mentioned that several counties in North America were named after Oranje in the seventeenth century. In the nineteenth century, Nassau came to be used in the nomenclature as well: in 1899, the county of Nassau in New York got its name because there was more interest in the past then. The title Oranje-Nassau is also one of the titles of William III, the Stadholder-King. The river and the county of **Nassau**, FL, were named after this title during the English government (1763-1783).
Nederland, CO. The town was named after a Dutch mining company that bought several mines in the area in the nineteenth century. The town was called Nederland, literally "low country" because it was situated to the south of the then flourishing town of Caribou and many people went to the lower Nederland to do their shopping. **Nederland**, TX, was founded by railway magnate Arthur Stillwell in 1897: he bought the land and attracted colonists; to thank his Dutch financiers he called the town Nederland

and arranged for Dutch families to come to Texas to grow rice.

Niekerk, MI. Founded in 1866 by Dutch colonists from Graafschap, MI, and named after the Dutch town of Nijkerk in the province of Gelderland. The town is now part of Holland, MI, and the name Niekerk has only been retained in proper names such as Niekerk Christian Reformed Church.

Noordeloos, MI. At first this town was part of Zeeland, MI, but in 1856, a group of villagers founded a new congregation. As an appeal for the support of the Dutch dominie Koene van den Bosch, they named the congregation after the dominie's Dutch birthplace, Noordeloos, to make it more attractive to him. The dominie established the Noordeloos Christian Reformed Church in 1857, with the result that Noordeloos was the first town with a Christian Reformed Church in the United States.

Oostburg, WI. So called in the middle of the nineteenth century by Dutch colonists from the Dutch town of Oostburg.

Orange City, IA. This town was founded in 1870 by Dutch colonists, most of whom came from booming Pella under the leadership of Pella's mayor, Henry Hospers. Orange City (in Dutch "Oranjestad") was named after the Dutch prince William of Orange.

Overisel, MI. Founded by dominie Seine Bolks and others from the Dutch province of Overijssel, after which they named the town.

Pella, IA. So called by the founder, dominie Scholte. He called it after the mountain town of Pella, which is located on the river Jordan, to which the parish of Jerusalem fled when the city was destroyed by the Romans in 70 A.D. Whoever fled and reached Pella was free. There used to be an expression in Dutch: *ze zijn in Pella* (literally, "they are in Pella"), meaning "they are safe, they have escaped from the oppression." The secessionists were also looking for a safe haven where they would be free to practice their religion. Colonists from Pella, IA, later transferred the name to the newly founded colony of **Pella**, Nebraska.

Rosiere, WI. Called after the Belgian town of Rosières by Belgian immigrants in the middle of the nineteenth century.

South Holland, IK. Dutch colonists settled there in 1847. At first, they called it De Laage Prairie, Holland Bridge, or Low Prairie to distinguish it from their other Dutch colony, higher up in the north, the Hooge Prairie ("High Prairie"), nowadays called Roseland. In 1870, a post office was established in the town and the name was changed to South Holland, to honor the Dutch province of Zuid-Holland from which many colonists originated. The Dutch reformed roots are still very much evident in daily life there: all shops and businesses are closed on Sundays, alcohol is not sold within the city limits, and the selling of pornography is prohibited. The town's motto is "a community of faith, family, future."

Vandervoort, AR. Arthur Stilwell named this town for the maiden name of the mother of his most important financier, Jan de Goeijen, which was Van der Voort; the town was first called Janssen, named after De Goeijen's wife's maiden name.

Vanoss, OK. This town, founded in 1908, was named by the inhabitants after the Dutch financier of the local railway, S.F. van Oss from The Hague.

Walhain, WI. Named after the Belgian town of Walhain by Belgian immigrants in the middle of the nineteenth century.

Walloon Lake, MI. At one time there were Walloons living near the lake; hence the name. Later it was called Bear Lake,

but when the original name was found on an old map, the name was changed.
Waterloo, NY. Named for the Belgian town where Napoleon Bonaparte was definitively defeated in 1815. The name was also used to refer to the expression *to meet one's Waterloo* "to be definitely defeated." Supposedly, **Waterloo**, OK, is named after the fact that this town is near a steep grade where a railroad engineer almost was "defeated". **Waterloo**, OR, according to Stewart's *Concise Dictionary of American Place-Names*, is supposed to have received its name after a severe court decision had been handed down. None of these Waterloos were named by Belgian immigrants.
Watervliet, MI. This town was founded as Waterford in 1833, referring to the running water of the Paw Paw River. When a post office was established there in 1849, the name had to be changed because another place in Michigan already used that name. The Dutch name Watervliet, literally "fleeting water," was opted. This choice is noteworthy, as it indicates that people apparently knew enough Dutch to be able to translate the English name into a Dutch one. Was the manager of the post office, Mr. Isaac Swain, of Dutch descent? The town **Watervliet**, NY, was founded in 1788 and got its Dutch name in honor of the original seventeenth-century Dutch colonists.
Westerlo, NY. Called after reverend Eilardus Westerlo (1738-1790) in 1815, who was born near the Dutch town of Groningen, became minister in Albany in 1760, and supported American Independence by holding a welcoming speech during General Washington's visit to Albany in 1782. The town, therefore, is not named after the Belgian town of Westerlo.
Wilhelmina, MO. Named by the Catholic Dutch founders of the settlement at the beginning of the twentieth century after Wilhelmina, who was at that time queen of the Netherlands.
Zeeland, MI. Founded by dominie Cornelis van der Meulen and others originating from the Dutch province of Zeeland, after which they named the town.
Zwolle, LA. Arthur Stilwell named this town after the birthplace of his main financier, Jan de Goeijen.
Zutphen, MI. Named for the Dutch town of Zutphen by Dutch colonists in the nineteenth century.

The places in the United States by the second wave of Dutch immigrants are more widely scattered about the US than those named by the first wave. The influence of the second wave on the American topography, however, is less extensive than that of the first wave: the colonists of the nineteenth and twentieth century primarily gave names to towns and counties, whereas seventeenth-century settlers also named many streams, rivers, and other characteristic physical features in the American landscape (see sections 1.3 and 2.5).

1.7 The Dutch language and culture in the US, anno 2009

Currently, there are very few speakers of American Dutch, American Flemish, or American Frisian; most of these are elderly, and their number is diminishing. According to the US Census from 2000, only 150,000 people stated that they spoke Dutch at home (see www.mla.org/map_data). Five years later, in 2005, this number had decreased to around 130,000. At this rate, Dutch will become extinct in 32.5 years, but in view of the age of most speakers, that figure seems to be optimistic. From the Census, moreover, it seems that most Dutch speakers reside in California (over 27,000), Pennsylvania, Florida, and New York (with a good 10,000), Ohio (with 9,500). Dutch is also spoken, albeit to a lesser extent, in (listed in decreasing order of speakers) Michigan, Indiana, Texas, New Jersey, Washington, Illinois, and Wisconsin. In each of the remaining states there are fewer than 3,000 Dutch speakers. Incidentally, no fewer than 387 different languages are spoken in American households. Nevertheless, Dutch culture has not completely dissolved in the famous American melting pot. The same US Census from 2000 shows that 4.5 million Americans consider themselves to be wholly or partly descended from Netherlanders; this is 1.6 percent of the population. Just as many Americans see themselves as being Norwegians, and slightly more (4.9 million) as Scots. In comparison: 42.8 million people (15.2 percent) regard themselves as German. Since 2000, the number of people claiming to have Dutch roots has even risen: it is now over five million.

It looks as if the more the Dutch language loses ground, the more emphatically Dutch or Flemish ethnicity is emphasized, albeit in a slightly folkloristic fashion. Apparently, one can be proud of one's Dutch background without being able to speak the Dutch language. In Pella, Iowa, around 1980, stickers could be seen on car bumpers reading *You're not Mutch* [sic] *if You're not Dutch*, and in Victor, Iowa, where many Flemings had settled, *Being Belgian is Beautiful* – in English, mind you. *You're not much if you're not Dutch* is still in use, as is evident on the Internet, in all kinds of variants, and even printed on tiles. Facebook has a discussion group called "If You Ain't Dutch, You Ain't Much," "A Group For Those Who Love The Dutch." A blogger named "Angie" from Colorado ("growing up in Iowa, I learned many 'frugal Dutch' tips from my mom and grandma") keeps a weblog entitled "Being Dutch, gets you much."

During special gatherings such as family reunions or funerals in the original Dutch enclaves such as Pella and Holland, some people use Dutch words or phrases to strengthen a feeling of unity – showing their Dutch background by using the odd Dutch word in a conversation, such as *goeie morrege, alles goed?*("Good morning, all is well?") or *potdorie!* ("darn!"). In Pella in the 1980s, people would greet each other with "How are you doing, you old *lamzak*?" (or *mieter*, *smeerlap*, *paardedief*, etc.). Especially the latter sounds a little strange to Dutch people: the good-natured terms *lamzak*, *mieter*, *paardedief* ("lamebrain," "sod," and "horsethief") have become totally obsolete in European Dutch, and *smeerlap* ("son of a bitch") is a relatively strong term of abuse. On Pella's website you can find - in English - "Old Dutch recipes" for amongst others Sint Nickolaas Koekjes (Santa Claus Cookies), Nieuwjaarskoekjes (New Years Cookies), Poffertjes (Holland Fritters), Balken Brij (Breakfast Dish), Hoofd Kaas (Head Cheese) and Erwten Soep (Pea Soup). Dutch enjoys prestige in all these settlements, and people take pride in being able to speak it, even if it's a matter of only a few words or phrases. At Central College in Pella and in Orange City, Iowa, Dutch courses are taught to improve that Dutch a little.

There are many kinds of festivities to keep up "Dutch" traditions. In Pella and Orange City, Iowa, and in Holland, Michigan, the Tulip Time Festival is celebrated every year (in Pella since 1929 and in Orange City since 1937) – there are parades with decorated floats, participants wearing Dutch costumes and *klompen* (clogs), and people scrub the streets - for which the Dutch are renowned. There is a Dutch market where *drop*, *pindakaas* and *gestampte muisjes* (licorice, peanut butter, and aniseed comfits) are sold, and clog dancers perform folk dances. These Tulip Time Festivals do not have direct roots in the Netherlands or Belgium: they can perhaps be traced back to the May festivals that used to be celebrated in the Low Countries, but the American festivals have a character all their own. Meanwhile, in the Dutch bulb belt, so-called tulip festivals are now being organized when the tulips bloom – it is an interesting thought that the name *tulpenfestival* may have been introduced from America. Many of the items on the programs, such as clog dances and walking around in traditional costume, have more or less disappeared in the Netherlands; might some of the so-called "Old Dutch traditions," in American form, perhaps be saved in the US after they have become extinct in the Netherlands? And then ... perhaps, return to the Low Countries completely renewed? In Pella, in addition to Tulip Time Festival in May, *Sinterklaas* is celebrated in December, and *kermis* in July; Americans will get a rather peculiar idea of the Netherlands on the basis of the annual festivals – but they will learn a few Dutch words, such as **kermis** (see 2.7), *klompen*, and *Sinterklaas* (see **Santa Claus** in section 2.11).

Since 1990, 16 November has been Dutch-American Heritage Day, and 19 April is Dutch-American Friendship Day. Since 2005, "5 Dutch Days" is celebrated in New York in November – this event focuses on the continuous influence of Dutch art and culture in New York City. The festival was started by the three then-directors of Dutch-American sites in New York City, Sean Sawyer of the Wyckoff Farmhouse Museum, Felicia Mayro of St. Mark's Historic Landmark Fund, and Susan De Vries of Dyckman Farmhouse Museum. Elsewhere, too, there are museums supplying information about the first or second wave of Dutch immigrants: Holland, Michigan, has its Holland Museum, Calvin College in Grand Rapids, Michigan, has a Heritage Hall, where material on the Dutch settlements in America from the nineteenth century (particularly about the Christian Reformed Church) is kept. Northwestern College in Orange City and the Pella Public Library have a Dutch Heritage Room. In the 1960s, some Dutch colonial houses from the seventeenth century were reconstructed, such as the Jan Martense Schenck house from 1675 in the Brooklyn Museum, and the Voorlezer House in Richmond, Staten Island.

Dutch and Belgian immigrants can become members of a vast number of societies that promote contact and mutual friendship between the Netherlands, Belgium, and the US. These societies organize meetings on important festival days such as Koninginnedag (Queen's Day) and Sinterklaas. The largest Dutch Heritage society in the US is the Dutch International Society (DIS) in Grand Rapids, Michigan, which started out as the Dutch Immigrant Society; this society publishes the *DIS Magazine*. The most influential bilateral foundation is the Netherland-America Foundation (NAF), which was founded in 1921 by, among others, Franklin D. Roosevelt; this foundation, of which Princess Margriet and her husband are patrons, initiates and supports exchange programs between the Netherlands and the US in the fields of education, arts, sciences, and so on; Fulbright fellowships and grants are available to support these programs. In 1965 the state news agency ANP started a newsletter in English for the foreign community, called *ANP News Bulletin*. In 1997, Netherlands Info Services BV (NIS) acquired the journal and continued it under its current name, *NIS News Bulletin*. It is the longest-running Dutch daily newspaper in English.

In addition to these, there are a variety of local societies throughout the US. The website of the group NY400 Holland on the Hudson (specially set up for the commemoration of 400 years of permanent friendship between Holland and the US) lists as many as 75 of these organizations (www.ny400.org/get_in_touch.php). Most of these groups have English names or are formed with international words, with a few interesting exceptions: the Hollandse Jonkies in America (Dutch "Young ones" in America) in Gillette, New Jersey; the Wapenbroeders ("Brothers in Arms") in Corona, California; Voor Elk Wat Wils ("Something for Everybody") in Grand Rapids, Michigan; and De Wieken ("The Sails") in Raleigh, North Carolina. Some of the societies were set up as social clubs, others for the promotion of cultural or business interests, one or two are for sport or drama, one is for homosexuals only. Most of them admit Dutchmen, Flemings, and interested people. Many of them have a website, and some publish newsletters. In fifteen states, socials are organized for the Dutch expat network (see www.nlborrels.com).

The website www.goDutch.com gives a comprehensive list of firms that concentrate on the Dutch market in the US: they offer Dutch products or are run by Dutchmen. It costs money to advertise on this website, but apparently many firms think it is important to be seen there. In February 2009, Flanders House was opened in New York; this is a non-profit organization that co-ordinates all Flemish activities in the US in the fields of trade, tourism, and so on. The organizers aim to create a consistent image of Flanders in the US. On the Internet, an English-language independent newsletter about Flanders called *Flanders Today* is published weekly (www.flanderstoday.eu). For Americans wanting to know who their Dutch ancestors were, there are special websites such as www.traceyourdutchroots.com/roots and www.genlias.nl/en. The Internet has much to offer for Americans nostalgic for their "Dutch Heritage." There are various websites where one can indulge in reminiscences and exchange views with other like-minded spirits; at www.goDutch.com, one can subscribe to the *Windmill Herald*, "Your Dutch North American newspaper"; one can order quality food at websites featuring "traditional" Dutch baking and catering. In and around Detroit or in Victor, the Flemings, too, need not be deprived of reminiscences of their motherland; they can read the *Gazette van Detroit*, written by and for (descendants of) Flemish immigrants, which was completely restyled in 2006, and they can drown their homesickness in Flemish bars. Once a year, they can play ball games such as **rolle bolle** (see 2.11) – which has since disappeared in their country of origin. Or they can read the twice-yearly periodical *Flemish American Heritage Magazine*, published since 1983 by the Genealogical Society of Flemish Americans in Roseville, Michigan.

In the last few decades, Dutch culture has figured in a number of American literary works; these contained a variety of Dutch words added for *couleur locale*. In 1995, Michael Pye published *The Drowning Room*, a story set partly in Amsterdam and partly in New Amsterdam in 1642, featuring a protagonist named "Gretje Reyniers". In 1998, Tracey Chevalier wrote *Girl with a Pearl Earring*, about the servant girl in the painting of the same name by Johannes Vermeer. *City of Dreams: A Novel of Nieuw Amsterdam and Early Manhattan* by Beverly Swerling (2002), and *The Mevrouw Who Saved Manhattan: A Novel of New Amsterdam* by Bill Greer (2009) are both situated in New Netherland. In addition to these titles, as we can see on the website www.goDutch.com, there are numerous other works of fiction published about Dutch immigration, culture, design, cooking, and the Dutch language.

In the field of scholarship, too, there is ample interest in Dutch culture and history; one example of this is a project started in 1974 by Charles Gehring, at the request of the New York State Library. Gehring has translated the New Netherland documents in the New York archives into English; eighteen volumes have been published so far. His activities fall within the New Netherland Project – see the informative website www.nnp.org. The website shows a long list of biographies of famous "Dutch Americans," including Humphrey Bogart, Marlon Brando, Dick Van Dyke, Clint Eastwood, Thomas Edison, Audrey Hepburn, Willem J. Kolff, Willem de Kooning, Herman Melville, Piet Mondriaan, Meryl Streep, and Bruce Springsteen. The New Netherland Project is supported by the New Netherland Institute, which by means of a large number of activities disseminates information on the Dutch history of colonial America. It publishes a quarterly periodical called *De Nieu Nederlanse Mercurius*.

On the basis of new data made available through the New Netherland Project, several books have been written recently about the New Netherland period, including the earlier-mentioned book by Russell Shorto *The Island at the Center of the World*, written in 2004, and Dutch historian Jaap Jacobs's book *New Netherland: A Dutch Colony in Seventeenth-Century* America, written in 2005. In 2006, Hans Krabbendam published a book on Dutch emigration to America between 1840 and 1940.

Despite these examples of scholarly interest in Dutch history and culture, it's worth noting that there is a decline in the number of US universities that offer Dutch language as part of their curricula. In 1949 there were two: Columbia University and Calvin College. In 1960, this number had increased to 6 and, in 1977, even to 24. But after that, a new decline set in: as of 2009, Dutch is taught at only 15 institutions – three of them in New York: State University of New York in Albany; Cornell University in Ithaca; and Columbia University. Two of them were established by the Christian Reformed Church: Calvin College in Grand Rapids, Michigan, and Dordt College, Sioux Center, Iowa. The other places where Dutch is found in the curriculum are the University of Michigan, Ann Arbor; the University of Texas, Austin; the University of California, Berkeley; the University of California, Los Angeles; Indiana University; the University of North Carolina; the University of Maryland; the University of Wisconsin, Madison; the University of Minnesota; and the University of Pennsylvania. In the academic year 2007-2008, there were 915 students taking Dutch at a university in the US.

It seems as if in the last few decades of the twentieth century and the first decade of the twenty-first century in the US, there has been a slight increase in interest in the

Netherlands. Do we detect a new "Holland Mania" here, like that of the previous turn of the century, or is that just wishful thinking? Time will tell – the trend is perhaps invigorated by this commemoration year. For the Dutch language, this increase in interest won't make a difference: there's no chance that it is going to catch on as a home language in the US, nor will American English end up taking over any new Dutch loanwords from immigrants or their descendants from the nineteenth or twentieth century. Nevertheless, the contributions to American English from the Dutch language over the past four centuries certainly can be called substantial. What that contribution consists of will be discussed in the next chapter.

CHAPTER 2.

Dutch words that have left their mark on American English: a thematic glossary

2.0 Introduction: sources and structure of the glossary

The glossary in this chapter highlights Dutch loanwords in American English that still exist – although some of them have become historical terms – as well as words cited in multiple sources. Most of the words have been extracted from the many dictionaries that describe the distinct vocabulary of American English (see the bibliography at the end of this book). A minority of the words have disappeared from American English. Dutch loanwords in American English that are cited only once or a limited number of times have not been included. The following list from Mencken's *The American Language* (1937) may serve as an example. On pages 109-110, Mencken writes in note 2:

> "Mr. Karl von Schlieder of Hackensack, N.J., sends me a list of curious forms encountered near Kingston, N.Y. It includes *pietje-kamaakal* (unreasonable), *surallikus* (so-so), *zwok* (soft, slippery), *connalyer* (crowd), *klainzaric* (untidy), *haidang* (nothing), *onnozel* (outlandish), *poozly* (whining), *feaselick* (undesirable), *kanaapie* (child), *aislick* (no-account), *brigghity* (impudent), and *bahay* (confusion). That all of these are of Dutch origin is not certain …."

None of these words are found in any other American English source and they therefore have not been incorporated.

The glossary gives the contemporary meaning of each headword, followed by an indication as to whether the word is included in the four-volume *A Dictionary of American English on Historical Principles* by William A. Craigie and James R. Hulbert from 1938-1944 (abbreviated as Craigie hereafter), in the *Dictionary of American Regional English* (1985-) edited by Frederic G. Cassidy and Joan Houston Hall (abbreviated as DARE hereafter; volumes published so far: A through Sk-) and/or in *Webster's Third New International Dictionary* from 1961 (hereafter abbreviated as Webster). These three dictionaries were chosen because each represents the most comprehensive collection of words in American English in their respective fields: Craigie in the area of Americanisms, DARE with regard to regional American English, and *Webster's* as a contemporary document of the entire English vocabulary in the US. The source entry shows at a glance how current or frequently used a certain word is: a word that does not occur in any source other than DARE is only used regionally, while a word that is only included in Craigie is now regarded as archaic. A word that occurs in all three dictionaries is regarded as commonly known and widespread.

Following headword, definition, and source, a new line starts with concise information about the origin of the American English word, the period in which it was probably borrowed from Dutch, and how common or widespread it is (based on information provided in the dictionaries rather than scientific corpus research).

The period in which the words were borrowed is based on their first occurrence and their prevalence: a word that is used only in and around New York is likely to have been introduced by the seventeenth-century Dutch settlers. Only relative value is attached to a word's first occurrence: words appearing in the seventeenth or eighteenth century evidently stem from the first settlers, but words appearing in the nineteenth century did not necessarily originate from the second wave of immigrants. They may just as well be vestiges of the first settlers, as it usually takes some, if not many, years before a loanword is recorded in the adopting language. For example, *dobber* was first recorded in 1809; nevertheless, the word is assumed to have been borrowed in the seventeenth or eighteenth century because it was described in 1809 as a vernacularized Dutch word in New York. In other words, dictionaries and printed texts are generally slow in adopting certain words. What is more, it was not until 1781 that American English was found to be moving away from British English and going its own way; in fact, this was when the term "Americanism" was introduced. And it was not until the nineteenth century that attempts were made to describe the specific American English vocabulary. Occasionally, the age of the Dutch word is considered to determine when a Dutch loanword was adopted into American English: for example, the fact that Dutch *bok* ("zaagbok") was not known until the nineteenth century means that American English *buck* ("sawbuck") cannot date from an earlier period.

This concise information is again followed by a new line providing a more detailed description of the Dutch word's vicissitudes in American English, including quotes to explain the word's usage. The oldest known quote is always given, supplemented by other quotes that shed more light on the word's usage or meaning, as well as a modern quote that demonstrates the word is still present in the living language. The quotes are for the most part selected from Craigie, DARE, or both – anyone interested can look up the complete selection of quotes with the relevant word in these works, which also contains the exact bibliography for the quotes, which have been omitted from this publication for reasons of readability. For example, the glossary provides the following quotes under *boodle*:

1833 I know a feller 'twould whip the whool boodle of 'em an' give 'em six.

1884 At eleven o'clock the "whole boodle of them," as Uncle Nahum called the caravan, ... had to boot and spur for church.

The entry in the original (Craigie) reads as follows:

1833 J. NEAL *Down-Easters* I. 61, I know a feller 'twould whip the whool boodle of 'em an' give 'em six.

1884 HALE *Xmas in Narragansett* 272 At eleven o'clock the "whole boodle of them," as Uncle Nahum called the caravan, ... had to boot and spur for church.

Where possible, the sources of all quotes (Bartlett, Schele de Vere, Farmer, Clapin) from the principal nineteenth-century dictionaries of Americanisms are added. The original sources were always consulted, and although Craigie and DARE do not consistently include quotes from these dictionaries, for our purposes they often contain interesting information about the use of the Dutch loan. Where a quote comes from informants who completed a questionnaire for DARE, DARE is listed as the source between parentheses. Some maps from DARE are reproduced, showing the regional distribution of a word in the US (DARE maps appear distorted because they display population density rather than land area). For all quotes taken from Kurath's *Word Geography of the Eastern United States* from 1949, Kurath is acknowledged as the source. Finally, the online *Urban Dictionary*, "the slang dictionary you wrote" (www.urbandictionary.com), was consulted as a source for modern usage, while critically ascertaining whether the information was reliable and was provided by more than one informant.

It appears that Dutch loanwords in American English concern thirteen specific areas and hence can be reduced to thirteen semantic fields; only five loanwords do not fit any of these categories and are therefore dealt with last, under the heading "Miscellaneous." There are, of course, always words that can be included in more than one category. These are incorporated into the category where they fit best. The semantic fields are given in descending order, from the category that encompasses the largest number of loanwords to the one with the fewest. There are many similarities with Dutch loanwords in Amerindian languages (see chapter 3), where foodstuffs, household effects, and animals also rank in the top three. However, there is a difference: in American English, flora and fauna rank second place instead of third but, and possibly more importantly, the animal names that Native Americans adopted invariably involved European species that the Dutch had brought with them to the East Coast of the US, whereas the majority of words adopted into American English in this field are names for American species. Ranked fourth and fifth place in Amerindian languages are the names for money and measures and for clothing – these categories are also found in American English but are ranked lower. The Amerindian languages have not adopted any words in the polity and citizens' category, which, in terms of meaning, have definitely been the most important in American English, where, in terms of numbers, they rank fourth place.

The loanwords in each semantic field are listed alphabetically. Each semantic field begins with a general overview of the constituent words (printed in bold) without providing details, which are given in the more extensive etymology. The introductions and some entries include words that have not been addressed in detail in the alphabetical list because they are not so commonly used (these words are printed in bold italics and included in the index).

All loanwords in this list originated from Dutch immigrants in the US and are attributable to direct contact between Dutch and English speakers in North America. The last category, dealt with in section 2.15, includes a number of more recent loanwords from the Low Countries that spread to other languages, including American English, in the second half of the twentieth century. A limited number of examples will be given, as they are not the result of special contact between Netherlanders and Americans, but instead involve coincidental Dutch inventions that have conquered the world. Finally, section 2.16 provides a brief summary of the nature and scope of the Dutch influence on American English and discusses a number of phonetic changes that are characteristic of the loanwords.

2.1 Food, drink, and stimulants

The largest contribution made by the Dutch to American English proves to have been in the area of foodstuffs, where no fewer than 28 loanwords have been adopted. This is rather surprising, given that the Dutch are hardly renowned for their culinary achievements.

It is particularly the names of confectionery and candy that the Yankees adopted, such as **cookie**, **cruller**, **olykoek**, **pannicake**, and **waffle** in the seventeenth or eighteenth century, which are still fairly to considerably widespread in the US, and **banket**, **letter**, and **oliebollen** in the nineteenth or twentieth century, which are only known in a small circle. Considering all this confectionery, it is no surprise that the verb *snoepen* ("to eat sweets") was adopted as **to snoop**, although this verb has acquired an entirely different meaning in American English.

A number of names for cold meats or meat dishes have been adopted: **apples and speck**, **rolliche**, and **speck** in the seventeenth or eighteenth century, and **balkenbry**, **headcheese**, and **metworst** in the nineteenth or twentieth century. **Bry**, **erwten soup**, and **hutspot** were adopted as names for dishes in the nineteenth or twentieth century and **noodles** in the seventeenth or eighteenth century. With the exception of **apples and speck**, **speck**, and **noodles**, use of the Dutch names is not widespread, indeed these names were introduced not so much by the Dutch as by the Germans. Slightly more commonly known are the names of two types of cheese introduced by the Dutch (which is a small number, considering that the Netherlands is a cheese country par excellence): **pot cheese** in the seventeenth or eighteenth century and **smear-case** in the nineteenth century. By far the best-known word is **coleslaw**, which is currently regarded as a typically American product and is exported to other countries under its American English name. This word was borrowed in the seventeenth or eighteenth century. Finally, one name of a native dish, namely **sup(p)awn** "corn-meal mush" was taken over by the Dutch from the Native Americans, and subsequently passed on to the Yankees.
Various names involve food that farmers make from their own products, such as **apples and speck**, **balkenbry**, **coleslaw**, **erwten soup**, **headcheese**, **hutspot**, **metworst**, **pot cheese**, **rolliche**, and **smear-case**.

American English borrowed three Dutch liquor names: **brandy** in the seventeenth century (still widely known), and **advocaat** and **boerenjongens** in the nineteenth or twentieth century, which are less commonly known.

Illustration 2.1 – Webster's Dictionary (source: The Printing Art, vol. 5, #2, April 1905)

Dope in the sense of "sauce, gravy" was adopted in the seventeenth or eighteenth century. The word has since undergone a drastic change in meaning in the US. Another Dutch word that was originally used to refer to a (savory) sauce is ***pickle***, which stems from Dutch *pekel* and has been used in British English since the fifteenth century. The sauce was first used to flavor meat and later to conserve fruit and vegetables. *Pickle* then began to mean vegetables kept in vinegar or salt water. According to the OED, the next step was made "primarily" in the US, where *pickles* was increasingly used to refer to sour cucumbers or gherkins. A 1715 text states: "At the Store-House ... are to be Sold ... Cases of Pickle on reasonable terms." In this sense, the word probably returned to the Low Countries via international trade. Although this originally Dutch word underwent a development of its own in the US, it entered the American continent via British English rather than Dutch.

Dutch influence in the area of smoking was insignificant, despite the nation's image as a country of pipe smokers. A brand of cigarettes was named after the Dutch governor, Peter **Stuyvesant**, in the twentieth century, and the Dutch introduced the word **cuspidor** (see 2.3). Furthermore, Mahican adopted the Dutch word *snuif*, meaning "stimulating powdered tobacco that is snorted."

Some Dutch words were insufficiently widespread to be included in the alphabetical list below. DARE cites American English ***kliekies***, also *klikkes*, derived from Dutch *kliekjes*,"leftovers." This was reported by only two informants, once in 1969 and once in 1993. Another term cited once, in 1940, is ***pot eten***, "a dish of potatoes, other vegetables, and sometimes meat boiled together," derived from Dutch *poteten*, meaning "cooked food," literally "pot meal." In areas where Dutch people settled, DARE reports the use of words such as ***snert***, meaning "pea soup" (synonym of **erwten soup**) and ***vetbollen***, meaning "fat dumpling(s)" (synonym of **oliebollen**). Kurath (1949: 24, 71) also mentions ***thick-milk*** for "buttermilk," derived from Dutch *dikke melk*, which was still used in 1949 in areas where Dutch people had settled, noting: "Some food terms of Dutch origin ... such as *thickmilk* for curdled milk, have probably always been Dutch family words and are disappearing fast." *Thick-milk* is also used in areas where Germans settled, where it is based on Pennsylvanian Dutch *Dickemilch*.

Slightly more than half of the Dutch loanwords in the field of food date from the seventeenth or eighteenth century, the rest are from the nineteenth or twentieth century. Most of the words from the former period are relatively widely known and are often used throughout the United States. The later derivations are mostly common within a small area. Of the 28 Dutch loanwords in the area of foodstuffs, at least 10 – more than a third – are used on a daily basis throughout the US: **apples and speck**, **brandy**, **coleslaw**, **cookie**, **cruller**, **dope**, **speck**, **noodles**, **to snoop**, and **waffle**.

Finally, it is interesting to note that thanks to Dutch, two dishes originating from Indonesia became internationally known in the twentieth century and entered American English: ***sambal oelek***, a hot, spicy relish, and ***rijsttafel***, a comprehensive meal. The words were probably imported by (Indonesian) Dutchmen who, after Indonesia became independent in 1949, left the country and chose America as their new home rather than the Netherlands. The assumption that *sambal oelek* was spread via Dutch is supported by the way the word *oelek* is spelled: in modern Indonesian, it is written as *ulek*, but in Dutch as *oelek*. *Rijsttafel* has an interesting history. It was customary among the Dutch in Indonesia to have a midday meal consisting of rice and many side dishes; the rest of the population ate a simple rice meal without side dishes three times a day. The Dutch dubbed this meal *rijsttafel*, a term which was subsequently adopted into Indonesian as well as American English. The word was included in the 2004 Scripps National Spelling Bee for children under sixteen ("Yes, it's a real word, not a Scrabble accident," said *The Charlotte Observer*). The word's spelling discomfited the participants, or as another paper commented: "'Rijsttafel' might be a delicious Indonesian dinner, but on Tuesday it upset the stomachs of the 275 youngsters attempting to spell it correctly."

advocaat, a drink somewhat similar to eggnog (Webster).

- From Dutch *advocaat* (a kind of liquor); borrowed in the nineteenth or twentieth century and still in use.

* The drink *advocaat* or its diminutive *advocaatje* is typically Dutch, akin to eggnog but by no means identical. *Advocaat* is a very sustaining drink composed of grape brandy, egg yolks, sugar, and grated nutmeg, which is so thick that it is usually eaten with a spoon rather than drunk. *Advocaat* was traditionally homemade. The drink has been known in the Netherlands since the late eighteenth century, but the etymology of its name is uncertain. There is a synonym, *advocatenborrel*, literally meaning "drink for a lawyer," which is explained by the fact that it is good lubricant for the throat and hence useful for lawyers, who have to speak a lot in public. This explanation may have been devised in retrospect, because it seems more likely that the beverage is named after the avocado, which provides a creamy, buttery, yellow substance that is used to make a thick mixture that looks like the drink advocaat. The fruit's name was adopted into Dutch from obsolete Spanish *avocado*, which in turn goes back to South American Indian Nahuatl.

Mencken reports that *advokat* was adopted from Dutch in Michigan (see quote). The word was probably introduced by nineteenth- or twentieth-century Dutch immigrants, and features in the 1961 edition of Webster's Third and in the OED with a quote from 1935. The drink is known in both the US and Great Britain, which is probably due to the international exchange of spirits and the fact that Dutch immigrants in America may have promoted familiarity with the drink. There are many recipes for "homemade *Advocaat*" on the Internet, but if that seems like too much trouble, one can just buy a bottle of Bols Advocaat, which is also available in the US.

> **1945** In the much larger Dutch colony of Michigan there are many more such [local] borrowings, *e.g.*, *advokat* (egg-nog). (Mencken, Suppl. I, 191)
>
> **2006** *Advokaat* is the Dutch word for "egg cognac." It is highly recommended for A.I. (Alcohol Imbibing) meetings. (on the Internet)

apples and speck, a certain dish (Craigie).

- From Dutch *appels en spek* (formerly *speck*); borrowed in the seventeenth or eighteenth century and still in use.

* On the Internet a New York food critic wrote in 2008: "This could be followed by ... roasted potatoes apples and speck."

Most Americans believe this dish to be of German origin, but it was brought to the American continent by the Dutch. Various dictionaries of nineteenth-century Americanisms include *applejees* or *speck and applejees*, often with a concise recipe and associated with the Dutch. In Dutch, *appels en spek*, *appeltjes en spek*, or *spek en appels* is the name of a dish, or actually the constituents of a dish: it is usually a hodgepodge of mashed potatoes and sometimes a type of vegetable into which apples and bacon are mixed, thus combining a variety of flavors. The same dish is called *Äpfel und Speck* in German, and Germany immigrants are bound to have played a key role in spreading the name and the dish in the US in the nineteenth century. However, it had already been introduced by the Dutch in the Dutch form *applejees*. For the *-jees* ending, see, for example, *blumachies* under **Easter flower** (in 2.2) and *rollichies* under **rolliche**. In American English, the name has since been anglicized to *apples and speck*, from which it is now impossible to tell whether it was derived from Dutch or German.

Finally, it is worth noting that the Dutch word *appel* was adopted into a number of Amerindian languages in the seventeenth century, namely Loup, Mahican, Mohegan-Pequot, and Munsee and Unami Delaware.

1848 *Spack* [ed. 2, *speck*] *and applejees.* (Dutch) Pork and apples, cooked together. An ancient Dutch dish made in New York. (Bartlett)

1863 "Speck and appeljees" is a slight modification of *spek en appeltjes*, the name for fried pork and apples among the Hollanders. (Craigie under *speck*)

1872 ... the famous *Spek en Apeltjees*, now commonly called *Speck and Applejees*, fat pork and apples cut up together and cooked. (Schele de Vere)

1902 *Applejees* or *Speck and applejees* (Dutch *apeltjees*). An old-fashioned Dutch dish still in favor in New York and consisting of fat pork and apples which are cut up together and cooked. (Clapin)

balkenbry, also **balken brie**, **balkenbrij**, a pork loaf (DARE).

- From Dutch *balkenbrij*, meaning "a pork loaf"; borrowed in the nineteenth or twentieth century and still used regionally. See also **bry.**

* This is a typically Dutch dish, originating from the province of Gelderland and prepared in the butchering season from the meat of a pig's head and other meat scraps, blood, and fat, cooked with buckwheat flour, currants, and raisins. In the olden days, it was wrapped in cloth and suspended from a rafter to mature. In Dutch, the word is now considered to be a compound of *balk* ("beam, rafter") and *brij* ("mush"). The first part, however, was transformed by folk etymology from *balch*, which means "intestines, tripe." In Standard Dutch, the name did not become known until the nineteenth century and was brought to the US by nineteenth- or twentieth-century immigrants, where, according to DARE, it is still known in areas of the US where Dutch people live.

1940 Balkenbry. A loaf made of pork liver and lean pork, cooked, and later sliced and fried.

1945 In the much larger Dutch colony of Michigan there are many more such borrowings, *e.g.*, ... *balkenbry* (a pork loaf). (Mencken, Suppl. I, 191)

1969 Balkenbry – mainly liver and pork; the mixture is cooked, stuffed into a cloth bag, spices added, then recooked; the slices are cut off and

fried ... similar to liver sausage. (DARE)
2007 Michiganites eat *balkenbry*, *erwten soup*, and *paczki*. (*The American Midwest, An interpretative encyclopedia*. 2007, p. 290)

banket, a rolled pastry filled with almond paste (DARE).
- From Dutch *banketletter* "puff pastry letter with almond paste," also shortened to *banket*, with the same meaning; adopted in the nineteenth or twentieth century and still known regionally in Dutch communities. Also see **letter**.
* In Dutch, *banket* refers to a particular type of pastry used to make confectionery in various forms, usually a letter, hence the name *banketletter* ("letter of banket"), also shortened to *banket*. In the Netherlands, it is a custom to eat *banketletters* during the St. Nicholas holiday (5 December, see **Santa Claus** in 2.11), and is known since the nineteenth century. In American English, the word is especially used regionally in the shortened form of *banket*; see the quotes from DARE. The Dutch word *banket* and English *banquet* (elaborate meal, formal dinner) are both derived, via French, from Italian *banchetto*, "bench," originally a snack eaten on a bench (rather than at a table), hence "a slight repast between meals." In Dutch, its meaning was then narrowed down to refer to a particular type of sweet pastry.
1982 This month we will be mailing a special Christmas catalog for chocolate initials, gingerbreads, banket, Christmas banket wreaths, marzepan, fancy tins with cookies and/or rusk.
1982 The original Dutch is *banket letters*, almond filling in puff pastry baked in the shape of your initial for your birthday ... In Dutch communities in America everybody recognizes the word *banket*, though sometimes it is not the most common word ... The Polish bakers on the West Side of Grand Rapids make *banket* and do not know it is Dutch.
1982 I make banket in pieces about 12 inches long and about 2 inches in circumference. It can also be shaped into letters, like if you want to give it as a Christmas gift. Then you might shape it into the form of someone's initial.

boerenjongens, a drink usually made with whiskey and raisins, usually served around Christmas time (DARE).
- From Dutch *boerenjongens*, meaning "type of spirits"; adopted in the nineteenth or twentieth century and regionally used in areas inhabited by Dutch people.
* The Dutch word literally means "country boys"; it is short for the Frisian name *brandewyn mei boerejonges*, literally "brandy with country boys." It is unknown how "raisins" came to be referred to as *boerejonges* – the name was probably used for humorous effect. The term has been known in Dutch since the nineteenth century. The immigrants who brought it with them apparently adjusted the recipe to the American situation, replacing the Dutch brandy with whiskey. ***Boerenmeisjes***, literally meaning "country girls," particularly popular in the eastern part of the Netherlands, is also known in the US. There are many recipes to be found on the Internet for *boerenmeisjes* or *boerenmeisjes cocktail*. The drink is sweeter than boerenjongens, and usually made with dried apricots, water, sugar and brandy or whiskey.
1940 *Boerenjongens*. A popular drink of brandy and raisins.
1945 In the much larger Dutch

colony of Michigan there are many more such borrowings, *e.g.*, ... *boeren-jongens* (a drink made of brandy and raisins). (Mencken, Suppl. I, 191)
1976 *Boerenjongens cocktail* ... Served especially during the Christmas season in Dutch homes.

brandy, spirit originally distilled from wine (Craigie, Webster).
- From Dutch *brandewijn*, meaning "an alcoholic liquor"; borrowed in the seventeenth century and currently very widespread.
* The discovery of brandy is probably attributable to a sixteenth-century Dutch shipmaster, who, before setting sail, concentrated wine with the intention of adding water immediately on reaching the home port. However, the concentrated drink was an immediate success and required no watering down. In Dutch, the drink was dubbed *brandewijn*, meaning "burnt, distilled": the verb *branden* "to burn" was used in the sense of "to distil." In British English, *brand-wine* was found in 1622 and shortened to *brandy* as early as 1657, while the unabbreviated form was still used in official texts (excise and parliamentary documents), but this came to be regarded as a compound of *brandy* and *wine* and was therefore spelled *brandy wine*.

There are extremely early records of use of the word *brandy* in American English, which may have been borrowed directly from Dutch rather than via British English. In any event, the word is included in Craigie's dictionary of Americanisms, although he does not mention that it originated within the present limits of the US. The oldest quote from the American continent containing the word *brandy* is only nine years younger than the oldest British quote, and the fact that the beverage was also

Illustration 2.2 – Brandy, sign from North-Holland, ninetheenth century, reading "The Three Little Bantams – Wine, Beer and Brandy" (source: Van Lennep & Ter Gouw, De uithangtekens, part 2, 1868)

known by its Dutch name is evidenced by the name Brandywine River, known on account of the Anglo-American Battle of Brandywine that was fought there in 1777. The origin of the name Brandywine River is obscure, but what is certain is that it was associated with the Dutch word *brandewijn* in the seventeenth century. In 1638, a Swedish colony headed up by the Dutchman Peter Minuit – the same Peter Minuit who had "bought" Manhattan from the Native Americans and who was later expelled from the Dutch colony – settled in the vicinity of the river. The settlers named the river Fish-kiln or "Fish Creek." However, a map dating from 1681 includes the name *Brande wine Creek* (apparently Dutch *brandewijn*), while another from 1687 has Brandy Wine. Some sources assert that the river is named after a settler by the name of Andrew Braindwine, Brainwende, or Brantwyn, and that the transformation into Brande wine or Brandywine is an instance of folk etymology. Irrespective of whether or not this is true, it does prove that they were familiar with the Dutch word *brandewijn*.

Dutch *brandewijn* was also adopted into Delaware Jargon, the lingua franca that the Native Americans and settlers used with one another, and into the Amerindian language Mahican.

The production of brandy was set up on a large scale in the US in the nineteenth century, particularly in California, which had an extremely favorable climate for growing the grapes from which wine was made that was, in turn, suitable for making American brandy. This American brandy conquered the world, and many languages adopted the word *brandy* from American English. The Dutch, too, have been drinking brandy instead of *brandewijn* since the nineteenth century.

> **1666** For wine per gallon ... For Brandy per gallon.
> **1675** Capt. William Hudson and Lt. John Smith [are licensed] to sell beere wine and brandy.
> **1887** The brandies of California did not strike me very favourably.

bry, also **brie**, **brij**, a buttermilk pap usually made with barley and eaten with sugar or syrup (DARE).
- From Dutch *brij*, meaning "porridge"; adopted in the nineteenth or twentieth century and only used in areas where Dutch people settled. See also **balkenbrij**.
* In the Netherlands, *brij* was a normal everyday food; it was a semi-solid, semi-liquid concoction of ground grains and milk or water. In the US, the ingredients of the dish were slightly modified.

> **1970** Something she used to fix [was made] with barley and she called it [brai] ... You'd eat it with brown sugar on it ... It's not as thin as soup. It's more like rice pudding except that it's barley. And that's a typically Dutch dish. (DARE)
> **1981** The word *brij* occurs especially in the names of two Dutch dishes, both of which involve a brewing or mixing process— *balken brij*, and *soepen brij* (which is also simply called *brij*). Soepen brij is white. It's a buttermilk pap—barley boiled in buttermilk. It has to be eaten with syrup on it. Balken brij contains scrap meat from a hog. Traditionally, the mixture was placed in a flour sack and hung from the balken (beams or rafters) where it cured and dried for at least a month or two. It is eaten sliced and fried, with syrup. Balken brij is usually made in early November at hog-butchering time and often eaten around Christmas. (DARE)

Illustration 2.3 – Cole (source: Menu Designs, Amsterdam 1999)

coleslaw, a salad made of sliced cabbage with condiments (Craigie, DARE *cold*, *hot slaw*, Webster).
- From Dutch *koolsalade* or *koolsla*, meaning "salad made of uncooked, finely sliced red or white cabbage," from *kool* ("cabbage") and *sla*, a reduced form of *salade* ("salad"); borrowed in the seventeenth or eighteenth century and currently very widespread.
* According to Flexner (1976), Dutch colonists near Setauket, Long Island, were the first to grow cabbage (and cauliflower) in America, which is further supported by the fact that the Dutch word *kool* was adopted into Mahican and the Dutch word *sla* borrowed by Munsee Delaware.

The word *coleslaw* was recorded in American English for the first time in 1794 but it is bound to be older, as is evident from the fact that it was transformed in even the oldest quotes: it was at one time – quite aptly – called *cold slaw*. This transformation is probably based on folk etymology, as the Americans did not recognize the first part *cole*, calling this plant *cabbage* instead. Alternatively, the first part of the word, which rhymes with *cole*, may have been pronounced as *cool* by the Americans. The step from *cool* to *cold* is only a small one.

The spelling *cold slaw* persisted for a long time, at least until the 1860s. This term is still used regionally, as a larger number of informants of DARE responded in 1965-1970 to "dishes made with fresh cabbage" *cold slaw*; its use was least prevalent in the south of the US.

Coleslaw also used to be shortened to ***slaw*** in American English. Theoretically, this word could also have been derived from Dutch *sla*, except that in Dutch this only denotes a dish consisting of lettuce rather than cabbage. In American English, on the other hand, *slaw* is synonymous with *coleslaw*. In 1913, Webster described *slaw* as "sliced cabbage served as a salad, cooked or uncooked." *Slaw* was used for the first time in 1861: “Plate of slaw, ready vinegared.”

The counterparts of *cold slaw* that were coined for warmed up coleslaw were *warm slaw* and, more commonly, *hot slaw*. In the olden days, people used to make a salad seasoned with salt, pepper, and vinegar that was eaten either hot or cold. That custom as well as the name *hot slaw* are still used regionally, both around New York and further afield, as evidenced by data from DARE; informants also mentioned *hot cabbage slaw* and *hot cole slaw*.

Eventually, under the influence of *cole*, the spelling was changed into *coleslaw*, in which form it was readopted into Dutch. These days, *coleslaw* is widely sold in Dutch supermarkets, as well as in those other countries into whose languages the American English form *coleslaw* has also been adopted. The recipe for the salad was changed in the US, with the primary addition being mayonnaise, which was lacking from the original Dutch cabbage salad, which was seasoned solely with vinegar, if only because mayonnaise was not recorded internationally until the first half of the nineteenth century, initially in French and somewhat later in English.

1794 A piece of sliced cabbage, by Dutchmen ycleped [called] cold slaw.
1796 A dish of stewed pork was served up, accompanied with some hot pickled cabbage, called in this part of the country “warm slaw.” (Craigie *warm slaw*)
1848 *Kool slaa*. (Dutch) Cabbage salad. Many persons who affect accuracy, but do not know the origin of the term, pronounce the first syllable as if it were the English word *cold*. (Bartlett)
1877 *Hot-slaw*. Cabbage minced and heated with vinegar; and thus named to distinguish it from *Kool Slaa* (mistakenly etymologized into *Cold Slaw*).
1902 *Cold-slaw* (Dutch *kool-slaa*, cabbage salad). A salad consisting of cabbage leaves cut fine, and dressed with vinegar and oil, pepper and salt. The term, it may be remarked, is a very curious corruption of the original word, the prefix *cold* having been substituted to *kool* from an utter ignorance of the latter’s foreign etymology, and simply through an innate desire to twist an unfamiliar word into a more pleasant shape ... *Hot-Slaw*. Minced cabbage, pickled in vinegar and made hot. So called to distinguish it from *cold-slaw*.

cookie, **cooky**, **cookey**, a small flat sweet cake (Craigie, DARE, Webster).
- From Dutch *koekje*, *koekie* “small cake”; borrowed in the seventeenth or eighteenth century and highly prevalent and productive, with various new meanings.
* Dutch *koekje* is a diminutive of *koek* – a word related to English *cake* and used to denote sweet pastries cut into pieces and presented as tidbits (see also **olykoek**). A *koekje* is comparable to what the British call *biscuit*. It used to be and still is a good practice in the Netherlands to offer guests a *koekje*. This custom was apparently taken along to other continents and adopted there. In American English, the word *cookie* was encountered for the first time in 1703; Judd’s *History of Hadley* from 1905, quoted by Mathews, states: “The Dutch in New York provided for funerals, rum, beer, gloves, rings; and in 1703, at a funeral, ‘800 cockies (cookies or cakes) and one and a half gross of pipes’ were furnished.”

Various sources reveal that it was customary in nineteenth-century New York to eat *cookies* on New Year’s day (a custom that was also extant in the Netherlands;

Illustration 2.4 – Cookies, engraving (source: Journal Panorama around 1955)

today, however, the Dutch eat *oliebollen* (see **oliebollen**) on New Year's eve. In the twentieth century, *cookies* were eaten year-round throughout the country.

> **1786** Idle boys, who infest our markets and streets, with baskets of cookies.
> **1803** When dears and sweets were as plenty as cookies on a new-year's day.
> **1843** But look a here, I'll bet a cookey you can't turn that into fust rate English as soon as I can.
> **1848** *Cookey*. A cake. A Dutch word used in New York. "Mrs. Child thinks it best to let the little dears have their own way in everything, and not to give them more *cookies* than they, the dear children, deem requisite." (Bartlett)
> **1902** *Cookey* (Dutch koekje, little cake). A little tit-bit ; a small, flat, sweet cake. Also used for small cakes of various other forms, with or without sweetening.

Cookie is one of the most frequently used Dutch loanwords in American English, and it is included in many expressions that do not exist in Dutch. Since the mid-nineteenth century, people say *to bet (or wager) a cookie*, to express assurance by pretending to wager a small amount. About a century later, the expression (*that's*) *how* (or *the way*) *the cookie crumbles* – meaning (that is) how a situation resolves itself; that is the way it is – was introduced. DARE cites for regional American English the facetious and euphemistic expression *to lose, spill, toss one's cookies* in the sense of "to vomit," particularly in the north and central parts of the US; see illustration 2.5. Another popular saying is *have your cookie (or cake) and eat it*.

Moreover, the word acquired many new meanings in American English. Since 1920, *cookie* has been used to refer to an attractive woman and somewhat later to a man ("he is a tough, smart cookie"). Such use is unknown in Dutch. In computer lingo, *cookie* recently acquired the specific meaning of "a packet of data sent by an Internet server to a browser to identify the user." Many languages, including Dutch, have adopted *cookie* from American English in that sense. According to the *Urban Dictionary*, young people use *cookie* to refer to "female genitalia, a nicer name for a pussy." Regionally, in the southern and central parts of the US, *cookie* is used to refer to what is called a *doughnut* elsewhere (DARE). And finally, there is the *Cookie Monster* that we know from Sesame Street. His favorite song "C is for Cookie (that's good enough for me") is known to many but apparently not to everyone, for the structure of the title has been used for many advertising slogans, particularly for cereal, chocolate, and other products and services starting with the letter c. *Cookie Monster* is used as a benign name for someone with a sweet tooth, but also for computer software that manages computer cookies.

1920 That girl friend of yours is a cookie – hey, what?
1942 Just about the toughest cookie ever born.
2008 Her cookie was so nicely shaven, mmm mmm! (*Urban Dictionary* on the Internet)

cruller, a sweet cake made in various shapes from rich egg batter and fried in deep fat (Craigie, DARE, Webster).
- Borrowed from Dutch in the seventeenth or eighteenth century and still commonly used. The form of the word was coined in American English.
* Dutch has a number of names for pastry or biscuits baked in the form of a curl, such as *krulkoek*, *gekrulde koek*, and the diminutives *krulkoekje* and *krulletje*. *Krul* is derived from the verb *krullen* ("to curl"); *gekruld* denotes "curled." *Koek(je)* is a "biscuit"; see **cookie.** In Dutch, *kruller* is not used to refer to pastry; a *kruller* is someone or something that curls, not something that is curled or curl-shaped. Accordingly, the word *cruller* must have been coined in American English, probably as an abridged derivative of the Dutch names – *cruller* is, of course, much easier to pronounce than, say, *krulkoekje* or *krulletje*. Furthermore, a *cruller* is a specific type of pastry in American English, a type of doughnut, whereas the Dutch name *krulkoek(je)* is normally used for any type of biscuit with curled up edges. In 1939, Van Loon cited a pretty poem that "was popular" among Dutch descendants and explained the origin of the *cruller*:

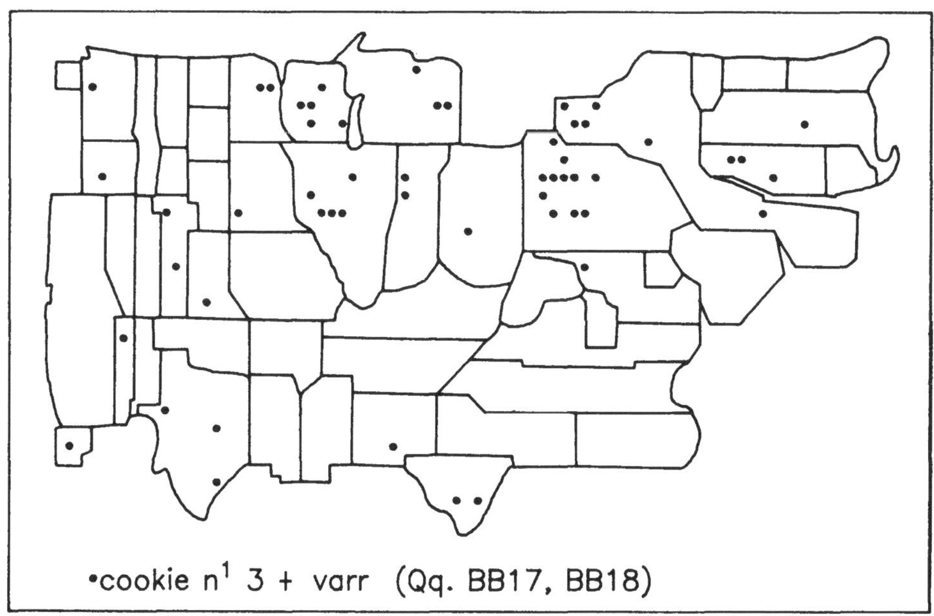

Illustration 2.5 – Map showing the distribution of to lose, spill, toss one's cookies *"to vomit" (source: DARE 1: 760)*

Der was 'n ouw vrouw,
dat koeke bakke zou.
Van haoze en patrijse,
en de koeke wou niet rijze.
De pat viel am,
en de koeke ware kram,
toe hiete zij krullers.
[There was an old woman,
who was baking cookies.
Of hare and partridges,
and the cake would not rise.
The pot fell over,
and the cookies were bent,
and then they were called crullers.]

Craigie reports that there used to be a variety of forms in American English, such as *croller*, *crueller*, and the short form, *crull*. According to Schele de Vere, *crullers* were simple, everyday tidbits, in contrast to *cookies*, which were specially baked for festive occasions. Today, www.cooks.com has a large number of recipes for *crullers*, such as *Christmas crullers*, *crusty crullers*, *French crullers*, *Spanish crullers*, and *snow ball crullers*, and elsewhere there is a recipe for *Dutch crullers*.

DARE reports the regional American English forms *cruller*, *crull*, *crawler*, *croiller*, *croller*, and *crueller* for: a small sweet cake made from a rich egg batter, formed variously but often into twisted strips, and deep-fried until brown; sometimes a cake doughnut. Illustration 2.6 shows that the word is used throughout the US, but particularly in the northeast. According to Carver's *American Regional Dialects*, the word came to be more widely used thanks to commercialization, starting in the nineteenth century.

1805 [Recipe for making] Crullers, Matrimony or Love Knots.
1831 The Yankee[s] ... tell us of their pies, doughnuts, crulls.
1835 At each of their meals, meats, and pastry, tea and coffee, in the provinces, with waffles, cruellers, dough nuts, sweet cakes, ginger-

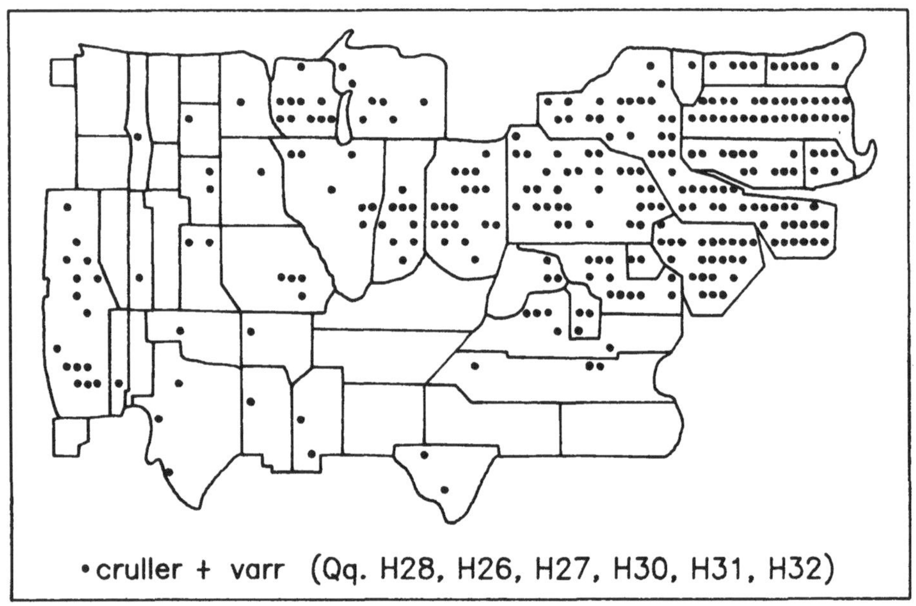

Illustration 2.6 – Map showing the distribution of cruller *(source: DARE 1: 870)*

bread, and quantities of preserved fruit are served up.
1848 *Cruller.* (Dutch *kruller*, a curler.) A cake made of a strip of sweetened dough, boiled in lard, the two ends of which are twisted or *curled* together. The New Yorkers have inherited the name and the thing from the Dutch. (Bartlett)
1855 Up to two o'clock he had redeemed two crollers and a dough-nut.
1872 If this dainty [a cookie] seems to be specially appropriated to great occasions, a *cruller* may, on the other hand, be found on many a cake-stand and in countless homes all the year round. Being made of a strip of sweetened dough, which is boiled in lard and then curled up at the two ends, it has received its name from a Dutch term *Kruller*, meaning a "Curler." (Schele de Vere)
1902 *Cruller.* A strip of sweetened dough, which is boiled in lard, and then loops up (curls) at the two ends. Also, doughnut, olycook. (Clapin)

dope, 1. a thick, heavy lubricant; 2. an absorbent element used in high explosives, a thick liquid or pasty preparation; 3. an illicit, habit-forming, or narcotic drug (Craigie, DARE, Webster).
- From Dutch *doop*, meaning "sauce, substance into which something is dipped," from *dopen*, meaning "to dip"; borrowed in the seventeenth or eighteenth century and still very widespread and productive, with a large number of new meanings.
* The Dutch word *doop* was used for "sauce, gravy," a liquid mixture used to season a dish to taste. The word is no longer used in Dutch. As they did with so many other names for dishes, the Dutch took their *doop* with them to the American East Coast, where the word was adopted into American English in its original meaning. Washington Irving, using the pseudonym Diedrich Knickerbocker, referred to it in *A History of New York*, published in 1809.
1807 Philo Dripping-pan was remarkable for his predilection to eating, and his love of what the learned Dutch call *doup*.
1809 The tea table was crowned with a huge earthen dish, well stored with slices of fat pork, fried brown, cut up into mouthfuls, and swimming in doup or gravy.

The word's meaning was quickly broadened in American English. *Dope*, originally a thick, edible sauce, was used to refer to all manner of viscous substances, such as lubricants, varnish and suchlike, as well as to "an absorbent element used in high explosives."
1876 Nothing was known of the mysteries of "dope" – a preparation of pitch which, being applied to the bottom of the shoes, enables the wearer to glide over snow softened by the warmth of the sun.
1880 Hercules powder ... contains a very large proportion of nitrate of soda, ... the remainder of the dope being incombustible carbonate of magnesia.

In 1851, the word began to be used to refer to a stupid, "thick-headed" person, nowadays often interpreted as "a person stupid from drugs." In 1889, it was used for the first time to refer to a viscous mixture of opium that was smoked at the time. In subsequent years it came to denote any narcotic drug – which is the most frequently used meaning these days. In 1896, the compound *dope fiend* and the derivative *dopey* "drugged, stupid" were found; in 1933, *dope addict* was used.

1895 Opium-joints—those mysterious dens in which ... the fumes of the burning "dope" cloy the senses.

1920 The death of a fascinating actress from an overdose of "dope."

In 1900, *dope* was used for the first time to refer to a preparation of drugs influencing a racehorse's performance. Only one year later it was used in the sense of "stuff, information, or knowledge, especially of a kind not widely disseminated or easily available": "I've known Tommy for a long time, so he feels free to read his dope to me." According to Barnhart, it was possible that this originally referred to the knowledge as to which horse was doped and therefore most likely to win.

A great many languages adopted the word *dope* in the meaning of "hard drugs" from American English, including Dutch, in which the original *doop* ("sauce") is no longer extant. In Dutch, *doping* – in American English the present participle of *to dope* – is used to refer to the administration of performance-enhancing drugs.

In regional American English, the original Dutch meaning of "sauce," though chaic, has been preserved. As recently as 1968, an older informant of DARE mentioned *dope* as a synonym for "gravy." In Ohio, *dope* is used specifically to refer to a sweet mixture, a dessert topping, usually for pudding or ice cream; rarely, an ice cream sundae (see illustration 2.7). The word is also used regionally to refer to "any medicine, vaccine, anesthetic, or stimulant." In the south, it is used particularly to denote "a carbonated beverage, usually one flavored with cola" (see illustration 2.8). The origin of this last meaning is not entirely clear: according to DARE, it may have evolved from *dope*, meaning "medicine in general," "in allusion to the supposed 'tonic' effects of some early soft drinks." However, folk wisdom has it that *dope* recalls the inclusion of minute amounts of cocaine in the

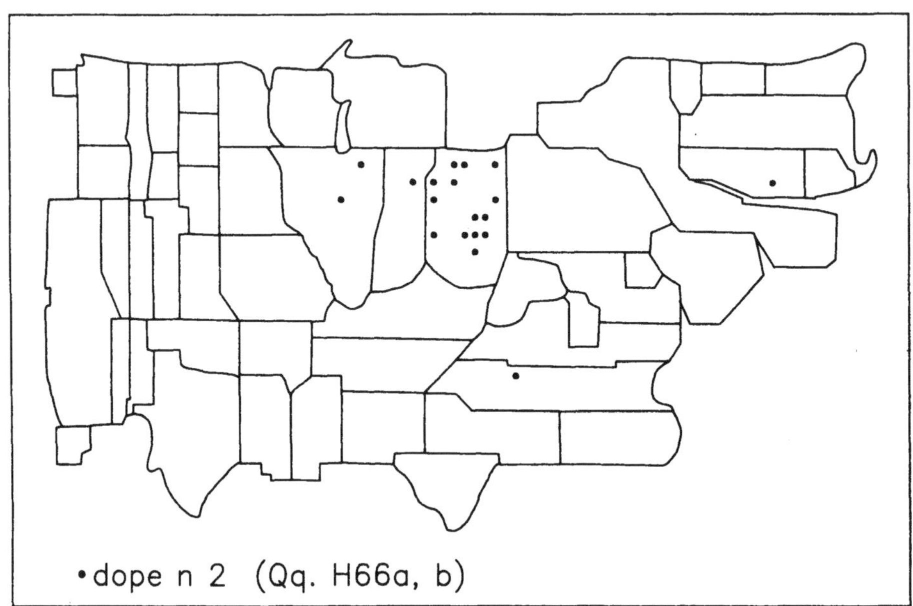

Illustration 2.7 – Map showing the distribution of dope *"dessert topping" (source: DARE 2: 140)*

original recipe for Coca-Cola, which was named after this exotic ingredient.

erwten soup, pea soup (DARE).
- From Dutch *erwtensoep*, meaning "pea soup," from *erwt* ("pea") and *soep* ("soup"); adopted in the nineteenth and twentieth centuries and still known regionally.
* In Dutch, *erwtensoep* is regarded as a delectable winter meal. The recipe and name were imported by Dutch immigrants but did not become widely known outside this circle.

1940 These expressions ... seem to be common ... wherever Dutchmen reside [in the US]. *Erwten soep* or *snert*. Pea soup.

1945 In the much larger Dutch colony of Michigan there are many more such borrowings, *e.g.*, ... *hutspot* (a combination of potatoes and some green), *balkenbry* (a pork loaf), *erwtensoep* (pea soup), and *boerenjongens* (a drink made of brandy and raisins). (Mencken, Suppl. I, 191)

1964 *Erwtensoep* – Dutch Pea Soup – 1 lb. peas, 1 medium pig hock or shoulder pork.

headcheese, the meat of the head of a pig, boiled, chopped, and pressed into a firm jellied mass or made into a sausage (Craigie, DARE, Webster).
- Probably a translation of Dutch *hoofdkaas*; adopted in the nineteenth century and still in use.
* It is likely, if not entirely certain, that American English borrowed *headcheese* from Dutch. British English has the word *brawn* and German has *Schweinskopfsülze* or *Presskopf*, which disqualifies these languages as factors of influence in this case. Dutch and American English, on the other hand, both use *headcheese* to refer to the same thing: the meat of the head (and sometimes feet and inner organs) of a pig, boiled, chopped, and then molded

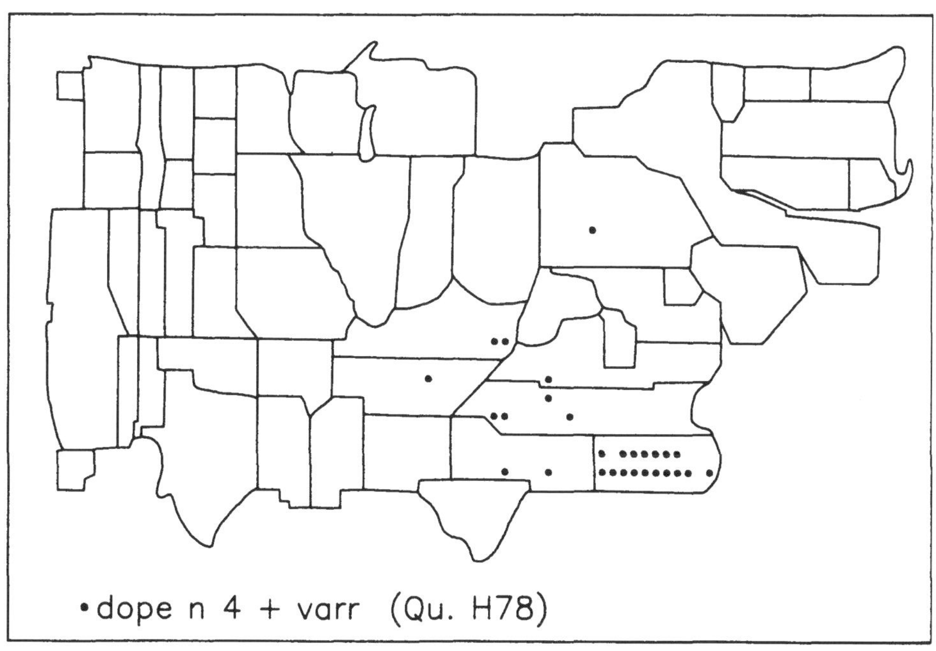

Illustration 2.8 – Map showing the distribution of dope *"carbonated beverage" (source: DARE 2: 140)*

into the shape of a cheese or sometimes prepared as a sausage and eaten on bread, like cheese. What is more, this name has been common in American English since the mid-nineteenth century, a period in which many Dutch immigrants moved to the US. It should be noted, however, that in the nineteenth century the word was no longer regarded as a Dutch loanword, but it does fit in with the general observation that American English adopted many names for food from Dutch, particularly for food that farmers made from their own products, such as *apples and speck*, *balkenbry*, and *erwten soup*. According to DARE, the name is now particularly prevalent in the northern, central, and western parts of America. Since 1942, *headcheese* has been used regionally to refer to "smegma," "cheesy matter collecting under the prepuce behind the glans of the penis," a meaning that has also been given by young people in the 2009 *Urban Dictionary*. This may be a figurative meaning, but the word may also have been coined independently of the meat dish. In Dutch, *kopkaas* is also used as an informal synonym of *smegma*.

Illustration 2.9 – Headcheese, Dutch hoofdkaas or zult. Cartoon by the Brabant draughtsman Cees Robben. Caption: "Headcheese? Well eh... ma'am, that's a pig, but all mixed up. But very tasty!" (source: Archive Cees Robben Foundation; published Nov. 23, 1973 in the Nieuwsblad van het Zuiden)

> **1841** The animal ... may be traced in the stewed chine and souse, the head-cheese and sausages.
> **1848** *Head-cheese.* The ears and feet of swine cut up fine, and, after being boiled, pressed into the form of a cheese. (Bartlett)
> **1948** They see nothing wrong with calling something "head cheese" or "hog maw," and any outlander who can overcome a slight shuddering repugnance to taste them will wonder why he never even heard of such dishes before.
> **1966** *Head cheese* is the usual name everywhere north of the Ohio, and appears to be a term which originated in the North Midland.
> **1973** *Head cheese* ... is common both on the East Coast and in the U[pper] M[idwest].

hutspot, a dish of potatoes and other vegetables, usually simmered with meat (DARE).
- From Dutch *hutspot* (a certain dish); adopted in the nineteenth century and still known regionally.
* The Dutch dish *hutspot* consists of a mixture of mashed potatoes, carrots, onions and beef; the name is composed of *hutsen* ("to mix") and *pot*. This easy to prepare, typical winter meal was taken to the US, where it gained some measure of popularity in Michigan outside the immediate circle of Dutch immigrants. It is sometimes abridged to ***pot eten*** – see the quote from 1940.

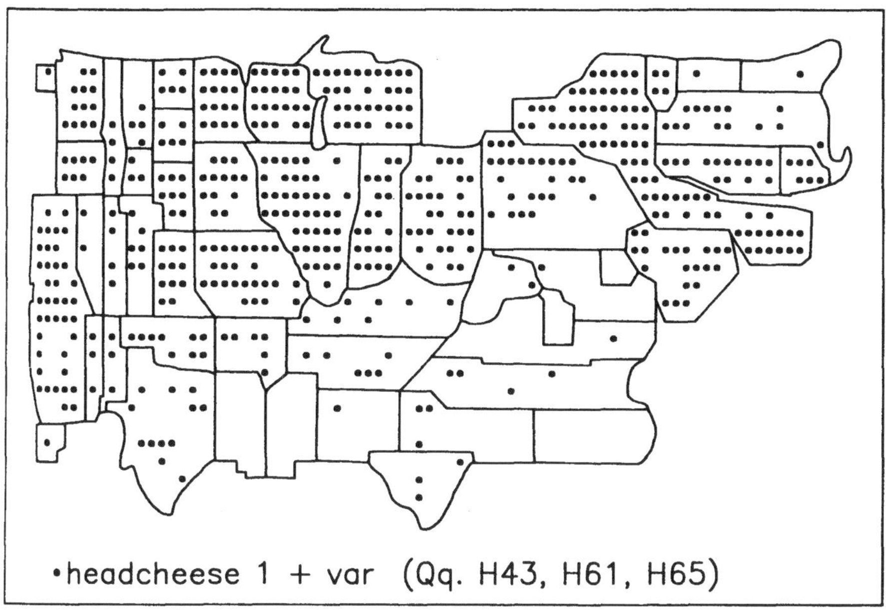

Illustration 2.10 – Map showing the distribution of headcheese *(source: DARE 2: 937)*

1940 *Hutspot* or *pot eten.* A combination of potatoes and cabbage; potatoes and carrots; potatoes and kale, or other vegetable boiled together and crushed.
1945 In the much larger Dutch colony of Michigan there are many more such borrowings, *e.g.*, ... *hutspot* (a combination of potatoes and some green), *balkenbry* (a pork loaf), *erwtensoep* (pea soup), and *boerenjongens* (a drink made of brandy and raisins). (Mencken, Suppl. I, 191)
1969-70 Hutspot – carrots, potatoes, onions, cooked in beef broth and mashed, served with short ribs (DARE)

letter, an almond-filled pastry originally made in the shape of a letter of the alphabet (DARE).
- Shortened from Dutch *banketletter* ("almond filling in puff pastry baked in the shape of your initial"); adopted in the nineteenth or twentieth century and still known regionally; see also **banket**.
* The Dutch delicacy was introduced by immigrants. In American English, the Dutch name *banketletter* was shortened to both *banket* (also used in Dutch) and *letter* – which is used sporadically in Dutch and only in contexts from which the meaning can be immediately inferred. Other names used for this pastry in American English are ***almond letter***, ***butter letter***, and *Dutch letter*. The first two names are derived from Dutch and are literal translations of the Dutch synonyms *amandelletter* and *boterletter*. These names are unknown outside the Dutch community and, according to DARE, the names are primarily found in areas where Dutch immigrants settled, especially in New Jersey and Iowa.
1982 The original Dutch is *banket letters*, almond filling in puff pastry baked in the shape of your initial for your birthday ... In New Jersey

they are called *almond letters*, even though they are never made in the shape of letters anymore ... In Pella [IA] they are called *Dutch letters*, or *letters*, again always sold in sticks. I once saw a bakery sign in Pella for *ledders*. When I asked ... he said... "It's a Dutch word for almond pastry!" (DARE)
1982 I make banket in pieces about 12 inches long and about 2 inches in circumference. It can also be shaped into letters, like if you want to give it as a Christmas gift. Then you might shape it into the form of someone's initial. (DARE)
1984 Our Dutch relatives here call *banket* "butter letters." (DARE)
1994 I bought an almond-flavored pastry called a *Dutch letter* in Pella, Iowa. (DARE)

metworst, a spiced pork and beef sausage (DARE, Webster).
- From Dutch *metworst*; adopted in the twentieth century and still in use, but only in the German form *mettwurst*.
* DARE reports the infrequent use of the form *metworst* in regional American English alongside the more common *mettwurst*. The latter form is borrowed from German, while the former comes from Dutch. *Metworst* is in fact *worst* (sausage) filled with *met* (a sort of minced meat), an archaic word in Dutch related to English *meat*.
1967-70 (*Foreign foods favored by people around here*) Metworst. (DARE)
1970 The Polish have a kind of sausage that they call kielbasa, and we [= the Dutch] have a sausage that we call metworst, and it's sausage with different spices in it. They don't taste alike, but it's the same base, which is the sausage, but with different spices in it. (DARE)

noodles, food paste made with egg and shaped typically in ribbon form (Webster, Craigie).
- Derived from both Dutch *noedels* and German *Nudeln*; adopted in the seventeenth or eighteenth century and still in use.
* *Noodles* can be eaten everywhere in the US where, in contrast to Great Britain, it is often used to denote "any style of pasta"; according to the OED, in Great Britain it refers specifically to "a long string-like piece of pasta or similar flour paste cooked in liquid and served either in a soup or as an accompaniment to another dish." In the US, however, Malaysian restaurants serve "noodles" that consist of long, wondrous strands, and people exchange recipes for "Asian noodle salad made of spaghetti." The German inventor is probably turning in his grave. The dish and hence the name both stem from Germany, and Dutch *noedel* was borrowed from German.

American English has had the form *noodle* since 1812, from which it is impossible to tell whether it was borrowed from Dutch or German, although German seems more likely. Then again, a different form was used in the same century, namely *noodlejees*, which form can only stem from Dutch given the diminutive *-jees*, which also appears in, for example, *applejees* (see **apples and speck**) and is the American English rendering of Dutch *-tjes*. The term was probably introduced in and around New York by the Dutch – at least that is what Schele de Vere suggests – and subsequently spread by the Germans. Unlike in the Netherlands, noodles are more or less a national dish in Germany, which is why the German form became prevalent in American English.

1848 *Noodlejees*. (Dutch.) Wheat dough rolled thin and cut into strings like maccaroni. It is used for the same purpose. (Bartlett)
1872 *Noodlejees*, an humble imitation of maccaroni and used like them for dumplings and in soup, retain in New York at least their old Dutch name, but are hardly known elsewhere. (Schele de Vere)
1896 *Noodeljees*, ... "noodles."
1902 *Noodlejees* (Dutch). A term hardly known outside of New York city, and designating strips of dough cut like vermicelli, and used in dumplings and in soup. *Noodles* (Ger. *nudeln*). A kind of vermicelli, differing from the Italian only in the addition of eggs. (Clapin)

oliebollen, oil dumpling(s) (DARE).
- From Dutch *oliebollen*, meaning "oil dumplings"; adopted in the nineteenth or twentieth century and still used regionally.
* In the Netherlands, *oliebollen* are almost exclusively prepared and eaten on New Year's eve these days. Oliebollen are ball-shaped cakes ("balls") with raisins or currants, deep-fried in *olie* ("oil"). Dating from the nineteenth or perhaps the eighteenth century, the name *oliebol* is relatively young in Dutch. An older name for a similar type of pastry is *oliekoek*, see **olykoek**. In the nineteenth century, Dutch immigrants in New York ate a different type of sweet pastry, made of more delicate and fancy dough, namely *cookies* (see **cookie**).

Dutch immigrants brought the preparation of oliebollen to the US, and in areas with inhabitants of Dutch origin, this custom has been preserved, no doubt for nostalgic reasons, but the name and product did not spread across the rest of America. The name's obscurity is evident from the fact that various informants of DARE in 1969 were not aware that the word *oliebollen* is plural.

1941 Sunday dinners are prepared on Saturday by Dutch housewives who still cook the good things their mothers made – *khuete*, a vegetable and pork roast stew; *oliebollen*, fried dumplings.
1969 (*A round cake of dough, cooked in deep fat, with a hole in the center*) Oliebollen – used by the Dutch, like a doughnut, but no hole. (DARE)
1969 (*Different shapes or types of doughnuts*) Oliebollen – a Dutch food, doughnut-like batter, drop a spoonful of it in hot fat or oil, has raisins or currants in them. (DARE)

olykoek, also **olycook**, a small sweetened cake fried in deep fat (Craigie, DARE, Webster).
- From Dutch *oliekoek*, meaning "round cake, deep-fried in rape oil"; adopted in the seventeenth or eighteenth century and still used regionally.
* In Dutch, the name *oliekoek* has been used to refer to a round cake, consisting of flour, currants, eggs and pieces of apple since the sixteenth century.
It is not regarded as a luxury food.
The article and name were brought by the first settlers. In American English, the word is spelled in different ways, probably because it was handed down orally, such as *olecoke*, *olekoek*, *olicook*, *oliekoek*, and *olycoke*, in which *koek* was regularly changed into *cook* (cf. **cookie**). Apparently, the first morpheme *olie* was not associated with the English equivalent *oil*. According to DARE, the word is now archaic and chiefly prevalent in the Hudson Valley, New York. In 1949, Kurath

wrote in his *Word Geography of the Eastern United States*: "Some food terms of Dutch origin have spread beyond the Dutch area, ... but others, such as *olicook* for a doughnut ... have probably always been Dutch family words and are disappearing fast." According to some, the delicacy *doughnut* originates from the Dutch *olykoek*, but this is uncertain. From the first citation below it appears that Knickerbocker (Irving), for one, linked the two.

1809 The table ... was always sure to boast an enormous dish of balls of sweetened dough, fried in hog's fat, and called dough nuts, or oly koeks.
1848 *Olycoke*. (Dutch, *olikoek*, oil-cake.) A cake fried in lard. A favorite delicacy with the Dutch, and also with their descendants, in New York, There are various kinds, as doughnuts, crullers, etc. (Bartlett)
1881 His favorite city has surpassed all others in ... oliekoeks, and New Year cookies.
1932 *Ole Koeks* (Albany, New York) ... Dough for Cinnamon Buns ... raisins ... cognac.

pannicake, also **panicake**, **pan(n)acake**, **panniecake**, **pannycake**, pancake (DARE).
- Probably variants of British English *pancake* influenced by the Dutch counterpart *pannenkoek*; probably adopted in the seventeenth or eighteenth century and still known regionally.
* British English *pancake* and Dutch *pannenkoek* (pronounced and previously spelled *pannekoek*) are both transparent compounds denoting a flat cake fried in a pan. The names were undoubtedly coined independently of one another. American English has, in addition to the common *pancake*, a substantial number of regional variants that, like Dutch *pannenkoek*, have a linking phoneme and are particularly prevalent in New York and Wisconsin, which attracted many Dutch immigrants. In addition, DARE points to the possible influence of Norwegian immigrants. The Norwegian word is *pannekake*.

It is impossible to conclude from the American English material exactly how old the Dutch influence is, given that all quotes date from the twentieth century. The word was chiefly used in places where Dutch immigrants had settled as early as the seventeenth century. Thanks to Amerindian languages, however, we know that the Dutch dish *pannenkoek* had been brought directly to the East Coast of the US, as the word *pannenkoek* was borrowed by Loup, Munsee Delaware, and Western Abnaki. It would seem obvious, then, that the Yankees came into contact with it in this period as well.

1941 [fieldwork], A three-syllable form was used by three [of 50] informants, with middle syllable unstressed and varying from [i] to [e]: [the first informant] (Dutch deriv.) *pannacake*, [the second] ... (Belgian deriv.) *pannycake*, [the third]. (Vermont deriv.) *pancakes*, "but *pannycakes* is the real name." ... Most current is *pancake*.
1949 *Pannacakes* – country version of pancakes.
1953 (as of late 19th cent.), There are plenty of oldsters who would deny that the phrase "in excess" had any meaning when applied to the laudable habit of riotous consumption of buckwheat "pannie-cakes."
1973 *Griddle cakes* (of wheat) ... The older variant *pani-cake* or *pannicake*, recorded 3 times in Wisconsin fieldwork, has echoes in Minnesota and was overheard locally by an inf. in a Dutch community in North

Illustration 2.11 – Pannicake (source: Internet http://graphic-design.tjs-labs.com/index)

Dakota. This variant may be derived from Dutch *pannekack*.

pot cheese, usually a dry form of cottage cheese (Craigie, DARE, Webster).
- From Dutch *potkaas* ("soft, rindless cheese"); adopted in the seventeenth or eighteenth century and still in use.
* American English *pot cheese* is a translation of Dutch *potkaas*, the name for a soft cheese kept or prepared in jars. The regional prevalence of the word demonstrates that it came with the first Dutch settlers, although it is occasionally used outside New York State as well (see illustration 2.12). In his *American Regional Dialects* Carver adds: "Given the widespread commercial preparation of this food and the according predominance of the term 'cottage cheese,' which has virtually displaced the numerous other old dialect terms for it, it is surprising that *pot cheese* has survived for so long. Of the forty-four informants [of DARE], however, three-quarters were old speakers and only two were under thirty-five years of age."

1812 Tell me thou heart of cork, ... and brain of pot-cheese.

1847 *To Make Pot Cheese.* – Put buttermilk and thick sour milk together, ... make it scalding hot, then take the curd from the whey with a skimmer, put it into a muslin or linen bag, tie it up and hang it to drain; after an hour or two, ... moisten it slightly with sweet cream, put a little salt to it, work the salt into it, and make it in balls the size of a teacup ... Potcheese should be made fresh, once or twice a week.

1859 *Smear-case*, ... a preparation of milk; ... otherwise called Cottage-Cheese. In New York it is called Pot-cheese. (Bartlett)

1980 Cottage cheese is one of the first stages ... Pot cheese is left to drain for a longer period. More whey drains away and it becomes a drier cheese. Farmer's cheese and pot cheese are practically identical, except that farmer's cheese is generally molded.

The cheese is also called *Dutch cheese*, about which Kurath writes (1949: 18): "*Dutch cheese* is the most widespread Northern term for cottage cheese. It was coined in Western New England with reference to the Dutch of the Hudson Valley and spread eastward in New England almost to the Atlantic Coast. It is used on Narragansett Bay and on the Merrimack in New Hampshire but not on the Massachusetts coast or in Maine. From Western New England *Dutch cheese* was carried westward into Upstate New York, the Western Reserve of Ohio, and into northern Pennsylvania, where the boundary over against the Midland *smear case* is clear-cut." For the present-day distribution of *Dutch cheese* see illustration 2.13. Other names are *farmer's cheese*, **smear-case** and *stink cheese*.

rolliche, a dish made of seasoned beef wrapped in tripe, and usually boiled, pickled, and cut into rounds (Craigie, DARE).

- From Dutch *rolletje*, diminutive of *rol* ("roll"); adopted in the seventeenth or eighteenth century and still used regionally.

* In Dutch, a dish made of seasoned beef wrapped in tripe is called *rolpens*, a compound of *rollen* "to roll" and *pens* ("tripe"). In the past, this was sometimes briefly referred to as *rol*, if the context was clear, or as *rolletje*. However, *rol* and *rolletje* have so many meanings in Dutch that they are no longer used to denote "dish with tripe." In American English, however, the lack of ambiguity allowed the Standard Dutch word *rolletje* to become the name of a dish. According to DARE, the word is prevalent in New York and in New Jersey, which suggests that it arrived with the early Dutch immigrants. The word was adopted in everyday speech, hence the large number of spellings, such as *relliche*, *rollejee*, *rollichie*, *ruletji* and *rullichie*. In 1847, an American cookbook mentions *rolla-cheese*, whose form must have been modified by folk etymology under the influence of *cheese*.

> **1830** If reading the above has given you the lock-jaw, why then certes [certainly], you will lose your share of the *oley cooks*, *ruletjis*, *smoked geese and sour krout*.
>
> **1848** *Rullichies*. (Dutch.) Chopped meat stuffed into small bags of tripe, which are then cut into slices and fried. An old and favorite dish among the descendants of the Dutch in New York. (Bartlett)
>
> **1949** Some food terms of Dutch origin have spread beyond the Dutch area [= the Hudson Valley, Catskills, and upper Delaware] ..., but others, such as ... *rollichies* for meat roulades ... have probably always been Dutch family words and are disappearing fast. (Kurath)

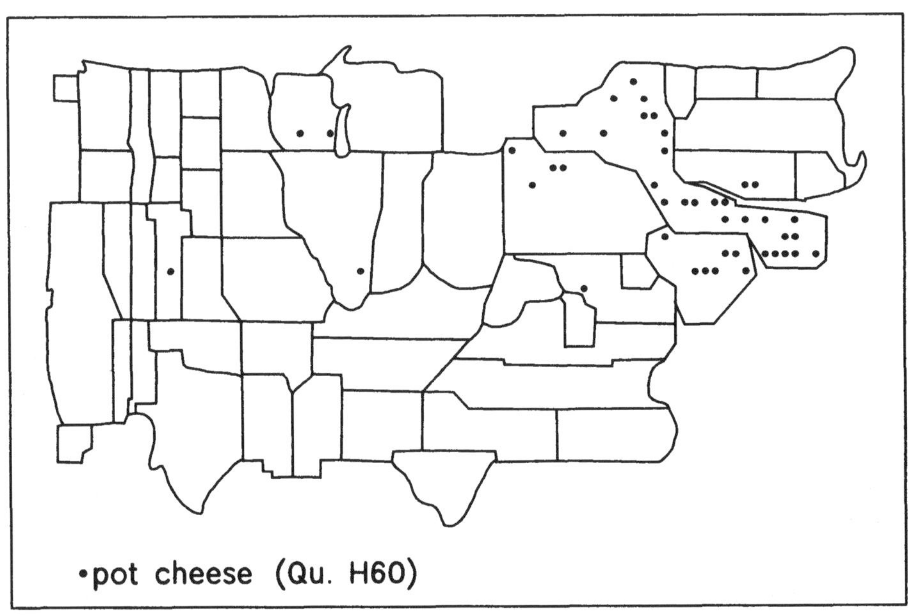

Illustration 2.12 – Map showing the distribution of pot cheese *(source: DARE 4: 308)*

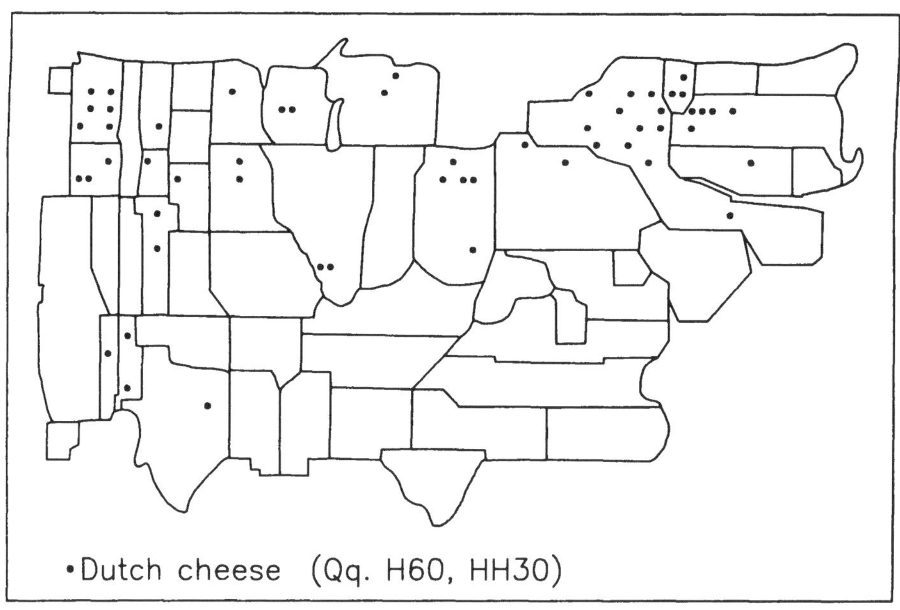

Illustration 2.13 – Map showing the distribution of Dutch cheese *(source: DARE 2: 243)*

1969 Of course, regarding food some of the old Dutch relliches. Do you know what relliches are? That's a meat dish. It's made from the stomach of a cow. ... (DARE)
2008 Listen up all you sausage lovers, a new temple just opened to fulfill your banger, bratwurst, frankfurter, kielbasa, rolliche and wienerwurst cravings. (gothambread.blogspot.com)

smear-case, a preparation of milk made to spread on bread (Craigie, DARE, Webster).
- From Dutch *smeerkaas* and from German *Schmierkäse*; adopted in the nineteenth century and still in use.
* In all languages, this cheese owes its name to the fact that it is spread on bread. The product and name originated in Germany, so the American English translation *smear-case* is derived in part from the German form *Schmierkäse*, as in the oldest quote in Craigie dating from 1829: "A dish, common amongst the Germans, ... is curds and cream. It is very palatable, and called by the Germans *smearcase.*" However, other sources state that Dutch *smeerkaas* has also played a part in the word's prolifcration in thc US. It is therefore unmerited that most dictionaries, including Webster, only cite German as the source. Webster mentions the variant *smier-case*, which does, of course, come from German. According to Webster, the word is used mostly in the central part of the US, but whether the same goes for the variant *smear-case* is not clear. The quotes below are all instances of Dutch influence.

1846 Their cheese is ... made on the same principle as the Dutch smerecase.
1848 *Smear-case.* (Dutch, *Smeer-kaas.*) A preparation of milk made to be spread on bread, whence its name; otherwise called Cottage-cheese. (Bartlett)

1872 *Smearcase*, from the Dutch smeer-kaas, a preparation of curds spread on a flat surface to make into cheese, is the same as the more familiar cottage-cheese and as familiar to Germany under the name of Schmier-Kaese as to Holland. It occurs as early as 1842 in the Philadelphia "Price-Current." (Schele de Vere)
1894 The "cookey" (koekje), noodles, hodgepodge, smearcase, rullichies, cold-slaw, and other dishes that survive in New England.
1902 *Smearcase* (Dutch *smeer-kaas*). A preparation of curds spread on a flat surface to make into cheese. Otherwise known as *cottage-cheese*. In New York city, also called *pot-cheese*. (Clapin)

to snoop, to go about in a sneaking way, to pry into (Craigie, Webster).
- From Dutch *snoepen*, meaning "to eat sweets," whose literal meaning was probably adopted as early as the seventeenth or eighteenth century; still widely used but with different meanings and all sorts of derivatives.
* The Dutch verb *snoepen* literally means "to eat sweets," and this often was done surreptitiously – in American English the word has also had the meaning "to eat (sweets) on the sly," as stated in Bartlett:
1848 *To snoop*. (Dutch, *snoepen*.) Applied to children, servants, and others, who clandestinely eat dainties or other victuals which have been put aside, not for their use. A servant who goes slyly into a dairy-room and drinks milk from a pan, would be said to be *snooping*. The term is peculiar to New York. (Bartlett)
The meaning in American English then shifted to "to go around in a sly or prying manner," "to pry into." While this meaning was found before the word's literal meaning, the latter meaning is of course older, dating from the seventeenth or eighteenth century, also due to the fact that this literal meaning was peculiar to New York. Examples of its figurative sense are:
1832 The world has realms wherein to *snoop*.
1840 Both he and Bradshawe are snooping about the country.
1891 In Worcester [MA], where there are no resident families of Dutch descent ..., it would be said: "They caught him snooping at the door," that is, peeping and listening.
1891 This word I have frequently heard in New England, used both as a verb and as a noun. It implies sneaking, spying, prying around.
In American English, the verb's new meaning spawned all kinds of derivatives, such as *snooper*, *snoop* (1891), meaning "prying medler" and *snoopy* (1895), meaning "inclined to snoop." The verb and its cognates were adopted into British English. *Snoopy* has become known inside and outside of the US through the eponymous dog, Charlie Brown's favorite animal in the comic strip *Peanuts* by Charles M. Schulz. Although the name fits the dog well, it is purely coincidental: the name is a mix of the two dogs that Schulz had as a child, Snooky and Spike.

speck, bacon (Craigie, DARE, Webster).
- From Dutch *spek*, previously also *speck*, or German *Speck*; adopted in the seventeenth century and still in use.
* The word *speck* occurs chiefly in the combination **apples and speck** (see relevant entry). At a very early date, *speck* was also used separately, which, given its age, must have originated from Dutch. In the

early nineteenth century, it reemerged on its own, but as it appears in a quote from Pennsylvania, it probably involves the German loanword.

> **1691** The plaintiff demands 180 lb. *speck*.
>
> **1809** He goes out almost every week to eat speck with the country folks.

The Dutch loanword *speck* became widely known through the word *specksynder*, which is the title of Chapter 33 of Melville's *Moby Dick* from 1851 (the correct form *specksnyder* is used elsewhere), which reads:

> **1851** The large importance attached to the harpooneer's vocation is evinced by the fact, that originally in the old Dutch Fishery, two centuries and more ago, the command of a whale ship was not wholly lodged in the person now called the captain, but was divided between him and an officer called the Specksynder. Literally this word means Fat-Cutter; usage, however, in time made it equivalent to Chief Harpooneer. (...) In the British Greenland Fishery, under the corrupted title of Specksioneer, this old Dutch official is still retained, but his former dignity is sadly abridged.

stuyvesant, brand name of a cigarette.
- From the Dutch name Peter *Stuyvesant*, the last director-general of New Netherland.
* The name of Peter Stuyvesant still lingers on the new continent, where he had been instrumental in expanding the Dutch colony: it was under his rule that Wall Street (from Dutch *wal*, meaning "wall") and Broadway (Dutch *de Brede weg*) were built. In 1664, he was forced to hand over the colony to the English. The hamlets of Stuyvesant and Stuyvesant Falls in Columbia County, New York, and Stuyvesant Street in New York, leading to the **Bowery** (see 2.8), still exist today. His name also lives on in computer games, for example. The fact that his name is still so prevalent in the US is due to a number of reasons. He played a central role in Diedrich Knickerbocker's *A History of New York*. He was a peculiar administrator, whose wooden leg appealed to people's imagination, and he had descendants named Stuyvesant living in New York until 1953. All in all, he had all the attributes required to become part of the American myth.

The name *stuyvesant*, like **knickerbockers** (see 2.13), has also become a generic name or rather a brand name: the name of a well-known cigarette brand. Sentences like "Give me a stuyvesant light anyday" and "all I ever used to smoke were stuyvo lights" can be found on the Internet. The association of the name Stuyvesant with smoking is probably once again attributable to Irving, who described the seventeenth-century Dutch settlers as chubby men in knickerbockers who were inseparable from their pipes – cigarettes had not been invented yet. To quote Irving: "The pipe, in fact, was the great organ of reflection and deliberation of the New Netherlander. It was his constant companion and solace – was he gay, he smoked; was he sad, he smoked; his pipe was never out of his mouth; it was a part of his physiognomy; without it, his best friends would not know him. Take away his pipe? You might as well take away his nose!" It is therefore understandable that advertisers used the image of the smoking Dutch for the name of a new cigarette brand.

Contrary to what many people believe, however, the *Stuyvesant* cigarette brand does not come from the US.

The Hamburg-based company Reemtsma (part of the international Imperial Tobacco Group since 2002) invented the name Peter Stuyvesant, and the Swiss Fritz Bühler came up with the first slogan in 1958: "the smell of the large far world: Peter Stuyvesant." The cigarette was made of one of the new "American blends" that became popular after the Second World War. A Peter Stuyvesant cigarette contained a blend of tobacco from no fewer than four continents, and it was directly associated with the far, new, and large world that had been opened up by Stuyvesant. The following slogans and commercial messages also alluded to a new world that Stuyvesant (the man or the cigarette) had at his feet: "The international passport to smoking pleasure," and "Find your world." TV commercials showed cosmopolitan images of modern art, ships, airplanes, metropolises, and so on.

Stuyvesant's name lives on in young people's lingo for another reason, as evidenced by the online *Urban Dictionary*. All quotes included in this dictionary refer to the prestigious public high school in the TriBeCa area of New York City. "Students are often characterized by drug usage, lack of sleep, nerdiness, high SAT scores and physical dependency upon escalators," one of the descriptions states. The school is lovingly referred to as *stuy* ("Yo, you go to stuy?") – a name with which the original name-giver undoubtedly could not have identified.

sup(p)awn, boiled corn meal; mush (Craigie, DARE, Webster).
- From seventeenth-century American Dutch *sapaen* (unknown in European Dutch); borrowed in the seventeenth century and still known.
* *Sapaen* is one of the few words that Dutch borrowed from an Amerindian language, specifically from a language of the Algonquian family – it is not certain which. The word is related to Massachuset *saupaun* "corn-meal porridge," literally "soaked, softened in water." Judging by the earliest forms, linguists have concluded that the word was borrowed by American English via Dutch rather than direct from an Amerindian language; Knickerbocker (Irving), too, assumes that, see the quotation for 1809. According to Webster, *sup(p)awn* is found mainly in New England. Kurath gives it for 1949 as a term particular to the Hudson Valley; but in his *American Regional Dialects* (1989), Carver points out that the word is practically unknown in 1965. He assumes that the reason why the word became obsolete so suddenly after 300 years lies in the commercialization of food terminology.

ca. 1627 When they wish to make use of the grain (maize) for bread or porridge which they call 'Sappaen,' they first boil it and then beat it flat upon a stone; then they put it into a wooden mortar ... and ... pound it small, and sift it through a small basket ... of the rushes before mentioned. (Mathews)
1671 Their general Food is Flesh, Fish, and *Indian Wheat*, which stamp'd, is boyl'd to a Pap, by them call'd Sappaen. (Mathews)
1754 Now [we] must eat Sapan (Indian Corn Porridge) alone, it is well that we have cows, which affords a little milk to it.
1809 [The Van Brummels] were the first inventors of Suppawn, or Mush and milk.
1835 I helped myself with an iron spoon from a dish of suppawn.
1949 The Midland and the South

have *mush*, and this expression is also used to some extent in the New England settlement area beside the terms containing *pudding*, in the Hudson Valley beside the local *suppawn*.

waffle, a crisp cake made of pancake batter baked in a waffle iron, eaten hot with butter or molasses (Craigie, Webster).
- From Dutch *wafel*, meaning "a light, flat pastry with a diamond-shaped pattern"; adopted in the seventeenth or eighteenth century and still widely used.
* The Dutch pastry name *wafel* is derived from *weven* ("to weave") and related to German *Wabe* ("honeycomb"). *Wafel* also has the same meaning in Dutch dialects and is therefore assumed to have been named after the honeycomb on account of its similar form.

The Hollanders took their waffles to America, and apparently made a big festive to-do out of baking them, for the word *wafel* first appears in American English in the compounds *waffle frolic* and *waffle party*. *Waffle parties* continued to be held at least until the end of the nineteenth century.

> **1744** We had the wafel-frolic at Miss Walton's talked of before your departure.
> **1744** For my own part I was not a little grieved that so luxurious a feast should come under the name of a wafel frolic. (OED citing US source)
> **1808** They are going to have a fine waffle party on Tuesday.
> **1882** She tells him of "little waffle parties" formed by her intimates.

In the Low Country, waffles were and are eaten both hot and cold, topped with butter and/or sugars, although this is not strictly necessary. The custom of eating waffles with butter or molasses

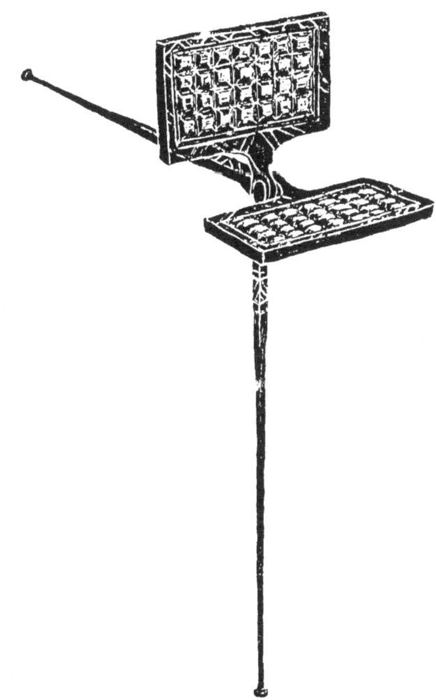

Illustration 2.14 – Waffle iron (source: Kroniek van de Kempen, Frans Hoppenbrouwers et al., Hapert, 1984)

for breakfast originated in the US, and was reported on as early as the nineteenth century.

> **1817** Waffles (a soft hot cake of German extraction, covered with butter).
> **1870** The Americans are all fond of molasses; using them regularly at breakfast and supper to their buckwheat cakes and waffles.
> **1906** Before she could reply, Sarah came in with hot waffles.

The waffles are baked in waffle irons – a word that was imported into the US by the Dutch together with their waffle baking. ***Waffle iron*** is a semi-translation of Dutch *wafelijzer*. The oldest quote refers to *woffle iron*, in which Dutch *a* has been changed into *o*, as it has countless other times (cf. *boss*).

> **1794** Woffle irons [advertised].
> **1828** Heat your waffle-iron ... Shut the iron tight, and bake the waffle on both sides.
> **1889** One of the commonest decorations of the nation was the waffle-iron face.

According to Flexner (1976: 266), the verb *to waffle* acquired the meaning of "to vacillate or to claim to be on both sides of a controversy in order to try to please everyone" in the 1960s. This meaning is also known in a slightly different form, for many of the meanings listed for *waffle* in the 2009 edition of the online *Urban Dictionary* are: "to change sides on an issue. One day you support something, the next day you oppose it."

2.2 Flora and fauna

"O this is Eden!," says Jacob Steendam in 1661 in his poem *'t Lof van Nuw-Nederland* ("In Praise of New Netherland"). Like Adam in paradise, the Dutch in America were faced with a natural environment for which they lacked words. Of course, they first tried to refer to animals and trees using words from their native tongue. Sometimes, they also made up new words and compounds that did not yet exist in Dutch. Some of these old and new names later ended up in American English. Or rather: they form the second largest contribution that Dutch has made to American English: twenty plant and animal names have been borrowed, most of which refer to species indigenous to America.

Borrowed plant names include **abele tree**, **Easter flower** (also **pass blummies**, **poss flower**), **fetticus**, **pinkster flower**, **pit**, and **sap bush**. These were all adopted in the seventeenth or eighteenth century, with the probable exception of **abele tree**. The Dutch names were transferred to American plant species that were identical or similar to European species; only the compound *sapbosch*, from which **sap bush** was derived, is coined in seventeenth-century American Dutch.

Various compounds or cognate animal names were coined in North American Dutch and never entered European Dutch, such as the fish names **killifish** and **weakfish**. The fish names **corporal**, **mossbunker**, **sea bass**, and **spearing**, on the other hand, were transferred from European to American species. With the possible exception of **corporal**, all these names were adopted into American English in the seventeenth or eighteenth century.

The names **blauser** for a certain type of snake and **groundhog** for a specific type of marmot were coined in Dutch in America; in contrast, the name **skillpot** was transferred to the American turtle, and **punkie**, the name for a biting midge, was borrowed from Munsee Delaware by the Dutch settlers.

Finally, American English also borrowed some names from Dutch for animals indigenous to Europe. **Kip** was borrowed regionally in the seventeenth or eighteenth century and the call **kish** in the nineteenth or twentieth century. The word *kip* was also adopted into Amerindian languages, in which the Dutch names for animals indigenous to Europe rank as high as third place in terms of number of loanwords. Widely known in American English are **span**, borrowed in the seventeenth or eighteenth century, and **Antwerp**, borrowed in the nineteenth or twentieth century.

abele (tree), **abel-tree**, the white or silver poplar tree (Craigie, Webster).
- From Dutch *abeel(boom)*, meaning "a white or silver poplar"; borrowed in the nineteenth century and still in use.
* The tree, whose timber is used in housing construction and its resin for medicines, is indigenous to Europe and must have been imported by Europeans. The name *abele* is Dutch, which makes it likely that the Dutch brought the tree to the US. Theoretically, it may also have been imported by the English, for British English also borrowed the Dutch word (it was included in the OED for the first time in 1681), but this Dutch word never really caught on in British English and is called "old-fashioned" in the *Encyclopaedia Britannica* of 1823, the ordinary English name *white poplar* being the preferred term. The OED provides few quotes, mostly from poems and none dating from after the second half of the nineteenth century, whereas this tree was planted on a fairly large scale in the US in this period (see the quote from 1852 in Craigie). The tree was probably imported into the US in the nineteenth century by Dutch or Flemish immigrants.

> **1828** The abele, the white poplar, the black poplar (Webster).
> **1847** Abele or Silver-leaf Poplar, ... a highly ornamented tree, native of Europe.
> **1852** If the nurserymen *will* raise Ailanthus and Abeles by the thousands ... and tell us nothing of pestilential odors and suckers.

Antwerp, 1. a variety of raspberry, usually *Red Antwerp*; 2. a variety of homing pigeon (Craigie, Webster).
- After the Belgian city *Antwerpen*; borrowed in the nineteenth century and still in use.
* The proliferation of the plant bearing the name *Antwerp* or *Red Antwerp* appears from the following quotes in Craigie.

> **1847** Antwerp Raspberry, Garden Raspberry,...is much cultivated for its favorite fruit.
> **1859** It is rare that the true Red Antwerp raspberry is found West of the State of New York.
> **1862** We are told that on the Hudson river fields are planted with a variety of the Red Antwerp, which has received its American cognomen from that stream, the Hudson River Red Antwerp.

But where does the plant's name come from? F.W. Card wrote the following about this in *Bush-fruits* in 1898:

> **1898** *Red Antwerp* (Old Red Antwerp, Knevett's Antwerp, True Red Antwerp, Howland's Red Antwerp ...). – One of the oldest European varieties, probably having been in cultivation more than a century. It is supposed to have derived its name from the city of Antwerp, in Belgium, though the plant itself is said to have come from the Island of Malta. It is one of the best European sorts, and is still grown, even for market, in the United States. ... Many other varieties have received this name at times. It is figured in the Report of the United States Department of Agriculture of 1866.

Based on this, the popular variety was most likely imported from Europe, possibly from the port of Antwerp. The plant may have been introduced earlier but, according to Craigie, the name *(Red) Antwerp* was not used until the mid-nineteenth century. However, the variety and name are unlikely to have originated from Dutch or Flemish immigrants who settled in the US in the nineteenth century – the berry has many different names in Dutch but none of them refers to Antwerp, nor is this area the berry's original habitat. The long name *Hudson River Red Antwerp* has become obsolete, but the short form *Red Antwerp* still exists. The name does not exist in British English, however, at least it is not listed in the OED.

The name for the type of pigeon was, however, derived from a Dutch name. Around 1840, two special types of carrier pigeon were bred by means of cross-breeding, called *Antwerpse duif* and *Luikse duif* in Dutch. The first name was adopted into American English as *Antwerp pigeon*, also abbreviated to *Antwerp*, according to the 1961 edition of Webster's Third.

Illustration 2.15 – Abele tree (source: J.G. Heck, The Complete Encyclopedia of Illustrations, 1879)

Illustration 2.16 – Blauser (source: Grosser Bildvorlagenatlas, Amsterdam 2001)

The name, which has existed in British English since 1839 (OED) and in American English since 1890, was probably adopted into American English from Dutch and Flemish immigrants, independently of British English.

> **1890** Some of these names [of fancy pigeons] are from localities, actual

or alleged, as Antwerps [etc.]
1905 Two main types of the Belgian homer have been distinguished as the Antwerp and the Liege varieties, the former being larger but less graceful in form than the latter.
1918 An Antwerp, or homing pigeon, commonly called carrier pigeon.

blauser, the hog-nosed snake (International Herpetological Society).
- From seventeenth-century American Dutch *blazer* ("blower"); borrowed in the seventeenth century and still known regionally.
* In European Dutch, *blazer* is not used as an animal name, so the Dutch settlers from the seventeenth century must have added this meaning to the word. The *-au-* spelling probably indicates that the pronunciation of the Dutch word has been adjusted to American English over time. The 1985 edition of the *Handbook of Snakes* and the International Herpetological Society (list of reptiles, 2008) still list the popular name *blauser*, in addition to many other names, including *blower*, which may be a translation of the Dutch name but may just as well have been coined in English, as blowing up the skin on its head is one of the snake's most typical characteristics.
1848 *Blauser*. The name given by the Dutch settlers to the hog-nosed snake, from its habit of distending or blowing up the skin of its neck and head. The other popular names in New York are Deaf-adder and Buckwheat-nosed. (Bartlett)
1872 Among the almost local terms of Dutch origin, which barely survive in districts inhabited by Dutch families, but which every now and then startle us by their sudden reappearance in poetry or in local description, are the following: ... *Blauser*, from the Dutch *blazer*, is still the name of the Deaf Adder (Vipera berus), which blows up its neck and head, and therefore, well deserves its graphic name. (Schele de Vere)
1902 *Blauser* (Dutch *blazer*, a blower). A typic and graphic name for the Deaf Adder (Vipera berus), which, as is well known, has the habit of distending or blowing up the skin of its neck and head. (Clapin)

corporal, a cypriniforme (*Semotilus corporalis*) (Craigie, DARE).
- Probably from Dutch *corporaal*; probably adopted in the nineteenth century and still used regionally.
* According to many standard works about American fish, starting with G. Brown Goode's *American fishes* from 1888, the name *corporal*, in the American English meaning of *fallfish*, is derived from Dutch and/or German. And considering the location – in the central and eastern part of the US – the word is likely to have been adopted in the nineteenth century.
The derivation is obscure: in Standard Dutch, *korporaal* is an army rank.
In the dialect of the province of North Brabant, however, *korporaal* is the name of a certain black-and-white water bird, the goosander. This bird was not named after the army rank but after *corporaal* or *corporale*, meaning "a white linen cloth underneath the ciborium and paten in Roman Catholic churches": the bird was named after this cloth on account of its white belly. Since the fish *corporal* also has a white belly, it was perhaps given that name for the same reason. I have found no similar name in German.
1887 The name Corporal seems to have derived from the Dutch or German settlers of the Middle States.

"Corporaalen" is one of its common names in that region.
1896 Mitchell calls the fish *Corporal* or *Corporaalen.*
1964 The fallfish is known to many anglers as chub, silver chub, chivin, windfish, and corporal.

Easter flower, an anemone, daffodil (Craigie, Webster), also hepatica (DARE); **pass blummies**, hepatica, **poss flower**, daffodil (DARE).
- Adopted as a translation and loanword, respectively, from Dutch *paasbloem* or its diminutives *paasbloempje*, *paasbloemetje*, a compound of *Paas-* ("Easter") and *bloem* ("flower"); borrowed in the seventeenth or eighteenth century and still known regionally.
* In Dutch, the word *paasbloem* is used to refer to various plants that flower around Easter time, particularly the anemone, daffodil, and hepatica – precisely the plants referred to by a similar name in the US. The names *pass blummies*, *paas blumes*, and so on, were adopted as loanwords from Dutch; the second part of *poss flower* is an English translation.
1859 *Paas Bloomachee*, i.e. Easter flower. *(Narcissus pseudo-narcissus.)* Not the Pasque Flower of botanists, but the common Yellow Daffodil. (Bartlett)
1872 *Paas-Blummachee* are well known in the flower-markets, and designate the common yellow Daffodill. (Schele de Vere)
1896 *Hepatica acutiloba* ... pass blummies, Alcove, N.Y. [Footnote:] Probably corrupted from *Pasque Blumen.*
1940 *H[epatica] triloba* ... paas blumes.
1957 Poss flowers, the old-fashioned, early double daffodils with the fragrance. My mother ... , now 96 years

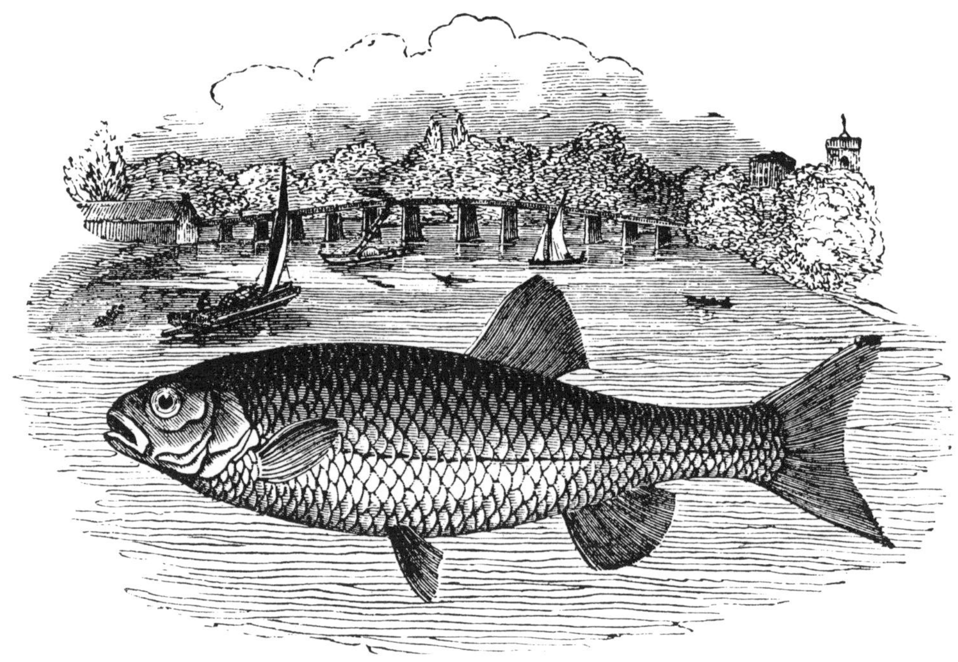

Illustration 2.17 – Corporal (source: Grosser Bildvorlagenatlas, Amsterdam 2001)

> old … , tells me that in her girlhood, these were always called Poss flowers. They were very important as Easter flowers in those days since there were few cultivated flowers.

In *Easter flower*, both parts have been translated into English. This name could have been coined in English, except that it does not exist in British English as a name for a plant species, so it is an American English neologism, which, in all likelihood is based on the Dutch name *paasbloem*.

> **1863** Beautiful wood-anemones I found to be sure, trembling on their fragile stems, deserving all their pretty names, – Wind-flower, Easter-flower, Pasque-flower, and homoeopathic Pulsatilla.
> **1877** Easter flower *(Narcissus pseudo-narcissus)*. (Bartlett)
> **1892** *Narcissus Pseudo-Narcissus*, Easter-flower.
> **1894/6** *Narcissus Poeticus*,. . . *Narcissus Pseudonarcissus*, … Easter flowers, Lincolnton, N.C.
> **1968** Wind flowers, anemone, Easter flowers [are] all the same thing – lavender, shaped like little tulips. (DARE)
> **1968-69** Easter flower [and] hepatica [are the] same. (DARE)
> **1974** Audrey Wilson was … looking at a clump of pale-yellow jonquils, … "I think Grandma Fannie must have planted these Easter flowers," she said.

The Dutch word *bloem* ("flower"), diminutives *bloempje*, *bloempie*, *bloemetje*, plural *bloemetjes*, was previously adopted into American English as a simplex, which probably also dates from the seventeenth or eighteenth century, as evident from the area where the words are used (New York) and the fact that many different

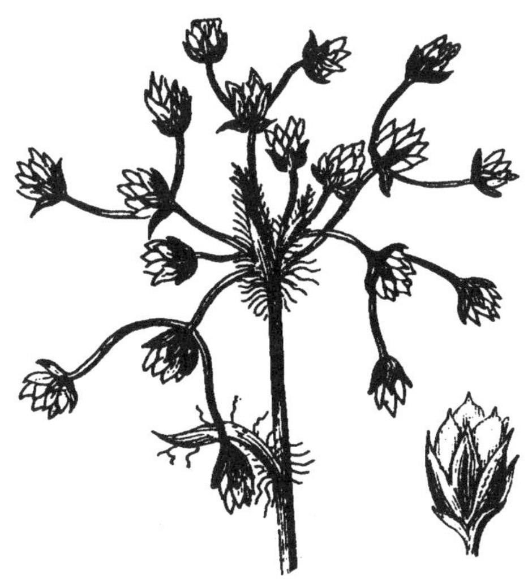

Illustration 2.18 – Easter flower (anemone) (source: J.G. Heck, The Complete Encyclopedia of Illustrations, 1879)

spellings have been found, including ***blumachies*** and ***blummie***. The words were found in the vicinity of New York until the twentieth century but have since disappeared altogether. In any event, they prove that the early Dutch settlers grew a variety of plants to sell flowers in markets. Nowadays, the Dutch are particularly associated with tulips, which they are likely to have sold in the old days as well, but there is no linguistic proof for this: the word *tulp* and English *tulip* were so similar that the pronunciation of the Dutch word was immediately anglicized.

> **1848** *Blumachies*. (Dutch.) This Dutch word for flowers is still preserved in the New York markets. (Bartlett)
> **1902** *Blummie*. A Dutch word still in use for flowers in New York City, and along the Hudson and Mohawk rivers. The diminutive form *blummachee* or *blummechie*, meaning small flower, is also well known in the New York markets. (Clapin)

1908-1909 *blum'mie, blum'mey*, flower, blossom [Du. *bloempje* (dim.), same meaning]. Mohawk valley, *blum'machie*, n., flower, blossom [Du. *bloemetje* (dim.), same meaning]. Mohawk valley. (Carpenter)

fetticus, corn salad or lamb's-lettuce (one of the names of *Valerianella locusta*) (Craigie, DARE, Webster).
- From Dutch *vettekost* or *vettekous*, meaning "veldsla"; adopted in the seventeenth or eighteenth century and still in use.
* In the Low Countries, there are many names for lamb's lettuce (*Valerianella locusta*) that refer to the fact that the leaves of the young plants feel slightly fatty to the touch, such as *vettik*, *vetsla*, *vettekool*, *vetzaad*, *vettekost*, and *vettekous*, literally meaning "fatty, fat salad, fat cabbage, fat seed, fat food, and fat stocking." Apparently, the Dutch brought these names to the American continent, together with the lettuce plant, which was native to Europe but not the US. The plant is still grown on the East Coast in particular.

The name *vettekost* was adopted into American English and pronounced and spelled in various ways, including *fetticus*. Various nineteenth-century dictionaries of Americanisms devoted attention to this name, crediting the Dutch with a greater sense of humor than reality warrants: according to these dictionaries, the Dutch had ironically named the low-calorie corn salad *vette kost* ("fat food"), failing to recognize the name's genuine reference to the leaves' texture. None of the Dutch sources explain the name with the same degree of humor.

When the word was adopted into American English, the Dutch name still shone through in the spelling, such as in *vettikost*, but the word would soon undergo all manner of morphological changes. For example, the first part was aptly anglicized to *fat*. The second part was probably influenced by *cow*, resulting in such spelling as *fatticows*, *fattikow* and *fattycows*. The final ending *-us* was undoubtedly due to the influence of modern Latin plant names, such as *crocus* or *hibiscus*.

According to DARE, the name *fetticus* is used regionally, particularly in New York. The 1961 edition of Webster's Third explains the name as being an adaptation of Dutch *vettekous*, literally meaning "fat stocking." This explanation is not inconceivable: both *vettekost* and *vettekous* were common names in Dutch; *vettekous* still exists as a common name. The pronunciation of both names is also similar, as the *-t* in *vettekost* is usually not pronounced. I suspect that the original form was *vettekost* – the lettuce is used as *kost* ("food") and feels *vet* ("fatty") to the touch – and that *vettekous* is a variant of it. The converse might also be true, but it is hard to account for the element *kous* "stocking."

1848 *Fetticus. Vettikost*. Vulg. *Fátti-kows*. (Bot. *Valerianella* ...) Corn-salad, or lamb's-lettuce. A word used in New York. (Bartlett)
1872 Vegetables were evidently not much to the taste of the old burghers, for it seems they called Corn-salad *(Valerianetta)* [sic] with biting irony *Vettikost*, something like rich fare. (Schele de Vere)
1889 The plant called corn-salad, or lamb-lettuce, is called *fetticus*, or *vettekost*, by gardeners. In the New York market I believe it is called fatty-cows. It appears to be the Dutch *vette kost*, "fat food;" but perhaps the *kost* is the same which appears in alecost,

Illustration 2.19 – Fetticus (source: Wikimedia Commons)

costmary, and other plant names.
1891 *V[alerianella] olitoria* ... is now often cultivated under glass as an early salad under the name *of fetticus*.
1902 *Fattikows*, *Fetticus* (Dutch *vettikost*, meaning, by irony, something like rich fare). A local term, in New York City, for corn-salad, or lamb's lettuce (Valerianella). (Clapin)

groundhog, the woodchuck, a heavy-bodied American marmot (Craigie, DARE, Webster).
- Translation of the Dutch name *aardvarken*, literally meaning "earth pig"; borrowed in the seventeenth century and still commonly used.
* As the Dutch scattered across the globe in the seventeenth century, they encountered a larger number of new animals and plants for which they had to find names. The easiest solution was to name new animals after ones they knew or with which they shared one characteristic or another. The same Dutch name was often used on various continents to refer to different animals. In South Africa, for example, a specific termite eater was called *aardvarken* (which still lives on in Afrikaans *aardvark*), and the same name was given to the woodchuck on the American continent. Both animals look like a pig rooting in the earth. In North America, *aardvarken* occurs for the first time in the *Beschryvinge van Nieuw-Nederlant* ("Description of New Netherland"), which Adriaen Cornelissen van der Donck published in 1655, the year in which he died, and it was one of the first books about New Netherland written by someone who had actually lived there. For more information about him, see **yonkers** in 2.4.

1655 Van der Donck: Daer zijn ooch *Aertoerckens*, ... *Trommelslaghers*, en verscheyde andere soorten die wy niet kennen ofte gesien hebben.
[= There are *also groundhogs*, ... *drummers*, and various other kinds which we have not known or seen.]

The normal American English name *groundhog* is a literal translation of Dutch *aardvarken*, which can be no coincidence: the English probably knew and understood the Dutch name and translated it into their own language.

Since the nineteenth century, the expressions *groundhog case*, meaning "a situation in which one has no choice," and *groundhog day* have been used. The meaning of the latter expression is no longer a mystery to anyone in or outside the US since the movie *Groundhog Day*, which was released in 1993. The movie tells a story that takes place on 2 February, the day that, as folklore has it, the groundhog crawls out of his burrow to predict the weather: if he perceives his shadow, he retires again to his burrow, which he does not leave for six weeks – weeks of stormy weather. But if he does not see his shadow, for lack of sunshine, he stays out of his hole, and the weather is sure to become mild and pleasant. Thanks to the movie, which is about a weatherman who wakes up every morning to experience Groundhog Day over and over again, *groundhog day* has acquired the meaning of "the same (unpleasant) thing over and over again": "My life never changes. Every day is groundhog day. Eat, work, sleep," somebody wrote in the *Urban Dictionary*.

DARE includes a map of the locations where *groundhog* is used to refer to woodchuck (illustration 2.21); the name is widespread but particularly prevalent in the Midland. Regionally, the name *groundhog* is also used to denote other animals. These are all American developments that have nothing to do with Dutch, for even though the Dutch were the first to use the name *aardvarken* to refer to an American groundhog, neither the name nor the animal ever became common in the Low Countries. It was not until recently that the acquaintance was renewed, and these days the groundhog is called *bosmarmot* in Dutch, literally "bush marmot."

> **1742** The *Monac*, or groundhog ... will be as tame as a cat (for I gave one to Sir Hans Sloane, who was much delighted with it).
> **1859** Then there is the ground-hog. As his name indicates, he burrows in the ground, and, like the prairie dog, builds a perfect city. He is about as large as a medium-sized opossum, and has similar hair. His color is a sort of dark gray.
> **1960** *Groundhog* is the only name for the animal in the area, except for an occasional extra – *whistle pig*.
> **1966-70** We have groundhogs; they dig holes in the fields.
> **2008** Somewhere between Texas and Ohio on Tuesday night the Democratic political groundhog saw his/her shadow and decreed at least another six weeks of campaigning. (www.theroot.com, 5 March 2008 under the headline: "Groundhog Day for the Dems")

killifish, a fish of the family Cyprinodontidae (Craigie, DARE, Webster).
- From seventeenth-century American Dutch *kilvis*, a compound of *kil'* ("stream, creek, channel") and *vis* ("fish"); adopted in the seventeenth century and still known.
* The creeks that the Dutch called *kil* (see 2.5) were home to special fish that were new to the Dutch, who probably called them *kilvis* or in the old spelling *kilvisch* ("fish from the kil"). The name *kilvis* was not known in the Netherlands, but nor were these animals. It is also possible that the name *killfish* originated in American English, after the Yankees had adopted Dutch *kil* to denote "creek." Whatever the case may be, in American

Illustration 2.20 – Groundhog (source: Grosser Bildvorlagenatlas, Amsterdam 2001)

English, the fish was called *killfish*, which rapidly changed into *killyfish* or *killi(e) fish*. The name was later shortened to *killie*.

1787 Diese beyde Fische, der Yellow bellied Cobler und Killfish, halten sich um Neuyork, in Kriken [sie] und Teichen ... auf. [= Both these fishes, the Yellow-bellied Cobbler and Kill-fish, are found in creeks and ponds about New York.]

1814 *Sheep's-Head Killifish. (Esox ovinus.)* ... Length about an inch and a half; and remarkably large in the girth.

1842 Its [= the striped killifish's] popular name is derived from its abundance in creeks and estuaries, which our Dutch ancestors termed "kills."

1848 *Killifish* ... A small fish found in the salt water creeks and bays, from one to five inches in length. It is only used for bait for larger fish. The name is Dutch from *kill*, a channel or creek ..., where the fish is only found. They are often called *killies*. (Bartlett, Appendix)

1993 I don't use *kill* as a small stream but the minnows that live in them ever were *killies!* I was raised on southern Long Island. (DARE)

The change from *killfish* into *killyfish* or *killi(e)fish* probably occurred because people did not associate the beautiful, charming little fish with the verb *to kill*. However, there were some people who did associate *kill* ("stream") with *to kill*, as became apparent in 1996 from a controversy about the name of the small town *Fishkill*. On September 6, 1996, CNN reported in a hilarious tone (http://edition.cnn.com/US/9609/06/fishy.name/) that an animal rights organization, PETA (People for the Ethical Treatment of Animals) had proposed to change *Fishkill* into *Fishsave*, claiming that *Fishkill* suggested cruelty to fish.

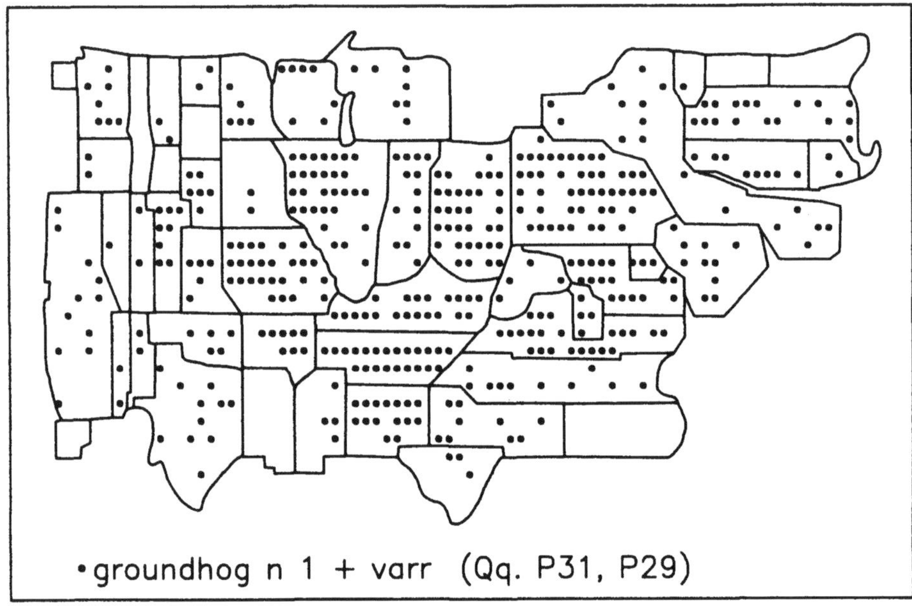

Illustration 2.21 – Map showing the distribution of groundhog *(source: DARE 2: 819)*

An alternative explanation for the form *killifish* is that the word is derived from a Dutch compound *killevisch* (*kille* was previously used alongside *kil* in Dutch); the linking phoneme *-e-* was adopted into American English as *-i-*, as it was in *pannicake*.

In regional American English, the name *killifish* is particularly prevalent in the southeast of New York State (see illustration 2.22). But the name of the little fish from the New York creeks has since spread enormously. Other groups of related fish were also named *killifish*, and the name is now a generic one for oviparous toothcarps (*Cyprinodontiformes*). *Killifish* are currently subdivided into ten families that inhabit Asian, African, and Central and South American waters. They are popular among aquarists and *killifish*, *killivissen* of *kilis* are kept frequently in the Netherlands as well. The most well-known *killifish* is undoubtedly the guppy.

kip, a young chicken (DARE).
- From Dutch *kip*, meaning "hen, fowl, chicken"; adopted in the seventeenth or eighteenth century and still known regionally.
* The Dutch word *kip* and the call *kipkip*, were adopted into the Amerindian languages Loup, Mahican, Mohawk, and Munsee Delaware. This means that the Dutch word was used very early on on the East Coast. The word also exists in American English and, according to DARE, is mostly found in New Jersey and New York, and particularly in areas with citizens of Dutch descent. Although the word was not found until the late nineteenth century, this loanword is bound to be much older. According to Carver's *American Regional Dialects* the word *kip* is probably dying out, just like the call *kipkip*, that has been noted in American English too.

> **1895** *Kip:* young chicken. (Used also as call – "kip, kip.")
> **1908-09** *kip*, n., a word used in call-

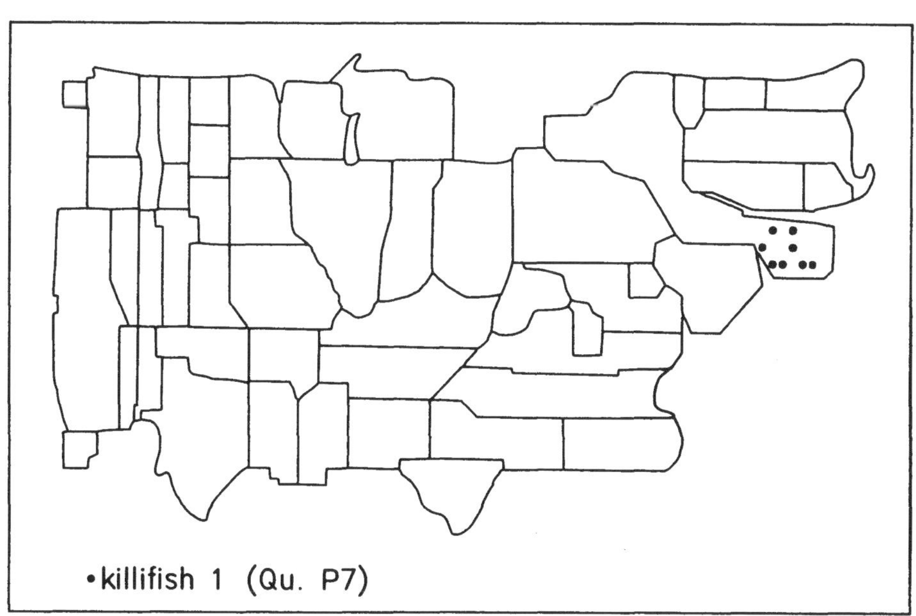

Illustration 2.22 – Map showing the distribution of killifish *(source: DARE 3: 216)*

ing chickens, e.g., “come *kip*, *kip!*” [Du. *kip*, hen, fowl]. Schenectady Co. (Carpenter)
1949 The chicken call *kip!* ... has survived all the way from Bergen County, New Jersey, to the Mohawk Valley. None of these calls *[=kip!, kees!, kish!]* occurs outside the Dutch settlement area, and they are, therefore, presumably of Dutch or Flemish origin. (Kurath)
1967-69 *(How do you call the chickens to you at feeding time?)* (Here) kip [sometimes repeated]. (DARE)
1986 Kip, chicky.

kish, also **kees**, **kissy**, used as a call to cows or calves (DARE).
- From Dutch *kis*, *kies*, *kiesie*, calls to a cow or calf; adopted in the nineteenth or twentieth century and still known regionally.
* The Dutch dialects have various calls for cows and calves, such as *kis*, *kies*, *kiesie* or *koes* and *kuus*. It is possible that these are corruptions of the diminutive *koetje* meaning “little cow, calf” or the word *koe* meaning “cow.” While documentation on the use of this word in American English is scarce, that says little about the frequency of use, as calls are seldom recorded. Since all documentary evidence dates from the twentieth century, it is

Illustration 2.23 – Kip (source: J.G. Heck, The Complete Encyclopedia of Illustrations, 1879)

unlikely that the word was already in use in the seventeenth or eighteenth century. Or is it? In 1949, the word was reportedly used along the Delaware and in the Catskills, and it is worth noting that the Dutch word *koe* was adopted into the Amerindian languages Loup, Mahican, and Munsee Delaware.

> **1949** *Kees!* or *kish!* ... is occasionally heard on the upper Delaware and in the Catskills ... None of these calls [to cows] occurs outside the Dutch settlement area, and they are, therefore, presumably of Dutch or Flemish origin. (Kurath)
> **1967** *(Call to calves)* Kees!; Kish!
> **1973** *Calls to calves ... kissy* is the term of a North Dakota inf. both of whose parents came from The Netherlands.

Another call that Kurath (1949: 24) mentions for calves is ***tye***, a word that rhymes with *high*. It is used in New Jersey, but only in Dutch settlement areas and is therefore likely to have been derived from a Dutch call; in Dutch dialects, *tuuk*, *tui*, *teu* and variations on these are used to call a cow or calf. On p. 26, Kurath adds: "In the northern part of East Jersey, notably in Bergen County, Dutch could be heard until recently, and there are a few individuals even now who still know Dutch. It is, therefore, not surprising that unique relics of Dutch calls to farm stock are current here such as *kush!* to cows and *tye!* to calves."

mossbunker, **mossbanker**, **marshbanker**, menhaden (fish) (Craigie, DARE, Webster).
- From Dutch *marsbanker*, also *masbanker*, meaning "type of horse mackerel"; adopted in the seventeenth century and still in use.
* Dutch *marsbanker* ("type of horse mackerel") was named after the shoals in Marsdiep, a channel between Den Helder and Texel, where the fish used to be abundant. When the Dutch moved to the American East Coast, they saw what is currently called the "Atlantic menhaden," which, like the Dutch horse mackerel, swam in shoals, which is why they called the fish *marsbanker*. The Dutchman Jacob Steendam, who is considered to be the first American poet, was the first to use the word *marsbanker* to refer to an American fish species. Steendam lived in New Amsterdam from 1650 to 1662, where he was a merchant. In 1659, he published *Klagt van Nieuw-Amsterdam* ("Complaint from New Amsterdam"), in which he blames the Dutch Republic for not doing enough for the new colony) and in 1661 *'t Lof van Nuw-Nederland* ("In Praise of New Netherland"), in which he glorifies the new world in rhyming verse, referring to the clean air and the many types of fish such as:

> Swart-vis, en Roch, en Haring, en Makreel
> Schelvis, *Masbank*, en Voren die (so veel)
> Tot walgens toe, die Netten vuld: en heel
> Min word ge-eeten.

Which translates as: "Black and rock, herring, mackerel, / Haddock, mosbankers and roach which fill / The nets to loathing; and so many, all / Cannot be eaten."

The Yankees adopted this name from the Dutch as early as 1679. In American English, it underwent all manner of changes: Dutch *a* changed into *o*, as it did so often (compare *boss*), the *r* in the middle of the word disappeared (although this occurred occasionally in Dutch too), *-banker* became *-bunker*, and the first part sometimes became *marsh*, probably under the influence of the homophonous word for "swamp," even though this is no habitat for menhaden. The form *mossybunker* also existed, probably under the influence of *mossy* "covered with moss." Information in DARE shows that all these names are mostly confined to New Jersey and New York.

> **1679** 100 Marsbanckers.
> **1803** The fish which Mr. Latrobe describes is the *morsch-banker* of the Dutch settlers about New-York, and the *menhaden* of the Mohegan natives.
> **1809** He saw the duyvel, in the shape of a huge Moss-bonker.
> **1814** Bony-fish, Hard-heads, or Marsbankers ... [are] about fourteen inches long.
> **1902** *Mossybank* ... A variation of mossbunker. (Clapin)
> **1990** The good ship *Riga* ... was fishing for menhaden, called mossbunkers down here in New Jersey.

In the nineteenth century, the word was abridged to ***bunker***. According to DARE, this name, which is also listed in Webster, for example, is particularly prevalent in the northern and central states situated along the Atlantic Coast.

> **1842** The Mossbonker ... Alosa menhaden ... At the end of the island [=Manhattan], they are called *Skippangs* or *Bunkers.*
> **1884** New Jersey uses the New York name with its local variations, such as "Bunker" and "Marshbanker."
> **1976** The menhaden has even more names than the herring ... Chesapeake watermen simply say menhaden or bunker.

pinkster flower, **pinxter flower**, rhododendron (Craigie, DARE, Webster). - From Dutch *pinksterbloem*, a compound of *Pinkster-* ("Whitsuntide") and *bloem* ("flower"); adopted in the seventeenth or eighteenth century and still in use.

* In Dutch, *pinksterbloem* is used to refer to various plants that flower around Whitsuntide. According to a detailed book containing descriptions of plants, animals, and minerals based on the work of the Swedish botanist Carl Linnaeus, written by M. Houttuyn in 1775, the name *pinksterbloem* is used in North America to refer to what used to be called "azalea" and is currently named "rhododendron": "Such flowers [*Azalea viscosa*] are found in North America... they [are] called May Flowers by the Swedes and Pinkster Flowers by the Dutch or Germans." This is exactly the meaning that *pinkster flower* still has in American English, particularly that of *Rhododendron periclymenoides.* This means that the settlers assigned an existing Dutch name to a new American species.

In American English, the plant's name is also abridged to simple *pinkster* or *pinxter*, which is impossible in Dutch on account of possible confusion with the name of the festival of Pentecost. This restriction does not apply to American English, since *pinkster* for Pentecost is rapidly disappearing. American English has and had all kinds of spellings and forms in addition to *pinkster flower*, such as ***pinxter bloom*** (in which Dutch *bloem* was adopted phonetically instead of being translated into *flower*), *pinkster blossom*, and *Pinxter blummachee* from the Dutch diminutive *pinksterbloemetje.* In 1881, *Pinkster Mummies* was found – if this is not a misprint, the author probably did not understand the form *blummies* and wrote it phonetically. Finally, "oak apple" is sometimes referred to as *pinkster apple* in American English.

> **1739** *Azalea* ... Caprifolio simili ... *Pinxterbloem.* [= *Azalea* ... resembling honeysuckle ... *Pinxterbloem.*]

Illustration 2.24 – Pinkster flower (source: J.G. Heck, The Complete Encyclopedia of Illustrations, 1879)

1822 *[Azalea] nudiflora [= Rhododendron periclymenoides]*, ... pinxter blomache ... Flowers abundant not viscous.
1833 He ... plucked for her the most beautiful pinkster blossoms.
1859 *Pinxter blumachies* ... A familiar name in the State of New York for the Swamp Honeysuckle and other early flowers. (Bartlett)
1869 Another species of Azalea, the *calendulaceum*, ... is found in some parts of Pennsylvania and Ohio, and still further south. The flowers are a reddish yellow, so bright it is often called the *Flaming pinxter*.
1872 The early azalea of our woods (Azalea nudiflora), is in like manner called *Pinxter Blummachee*. (Schele de Vere)
1881 The Pinkster king ... and his followers were covered with Pinkster *Mummies* – the wild azalea, or swamp-apple.
1902 Several Whitsuntide flowers, and especially the early azalea of our woods (Azalea nudiflora) are similarly called *Pinxter blummachees*, or *blumachies*. (Clapin)
1948 Sometimes called June pinks or Pinxters, this shrub [= the azalea] is quite common throughout the region.

An abridged form is *pink*, which was already cited in 1902 by Clapin, and later associated with the color *pink*.

1902 *Pink* (Dutch *Pinkster*, Whitsuntide). In New York city, a flower owing its name to the season of its blooming, i.e. Whitsuntide. (Clapin)
1969 Pinksters ... grow on a low bush, and they're very pink; they have long tongues, stamens. It really is a wild azalea... Some of ... the older ones in the family called those mayflowers. (DARE)
ca. 1985 As a child in grade school, I learned the name *pinxter* for our wild azalea. I did not know I was using a Dutch word and that the name was

really *pinxter bloom* or *pinxter flower.* I thought the name came from the color – pink.

pit, the hard stone or seed of a fruit (Craigie, DARE, Webster).
- From Dutch *pit*, meaning "hard stone or seed of a fruit"; adopted in the seventeenth or eighteenth century and very widespread.
* What the British call a *stone* or *seed* is referred to as a *pit* in American English, which was adopted from the Dutch. Today, it is used throughout the entire US. DARE has studied where the stone of a cherry, plume, and peach is called *pit*, and there appear to be differences. Particularly in the central and southern parts of the US, the word is used less frequently than elsewhere, but it is still a highly prevalent word, which spread from New York to the other states.
In 1848, Bartlett still called it typical of New York.

1828 In August, 1826, a Mr. Robert Martin, of Blenheim, in this county, ate a quantity of plumbs, and under the impression that they would be less liable to injure him, swallowed pits and all.
1847 We ate cherry pie and flung the pits at old codgers passing in the streets.
1848 *Pit.* (Dutch, *pit*, a kernel.) The kernel or nut of fruit; as, a cherry-*pit*. Peculiar to New York. "You put an apple-seed or a peach-*pit* into the ground, and it springs up into the form of a miniature tree." (Bartlett)

The word spread particularly in the twentieth. Interestingly, various statements (see the quotes below) reveal that the word did not spread among farmers but rather among the more highly educated, partly due to the inscriptions on cans. In the twentieth century, the word *pit* became more prestigious than its synonyms. By that time, however, there was not a living soul who knew the word was once adopted from Dutch, a fact that had not yet faded into oblivion in the nineteenth century. The word *pit* also spread from American English to British English. Derivatives of the noun are the verb *to pit*, meaning "to remove the pit," and the noun *pitter*, meaning "fruit stone extractor."

1968 Vocabularies sometimes change because a word from one dialect appears to have more prestige than that of another dialect ... The Midland *(peach) seed* appears to be replacing the Northern *(peach) stone; (peach) pit*, another Northern term is perhaps also on the increase (field informants, 31%; students, 49%).
1970 The hard center of a peach is regularly called a seed ... *Pit* is a nonrural term found only among the highest educational bracket.

1970 As in the case of peaches, *seed*

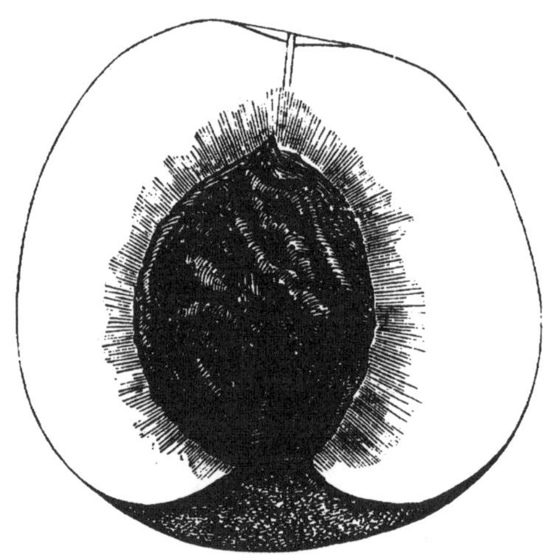

Illustration 2.25 – Pit (source: Vignettes, Paris 2001)

is the name given most often to the hard center of a cherry. *Pit*, a word unknown to the least educated and rare in rural communities, is used by 19.5% of the [200] informants, many of whom indicate they learned it from labels on cans of cherries.
1972 *Pit* is generally restricted to educated usage (5 of the 7 occurrences).

punkie, **punky**, biting midge (Craigie, DARE, Webster).
- From seventeenth-century American Dutch *punkje*, *punkie*; adopted in the seventeenth century and still known.
* *Punkie* is one of the few words that Dutch borrowed from an Amerindian language, Munsee Delaware in this case, where the mosquito is called *pónkwes*, which, with the diminutive ending *-ehs-* is derived from a word denoting "dust, ashes." The insect's bite causes an unbearable itch and pain, which is why the Native Americans compared the insects to "live sparks": they are so small that they are barely visible and their bite is as painful as a piece of coal scorching the skin.

In Dutch, the word's ending was replaced by the Dutch diminutive *-je* or *-ie*, which was adopted into American English as *-ie*, as was customary; compare *cookie*, for example. This ending shows that American English did not borrow the word directly from Munsee Delaware but from Dutch. This Amerindian word still lives on in American English, albeit via Dutch, particularly in Upstate New York (see illustration 2.27). Variants include *ponki*, *pungie*, *punk(ey)*, *punkie gnat* and *punkie fly*. Occasionally, it is also used as a synonym of *gnat*. In European Dutch, *punkje*, *punkie* remained unknown as a name for mosquitoes, which is logical because this particular type of mosquito does not exist in the Low Countries.

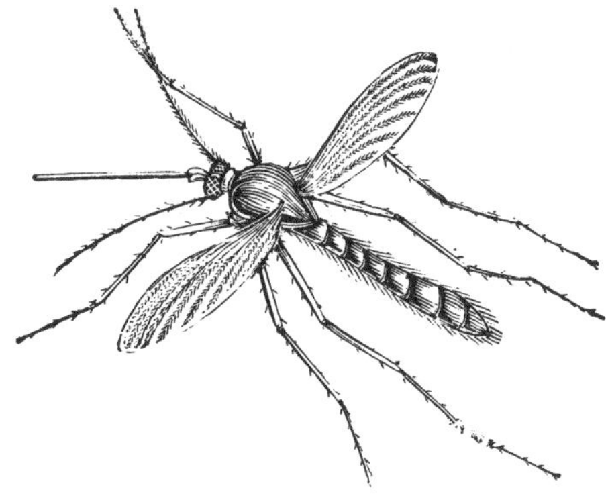

Illustration 2.26 – Punkie (source: Grosser Bildvorlagenatlas, Amsterdam 2001)

1769 We begin to be teazed with Muscetoes and little Gnats called here Punkies.
1840 Of all the tortures of this nature, that inflicted by the *gnat*, (sand-flies, punkies, brulos, for they bear all these appellations,) is the least endurable.
1910 *Punky*, or *punkie*, is from the Dutch of New York and New Jersey *pûnki*, pl. *pûnkin*, from (by vocalic addition) Lenape *pûnk* or *ponk*.
1965-70 Punkie gnat – Williams River is full of them – drive you off the river about 4 p.m. (DARE)
ca. 2008 To get rid of punkies gnats (yet another species of gnats) you need only move away from the lakeshore. Punkie gnats are generally found near moist, swampy areas and found near the muck that builds up on lakeshores. Punkies feeding zones are fairly small, so if you want to stop being bitten, just move a short distance away. (www.getridofthings.com)

sap bush, sugar bush, grove of sugar

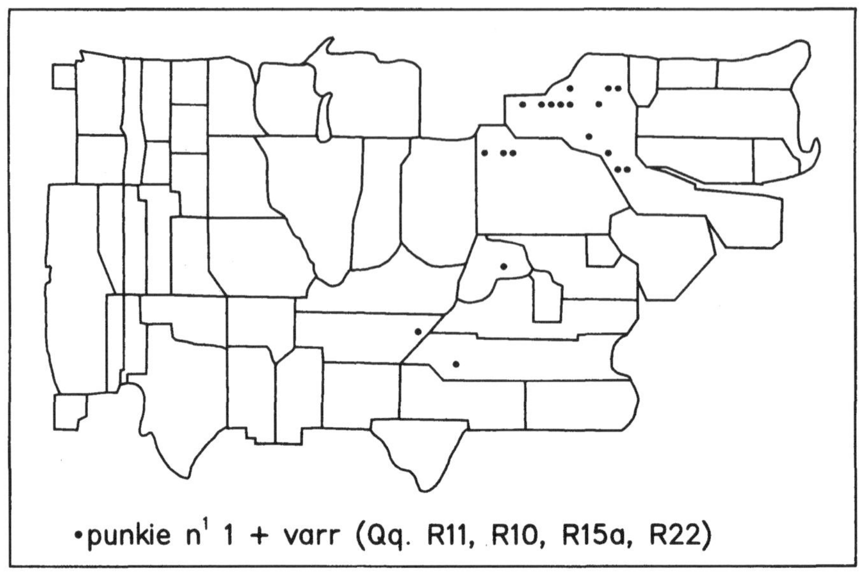

Illustration 2.27 – Map showing the distribution of punkie *(source: DARE 4: 380)*

maples (DARE).
- From seventeenth-century American Dutch *sapbos*, older *sapbosch*, literally meaning "sap grove"; adopted in the seventeenth or eighteenth century and still known regionally.
* *Sapbos* is a compound of two Dutch words, but it does not exist in European Dutch. The name for a plantation of sugar maples – a phenomenon that never existed in the Low Countries – was coined by Dutch settlers in the US but never transferred to Europe. Today, it is particularly prevalent in central New York, according to DARE.

> **1828** The daughter of Mr. Hunsinger, of Camillus, Onondagua County, N.Y. ... , was burnt to death last week, in consequence of her clothes taking fire in a *sap bush*. This is understood to be a temporary settlement for boiling the sap of the maple tree into sugar.
> **1913** *Sap-bush* ... A place where maple sap is gathered, with especial reference to trees. "Sam Jones has quite a large sap-bush."
> **1949** The Hudson Valley has two expressions for the sugar maple grove, *sugar bush* and *sap bush*. ... *Sap bush* ... occurs only in the valleys of the Hudson and the Mohawk. *Sap bush* is an Anglicized form of the Dutch term. (Kurath)
> **1950** (*To do something in an unnecessarily roundabout way: "I don't know why he had to go to do that"*) All around the sap bush.

sea bass, any of the fishes of the family Serranidae, especially the black sea bass, found along the Atlantic coast (Craigie, DARE, Webster).
- Probably from Dutch *zeebaars*; adopted in the seventeenth or eighteenth century and still in use.
* The Dutchman Jacob Steendam, already referred to under **mossbunker**, was the first to use the word *zeebaars* for an Ameri-

can fish species. In the above-mentioned *'t Lof van Nuw-Nederland* dating from 1661, he wrote:

> So gaat het hier: dat's Werelts overvloed,
> (Waar mee de Mensch word koninglijk gevoed
> Door gulle gunst des milden gevers) doet
> Hem vaak vergeeten.
> Steenbrassem, Steur en Dartien en Knor-haan.
> En *Zee-Baars* die geen vorst sal laten slaan
> En Kabellau: en Salm, die (wel gebraan).
> Is vet, en voedig.
> [That's how it goes here: the world's plenty,
> (With which Man is royally fed
> Through the generosity of the charitable giver)
> often causes Him to be forgotten.
> The bream and sturgeon, drumfish and gurnard,
> The sea-bass which a prince would not discard;
> The cod and salmon cooked with due regard
> Most palatable.]

G. Brown Goode cites this poem without a translation in his well-known *American fishes* from 1888 – did he assume that his readers would understand this Dutch poem without a translation?

Zeebaars is compounded of *zee* ("sea") and *baars* ("bass"). Steendam used an existing Dutch word (*zeebaars*) to refer to an American fish species, but the Dutch word denotes a different type of fish. Since both elements, *sea* and *bass*, also exist in English, it is of course possible that the English coined the compound independently. However, since it goes back such a long time in American Dutch, it is more likely that the Dutch gave the fish its name and the English adapted the name to their vernacular. In any event, the name *sea bass* is American English and not British English.

The name *sea bass* was originally used to refer to the "black sea bass," which lives on the East Coast of the United States According to data from DARE, the name for this specific species is particularly prevalent in the northern states along the Atlantic Coast. Nowadays, the name *sea bass* is also used to refer to different, related types on the West Coast and in the central and southern parts of the United States. In other words, the name has spread across the larger part of the United States.

> **1760** These waters afford various kinds of fish, black fish, sea bass, sheeps-heads, rock-fish, lobsters, and several others.
>
> **1765** In the sea adjacent to this island [Long Island] are sea-bass and black-fish in great plenty, which are very good when fresh.
>
> **1842** This *[=Centropristis striata]* is one of the most savory and delicate of the fishes which appear in our markets from May to July. Its most usual name with us is *Sea Bass.*

Illustration 2.28 – Sea bass (source: Grosser Bildvorlagenatlas, Amsterdam 2001)

1976 He diversifies, making strong rectangular pots for the ocean capture of "blackfish" or sea bass, as practiced in the Carolinas.

skillpot, also **skillipot**, **skilpot**, usually a red-bellied turtle, but also a mud turtle or musk turtle (Craigie, DARE).
- From Dutch *schildpad*, meaning "turtle," from *schild* ("shield") and *pad* ("toad"), so literally "shieldtoad"; adopted in the seventeenth or eighteenth century and still used regionally.
* The Dutch settlers referred to a turtle with which they were unfamiliar using the Dutch word *schildpad*, which does not denote a specific type, as there were no wild turtles in the Netherlands in the seventeenth century. The existence of the name and the animal was, however, known in literature.

The Dutch word *schildpad* was transformed in American English by folk etymology: the second part was changed into *pot*, an interpretation that makes sense, given the shape of the shell. The first part of the word appeared in many variants, including *shellpot*, *skillipot*, *skilliput*, *skillypot*, *skilpot*; the form *skillpot turtle*, where *turtle* has been added for clarification, also exists. Since the words have been so corrupted, it is not inconceivable that the American English word was influenced by immigrants speaking a Scandinavian language: the animal is called *skildpadde* in Danish, *skilpadde* in Norwegian and *sköldpadd* in Swedish – three words that were all derived from Dutch or Low German. In the US, the word *skillpot* (and variants) is particularly prevalent in Washington, D.C., Maryland, Virginia, and West Virginia (see illustration 2.29); that is, somewhat to the south of the original Dutch settlements, but the word is also used in Delaware. To the north of New York lies the small Skillpot Island in the Hudson River.

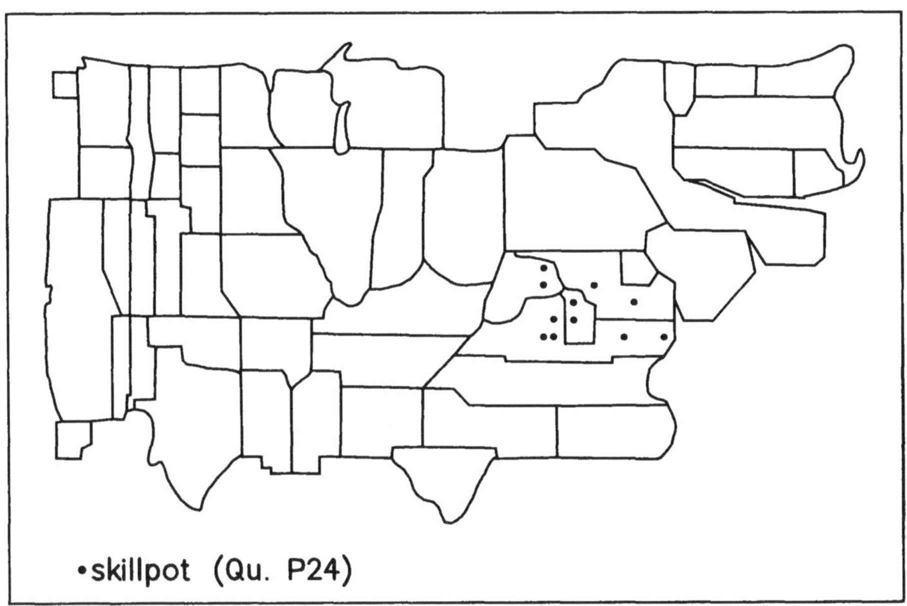

Illustration 2.29 – Map showing the distribution of skillpot *(source: DARE 4: 995)*

1790 A negro man ... saw, and caught, a small turtle (*or* what is more generally known by the name of shellpot).
1807 Famous place for *skilly-pots;* Philadelphians call 'em tarapins.
1851 *Skillpot Turtle, Testudo Picta*, or *Emys Guttata*, the most common kind here, seen by dozens in spring and summer...
1868 It was a bright idea of his ... to found a Turtle Club. The Delaware Indians believe that this world is supported by an enormous skilliput.
1948 A yellow-belly skilpot is the small kind, the red-belly skilpot the kind that gets as big as a small snapping turtle – maybe four pounds ... [H]ere in Delaware it is commonly called a skilpot from Indian River clear up to Shellpot Creek.
1986 Skillpot – not edible, small, like turtle...

span, a pair of horses, mules, or other animals usually matched in looks and action, and driven together (Craigie, Webster).
- From Dutch *span*, meaning "two (or more) yoked draft animals," adopted in the seventeenth or eighteenth century and still in use.
* Dutch *span* literally means "two (or more) yoked draft animals," hence "two matching draft animals," which was later also used to denote "two matching things or people." *Span* is derived from the verb *spannen*, meaning "to attach to a vehicle or in a harness." Although the yoked animals may be similar in terms of color, build and suchlike, this is not strictly necessary for Dutch *span*. In American English, however, this has become typical, and the Dutch word is likely to have been adopted with this narrowed meaning, to distinguish it from the more general English *team* or *yoke*. The word *span* may, of course, also have been borrowed in conjunction with **sleigh** (see 2.12). The verb *to span*, meaning "to agree in color, or in color and size," was derived from the noun (1828).
1769 Wanted, a Spann of good Horses for a Curricle.
1828 A span (pair) of horses is a common expression through all the state of New York, and even as far as Upper Canada. (OED)

Illustration 2.30 – Span (source: Vignettes, Paris 2001)

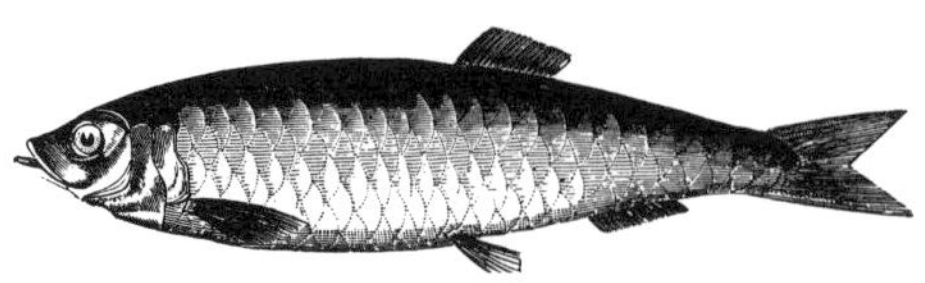

Illustration 2.31 – Spearing (source: Grosser Bildvorlagenatlas, Amsterdam 2001)

Illustration 2.32 – Weakfish (source: J.G. Heck, The Complete Encyclopedia of Illustrations, 1879)

> **1848** *Span.* A span of horses consists of two of nearly the same color, and otherwise nearly alike, which are usually harnessed side by side. The word signifies properly the same as yoke, when applied to horned cattle, for buckling or fastening together. But in America, *span* always implies resemblance in color at least; it being an object of ambition with gentlemen, and with teamsters, to unite two horses abreast that are alike. – *Webster.* This use of the word is not mentioned in any of the English dictionaries or glossaries. (Bartlett)
> **1945** I got a span of mules from the ranche. (Mathews)

spearing, the young of the herring (Craigie, DARE, Webster).
- From Dutch *spiering*, meaning "small silver white fish (Osmerus eperlanus)"; adopted in the seventeenth or eighteenth century and still used.
* The Dutch name *spiering* is used to refer to a type of fish that is indigenous to Europe and is called *smelt* in British English. In American English, the Dutch name was borrowed as *spearing*, but this refers to a young herring or anchovy (which belongs to the herring family), a meaning that the word *spiering* does not have in Dutch. The silver white color is a shared characteristic, and smelt do in fact bear some resemblance to young herring or anchovies.

> **1884** Our Anchovy has recently been sold in considerable numbers in New York under the name "Whitebait," although the fisher--men distinguish it from the true "Whitebait," the young of the herring, calling it "Spearing."
> **1903** The common silversides, or spearing, lives in Gravesend bay almost all the year.
> **1911** The silver anchovy (*Anchovia browni*) ... is also known as "sardine" and "spearing."

weakfish, an edible marine fish of the genus *Cynoscion* and allied genera of the family *Otolithidae* (Craigie, DARE, Webster).
- From seventeenth-century American Dutch *weekvis*, older *weekvisch*, literally "soft fish"; adopted in the seventeenth century and still in use.
* In the European Dutch, the word *weekvis* does not denote a specific type of fish but was coined in New Netherland from two existing Dutch words (*week* meaning "soft" and *vis* meaning "fish") to refer to a new species that did not exist in the Low Countries. The word *weekvis* was used for the first time by the Dutchman Jacob Steendam, who has already been mentioned under **mossbunker**. In 1661, he wrote in his *'t Lof van Nuw-Nederland* about the many types of fish in the area, such as:

> Weekvis, en Schol, en Carper, Bot, en Snoek,
> Ja gy en hebt geen poel, geen water-hoek.

> Of't krielter vol von Visschen; die (te soek)
> Ticht zijn te vinden.

The poem is cited in G. Brown Goode's famous *American fishes* from 1888, in which it is translated as:

> You've weak-fish, carp and turbot, pike and plaice;
> There's not a pool, or tiny water-trace
> Where swam not myriads of the finny race
> Easily taken.

The word was found in American English for the first time in 1791, but is bound to have been used before.

> **1791** Went a fishing ... had 350 weekfish. (OED, citing US source)
> **1796** Bony Fish [found in the US include the] ... Minow, Week fish, King fish.
> **1903** The soft fish without strong and flabby flesh – such as the bluefish and weakfish – spoil quickest.

However, where does the name *weekvis* come from? In the 1903 quote, it is suggested that it has to do with the texture of the meat, which seems most likely. The 1838 edition of the *Encyclopaedia Metropolitana* gives two other reasons, neither of which seems plausible, stating: "This species ... is known to the Anglo-Americans by the name of *Weak-fish*, because considered by some as a debilitating food, and by others from it pulling but slightly on the line with which it is caught." As long as we can find no documentation about the reasons for this name, it will continue to elude us.

The name *weakfish* was initially used to refer to one specific type, as evident from *Bass, Pike, Perch and Other Game Fishes of America* by James Alexander Henshall from 1919: "The weakfish, or squeteague, was first described by Bloch and Schneider, in 1801, from the vicinity of New York. They named it regalis, or 'royal.' In the Southern states it is called gray-trout and sea-trout." The name has since come to be used to refer to other varieties, such as the spotted weakfish, *C. nebulosus*, and the white or bastard weakfish, *C. nothus*.

The name of the fish was verbalized to *to weakfish*, which refers to the activity of catching this fish, mentioned for the first time in 1888 by the aforementioned Goode: "Much the same rig as is used in weakfishing."

2.3 Household effects and everyday implements

American English adopted eighteen words from the category of household effects and implements, which thus ranks third place (after foodstuffs and flora & fauna). General terms, adopted in the seventeenth century and currently very widespread, are **boodle** and **caboodle**. Concrete names of objects are **bake-oven**, **bake-pan**, **bed-pan**, **blickey**, **bockey**, and **cuspidor** – all of which, except for the last one, borrowed in the seventeenth or eighteenth century. With the exception of **blickey** and **bockey**, all these words are still commonly used. This category also includes the word ***trummel***, from Dutch *trommel*, which is listed only once, by Clapin in 1902, who wrote: "An old word, derived from the Dutch, and still lingering in NYC and surroundings in the sense of a round tin box used for cake or bread."

Names for tools include **buck**, **lute**, **sawbuck**, and **skein**: all four were adopted in the nineteenth century and are still in use. Fishing terms adopted in the seventeenth or eighteenth century include **dobber** and **fyke (net)**, which are still used, although **dobber** only regionally. Dutch cleanliness is demonstrated by such words as **boonder** and **file**; both words were adopted in the seventeenth or eighteenth century and are now virtually or completely obsolete. The last two words relate to woolen items: **barraclade**, borrowed in the seventeenth or eighteenth century and now obsolete, and **bed-spread**, borrowed in the nineteenth century and still in use.

Twelve of the eighteen words were borrowed as early as the seventeenth or eighteenth century. All but three are still in use, although some only regionally, which is definitely a high percentage.

A Dutch name for a tool that was adopted in British English as early as the fifteenth century is *schop*. The borrowed noun ***scoop*** was verbalized to *to scoop*, which means "to take up or cut with a scoop." The British – rather than the Dutch – imported it into the US, where it underwent a remarkable change in meaning which, although not attributable to Dutch influence, is interesting enough to mention. At the end of the nineteenth century, American journalists started using *to scoop* in the sense of "to 'cut out' a rival reporter or editor, or his paper, by obtaining and publishing exclusive or earlier news," from which *a scoop*, meaning "news published before any other paper has published it" was derived, which has been used since 1874. This word was readopted into Dutch in the second half of the twentieth century.

bake-oven, an oven used for baking, a Dutch oven, a heavy pot used for baking over an open fire, an outdoor oven (Craigie, DARE).
- After Dutch *bakoven*, meaning "oven used for baking"; borrowed in the seventeenth or eighteenth century and still in use.
* On their travels, the Dutch took with them portable ovens that were new to the English in terms of their shape and appearance. Accordingly, they referred to the object as *Dutch oven* or, with a Dutch name, *bake-oven*, or pleonastically *Dutch bake-oven*. The oven was an ideal travel item for the major westward migration in the nineteenth century. According to Bartlett 1859, the term was often used in the West for the simplex *oven* in a bakery, and it was also applied to the iron bake-pan. The word is still regularly found in American English, even though it is not listed in Webster's Third. DARE points out that in regional American English the meanings "oven used for baking" and "Dutch oven" are nowadays somewhat old-fashioned. In American English, however, the term has adopted an entirely new meaning among loggers, which is unknown in Dutch, namely, a "tent constructed to capture heat from a campfire." The word *bake-oven* is also found in British English dialects, but only since 1886 and borrowed independently.

> **1777** A good two-story brick house ... [with] bake-oven, a cedar log barn, and stables.
>
> **1848** The furnaces are of the simplest construction exactly like a common bake-oven.
>
> **1862** Those three-legged iron conveniences known to the initiated as a "Dutch bake-oven."
>
> **1891** Without looking up from the

eggs she was scrambling in the bake-oven of a few minutes before.
1967 We had what they called a bake-oven ... big enough for eight loaves of bread and twelve to fifteen pies. (DARE)
1969 *Bake-oven* – A cruiser's tent with one sloping side and two ends.

bake-pan, a pan or similar utensil in which bread, etc., can be baked (Craigie).
- Possibly influenced by Dutch *bakpan*, meaning "pan in which something is baked"; borrowed in the seventeenth or eighteenth century and still in general use.
* The compound *bake-pan* may have been coined in English, although its formation was probably influenced by the Dutch word. In the quote from 1879, *Dutch oven* is cited as a synonym for *bake-pan*. A number of Dutch names for household effects were also adopted into Amerindian languages, such as the Dutch word *pan* into Munsee Delaware.
1790 William Robinson ... hath for sale ... iron castings, consisting of tea kettles, bake pans, spiders, ...
1879 One of those flat-bottomed, three-legged, iron-covered vessels, which my reader will now recognize as the bake-pan, or Dutch oven.

barraclade, a home-made woolen blanket without nap (Craigie).
- From Dutch *baar kleed*, *bare kleden*, from *baar* ("naked, having no nap") and *kleed* ("cloth"); adopted in the seventeenth or eighteenth century and no longer extant.
* The word is mentioned only in dictionaries and wordlists (Farmer, Clapin, Carpenter, Webster 1913, Neumann), all based, it seems, on Bartlett 1848. It is not even mentioned in Schele de Vere's *Americanisms*, published in 1872. It may be a relic of the oldest Dutch settlers – which its corruption in American English suggests – and was virtually obsolete by the nineteenth century.
1848 This word is peculiar to New York City, and those parts of the State settled by the Dutch. (Bartlett)
1889 *Barraclade*. – A term which has descended from the old knickerbocker days and is now almost exclusively confined to the regions settled by the Dutch. *Barraclade*, from the Dutch *barre kledeeren* is a home-spun blanket destitute of nap.

bed-pan, 1. a warming pan; 2. a sanitary vessel for use in bed (Craigie, Webster).
- From Dutch *beddenpan*, *bedpan*, meaning "pan filled with coal to heat beds" and "bedpan"; borrowed in the seventeenth century and still in general use in the meaning of "sanitary vessel for use in bed."
* The history of **bake-pan** already showed that the Dutch took all manner of household effects to the US, including

Illustration 2.33 – Bake-oven with bake-pan (source: Menu Designs, Amsterdam 1999)

the *bed-pan*. With the introduction of central heating in both the Netherlands and the US, the term in the sense of "warming-pan" became a historical term. The Dutch word has also existed in this meaning in British English since the sixteenth century, but the European and American continents must have borrowed it separately from one another, as the quotes demonstrate that the first Dutch settlers had brought the item to the American East Coast and that it was a frequently traded commodity.

1635 A bedd pan, 5s.

1648 (in *Mayflower Descendants* X). 199 Item one bedpan, [5s.].

1679 1 smoothing yron & bed pan.

In the sense of "sanitary vessel for use in bed," the word was found in American English as early as the seventeenth century and in British English as late as the nineteenth century, from which it follows that British English and American English adopted this meaning from Dutch independently of one another.

1678 Twoo Earthen bed Pans.

1711 A bed pan & stool pan.

1756 Half a dozen Bed-panns for the Hospital.

Finally, it is interesting to note that the Dutch word *bed* was probably adopted into Mohegan-Pequot in the seventeenth century.

bed-spread, a coverlet or counterpane (Craigie, Webster).
- Perhaps after Dutch *beddensprei*, *bedsprei* ("bed cover"), probably borrowed in the nineteenth century and still widely used.
* The word may have been borrowed from Dutch, but may just as well have been coined in American English; the British English equivalent is *coverlet*. Craigie tentatively refers to Dutch, while Bartlett and Webster (1913) include it without any etymological reference. In 1976, Flexner stated plainly that it is a Dutch loanword, which seems very likely, as it was customary for Dutch housewives to lay a coverlet on the bed. In 1908-09, Carpenter stated that inhabitants of the Hudson Valley used ***spree*** to refer to "a homewoven

Illustration 2.34 – Bed-pan (warming pan) (source: private collection)

bed-quilt, usually blue and white"; this word is derived from *sprei*, a Dutch synonym for *bedsprei*; *bed-* was prefixed to *bedsprei* for clarification.

ca. 1845 I made a bed-spread of his skin, and the way it used to cover my bar mattress ... would have delighted you.
1848 *Bed-spread.* In the interior parts of the country, the common name for a bed-quilt, or coverlet. (Bartlett)
1904 500 honeycomb and crocheted bed-spreads, hemmed, double bed size.

blickey, also **blickie**, **blicky**, a pail or bucket; a lunch pail (Craigie, DARE, Webster).
- From Dutch *blikje*, *blikkie*, meaning "tin, can," diminutive of *blik* ("tin, a pail"); borrowed in the seventeenth or eighteenth century and still used regionally.
* Craigie reports that the word originated within the present limits of the US, and DARE notes that the word is chiefly prevalent in southeastern New York, New York City and New Jersey – all traditional Dutch settlement areas from the seventeenth century onwards. It is noted, however, that the word had spread further in 1894: "*Blicky (blickie, blickey)*: a small bucket or pail. Said to be Dutch in its origin, but used extensively in S[outh] J[ersey], where there are no Dutch." Funnily enough, there were two varieties in 1902: "*wooden* and *tin* blickey," which goes to show that the original meaning of the word had faded in American English, because a Dutch *blikje* is made from tinned sheet iron, and there is no such thing as a "wooden blikje." Likewise, it is interesting to note that the diminutive ending *-ie*, *-ey* was not recognized as such, as American English *blickey* refers to a much larger object than Dutch *blikje*.

1859 *Blickey* ... In New York, a tin pail. (Bartlett)
1881 The tin dipper that hung at the well curb was a "blikke," from the Dutch word "blik," for tin.
1902 *Blick*, *Blickey* (Dutch *blick*, tin). Used for a small bucket or pail, in parts of the States of New York, New Jersey and Pennsylvania. The variety is distinguished by an adjective, as "wooden" or "tin" blickey. (Clapin)
1967 *Blicky* – a pail, usually about four quarts. A woman might use one of these to gather berries. (DARE)
2008 That evening, I went back to the tree with a makeshift blickey (a basket tied around your waist, leaving both hands free to pick) and a berry hook (*The Honest Angler*, June 16)

bockey, a bowl or vessel made from a gourd (Craigie).
- From Dutch *bakje*, *bakkie*, diminutive of *bak*, meaning "bowl"; adopted in the seventeenth or eighteenth century but now obsolete.
* Both Clapin and Farmer have etymologized *bockey* as stemming from Dutch *bokaal* "large drinking cup or bowl," but this is unlikely: the word *bockey* corresponds exactly to Dutch *bakje*, *bakkie*, in which Dutch *a* was transformed into *o* in American English, as it did in *boss* (from Dutch *baas*), for example. However, more interesting is its change in meaning: in American English, the word referred specifically to a gourd, whereas in Dutch it is a general name for "bowl." The word is mentioned only in dictionaries and wordlists (Schele de Vere, Farmer, Clapin, Carpenter, Neumann), with strikingly similar definitions, all of which seem to be based on Bartlett 1848. Apparently, the word had become virtually obsolete by the nineteenth century.

1848 *Bockey*, a bowl or vessel made from a gourd. A term probably derived from the Dutch, as it is peculiar to the city of New York and its vicinity. (Bartlett)
1857 "Yes, Miss Gracey; I wants to git some sugar for de pies in dis bockey," and she exhibited the little wooden bowl, as white as pine could be, which she had been holding in her hand during her conversation with Annie. (Sallie Rochester Ford, *Grace Truman*, p. 415)

Illustration 2.35 – Bockey, advertisement for Saratoga Springs & healthy water (source: The Printing Art, vol. 3, #3, May 1904)

boodle, 1. collection, crowd (*the whole boodle*, the whole lot); 2. counterfeit money; bribe money; a lot of money (Craigie, DARE, Webster).
- From Dutch *boedel*, meaning "estate, property," also "a large quantity" (today the word is only used in the latter meaning in the contracted form *boel*); borrowed in the seventeenth century and still commonly used in slang. See also **caboodle**.
* The word *boedel* was found in American English in the late seventeenth century in the archaic meaning of "property, goods, effects," which is exactly the meaning it has in Dutch and it is also spelled the same way as in Dutch; the quote comes from Craigie:

1699 Elisabeth ... hath the boedel of Jan Verbeek, deceased, in hands.

In the nineteenth century, the slang expression *the whole boodle* emerged, which corresponds to modern Dutch *de hele boel*, or *de hele boedel* in the olden days and dialects. While in Dutch *de hele boel* only refers to objects, in American English *the whole boodle* only refers to people, although in Dutch one can say ***een** heleboel (mensen), meaning* "a whole lot of people." Evidently, the word went its own way in American English.

1833 I know a feller 'twould whip the whool boodle of'em an' give'em six.
1884 At eleven o'clock the 'whole boodle of them,' as Uncle Nahum called the caravan, ... had to boot and spur for church.
1969 She has a whole boodle of cousins. (DARE)

In the nineteenth century, *boodle* acquired all kinds of meanings associated with "money." The general meaning of "money" no longer exists in American English, but it is, however, used regionally, according to DARE, in which informants stated in 1965-70: "He's got boodles [of money]," "He made a boodle [of money]." The shift in meaning from "property, goods" to "money" is obvious; in Dutch too *boedel* was occasionally used to refer to somebody's money and property.

The step to "bribe money" and "illegal money" was made in the US on account of a historical event in which corrupt New York dignitaries were involved; see the quote from 1902.

1858 "Boodle" is a flash term used by counterfeiters ... The leaders [of the gang] were the manufacturers and bankers of the "boodle."
1902 *Boodle*. A word now immensely popular in its present meaning of bribery, plunder, owing its sudden prominence to a corrupt board of elderly New York aldermen, many of whom were convicted of having accepted bribes or boodle for their votes. Was probably thieves' argot a long while, before generally known, meaning the "bulk of the booty." We read in Macaulay's Political Georgies (1828): "And *boodle's* patriot band," with evident sense of bribery and plunder. The word was also current in the West about 1870, with a meaning not far wide of its present signification in American politics. ... Among the thieving fraternity *boodle* is used to denote money that is actually spurious or counterfeit. – Fake *boodle* is a roll of paper, over which, after folding, a few bills are so disposed that it looks as if the whole was made up of a large sum of money. – *To carry boodle* is to utter base coinage, *boodlers* being the men who issue it. *Boodle* is also sometimes identical with the slang expressions *dust*, *rhino*, for money. (Clapin)

boonder, a brush used in scrubbing (Craigie).
- From Dutch *boender*, meaning "brush," a derivation of *boenen*, meaning "to scrub"; adopted in the seventeenth or eighteenth century and now obsolete.
* The word, frequently associated with the cleanliness of Dutch housewives, was probably adopted at an early stage, but never became current outside the East Coast of the US.

1791 Fate early had pronounc'd this building's doom, ne'er te bo vex'd with boonder, brush or broom.
1826 The scrubbing is done with a small broom, made of a blak ash or hickory sapling, after the Indian manner; the body of it is two and a half or three inches thick, and about four inches long; the handle five or six. It is called a *boonder*. (*The American Farmer*, Vol. 8., 1826, No. 7, p. 49)
1889 *Boonder*, ... a brush. Still commonly used in New York and New Jersey.
1902 *Boonder* (Dutch). A word still in use in New York City for a scrubbing-brush. (Clapin)

buck, a sawhorse (Craigie, Webster).
- From Dutch *bok*, meaning "sawhorse," probably borrowed in the nineteenth century and still in use.
* The Dutch word *bok* is probably a shortened form of *zaagbok* (see **sawbuck**), the name of a rack whose shape resembles a billy goat and is used to support a piece of wood while it is being sawed. As far as is known, the word was not recorded in Dutch until the nineteenth century.

1817 He bought himself a buck and saw, and became a redoubtable sawyer.
1839 There were also woodsawyers sitting listlessy on their bucks.

caboodle, in: *the whole caboodle*, the whole lot (Craigie, DARE, Webster).
- Possibly derived from Dutch *kit en boedel*, meaning "house with furnishings"; probably borrowed in the seventeenth or eighteenth century and still commonly used in slang.
* *The whole caboodle* is colloquial, and the expression has been found in many different forms, all dating from the

nineteenth century, including *the whole kaboodle, keboodle, kerboodle, kitcaboodle.* Many different etymological explanations have been provided for the term, although none of them is beyond question. The second part of *caboodle* is probably *boodle*, which is derived from Dutch *boedel* (see **boodle**), but the origin of the first part is more difficult to explain. One theory is that *ca-*, *ke-*, and *ker-* represent an emphatic prefix, which would mean that it is an extended form of *the whole boodle*, which has been seen since the 1830s. *The whole caboodle* is noted somewhat later, namely in 1848 by Bartlett, in the appendix to his book.

An alternative explanation is that *the whole caboodle* is a blend of two expressions with the same meaning: *the whole kit*, listed in Grose's *Dictionary of the Vulgar Tongue* from 1785, and *the whole boodle*, used since 1833, which is believed to have led to *the whole kit and boodle* (an expression found in 1861), which, in turn, pronounced sloppily, is thought to have led to *the whole caboodle*. The form *the whole kitcaboodle* (found in 1891) could also suggest this origin.

This theory is based on the assumption that the word *kit* is British English *kit*, meaning "gear, tools" (which was derived from Dutch in its original meaning of "circular wooden vessel" as early as the fourteenth century), but it seems more probably that the entire expression was borrowed directly from Dutch, which has the slang word *kit*, which means "home, dwelling": *the whole kit and boodle*, which would be a translation from Dutch *de hele kit en boedel*, meaning "the entire house and everything in it."
The other variants such as *kerboodle*, *caboodle* are subsequent corruptions of the form *kit and boodle*.

1848 *Caboodle. The whole caboodle* is a common expression, meaning the whole. I know not the origin of the word. It is used in all the Northern States and New England. The word *boodle* is used in the same manner. (Bartlett, appendix)
1861 I motioned we shove the hul kit an boodle of the gamblers ashore on logs.
1877 *Kerboodle*, all; the whole.
1884 I wish the hull keboodle on ye a Merry Christmas.
1888 If any "railroad lobbyist" cast reflections on his character he would wipe out the whole kit and caboodle of them.
1891 *Kitcaboodle*, used in New England, in the same sense as the preceding *[kerhoot]*. "The whole kitcaboodle."

cuspidor, spittoon (Craigie, Webster).
- From Dutch *kwispedoor*, meaning "spit-box"; adopted in the nineteenth century and still in use.
* The majority of English etymological dictionaries claim that *cuspidor* is derived from Portuguese, which is in fact the ultimate source of the word, but it is likely that American English borrowed the word from the Dutch who, in the seventeenth century, adopted in Indonesia the custom of spitting a wad of chewing tobacco into a special container rather than onto the ground. Obviously, the tobacco plant and the custom of smoking or chewing its leaves come from America. In the sixteenth and seventeenth century, the Spanish introduced tobacco in Europe and subsequently in Asia.

About American English *cuspidor*, Mathews wrote: "The earliest Amer[ican] evidence at present available for this term is in the application papers filed Oct. 10,

1871, by E. A. Heath of N.Y. City, in connection with patents numbered 119,705 and 119,706. These papers use the spelling 'cuspadore.' The word was probably based upon Du[tch] *kwispedoor*, *kwispeldoor*, used of a spitbox, and derived in the East Indies f[rom] Portuguese *cuspidor*, spitter. The *OED* shows that in 1779 a British traveler in New Guinea recorded *cuspadore* meaning a spit-basin, but the word never caught on in British use."

The Dutch custom of chewing tobacco is described in Diedrich Knickerbocker's *A History of New York* from 1809. Chapter 31 states that Governor Willem Kieft wanted to prohibit pipe smoking in New Netherland and, by way of compromise, smoking short pipes was to be permitted. In Chapter 31, Knickerbocker continues as follows:

> From this fatal schism in tobacco pipes we may date the rise of parties in the Nieuw Nederlandts. The rich and self-important burghers who had made their fortunes, and could afford to be lazy, adhered to the ancient fashion, and formed a kind of aristocracy known as the Long Pipes; while the lower order, adopting the reform of William Kieft as more convenient in their handicraft employments, were branded with the plebeian name of Short Pipes. A third party sprang up ... These discarded pipes altogether, and took up chewing tobacco.

The oldest incidences of *cuspidor* in American English date from the late nineteenth century (from Mathews).

> **1875** Here [on a Miss. steamboat] ... bright, fanciful "cuspadores" instead of a broad wooden box filled with sawdust.
>
> **1891** The British Government does not provide cuspidores for its legislators.
>
> **1947** He ran me out of the office with a bust of Walton, a cuspidor, and a string of invectives which has left me permanently bald.

Today, *cuspidor* or *dental cuspidor* is still used to refer to a dentist's basin:

> **2009** Dentist work station/cuspidor or spitoon for sale. Excellent condition, water hydro all works well, asking $500.00.

dobber, a float to a fishing-line (Craigie, DARE, Webster).
- From Dutch *dobber*, meaning "float"; borrowed in the seventeenth or eighteenth century and still used regionally.
* Dutch *dobber* is derived from *dobberen*, meaning "to bob up and down." According to DARE, the word is used chiefly in New York and New Jersey, and is archaic. In 1970, an informant mentioned it as one of the jocular names for doughnuts.

> **1809** He floated on the waves ... like an angler's dobber.
>
> **1844** Sit all on a rock watching your float, or cork, or *dobber*, as the Dutch boys call it, dance merrily over the waves.
>
> **1848** *Dobber.* A float to a fishing-line. So called in New York. (Bartlett, appendix)
>
> **1872** The *dobber*, ... the float of the

Illustration 2.36 – Cuspidor (source: Wikimedia Commons)

[fishing] line, is peculiar to New York. (Schele de Vere)
1986 At home, around Catskill, we always went fishing with a worm and a dobber. (DARE)

file, a cloth used for wiping floors or tables; less frequently: a mop (Craigie, DARE, Webster).
- From dialectal Dutch *feil* "cloth used for wiping floors"; borrowed in the seventeenth or eighteenth century and still used regionally.
* The Dutch word *feil* is a dialect word, probably derived from the verb *vegen*, meaning "to brush." It was adopted into American English and, according to DARE, it still exists in New York, New Jersey, and Pennsylvania, where it is also archaic. Craigie also has the verb *to file*, meaning "to mop or rub with a file" (1850: I've seen you file off tables"), which is probably derived from the Dutch regional verb *feilen* that has the same meaning. There is one informant who mentioned it in 1983.
1850 "You never touch your fingers to a file now-a-days, - do you?" "A file!.".. "Margery calls it a dishcloth, or a floorcloth, or something else."
1859 *File.* A cloth used for wiping a floor after scrubbing. *File-pail*, or *Filing-pail.* A wash-pail. (Bartlett)
1889 *File.* - What is known to English servants as a house-flannel, and a house-maid's pail, goes by the name of *file-pail*, or *filing-pail.* (Farmer)
1983 Some women in Bergen County, N.J. (the "Jersey Dutch" area) still know the word *file* for a cloth with which to remove dirt, especially a floor cloth ... "After you file the floor, you wash out the file and hang it out on the grape arbor till you need it again."

fyke, also **fyke net**, a hoop net for catching fish (Craigie, DARE, Webster).
- From Dutch *fuik*, meaning "bow-net"; borrowed in the seventeenth or eighteenth century and still in use.
* American English adopted the Dutch name *fuik* for a piece of fishing gear that DARE defines as "a funnel-shaped net kept open by a series of hoops and often equipped with wing nets designed to funnel the fish or other catch to the mouth of the net." The name *fyke net* was also used in American English and may have been coined in English or be derived from Dutch *fuiknet*, which is and was used rarely, however. The word *fyke* became prevalent in the US in the rivers in and around New York, and is currently known at least among fishermen. DARE even mentions that it is particularly prevalent in the middle states along the Atlantic Coast.
1832 While some men were rowing up Newtown Creek ... they discovered a sea-dog stealing bass from a fuik of a bass-net.
1859 *Fyke.* (Dutch, *fuik*, a weel, bow-net.) The large bow-nets in New York harbor, used for catching shad, are called *shad-fykes.* (Bartlett)
1871 The meshes ... of fykes set in any of the waters surrounding Long Island, Fire Island, Staten Island ... [shall be] not less than four and one-half inches in size.
1872 The Anglicized term *fyke* from the Dutch *fuik* is however still in use among fishermen for a large bow net, with which certain fish, like shad, are caught in New York harbor (Schele de Vere)
1915 Farther down the river lots of fish are caught in pounds and fike nets.
1968 Snapping turtles in the Pine

Barrens are sometimes a foot and a half long and almost as wide... Pineys trap them in fykes, and fry their delicious white meat.

lute, tool used for scraping off and leveling the moulding floor, tool used to level off freshly poured concrete (Craigie, DARE, Webster).
- From Dutch *loet*, meaning "tool consisting of a handle with a wide iron front piece used to dig or scrape"; adopted in the nineteenth century and still in use.
* The Dutch tool *loet* is not so widespread in American English, but it is still listed in Webster's Third. The quote from DARE shows that it still existed in the twentieth century in the sense of "scoop." DARE suspects that this involves an expansion of meaning, but it seems more probable that the word was readopted from Dutch in the twentieth century, since this meaning of *loet* also exists in Dutch.

1875 *Lute*, ... a straight-edge employed to strike off the surplus clay from a brickmold.

1889 There is a tool used for scraping off and levelling the moulding floor ... It consists of a piece of light pine board, ... set upright, with a long light handle in the centre ... The tool is called a "lute."

1975 *Lute* ... A scoop used with a horse for excavating. It has two handles like a wheelbarrow, and when the handles are held down it digs. It then rides with the dirt flat on the ground, and dumps itself when the handles are lifted. Seems to be a word unique to Maine. It is also a verb: *to lute* a cellar hole. When similar tools became available for attaching to farm tractors, the manufacturers offered them as *scoops*, but Maine farmers continued to call them *lutes*. (DARE)

Today, the name of the tool is found particularly in the compound *scarifier lute*, which refers to an instrument used to level tennis courts and suchlike:

2009 This Scarifier Lute has a sawtooth design that makes this tool an excellent choice when breaking up & grading hard soils. This Scarifier Lute was originally designed for dressing clay tennis courts. The Scarifier Lute is also used by professional landscapers & grounds crews. (Internet)

sawbuck, a sawhorse, especially one with the legs projecting above the cross, any piece of furniture of similar construction (Craigie, DARE, Webster).

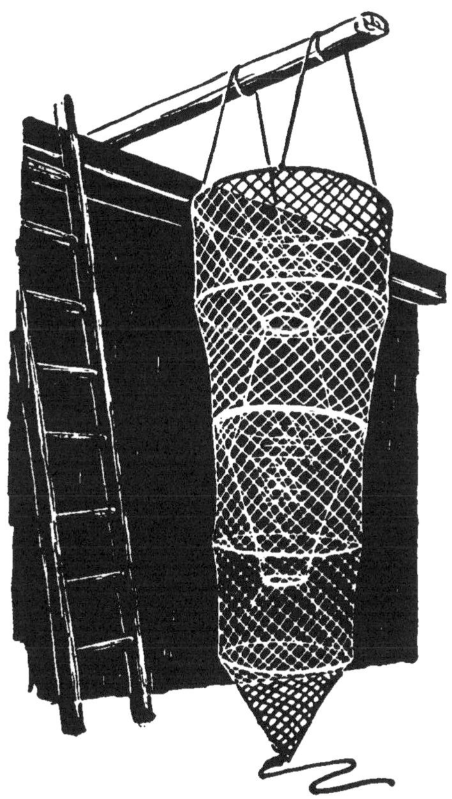

Illustration 2.37 – Fyke net (source: Mathews 1956: 676)

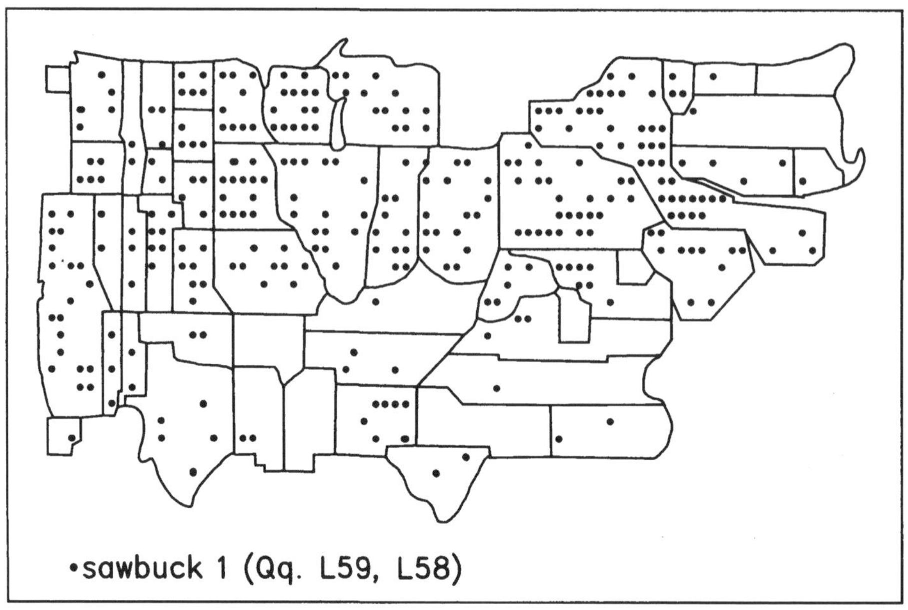

Illustration 2.38 – Map showing the distribution of sawbuck *(source: DARE 4: 759)*

- From Dutch *zaagbok*, meaning "sawhorse"; probably borrowed in the nineteenth century and still in use.

* Dutch *zaagbok* is a compound of *zaag* ("saw") and *bok* ("buck"); the word is occasionally shortened to *bok*, which was also adopted into American English (see **buck**). The rack owes its name to the fact that it is shaped like a billy goat. Or, as the comparison made in British English (i.e., *sawhorse*) indicates, a horse. As far as is known, the word was not recorded in Dutch until the late eighteenth century.

Information from DARE demonstrates that *sawbuck* is very common in various states, except in the south. It is probably on account of its currency that DARE does not state its Dutch derivation. In any case the oldest quote stems from New York and the quote taken from the 1949 Kurath shows that the word was probably adopted from both German and Dutch.

1851 Noon came and he sat down on his saw-buck to eat his frugal Christmas dinner.

1920 In back yards their sawbucks stood in depressions scattered with ... flakes of sawdust.

1949 *Saw buck*, *wood buck*, sometimes simply *buck*, are characteristic of the entire German settlement area in Eastern Pennsylvania, western Maryland, the Shenandoah Valley, the upper reaches of the Potomac in West Virginia, and on the Yadkin in North Carolina. These expressions are clearly modeled on German *Sagebock*, *Holzbock*. *Saw buck* also has rather general currency in the entire Dutch settlement area from Long Island and eastern New Jersey to Albany, whence it was carried into the rest of New York State, into the Housatonic Valley, along Long Island Sound into Connecticut, and into western

Vermont. Here *sawbuck* has the Dutch prototype *zaagbock*. (Kurath)
1985 *Saw buck* ... Device used for holding wood while it is being cut ([*saw*] *horse* 59% [of 60 infs], *saw buck* 20% [of 60 infs] ... [O]ne can no longer accept Kurath's claim ... that [*saw*] *horse* "is in rather general use throughout the Eastern States except for the greater part of Pennsylvania east of the Alleghenies, ... where *saw buck* dominates.")

In American slang, *sawbuck* acquired a meaning that does not exist in Dutch: "ten-dollar bill." This bill is named in allusion to the X-shape (Roman X = 10) of the sawyer's sawbuck; moreover, *buck* is slang for "dollar". The word is mentioned various times in the *Urban Dictionary*. Since the 1920s, it has also been shortened to *saw*.

1850 Send me the two double "sawbucks."
1870 In former years he was ever ready to ... risk what he called a "sawbuck" (a ten dollar note), on his success.
2009 Slap me a sawbuck and I'll get us some beers, fella. (*Urban Dictionary* on the Internet)

skein, a thin iron strip on the lower side of the arm of a wooden axletree to save wear (Craigie, DARE, Webster).
- From Dutch *scheen*, meaning "thin iron or wooden strip against wear"; probably adopted in the nineteenth century and still known regionally.
* The first meaning of the Dutch word *scheen* is "the front part of the lower leg," related to English *shin*. The word is derived from a verb meaning "to cut off," and its original meaning was "narrow, split piece of wood," from which the meaning of "front part of the lower leg" as well as that of "thin iron or wooden strip

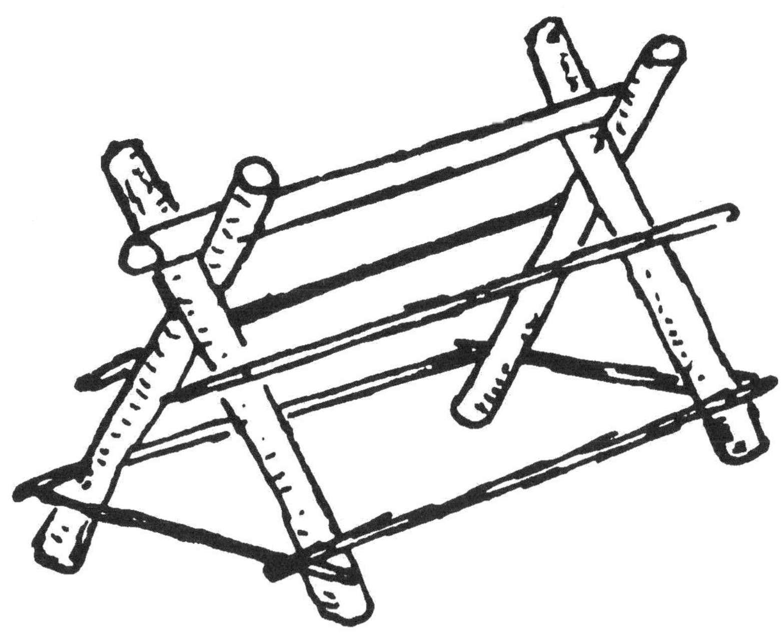

Illustration 2.39 – Sawbuck (source: Kroniek van de Kempen, Frans Hoppenbrouwers et al., Hapert, 1984)

against wear" are derived. The latter meaning was adopted into American English as *skein*, which is not related to the homophonous word that means "coil of yarn or thread." The days of *skein* are numbered in both Dutch and American English, as nearly all carts have been replaced by tractors. In American English, *skein* is pronounced and spelled in many different ways (see the quotes below), whose origins DARE is unable to explain.

1847 The lower "skeen" of the spindle was broken.
1850 Gun Carriage ... *Iron ... 8 axle skeans; 16 nails.*
1899 *Skene* ... A thin iron strip on the lower side of the arm of a wooden axletree to save wear.
1920 In those days [ca. 1865] wagons had wooden axles with an iron skean, and lynch-pins to hold the wheels on the axle.
1967 *Skeen* – the part that a wagon wheel turned on. (DARE)

2.4 Polity and citizens

The Dutch who moved to the US made a living as **boor** or **handler** – two words that were adopted in the seventeenth century but have since lost the meaning they had at that time. They were addressed as **frow** and **mynheer** – two words that were likewise adopted in the seventeenth century and are still known as historical terms. There was one person who behaved as though he were a nobleman, like a *jonker*, and the town **Yonkers** has him to thank for its name.

Although these insignificant and occasional derivations would seem to suggest otherwise, Dutch has had a profound impact on US polity, an impact still noticeable to this day, not so much by the use of Dutch loanwords, but rather by their meanings. For example, a Dutch person's name has become the general term to refer to a US citizen, a **Yankee**. When the Dutch transferred the administration of New Netherland to the English in 1664, the English adopted the Dutch administrative system. They drew up Articles of Capitulation, which conferred significant rights on the Dutch, more than on the people of any other English colony. As Shorto describes in chapter 15 of *The Island at the Center of the World*, it was stipulated that the Dutch "shall keep and enjoy the liberty of their consciences," meaning that they were to have freedom of religion, could go wherever they pleased and were permitted to conduct trade without limitations, for example. In addition, it was agreed that the political leaders of the colony were permitted to continue their work on condition that they pledged allegiance to the English king. In the future, "the city of Manhattan will elect representatives who will have a free vote in all public affairs," which laid an important foundation for the later democratic administrative organization of the independent US.

In concrete terms, this meant, for example, that the **burghers** in New York retained many civil rights that been bestowed on them in 1653 as citizens of New Amsterdam (see also section 1.1 in this book). Later, the meaning of the term **burgher** passed to English *citizen*, as a result of which the Dutch word as such disappeared, but its meaning has remained. The English adopted the Dutch city administration with its

burgomasters, **schepens**, and **scouts** – the latter title did not exist in England and was introduced in the US modeled on the Dutch example, later under the new name of *district attorney*. The name of the city administration's seat, **stadt-house**, was also adopted from the Dutch.

The fact that all Dutch names for important government officials – **burgomaster**, **schepen**, and **scout** – were used in American English for some time highlights the influence the Dutch had on US polity. A Dutch position that was also once adopted but has since vanished is the name for an official who was responsible for serving the interests of the treasury and was called *fiscaal* in Dutch. This name was known in American English for a brief period around 1680 in the shortened form ***scol***, *scule*. American English also had the name *fiscal* for "a revenue officer," but only to refer to an official in an Native American village, not in what were originally Dutch settlements; the oldest quote comes from Boston, which is unlikely to have been derived from *fiscaal*, but rather from Spanish *fiscal*. The reason why the *fiscaal* was the least known Dutch official in American English is probably that his position involved the same duties as that of a *treasurer* in Great Britain. Consequently, there was no reason to adopt the Dutch name and position this time, as was done in the case of *scout*.

Another demonstration of the Dutch influence is the fact that the Americans preferred the word **boss** over English *master* for socially critical reasons. The word **patroon** continued to be used to refer to a large landowner for a long time after the transfer of Dutch rule, but is now a historical term.

It is also interesting to note that the Americans reportedly called the annual date on which the rent expired **Moving Day**, translated from Dutch *verhuisdag*. The Dutch traders who bought fur from the Native Americans are responsible for the name of the Native American tribe the **Seneca**, which was adopted into American English. In the nineteenth century, US politics appropriated two Dutch words: **filibuster** and **overslaugh**.

Most of the seventeen words in the polity and citizens category, which ranks fourth place, were adopted in the seventeenth century and are now historical, the two principal exceptions being **boss** and **Yankee**. Nevertheless, the concepts underlying the Dutch terms in this area have had a permanent influence in the US.

boor, Dutch colonist of the farming class (Craigie).
- From Dutch *boer*, meaning "farmer"; adopted in the seventeenth century and now obsolete as a name for a Dutch settler.
* The Dutch who moved to the East Coast of the US were mostly fur traders and farmers. The Dutch word *boer* was adopted in this period by the English who settled in North America and eventually took over the Dutch colony. The word *boor* was also adopted into British English, but used to refer to the farmers in the Netherlands and Germany and in the nineteenth century to Dutch colonists in South Africa, currently named *Boers*. Webster's Third includes *boor* ("small farmer") and *boer* ("South African of Dutch or Huguenot descent"). The second word was probably adopted from Afrikaans; given its meaning, the first was probably

borrowed from British English and is therefore not a relic of the original Dutch settlers.

1649 We were then informed also of a Dutch ship lately arrived at Hudson's river sent to the free boors at Fort Orange.

1701 I cannot say I observed any swearing or quarrelling ... except once betwixt two Dutch Boors.

boss, 1. foreman; 2. the manager or dictator of a political organization (Craigie, Webster).
- From Dutch *baas*, meaning "master, foreman"; borrowed in the seventeenth century and currently very widespread and productive.
* A few Dutch loanwords in American English have conquered the world, *boss* being one them. Together with **Yankee**, *boss* is without a doubt the most important Dutch loanword in American English, as it is not the name of a hitherto unknown thing or a Dutch invention. On the contrary, the word *boss* reflects a new view on society.

Baas is the normal Dutch word used to refer to a master, foreman, someone who is in charge of servants. The Dutch brought the word to the new colony, where it was rapidly adopted into American English:

1649 Here arrived a small Norsey bark ... with one Gardiner, an expert engineer or work base, and provisions of all sorts, to begin a fort at the mouth of Connecticut.

1653 From our Place of Residence at the Basses house in the Monhatoes.

These oldest forms *base*, *basse* are still spelled with *-a-*, but at the beginning of the nineteenth century *-a-* became *-o-*, resulting in *bos* or *boss* ("I had to return, make an awkward apology to boss, and look like a nincompoop"). The cause of this shift is not entirely certain and may be related to the pronunciation of the Dutch who moved to the US: the pronunciation "boas" was and still is common in regional Dutch, in addition to the Standard Dutch pronunciation with a clear *a*, similar to the vowel in *father*. However, it may also have originated in American English speech.

The word *boss* spread from New York to other states, but it was not widely used until the nineteenth century. *Boss* was adopted widely in the US because it was an acceptable alternative to *master* – the word used in England to refer to a superior. The English who went to the new continent wanted to do away with the hierarchical relations customary in their homeland and therefore looked for an alternative to *master*. For many English settlers who had started their new life in the US as contract laborers, the word *master* had negative connotations. Moreover, white workers objected to *master*, because it was used by slaves. In 1858, Abraham Lincoln spoke the famous words: "As I would not be a *slave*, so I would not be a *master*. This expresses my idea of democracy. Whatever differs from this, to the extent of the difference, is no democracy."

Initially, *boss* was primarily used in everyday speech; a book on etiquette from 1833 states: "Such words as ... *boss* ... are rarely used by the better orders." However, the word gradually spread in the meaning of "boss, foreman," and as a form of address. In the nineteenth century, many instructive comments were made on the proliferation of the word, as evidenced by the quotes below.

1818 *Master* is not a word in the vocabulary of hired people. *Bos*, a Dutch one of similar import, is substituted.

The former is used by Negroes, and is by free people considered as synonymous with slave-keeper. (James Flint in *Letters from America*)
1823 No one, in this republican country, will use the term *master* or *mistress*; *employers*, and the Dutch word *boss*, are used instead.
1848 *Boss*. A master, an employer of mechanics or laborers. It probably originated in New York, and is now used in many parts of the US. The blacks often employ it in addressing white men in the Northern States, as they do *massa* (master) in the Southern States. (Bartlett)
1872 But of all Dutch words familiar to our ear, none has acquired a wider circulation and a stronger hold on our social system than the term *boss*, derived from the Dutch *baas*. It had, originally, with us as in its native land, the primitive meaning of "master," overseer, or superior of any kind, and retains it to this day in a large measure. Even now a *boss* shoemaker, or a *boss* bricklayer means thc hcad of a gang of workmen, who deals their work out to them, and pays their wages, as an English master does to his workmen and apprentices. ... For the proud Yankee, from the beginning, disliked calling any man his master, a word which, as long as slavery existed, he thought none but a slave should employ; and as the relation between employer and employed required a word, the use of *boss* instead of master, was either coined or discovered. (Schele de Vere)

Finally, the word acquired meanings in American English that *baas* does not have in Dutch. In politics, the word *boss* is used in the sense of "a bigwig, a honcho": *the Republican bosses*. How this came about appears from the following quote:

1902 *Boss*. ... In politics, the word *boss* generally carries with it an implication of corrupt or discreditable methods. The renowned Tweed was the first to wear the title in a semi-official way, and "political boss" has now become a familiar expression for a leader whose word is law to his henchmen, and who reigns supreme over them. (Clapin)

In nineteenth-century American English, *boss* also became common as a superlative adjective: *a boss sight* is "a cool spectacle." This meaning has existed since 1867. According to DARE, it is now particularly prevalent in the urban areas in the north, middle and along the Pacific Coast, particularly among African Americans.

1867 If all are fed together, the "boss" cattle fill themselves.
1880 If a coast man wants to express the superlative degree he says "That is a 'Boss' log or a 'Boss suit'."
1971 There was a boss flick on TV last night. (DARE)

The nineteenth century witnessed the coinage of the derivatives *bossy* and *to boss (about, around)*. In the twentieth century in particular, many other languages, including Dutch, adopted the word *boss* from the Americans, to provide for a need, it appears.

burgher, a citizen; a townsman (Craigie, Webster).
- From Dutch *burger*, meaning "resident of a city with all the associated rights"; borrowed in the seventeenth century and now a historical term.
* The Dutch word *burger* was also adopted into British English, but in the US it acquired a meaning and connotation of its own. The word *burgher* was introduced when the Dutch colony of New Amsterdam was granted city privileges on

2 February 1653 and all people automatically became citizens. They retained their existing rights and obligations towards the state, even after the English had taken over.

> **1677** The Court have ordered that the burgers in gennerall bee called together.
>
> **1899** This bald, middle-aged young man, not without elegance, yet a prosperous burgher for all that.

However, the English terms *citizen* and *citizenship* would soon replace their Dutch counterparts. The name *burgher* was, however, preserved but came to refer to a Dutch settler after the transfer of power. Thanks to Washington Irving's satirical *A History of New York, by Diedrich Knickerbocker* from 1809, the word *burgher* will evoke in most Americans' minds the stereotypical picture of a chubby, vest-wearing, pipe-smoking man who possesses all kinds of character traits that Irving subtly introduced by consistently having the word *burgher* preceded by ironically used adjectives such as "adventurous, christian, excellent, fat, good, honest, peaceful, ponderous, respectable, renowned, robustious, self-important, simple, somniferous, worthy": *the adventurous, christian, etc. burgher...*

Meanwhile, the Dutch word *burgher* has become a historical term in American English, but its special meaning has been preserved in the US as the word *citizen*. See also **burgomaster**.

burgomaster, the chief magistrate of a town (Craigie, Webster).
- From Dutch *burgemeester*, meaning "chief magistrate of a town"; borrowed in the seventeenth century and now a historical term.
* The history of the word *burgomaster* runs parallel to that of **burgher**. When the English took over New Amsterdam, the chief magistrate, the *burgomaster* (Dutch *burgemeester*) had to give up his title in exchange for *mayor*; the quote from 1665 already reports on the demise of the title. The word did, however, remain known as a historical term. In 1809, Irving could not resist the temptation of mockingly writing: "the porpoise is a fat, well-conditioned fish – a *burgomaster* among fishes."

> **1664** If the Fort [in N.Y.] be not capable of lodging all the soldiers then the Burgomaster by his Officers shall appoint some houses capable to receive them.
>
> **1665** I have thought it necessary to revoke & discharge the fforme and Ceremony of Government of this his Ma[jes]ties Towne of New Yorke, under the name or names ... of Scout, Burgomasters & Schepens.

The word *burgomaster* still lives on in a different meaning, as the name of a specific type of seagull. This is originally probably a mocking name, as a quote from 1678 states: "The Great grey Gull ... called at Amsterdam the Burgomaster of Groenland" (OED). However, this is no Americanism: the word was adopted into British English from Dutch, and was not found in American English until almost two centuries later, in 1858. Most Americans are likely to know the name from Celia Thaxter's famous poem "The Burgomaster Gull" from 1883 ("For every seabird, far and near, / With an atom of brains in its skull, / Knows plenty of reasons for hate and fear / Of the Burgomaster Gull").

filibuster, 1. one who practices obstruction in a legislative assembly; 2. an act of obstruction in a legislative assembly (Craigie, DARE, Webster).
- Ultimately from Dutch *vrijbuiter*,

meaning "freebooter, pirate"; adopted in the seventeenth century; the new American English meaning emerged in the nineteenth century and still exists.
* The history of the word *filibuster* begins in Dutch, passes through British English and Spanish, and ends in American English in its own form and with meanings entirely of its own. The word *filibuster* was born in the world of Dutch pirates and hijackers who roamed the oceans in the sixteenth and seventeenth century, with or without the permission of the authorities. They were called *vrijbuiters*, which in British English was literally translated into *freebooters* (from 1570). Somewhat later, from 1587 onwards, they were dubbed *flibusters*. According to the OED, the form with *fl-* may have been influenced by Dutch *vlieboot*, which was adopted into British English as *flyboat*. After this British episode, the word moved to the American continent.
In the mid-nineteenth century, Americans joined Spanish rebels who were engaged in fomenting insurrection in certain Latin American areas. In Spanish, these insurgents were called *filibustero*. By analogy with the Spanish name, the Americans who participated in these unlawful expeditions were called *filibusters*, a form that superseded the older *flibusters*.

In the second half of the nineteenth century, *filibuster* ultimately acquired the meanings that everyone thinks of today on hearing the word, namely "one who practices obstruction in a legislative assembly" and "an act of obstruction." The meaning of the term – obstructing political decision-making – already existed earlier, but a specific name for it had not yet been invented. Apparently, this had now become necessary. It was probably an opponent who compared someone who "hijacked" the decision-making of the Senate to a pirate. Unfortunately, it is unknown who used the name *filibuster* for the first time and under what circumstances. In any event, the name provided for a need, for many languages adopted the term *filibuster* from American English, and the freebooter returned in Dutch in a new form and with a new meaning.

According to DARE, the verb *to filibuster* is now particularly prevalent in the Mid- and South Atlantic states among African Americans in the sense of "to talk garrulously, sometimes in an attempt to show off, to stall, or to divert attention from one's own error."

1853 I saw my friend ... filibustering, as I thought, against the US.
1889 The surrender of legislative functions by the majority of the House and the carrying on of business ... only by a humiliating "treaty" with a single determined filibuster is something entirely anomalous in a country ... governed by majority action.
1890 A filibuster was indulged in which lasted ... for nine continuous calendar days.
1913 We intended to continue the "filibuster" until the leaders should give in.
1915 The Senate sits day and night, silently waiting for the time when nature can stand no more and the overwearied filibusters simply cannot talk.

frow, Dutch woman; preceding the name of a Dutch woman: mistress (Craigie, Webster).
- From Dutch *vrouw*, meaning "woman," also as a form of address; adopted in the seventeenth century and still in use,

under the influence of Afrikaans and German.

* The Dutch word *vrouw* was probably borrowed twice, once in the seventeenth or eighteenth century in the diminutive form *vrouwtje*, which can be both endearing and condescending. It was adopted into American English as ***frowchey***, being the form used in all quotes from the nineteenth and the early twentieth century given in the dictionaries of Americanisms.

> **1848** *Frowchey*. (Dutch *vrouw*, meaning "woman.") A furbelowed old woman. Local in New York and its vicinity. (Bartlett)
>
> **1872** ... a *Frowchey*, a wellnigh desperate attempt to render the staid old *Vrouwtje* ..., with which the wives of the good burghers used to be greeted. (Schele de Vere)
>
> **1902** *Frowchey* (Dutch *vrouwtje*). In city of New York and vicinity, a term applied to an old woman, with bent shoulders, and deep-wrinkled, furbelowed face. A wellnigh desperate attempt to render, into English the staid old greeting "Vrouwtje," so much in use amongst the good burgher's wives in Knickerbocker times. (Clapin)

The word was borrowed for the second time as *frow*. The discussion of the word *frow* in the various editions of Webster gives a fair impression of its development.

> **1828** *frow*, a woman. [Not used.]
>
> **1913** *frow*, a woman; especially, a Dutch or German woman.
>
> **1961** *frow* ... 1 a: a Dutch or German woman b: woman, wife, housewife (I'm not going to settle down into a ~ until I've had some fun – Joyce Cary) (a crocodile-hided ... old ~ – A.M. Mizener)
>
> **1961** *vrouw* or *vrow* ... 1: a Dutch or Afrikaner woman 2: mistress – usually used preceding the name of a Dutch or Afrikaner married woman.

It appears, then, that the word *frow* was regarded as unusual in the nineteenth century, but became common a century later, denoting both a Dutch and a German woman, probably on account of the many nineteenth-century Dutch and German immigrants – the Germany word *frau* was also listed in the dictionary at that time. In 1961, *frow* had also acquired the meaning of household drudge ("I'm not going to settle down into a frow") and was now also spelled as *vrouw* and *vrow*, thanks in part to Dutch and in part to Afrikaans. In the twentieth century, the German loanword *hausfrau* (a somewhat degrading name for a housewife) became popular as well.

In summary: in its earliest form, *frowchey* was handed down from Dutch, followed by *frow*, a word originating from Dutch, German and Afrikaans.

handler, one engaged in trade, especially among the Indians (Craigie).

- From Dutch *handelaar*, meaning "trader"; adopted in the seventeenth century and no longer used in this sense.

* In English, *handler* existed and still exists in the meaning of "one who handles something," but not in the sense of "trader," which was adopted from Dutch. For reasons of ambiguity no doubt, the word *handler* lost the meaning of "trader."

> **1697** Ordered the sheriffe to goe throw the handlers, and require them to rebuild the house.
>
> **1754** We, the traders (or handlers) to Oswego, most humbly beg leave to remonstrate to your Honor the many hazards and difficulties we are subject to.

Moving Day, a day on which leases typically expire, causing people to change residences at the same time (Craigie, DARE).

- Probably a translation from Dutch *moving day*; possibly adopted as early as the seventeenth century and still known regionally.

* It is likely if not entirely certain that American English *Moving Day* was informed by Dutch *verhuisdag*, in the specific sense of the "day on which leases expire and people change residences at the same time" – a tradition that is hilariously described by Irving in Chapter 12 of *A History of New York*, as being a custom dating from the time of the first Dutch settlers:

> **1809** It having been solemnly resolved that the seat of empire should be removed from the green shores of Pavonia to the pleasant island of Manna-hata, everybody was anxious to embark under the standard of Oloffe the Dreamer, and to be among the first sharers of the promised land. A day was appointed for the grand migration, and on that day little Communipaw was in a buzz and a bustle like a hive in swarming time. Houses were turned inside out, and stripped of the venerable furniture which had come from Holland ... By degrees a fleet of boats and canoes were piled up with all kinds of household articles; ponderous tables; chests of drawers, resplendent with brass ornaments, quaint corner cupboards; beds and bedsteads; with any quantity of pots, kettles, frying-pans, and Dutch ovens. ... This memorable migration took place on the first of May, and was long cited in tradition as the grand moving. The anniversary of it was piously observed among the "sons of the pilgrims of Communipaw," by turning their houses topsy-turvy, and carrying all the furniture through the streets, in emblem of the swarming of the parent hive; and this is the real origin of the universal agitation and "moving" by which this most restless of cities is literally turned out of doors on every May-day.

Irving was known to be less than particular about the facts, but he was conversant with Dutch traditions. Schele de Vere goes even further, stating:

> **1872** The readers of W. Irving's delightful work on the *History of New York*, in which fact and fiction are so amusingly interwoven as to have deceived more than one acute critic, are familiar with his quaint and graphic description of the origin of *Moving Day*. He ascribes the curious custom which makes the first of May a day of horror in that city, on which every one who is not the fortunate owner of a house, vacates his lodgings and seeks new ones for the coming year, to the first great *move* made by the Dutch inhabitants of Communipaw to New Amsterdam. ... The custom has certainly survived till now ... but it is older than even the ancient settlement called Communipaw. The Dutch settlers evidently brought the custom with them from their transatlantic home, and to this day, in Bruges and its neighborhood, in Verviers and many other parts of Belgium and Holland, the first of May continues to be the general day of moving. It has not only become a characteristic institution of the City of New York, but the tendency to *move*, constantly to shift and drift from one place to another, is, by the

home-keeping Scotch and Irish especially, not quite unjustly looked upon as a sign of instability in the national character.

The fact is that in the Netherlands of the seventeenth century and later, *verhuisdag* existed in the specific sense of "day of the year on which the annual lease expired, typically 1 May"; "May-day, moving day" was a popular expression for a long time, according to the comprehensive *Woordenboek der Nederlandsche Taal*, which describes Dutch from the sixteenth until the twentieth century, which is exactly what *Moving Day* means. Whether this meaning is attributable to the seventeenth-century Dutch settlers or Irving is not entirely clear. All quotes containing Moving Day in this sense postdate the publication of *A History of New York*. However, DARE states that the word is particularly prevalent in New York and Pennsylvania, which may indicate that it is a relic, at least partly, of the first Dutch residents. Whether there is any truth in Schele de Vere's statement that the capricious nature of the Americans is traceable to the same source is left aside here.

1828 "The first of May, what of the first of May?" "'Tis moving time." "Moving time! what is that?" "The time when every body moves."
1832 "Moving day" was, as now, the first of May, from time immemorial.
1841 A sudden light bursts upon me! 'tis "moving day" – the dreaded "first of May!"
1910 One of the inalienable rights of the free American is the privilege of insuring his domestic tranquility by leaving a domicile before it has become too familiar. An annual moving day fits nicely into our practice of the restless life.

mynheer, a polite or respectful form of address to a Dutchman (Craigie, Webster). - From Dutch *mijnheer*, previously also spelled *mynheer*, literally meaning "my sir"; adopted in the seventeenth century and still known.

* *Mynheer* also exists in British English but its derivation was independent from American English; in British English *mynheer* is also used to address an Afrikaner (therefore borrowed from Afrikaans) and, according to the OED, often used humorously or ironically as a form of address. Compare the following quote from 1868: "There is a well-known modern glee commencing –'Mynheer Van Dunk, Though he never got drunk.'"

Craigie lists two meanings for American English, the first being "a Dutchman" or "a generic name for Dutchmen." The original Dutch population of New Amsterdam was also referred to as *the mynheers*: "the mynheers of Nieuw Amsterdam." Apparently, women did not play a role of significance in that society (see also **frow**). *Mynheer* was also used in reference to the Germans of Pennsylvania (the Pennsylvania Dutch), in which the original word "Deutsch" was replaced by the homophonous "Dutch," although the mother tongue of this group was German rather than Dutch.

1701 *Frederick Philips* the richest *Myn Heer* in that place ... was said to have whole Hogsheads of Indian Money or *Wampam*.
1882 The portly "mynheers" turned out their cows to graze.
1890 It gave the good mynheers inexhaustible food for reflection.

The word *mynheer* was also used in American literary works for the purpose of atmospheric description, by who else but Diedrich Knickerbocker in 1809 ("And they all with one voice assented to this interpretation excepting Mynheer Ten Broeck"), but also in, for example, *Hans Brinker or The Silver Skates* (1865) by Mary Mapes Dodge, who wrote in the margins an explanation for each Dutch word that she used in the book, except for the word *mynheer*; evidently, this word was common enough to dispense with an explanation. At the very beginning of the book, she writes: "Most of the good Hollanders were enjoying a placid morning nap. Even Mynheer von Stoppelnoze, that worthy old Dutchman, was still slumbering 'in beautiful repose'."

overslaugh, to pass over (someone) in favor of another; to ignore the rights and claims of (someone) (Craigie, Webster). - From Dutch *overslaan*, which literally means "to pass over"; adopted in the nineteenth century and now archaic.
* New York politicians adopted the Dutch word *overslaan*, using it when someone, a soldier for example, was wrongly passed over for promotion. Hence the word also acquired the meaning "to hinder, bar, thwart or overwhelm." The same word was also adopted into British English, at an even earlier date, but with a different meaning, namely that of "to relieve of an obligation to be able to carry out a more important task." American English seems to have adopted the word separately and directly from Dutch immigrants who were engaged in American politics, perhaps even from the first president of Dutch-American descent, Martin van Buren (the two other presidents with a Dutch-American background were in office in the twentieth century).

Overslaugh was part of the nineteenth-century political jargon employed in New York. In a special message to the Senate, Abraham Lincoln wrote: "I therefore nominate Commander John J. Young ... to be a captain in the Navy ... from the 12th August, 1854, the date when he was entitled to his regular promotion had he not been overslaughed." This meaning of the verb *to overslaugh* is still given in Webster's Third and other modern dictionaries of American English, but it shared the fate of so much other popular political lingo: it was used so frequently that it became worn out, which necessitated the introduction of new synonyms, such as *pass over* and *disregard*.

1848 *To overslaugh.* (Dutch, *overslaan.*) To skip over; pass over; omit. A word used by New York politicians. Mr. Polk intended making Gen. Butler commander-in-chief, and to drop Gen. Scott. But it was found that public opinion would not be reconciled to *overslaughing* Taylor, and he [Gen. Taylor] was nominated. – *Washington Correspondent, N. Y. Com. Adv.*, Oct. 21, 1846. Van Buren is no longer feared as a candidate for the Presidency. He was *overslaughed* in May, when he was a candidate of some promise. – *Letter from Washington, N. Y. Com. Adv.*, Nov. 28, 1846. (Bartlett)
1872 The same verb [*overslaan*], it is well known, has given to English the familiar term of *overslaughing*, for the act of rewarding an outsider at the expense of the person entitled to the preferment by seniority in office. ... A prominent candidate for the presidency is thus said to have been *overslaughed* by his party if a man before unknown is nominated in his place, and army officers complained bitterly during the late Civil War when they saw themselves repeatedly *overslaughed* by civilians serving among the volunteers. "There is no danger that General Grant can be *overslaughed*," predicts the New York

Tribune (Jan. 19, 1871), speaking of the next presidential election. (Schele de Vere)
1903 The spirit of commercialism will overslaugh every less practical consideration.

patroon, the proprietor of one of the tracts of land with manorial privileges granted to members of the Dutch West India Company under the old Dutch governments of New York and New Jersey (Craigie, Webster).
- From Dutch *patroon*, meaning "owner"; adopted in the seventeenth or eighteenth century and now a historical term.
* The Dutch word *patroon* was adopted from French, as was the English word *patron*. Its general meaning is "protector," but in North America it acquired the special meaning of "owner of a large tract of land where the patron acted as lord and protector of a number of settlers" or "privileged large landowner." This meaning dates back to 1629, when the Dutch West India Company issued its charter of "Privileges and Exemptions" setting up the institution of "Patroon," or lord of the manor. The first to be awarded this title were the major investors in the West India Company. The *patroonschappen*, named ***patroonships*** in American English, were designed to attract more people to New Netherland. One of the patron's responsibilities was to entice at least 50 adults to emigrate from the Low Countries to the *patroonship* within four years. The patron had far-reaching privileges and rights. While tenants did not have to pay taxes to the state, they did have to hand over money and goods to the patron, whose patroonship comprised a small town, a church, and other amenities. In 1640, the system was amended to render every American Netherlander of good repute eligible for the position of *patroon*.

The oldest Dutch patroonships have left traces in the American landscape to this day: many of the original names of the patroonships were preserved.
For example, the name of Michael Pauw, who secured the region about Hoboken and Jersey City, together with the whole of Staten Island, still lives on in *Pavonia*. (Staten Island had received its name from Hudson in 1609 – so called in honor of the States General.) The largest colony or patroonship was set up by Kiliaen van Rensselaer, who acquired the greater part of what is now Albany and Rensselaer Counties. The area under the patroonship of Jonas Bronck was called Broncks Land and people who went there said that they were "going to the Broncks," which still lives on in the name *the Bronx*, preceded by the definite article "the." See also **yonkers**.

The word *patroon* was adopted in this meaning into American English, and both the word and what it referred to were preserved even after the English had taken over the settlements from the Dutch. The name *patroon* was used chiefly to refer to large landowners on the East Coast. In 1797, Thomas Jefferson, one of the main authors of the Declaration of Independence and later the third president of the US, wrote: "With the English influence in the lower, and the Patroon influence in the upper part of your State, I presume little is to be hoped." The rights of the patroons were only gradually curtailed after the American Revolution, at the end of the eighteenth century. *Patroon* thus became a historical term, unlike **boss**, which evolved together with the changing society. As late as 1945, however, Anya Seton's historical novel *Dragonwyck* set in 1844 was published, in which the patroon Nicholas van Ryn played a gruesome role; the novel became particularly well-known because it was filmed in 1946.

1744 Jeremiah Ranslaer ... is dignified here with the title of Patroon.
1776 Vast tracts of land on each side of Hudson's river are held by the proprietaries, or, as they are here styled, the *Patrones* of manors.
1781 Messrs. Smith and Livingston, and other pateroons in New-York, will find the last determination also to have been "founded in ignorance and fraud."
1838 They are addressed to a gentleman well known and highly appreciated in the annals of White Sulphur, the grand master of ceremonies for years on festive occasions, and by prescription the Patroon of the establishment.
1848 *Patroon*. (Dutch, *patroon*, a patron.) A grantee of land to be settled under the old Dutch governments of New York and New Jersey. (Bartlett)

schepen, a municipal officer with duties similar to those of an alderman (Craigie, Webster).
- From Dutch *schepen*, meaning "municipal officer"; adopted in the seventeenth century and now a historical term (as it is in the Netherlands but not in Belgium).
* In the olden days, Dutch towns and cities were governed by *schepenen*, assisted by a *schout*, who was the head of police and the judiciary. The day-to-day management of the cities was the responsibility of one or more burgomasters. This organizational structure was taken to the Dutch settlements or patroonships in New Netherland, which were governed by *schepenen* and a *schout*. After it had been granted city privileges, New Amsterdam was the only city with burgomasters. The word and position *schepen* lived on for some time after the assumption of power by the English. The oldest quote dates from the Dutch, New Amsterdam era; the following quotes pertain to the same position in New York.

1660 [They] verified their declaration ... before the court of the burgomasters & schepens of this towne of New Amsterdam. (Mathews)
1664 Jacob Kip, and Jaques Cousseau, are also Chosen to the Office of Schepens, in this City of New Yorke.
1673 Ye Schepens or Magistrates of respective Townes ... [shall] Governe as well their Inhabitants as Strangers.
1809 There is not a Burgomaster, Pensionary, Counsellor, or Schepen – and there are near five thousand of them all – who does not understand this subject better than Hamilton did.

scout: a good scout, a fine fellow (Webster).
From Dutch *schout*, meaning "a local officer vested with judicial functions"; adopted in the seventeenth century and still in use in this context (although it has become a historical term in its original meaning).
* The expression *a good scout*, probably does not refer to a scout "explorer" (a loanword from French), as this meaning differs completely from "reasonable fellow to live with, one who makes life comfortable for those with whom he associates." It is much more likely to be related to Dutch *schout*, the name of a city administrator heading the judiciary and the police. A *schout* had many powers and was therefore a much-feared figure; in addition, Krapp (1960: 158-159) points to

their bad historical reputation: "it would appear that a good scout in the days of New Amsterdam was notable chiefly because of his rarity, and the phrase may thus have persisted even after the schout, as a public officer, had passed into history." Whatever the case may have been, it is virtually certain that two originally different words coincided in modern English *scout*.

1912 Dad's a good old scout and he's pretty sure to do it.
1929 Be like Jerry Dillon now – good scout, Jerry – never sober no more.

It is certain that the Dutch name and position of *schout* were known in and had been adopted into American English at a very early date. The position of the *schout*, who prosecuted criminals on behalf of the government, was unknown in England, where the victim of a crime or their family was responsible for seeking justice. The Yankees found the Dutch system more objective and effective, prompting them to embrace the position of schout, initially under the name *scout*, and introducing this officer in other colonies as well. Eventually, the name *scout* was replaced by *district attorney* – a name that is not used in Great Britain. In 1789, the First American Congress decided: "I also nominate, for District Judges, Attorneys, and Marshals, the persons whose names are below." In 1809, Knickerbocker still mentioned the *schout* in his *History of New York*, but it had become a historical term by then, even in the Low Countries. Incidentally, the first Dutch *schout* was Adriaen Cornelissen van der Donck; see **yonkers**.

1664 Scout, Burgomastrs. & Schepens ordered to summon a court.
1673 91 Deputis ... [were] to make choice ... of one for a skoute and one for a secretary.
1674 At a Jenerall townd Meting ... Captin John semans was Elected ... to kepe Cort with the scaut at Jemeco (Krapp 1960)
1695 Wee doe give & graunt unto the said Pattentees ... full power & authoritie to Elect & nominate a certaine officer amongst themselves to execute the place of a Scoute.
1809 This potent body consisted of a schout or bailiff, with powers between those of the present mayor and sheriff.

Seneca, an Iroquoian people of western New York, a member of such people (Craigie, Webster).
- From Dutch *Sennecaas*, a term used collectively for the Indians in the Lake Oneida region of western New York; adopted in the seventeenth century and still in use.
* In the seventeenth century, an Iroquoian tribe that called itself *Onöndowága'*, meaning "People of the Great Hill," lived in the area around what is called Lake Seneca nowadays. It was the most important Iroquoian tribe in that region, and its members came into contact with the Dutch at an early date. Those Dutch people gave them the name *Sennecaas*, also spelled differently. The word *Sennecaas* is derived from an Iroquoian word, though it is unclear which. Two options have been suggested: it may be either a corruption of the name of their largest village, *Osininka*, or it is derived from *A'sinnika*, the Mahican name for the Oneida tribe, which is a translation of Iroquoian *Oneyode'*, which literally means "standing rock" – a name that goes back to a legend. Whichever is the case, the Dutch named the tribe *Sennecaas*, which was written on a card as early as 1614. In 1657 and 1658, diplomats of the tribe visited

New Amsterdam, and in 1659 and 1660, members of the tribe attempted to intervene in the first Esopus War (see 1.1), regularly urging the Dutch to end the war. As a consequence, the name of the tribe is found regularly in Dutch documents in various spellings, including *Senecke*, *Sinneque*, and *Siniker*.

The Yankees adopted the name from the Dutch, and also spelled it in different ways, with the spelling *Seneca* prevailing in the end, probably under the influence of the eponymous Roman philosopher.

At the end of the seventeenth century, the English called the Seneca together with the other Iroquoian tribes "People of the Five Nations." In the early eighteenth century, the Tuscaroras entered Iroquoian territory and the tribes have since been called "People of the Six Nations." Nowadays, there are still Seneca living in New York State, as well as Oklahoma and Canada. They even employ the name Seneca themselves and *Seneca grass*, *root*, *oil* and *Seneca Lake* were named after them. The tribe is even called Seneca in modern Dutch.

ca. 1614 (*map*), Sennecas.
1664 3000 of the Seneckes, a people in league with the Mohawkes beyond them, are gathered together.
1694 The Mennissinck Sachems ... are afraid that the Sinneques have killed them.
1699 At last one of the great men & one Siniker (Seneca) came over to us.
1709 300 Eastern Indians ... were gon to the 5 Nations to pray leave to dwell with them, and ... others refusing them, they were gon to the Senecas.
1789 The Ondawagas, or Senacas, Cayugas, Tuscaroras, Onondagas, and Oneidas, ... did make, and conclude upon the following articles.
1894 These various tribes of New York Indians, consisting of the remnants of the Senecas, Onondagas, Cayugas, Tuscaroras, Oneidas, St. Regis, Stockbridges, Munsees and Brothertowns, were called the "Six Nations."

stadt-house, a town hall (Craigie, Webster).
- Partial translation of Dutch *stadhuis* (formerly also spelled *stadthuis*), from *stad*, meaning "town, city" and *huis*, meaning "house"; adopted in the seventeenth century and now a historical term.
* A *stadhuis* is a public building housing the municipal council. The first town hall in New Netherland was, of course, erected in the only city, New Amsterdam. In 1653, the old city inn was turned into *Stadt Huys*, where the burgomasters and *schepenen* who formed the municipal council convened every Monday morning.

When the English took over New Netherland, they retained the name *stadhuis* to refer to the municipal center in the original Dutch areas, not outside of them, albeit in the adapted form *stadt-house*. The word *stadthouse* continued to be used until the late eighteenth century. Only after the American War of Independence, which spawned new names for public administration, did the Dutch term *stadt-house* become historical and was replaced by *town-hall*.

1666 The Upper House do think fit ... that Smith repay the Tobaccos next Year which he hath already received towards the building of the Great Stadt house.
1695 When he arrived he went to ye Stadt House.
1744 About 4 in the afternoon, the Company broke up, and from thence went to the Stadthouse.

1769 The stadt-house in the city of Annapolis is so much gone to decay that it is become necessary to build a new one, as well for the holding assemblies and provincial courts, as for providing safe and secure repositories for the public records.

In addition to *stadt-house*, American English also has ***statehouse*** for "the building in which the administrative affairs of a colony are carried on; the capitol of a colony." This word was probably also influenced by Dutch *stadhuis*.
Although the word was used somewhat earlier in British English (likewise informed by the Dutch word), it possibly originated in the US independently of this. It was used in Virginia as early as 1638, prompting some to question the Dutch influence – after all, the first was not built on the American continent until 1653 – but Dutch is likely to have advanced the use of *statehouse* and to have been instrumental in the word's proliferation (OED confirms this); the quote from 1671, for example, stems from New Amsterdam. Other than *stadthouse*, the first part of which is Dutch, the anglicized word spread to far beyond the area where the first Dutch immigrants had settled.

1638 A Levye ... is raised for the building of a State howse at James Cittie. (Virginia; Mathews)

1662 The Vpper howse took into Consideracion the place for the Seateing of the State howse. (Maryland; OED)

1671 The Stone Well in the State-House-Yard. (New Amsterdam)

The word was also used to refer to a building where Native Americans gathered for meetings:

1654 A State-house ... covered round about, and on the top with Mats.

1666 Before the Doore of their State-house is a spacious walke.

After American independence, *statehouse* became the name for "a state capitol" – a function that Dutch *stadhuis* never got to fulfill.

1786 The State House, the Capitol of Maryland.

Yankee, 1. a native or inhabitant of New England, or, more widely, of the northern States generally; 2. a native or citizen of the US (Craigie, DARE, Webster).
- From the Dutch personal name *Jan*, probably from *Jan-Kees*; adopted in the seventeenth or eighteenth century and widely used in a modified sense.
* *Yankee* is one of the most intriguing words in American English about which a great deal has been written, mostly nonsense. However, the question regarding the origin of the word, which is used outside the US to refer to an American, has never been satisfactorily cleared up. Before addressing this issue, let us first look at the changes in meaning that the word underwent. It was encountered in writing for the first time in the second half of the eighteenth century, when the British used it as a derogatory name for a New Englander. It was found for the first time in a letter from the British general Wolfe, who was fighting the French in North America in that year. About the troops from New England that served under his command, he wrote:

1758 My posts are now so fortified that I can afford you two companies of Yankees, and the more as they are better for ranging and scouting than either work or vigilance.

The next occurrence of *Yankee* is found in "Oppression, a Poem by an American":

1765 From meanness first this Portmouth Yankey rose. (OED)

Illustration 2.40 – Archibald Willard's painting "The Spirit of '76" (ca. 1895). Willard painted some variations of this scene: the march of the Yankees on the battlefield during the American War of Independence. The painting is also named "Yankee doodle". (Original painting in the Western Reserve Historical Society; source: Wikipedia)

The poem was published in England "with notes by a North Briton," who comments on this passage: "'Portsmouth Yankey', It seems, our hero being a New-Englander by birth, has a right to the epithet of Yankey; a name of derision, I have been informed, given by the Southern people on the Continent, to those of New-England: what meaning there is in the word, I never could learn." It would appear then that the nickname *Yankee* was not yet known in England, which means that it must have originated in the US, where General Wolfe is likely to have heard it for the first time as well. The following quote dates from 10 years later, in which, again, *Yankee* is not used complimentarily.

> **1775** They [*sc.* the British troops] were roughly handled by the Yankees, a term of reproach for the New Englanders, when applied by the regulars. (OED)

In the same year (1775), however, when the Battles of Lexington and Concord heralded the American War of Independence, the New Englanders adopted the epithet as an honorary nickname, while at the same time etymologizing it:

> **1775** We have by this action [at Concord and Lexington] got in reality the name Yankee, which is an Indian word, and was given our forefathers, signifying Conquerors, which these ignoramuses [i.e., the British] give us by way of derision. (Mathews)

In the same year, the American poet John Trumbull wrote:

> **1775** When Yankies, skill'd in martial rule, First put the British troops to school. (OED)

Added to this is an *Editor's note*: "Yankies – a term formerly of derision, but now merely of distinction, given to the people of the four eastern States." Apparently, the word had now come to be regarded as a neutral term, but the War of Independence (1775-1783) boosted its image considerably: during this war, *Yankee*, also abbreviated to *Yank*, definitively became a name for Americans to be proud of. During the war, the troops sang at the top of their voices ***Yankee Doodle***, a song whose origin is unknown to this day. In 1909, American music historian Sonneck summed up no fewer than sixteen theories, which he then refuted one by one. One of those theories, which is still regularly repeated, is that it is derived from a Dutch nonsense poem, which in turn was derived from a Low German harvest song, but such a song has never been found. This theory caught on thanks to Mary Mapes Dodge's famous children's book *Hans Brinker or the Silver Skates* from 1865, which (following the example of other sources) includes a "harvest song" that was assumed to be very popular in the Netherlands, "though no linguist could translate it":

Yanker didee dudel down
Didee dudel lawnter;
Yankee viver, voover, vown,
Botermelk and Tawnter!

Another theory, likewise regularly repeated and equally unproven, is that the melody was composed in 1755 by Dr. Shuckburgh, a medical officer in the British army commanded by Jeffrey Amherst. According to this theory, the song was originally British and was believed to have been sung by British soldiers between 1754 and 1763 when they fought with the Americans against the French and Native Americans, supposedly mocking the poorly organized Yankees, which General Wolfe also pointed out in 1758. In English, the word *doodle* means "silly or foolish fellow." The Americans then adopted *Yankee Doodle* as a freedom song, just like they upgraded *Yankee* from a condescending term to a complimentary name. The problem with this story is that not a single written record was ever found to confirm that the British had ever sung *Yankee Doodle*. The song was not reported until 1775, emanating exclusively from the throats of American soldiers. What is certain, however, is that the proliferation and appreciation of *Yankee Doodle* and *Yankee* went hand in hand.

From 1784 onwards, the British started using the word *Yankee* to refer to a resident of the US, an American, in general. This use was adopted by other nations and eventually by the Americans themselves. Over time, the negative connotation even transformed into a positive one, thanks in part to the American intervention in the two world wars fought in the twentieth century.

> **ca. 1784** I ... am determined not to suffer the Yankies to come where the ship is. (Nelson)
>
> **1796** Their wit was particularly directed against a "Yankee" who was one of the company. We apply this designation as a term of ridicule or reproach to the inhabitants of all parts of the US indiscriminately; but the Americans confine its application to their countrymen of the Northern or New England States. (OED)
>
> **1833** In England we are apt to designate all Americans as Yankees, whether they are born under the burning sun of Louisiana, or frozen up five months in the year on the shores of the Lake of the Woods.

In the nineteenth century, people from the southern states of the US started calling their northerly neighbors *Yankees*, without any friendly intentions. This use culminated in the American Civil War (1861-1865), but has not yet disappeared, and because the name *Yankees* had meanwhile come to be used as a complimentary name, people added *damned* to clarify how they meant it.

> **1812** Take the middle of the road, or I'll hew you down, you d'---d Yankee rascal.
>
> **1861** The soil may be sacred, but we sacrilegious Yankees can't help observing that it is awfully deficient in manure.
>
> **1865** [The] newspapers have persuaded the masses that the Yankees (a phrase which they no longer apply distinctively to New Englanders, but to every person born in the North) ... are arrant cowards.

In summary, then, the word *Yankee* underwent the following changes in meaning: the British first used it as derogatory name for New Englanders, who adopted it as an honorary nickname, after which it was used to refer to people from one of the northern states or even US citizens in general rather than just New Englanders. Depending on the user, the word has either a positive or a negative connotation.

But where does the word come from? This has been a matter of speculation since 1775, seventeen years after the words' first occurrence in writing. The first theories sought the word's origin in a Native American word. In 1775 (see also the above quote), it was suggested that the word was derived from the name of a Native American tribe, the *Yankoos*, which purportedly meant "invincible ones," but such a name was never found. In 1789, a British officer who had fought in the American War of Independence and can therefore not be called objective suggested that the name was derived from the Cherokee word *eankke* meaning "slave, coward" and that it alluded to the fact that the inhabitants had not helped the Native Americans in the past when they were at war. In the same year, William Gordon claimed in *History of the American War* that around 1713 it was a stopgap of a farmer named Jonathan Hastings of Cambridge, Massachusetts, who used it in the sense of "excellent." In 1822, it was suggested that the word was a corruption of the word *English*, as pronounced by northern Native Americans. Obviously, Washington Irving could not resist the temptation to have his spokesman Diedrich Knickerbocker put forward a new theory. In Chapter 21 of *A History of New York*, he writes:

> The simple aborigines of the land for a while contemplated these strange folk in utter astonishment, but discovering that they wielded harmless, though noisy weapons, and were a lively, ingenious, good-humored race of men, they became very friendly and sociable, and gave them the name of Yanokies, which in the Mais-Tchusaeg (or Massachusett) language signifies silent men – a waggish appellation, since shortened into the familiar epithet of Yankees, which they retain unto the present day.

While none of these claims have ever been supported by supplementary evidence, the list of possible theories is by no means exhausted. In his first supplement from 1945 on pages 192-197, Mencken sums up sixteen different etymologies that have been suggested for the word *Yankee* over time, one even more unlikely than the other. By now, there seems to be a certain degree of consensus that the word is derived from a form of the Dutch first name *Jan* – the equivalent of English *John* and for centuries the most common Dutch Christian name. However, scholars still do not agree on the exact form from which *Yankee* is derived. What is certain, however, is that Yankey was used as a personal name or nickname at a very early date, first as the nickname of a Dutch pirate captain whose real name was John Williams (Jan Willemsz?):

> **1683** [The pirates] sailed from Bonaco ...; chief commanders, Vanhorn, Laurens, and Yankey Duch. ... [They] put eight hundred man into Yankey's and another ship.
>
> **1684** A sloop ...unlawfully seized by Captain Yankey.
>
> **1687** Captains John Williams (Yankey) and Jacob Everson (Jacob).
>
> **1687-8** The pirates Yanky and Jacobs.

1725 Item one negroe man named Yankee to be sold.
1788 The students ... gave him [Jonathan Hastings] the name of Yankee Jon.

These are all references to a specific person rather than uses of the general word Yankee, but they prove that the name was commonly known on the East Coast of the US from the seventeenth century onwards.

Three names have been suggested from which *Yankee* or *Yankey* might be derived. The first, which is supported by the OED, Klein and Quinion, and included in numerous foreign etymological dictionaries, is the name *Janke*, an allegedly Flemish diminutive of *Jan*, the Dutch equivalent of *John*. (The Dutch diminutive of that name has been *Jantje* since the early seventeenth century and before then it was *Janneke*, which was used as a women's name or for little boys, but not for grown men.) An insolvable problem with this etymology is that the diminutive *Janke* has never existed in Flemish: the only form found is *Janneken*, with the linking phoneme *-e-*, exactly as it exists in Dutch. This Dutch linking phoneme was adopted into American English as *-i-*, as appears from *pannicake* and probably *killifish* as well. Compounding the problem is the fact that a substantial number of Dutch diminutives were adopted into American English, all derive from the Dutch form *-(t)je* rather than the Flemish form *-(e)ke*. Compare *blumachies* (from Dutch *bloemetjes*) and *frowchey* (from Dutch *vrouwtje*), referred to under 2.2 **Easter flower** and 2.4 **frow**, respectively, none of which has *-k-*. On www.rootsweb.ancestry.com/~nycoloni/daimm.html there is wonderful overview of the names of immigrants who emigrated to New Netherland between 1621 and 1664. The lists of passengers feature many people named *Jan* (119 times as a Christian name). The women's name *Jannetje* – a derivative of *Jan* and proof that the diminutive form in that period was *-tje* – appears eight times. Finally, there was one *Janneken* on board (with the linking phoneme *-e-*); she came from Noord-Brabant, where a southern dialect is spoken.

An alternative theory is that *Yankee* is derived from the name *Jan-Kees*, which was also a common Christian name and a combination of *Jan* and *Kees*, the latter being the familiar form of the name *Cornelis*. Logeman, who attempted to etymologize *Yankee* in 1929, did not regard *Jan-Kees* as being a double first name, but as a variant of *Jan Kaas*, which literally translates as John Cheese and is a general term to refer to a Dutchman, someone coming from the land of cheese, comparable to the English name John Bull. This explanation is still widely accepted, for example by Mencken in his first supplement and by Barnhart. Again this theory meets with an insolvable problem, this time of a chronological nature: although *Jantje Kaas* is in fact a nickname for a Dutchman, it stems from nineteenth-century Flemish. The name originated in the period when both the Netherlands and Belgium were part of the Kingdom of the Netherlands ruled by King William I, from 1815 until 1830, or immediately afterwards, when the Belgians had separated themselves from the Netherlands. "By ons heet elke hollander Jan-kaes" ("We call every Dutchman Jan Kaas"), wrote Jan Frans Willems, a member of the Flemish Movement. In the Flemish region, *Jantje Kaas* also became the nickname of King William I.

This leaves the Christian name *Jan-Kees* as the only explanation for

Yankee – the only explanation that is *not* suggested in the various etymological dictionaries. The shift in meaning is easy to explain. It was already established that *Jan* was a common name among the first Dutch settlers in New Netherland. The overview on www.rootsweb.ancestry.com/~nycoloni/daimm.html, moreover, shows that there were many men called Cornelis – shortened form *Kees* – (there were 44 men on the lists of passenger whose first Christian name was Cornelis), and that the name *Jan Cornelisz* – possibly shortened to *Jan-Kees* – also occurred a number of times. It is therefore highly conceivable that the English in New England contemptuously referred to the Dutch in the neighboring colony of New Netherland as the *Jannen en Kezen* or the *Jan-Kezen*. After the English had annexed New Netherland, the Dutch Jannen and Kezen simply continued living there. The name *Jan-Kezen* also continued to be used but now in reference to the entire population of New England, including the English-speaking part: *Jan-Kezen* became *Yankees*. The word *Yankees* was regarded as a plural, from which the singular form *Yankee* followed logically. The word was not found in written sources until the second half of the eighteenth century, but that is not surprising for a word originating in speech and starting its career as a – mostly derogatory – nickname.

Funnily enough, the original Dutch character of *Yankee* has been preserved, as appears from the definition in the 1961 edition of Webster that comes after the general definition of "a native or inhabitant of New England," namely: "a New Englander descended from old New England stock; *specifically*: one having qualities of character (as conservatism, thrift, pertinacity, or shrewdness) ... traditionally associated with inhabitants of New England." All these characteristics are generally associated with the Dutch and can probably traced back to the original Dutch settlers.

Nowadays, most Americans and many people outside the US, associate *Yankees* first and foremost with the professional baseball team in New York that has competed under this name since 1913 and is also referred to in full as the New York Yankees. It is therefore astonishing that American English dictionaries do not list "member of the New York Yankees baseball team" as the first definition of *Yankee*. Perhaps in the next edition.

yonkers, of or from the city of Yonkers, N.Y. (Craigie, Webster).
- From Dutch *jonker*, *jonkheer*, meaning "young nobleman, young man of high rank," a compound of *jong* ("young") and *heer* ("sir"); adopted in the seventeenth century and still in use.
* The Dutch nobility title *jonkheer*, also shortened to *jonker*, was adopted into British English in the sixteenth century and was also known in American English, thanks to the Dutch landowner Adriaen Cornelissen van der Donck. Van der Donck, already introduced under **groundhog** (in 2.2), served unsuccessfully as *scout* for *patroon* Kiliaen van Rensselaer from 1641 until 1644. This lack of success was due to the fact that Van der Donck was a rather obstinate man. In 1645, Van der Donck was thanked for his services to Governor Willem Kieft with a parcel of land that he called *Colen Donck*, meaning "Donck's colony." The area was so large that Van der Donck was henceforth called "de Jonker" in the Dutch archives, even though the title was never conferred upon him. People spoke of going to *de Jonker*, or going to *het Jonkers Land*, and in

the English period the name was changed to a phonetic spelling, and the article was dropped. The area retained the name *Yonkers* even after he died, and is called Yonkers to this day.

> **1666** Mary [Oneale] ... laid clayme to a certaine parcell of Land ... Commonly called ye Younckers Land ... [and] brought seuerall Indians before ye Governor to acknowledg the purchase of ye said Lands by Vander Dunck commonly called ye Younker.
> **1668** The Def[endan]t ... hath purchased Land near adjoyning that was the Youncker Van der Duncks.
> **1754** Even if the real line of Jersey is to run from the Forks of Delaware ... to the Station on Hudson's River opposite to the lower Yonkers.

However, there may well be a second reason why Yonkers is called Yonkers. Some years after the death of the original "jonkheer," the estate and surrounding sites came into the hands of a certain Frederick Philipse (more accurately: Flypse), from Friesland. He started out as a simple carpenter but worked his way up to large landowner, partly by marrying well-to-do ladies. He was sometimes referred to as "the Dutch millionaire." In 1693, he was granted the right to call himself "lord of the Manor of Philipsburgh." He possessed another plot of land that was called Fredericks-borough, where Washington Irving, alias Diedrich Knickerbocker, set *The Legend of Sleepy Hollow* – the town of Sleepy Hollow being tormented by a headless horseman. The story has been filmed many times, the 1999 version featuring Johnny Depp probably being the most famous one. Irving was buried there. The town was previously called North Tarrytown but was officially renamed Sleepy Hollow in 1977 to attract tourists. The great-grandson of this Frederick Philipse, who had inherited the title from his great-grandfather, was the last lord of the manor, for he was suspected of sympathizing with the English and therefore banned during the revolution; his estate was confiscated and he had to flee to Great Britain in 1783. According to Schele de Vere, Philipse was to thank for the name *Yonkers*:

> **1872** The Dutch word *Yonker* in the sense of the French Cadet and the German Junker, survives in the name of the town of *Yonkers*. The Right Reverend Bishop Kip states, in his charming sketches of former times, that he remembers visiting, in his early days, the old manor-house of the Phillipse family, still standing in Westchester on the Hudson. "When, before the Revolution, Mr. Phillipse lived there – lord of all he surveyed – he was always spoken of by his tenantry as the *Yonker*, the gentleman by excellence. In fact, he was the only person of social rank in that part of the country. In this way the town, which subsequently grew up around the old manor-house, took the name of *Yonkers*.

This definitely gives Philipse too much credit, but the grandeur surrounding him is bound to have contributed to the survival of the name *Yonkers*, which has grown to become the fourth city in New York State. The word Yonkers, generally spelled with a capital, is usually used to refer to someone or something from the city of Yonkers, New York, for example "a Yonkers resident," and *Yonkersite* is "a native or resident of Yonkers."

In addition, the 1961 edition of Webster also includes the entries *yonker* and *younker*, with meanings such as "a young man" and *archaic* "a junior seaman on board ship." These words are derived from the same Dutch *jonker* and *jonkheer*, but they are later derivatives that may have been adopted from British English, as the terms were known in that language from the sixteenth century onwards.

2.5 The American landscape

The American landscape was new and unknown territory to the Dutch, who were the first Europeans to name certain places on the East Coast of the United States. It is logical, therefore, that a number of those names – twelve, to be precise – ended up in American English, all of which were adopted in the seventeenth or eighteenth century. Half of them are names relating to water: **binnacle**, **binnewater**, **canal**, **fly**, **kill**, and **overslaugh**. **Binnacle** is based on a Dutch compound that was, in all likelihood, coined specially for the American landscape and does not exist in European Dutch.

A wooded and bushy area was called a **bush** or **cripple**, a ravine was called a **clove**, a small passage a **gat**, a sharp bend or point of land a **hook**, and a Dutch settlement a **dorp**. While all those names have been preserved, most of them only exist regionally or as proper names; only **bush** – which has Dutch to thank for an expansion of meaning only – is widespread.

binnacle, a side channel of a river; an inlet from a river into flat land (Craigie, DARE, Webster).

- From Dutch *binnen*, meaning "within, inner" and *kil*, meaning "water"; borrowed in the seventeenth century and still known regionally. See also **kill**.

* The usual Dutch word is *binnenwater*, which was also adopted into American English (see **binnewater**). Both *binnen* and *kil* are normal Dutch words, but the compound *binnenkil* is not mentioned in Dutch dictionaries, although it is a perfectly acceptable formation.

Possibly the compound was formed by Dutch settlers in the US to describe the natural conditions. A number of different spellings were found in American English, as the quote from 1960 shows. According to DARE, *binnacle* is old-fashioned and limited to the New York region. It has been preserved in some geographical names, for instance Binnacle Island and Binnacle Road. Probably the disappearance of the word is promoted by the existence of the homonym *binnacle*, meaning "box or stand for ship's compass," loaned from French.

1860 Commencing on the bank of the Delaware River ... to a point at the mouth of the binacle, thence up along the western side of said binacle at low water mark.

1881 There was a whirlpool, a rock eddy, and a binocle within a mile.

1901 There was a binnekill in the meadow near by.

1902 *Binnacle*. In parts of New York, the flume of a mill stream, a mill race.

1960 Several Dutch words of topographical meaning have survived in close connection with the landscape. ... The word *kill*, meaning creek, stream, of Dutch origin, appears ... in central New York in a word naming

> a bend, or eddy, or a branch of a stream, variantly spelled *binocle*, *binnacle*, *binnekill*, *bennakill*, *benderkill*, with a variant *binnewater* ... The spelling *binnekill* is etymologically the most correct. (Krapp 1960, I, 161)

binnewater, a small lake (DARE).
- From Dutch *binnenwater*, meaning "water that does not flow into the sea, a lake," a compound of *binnen* ("within, inner") and *water*; borrowed in the seventeenth or eighteenth century and still known regionally.
* DARE deems the word old-fashioned and limited to New York, and, like **binnacle**, it is likely to have been introduced by the original Dutch settlers. The word *binnewater* also lives on in geographical names in New York State, as in the town of Binnewater (Ulster County) and in Binnewater Lakes.

> **1901** In the vicinity of Kingston, two words exist side by side, *binnewater* and *binnekill* ... A *binnewater* is a lake.
> **1929** For a time *binnewater* and *cripplebush* were current.
> **1968** Binnewaters – a settlement of Protestants. (DARE)

bush, woods (Craigie, DARE, Webster).
- From Dutch *bos*, older *bosch*, meaning "woods, forest"; borrowed in the seventeenth century and still in use in, for example, place names. See also **cripple**.
* English *bush* and Dutch *bos* are related but differ in meaning: in British English, *bush* is a "shrub," whereas in Dutch *bos* is equivalent to *woods*. Thanks to Dutch, the meaning of English *bush* was expanded in American English. DARE comments that, although old-fashioned, the meaning of "a piece of land covered by forest or shrubbery" is especially common in New England.

> **1779** The Gentlemen took to the Bush and escaped being made prisoners.
> **1872** The word *bush* has in like manner retained in America the original meaning of the Dutch *bosch* more faithfully than in England, where it generally designates a single shrub, while here, as in most British colonies, it means rather a region abounding in trees and shrubs. ... During the war men "took to the *bush*" in the South as readily as at the North, and to this day Western papers report that the "Indians disappeared in the *bush*, when they saw the troops approaching." (Schele de Vere)

Since *bush* and *bos* sound very similar, the word *bos* or the older *bosch* have been replaced by English *bush* in many originally Dutch place names. However, if we look at the oldest incidences of the word, the spelling sometimes reveals its Dutch origins. For example, Bushwick was called *Boswijck* until it was transferred to the English in 1664. Flatbush was called *vlak-bosch* in Dutch, meaning "level forest," "an early spelling being *Flakkebos*. After the takeover of 1664 the name was shifted to an English form, probably by conscious design," Stewart states in his *Concise Dictionary of American Place-Names*.

Furthermore, various compounds with *bush* originated from Dutch *bos* in the sense of "woods, wilderness." In 1976, Flexner wrote: "The Dutch are responsible for such American terms as: ... *bush* (Dutch *bosch*, meaning 'woods, forest'), meaning 'wilderness', 1657; *bush country*, 1855. *Bush ranger*, frontiersman, 1756; *bush fighter*, one who fights from behind rocks and trees, 1760; *bushwacker*, a guerrilla soldier, one who ambushes the enemy in the bush (very popular during the Civil War), 1813."

Illustration 2.41 – Binnewater (source: Steel engraving after a drawing by William Henry Bartlett, 1837)

Dutch, in turn, adopted the word *bush* in the sense of "primeval forest" from English, coining the amusing reduplication *bushbush: hij woont in de bushbush*, meaning "he lives far from the civilized world."

canal, also **canal**, **canawl**, **canol**, **cunnal**, an irrigation ditch (DARE).
- From Dutch *kanaal*, meaning "channel, artificial watercourse, irrigation ditch"; borrowed in the seventeenth or eighteenth century and still used regionally in this context.
* The Dutch word *kanaal* is, like British English *canal*, derived from French for "artificial watercourse." The marshy soil of the Low Countries forced the Dutch to engage in water management at a very early stage, rendering them very skilful in irrigating and draining their farmland by digging drainage ditches which they likewise referred to as *kanaal*. The Dutch, then, were responsible for the word *canal* acquiring the meaning of "irrigation ditch" in regional American English. The word is pronounced in various ways, including *canol* with *a* instead of *o*, comparable to *boss* from Dutch *baas*, and as *canawl*, comparable to *crawl*. The Dutch also created ***polders*** (a word adopted into British English as early as 1604). A US government report from 1856 states: "Polders of three miles square, near the levees of the Mississippi, ... could be diked and drained at a small cost compared with their subsequent value."

1810 Both above and below Albuquerque, the citizens were beginning to open canals, to let in the water of the river.
1835 The Erie canal – here called *canol*.
1939 It is generally assumed that we got the pronunciation *canawl* from the Irish. Mr. Joel Munsell,

the antiquary-printer, maintained that it was of Dutch origin.
1970 They call them irrigation canals out here but it was a ditch to us. (DARE)

clove, a ravine or valley; a mountain pass (Craigie, DARE, Webster).
- From Dutch *kloof*, previously *klove*, meaning "ravine"; borrowed in the seventeenth or eighteenth century and still used regionally.

Illustration 2.42 – "Canal near Dordrecht", painting by Walter C. Hartson. The picture was awarded the $500 prize for Landscapes in The Osborne Company's Artists' Competition for 1905. (source: The Printing Art, vol. 5, #6, Aug. 1905)

* The Dutch settlers, who were used to the flat Dutch landscape, were astonished by the American landscape with mountains, valleys and deep clefts, referring to the latter with the Dutch word *kloof*. This has been preserved in the name Clove River in New Jersey. Regionally, *clove* still exists in New York State, particularly in the Hudson River Valley.

> **1777** The other Part [of Washington's army is] to be commanded by Mr. Green, at the Clove, and Parts adjacent.
>
> **1902** *Clove*. Along the Hudson river, and especially in the Catskills, a narrow gap or valley, a ravine, a gorge. Somewhat analogous to the *notch* of New England.
>
> **1983** *Clove* – As a term for a gap or pass or notch in the hills, the word appears in some place names in Rockland and Orange Counties, N.Y., and farther north in the Catskills. It seems to have been applied especially to a gap through which travelers could most easily cross a ridge.

cripple, low swampy ground usually covered with trees or underbrush (Craigie, DARE).
- Abbreviation of *cripplebush* from Dutch *kreupelbos*, meaning "thicket, undergrowth"; borrowed in the seventeenth century and still used regionally in an altered meaning.
* In the seventeenth and eighteenth century, American English also employed the long form *cripplebush* and the form *creuple*, in which Dutch *kreupelbos*, previously *kreupelbosch*, is easy to recognize. Dutch *kreupelbos* means "thicket, undergrowth," but immediately acquired the meaning of "swamp, swamp covered with underbrush" in the US, which became the meaning adopted into American English. The morphological change from Dutch *kreupel* to American English *cripple* is interesting, because had it been merely a phonetic change, it would probably have been adopted into American English as *crupple*, which sounds the closest to Dutch *kreupel*. In fact, the transformation into *cripple* can only mean one thing: that it is a loan translation, for the Dutch word *kreupel* literally means "lame," exactly the same as English *cripple*, to which it is related. The word must have been adopted by bilingual speakers, who were sufficiently conversant with Dutch to recognize *kreupel* as a term meaning "lame." Nevertheless, they did make a minor translation error, for although *kreupel* literally means "lame" as stated above, it has a different denotation in the *kreupelbos*, namely "crawling." A *kreupelbos* is "a thicket or underbrush, intertwined branches growing everywhere."

According to DARE, the word *cripple* is still used in eastern Pennsylvania, New York and New Jersey. It has also been preserved in a number of place names. In his *Concise Dictionary of American Place-Names*, Stewart writes: "it [*Cripple*] was used as a common noun or place-name generic, but its meaning was forgotten, and a new generic was often then supplied, with resulting names such as Big Cripple Swamp DE, Long Cripple Brook NJ. Also as Kripplebush, NY."

> **1675** The sd land ... lyeth between two Small gutts or Run's, and streatches into the woods as far as the great Swamp or Cripple wich backs the said two Necks of land.
>
> **1676** Martin Garritson was Imployed by Mr. Hans Block (Deceased) to make a way from his Plantation over ye valley & Creuple, into his Backward Land wch Lyeth behinde the Sayd Valley & Creuple.

Illustration 2.43 – Clove (source: The Printing Art, vol. 4, #4, Nov. 1904)

1765 The cripplebush ... lying between the lake and the river.
1929 *Cripple bush* ... a direct borrowing from the Dutch (Kreuple bush) seems to have been current in common speech. The first occurrences are Dutch, and already the word means *swamp* instead of *underbrush.* "Eastward to a certain swamp (kreuplebush)" is a translation from a patent of 1637.
1968 A low, wet area where the Atlantic white cedars grow is called a cripple.

dorp, a (Dutch) hamlet or village (Craigie, Webster).
- Derived from Dutch *dorp*, meaning "village"; borrowed in the seventeenth century and now only preserved in a number of place names.
* The Dutch called their settlements *dorpen*, except New Amsterdam, which acquired city privileges in 1653 and was permitted to call itself *stad* ("city"). The English referred to their own settlements as *villages*, and to those of the Dutch as *dorpen* by way of distinction. The word was therefore never really integrated into American English and would soon disappear, except in historical works and in a number of place names, notably New Dorp, NY.
1668 These are to give notice to all persons concerned in either of the new Dorpses or Villages lately laid out.
1668 We ... are willing to take o[u]r Dividend of Lotts at the furthest New Dorpe or Village.

fly, also **vly**, a swamp or marsh; also, a creek (Craigie, DARE).
- From Dutch *vallei*, meaning "valley"; borrowed in the seventeenth century and chiefly preserved in place names.
* The Dutch word *vallei* is derived from French *vallée*, as is English *valley*. These three words all have the same meaning. In Dutch, *vallei* was also referred to an area through which a river flowed. Dutch settlers used it to refer to a low-level valley or creek, that is, in a slightly different meaning than the word *vallei* had in Dutch. As the last syllable of the word is stressed, the vowel *a* is pronounced very briefly. It is not certain whether the Dutch already said *vlei*, but the English-speaking Americans adopted it as *fly* and *vly*. It is still found in the place names Fly Creek, NY and Vly Lake, NY, and DARE shows it still has some currency as a generic name.
1675 On part frunting on the lott of John Ellisons which lys in the fly.
1695 A valley begginning att the head of a flye or Marshe.
1809 The renowned feuds of Broadway and Smith fly – the subject of so many fly market romances and schoolboy rhymes.
1832 From the Fly or Vly Market, Maiden-lane commenced, exceedingly narrow; ...
1902 *Fly* (Dutch *vly*). In New-York, a swamp, a marsh. The "Fly market" of New-York is well known. (Clapin)

Flexner (1982: 480) also points to the famous Fly Market that was held at the bottom of Maiden Lane in New York City in 1816. The name was derived from the Dutch name *Valley Market* or *Vallie Market*, which was abridged to *Vly* or *Vlie Market*. Due to the phonetic similarity, most English-speaking Americans associated it with insects – flies or fleas – and spoke of Fly Market or Flea Market. The original American flea market was therefore really the Valley or Vlie Market in New York City. *Flea market* did not become a common name for a market sell-

Illustration 2.44 – Cripple, wood engraving around 1880 (source: private collection)

ing used goods in which fleas were often found until the 1920s – and then it was the translation of the name of the famous Parisian flea market, *marche aux puces*.

gat, narrow passage (DARE, Webster).
- From Dutch *gat*, meaning "hole," also "narrow passage"; borrowed in the seventeenth century and only preserved in a small number of place names.
* *Gat* generally means "hole," and was used by Dutch sailors to refer to a narrow and therefore dangerous passage. It still lives on in some place names assigned by Dutch settlers in the seventeenth century, the most of famous of which is Hell Gate in New York City, in which Dutch *gat* has been anglicized to *gate*. In his *Concise Dictionary of American Place-Names*, Stewart writes: "this venerable and wholly respectable name renders the Dutch Hellegat of the seventeenth century. 'Gate' is an approximate translation, since *gat* should be taken more widely, as 'passage.' It was named because of the difficult and dangerous tidal currents." Surviving in only a few place names, the word *gat* has vanished completely from American English. According to DARE *gat* was found in 1930 in Pennsylvania and Massachusetts in the meaning of "a natural sink filled with water, that has an outlet to a creek or river." This word may well have originated from Dutch immigrants in the nineteenth or twentieth century, which would mean that it was borrowed twice by American English, without catching on, however.

> **1848** *Gat*. (Dutch.) A gate or passage. A term applied to several places in the vicinity of New York, as Barnegat, Barnes's gate; Hellegat, now called Hell Gate. (Bartlett)
> **1872** The term *gat* also, meaning a hole, a pot, or a passage at sea, has survived in the name's of many maritime localities. Barnes' Gate, as the English would have called it, thus continues to be *Barnegat*. (Schele de Vere)
> **1902** *Gat* (Dutch). A term applied to several places in the vicinity of city of New York, and meaning a strait, a narrow passage at sea, as Barnegat, Hell-Gate (formerly Dutch *Helle-gat*). (Clapin)

hook, a sharp bend or curve, or a point of land (Craigie, Webster).
- From Dutch *hoek*, meaning "corner, angle, nook, point of land"; adopted in the seventeenth century and still preserved in place names. See also **hooker** in 2.12.
* While English *hook* and Dutch *hoek* are related, their meanings have diverged. Semantically, English *hook* corresponds to Dutch *haak*, and *fishhook* is called *vishaak* in Dutch. The first meaning of *hoek* in Dutch is "corner, angle," hence "nook, point of land," as in Hook of Holland. American English adopted the word in the meaning of "point of land," which has been preserved primarily in place names. In *A Concise Dictionary of American Place-Names*, Stewart states *Hook* is particularly prevalent in Delaware, New Jersey and New York, citing examples such as Bombay Hook Point, Marcus Hook and Hook Brook.

Dutch hooks that are still well-known include Ponkhockie ("little point-hook," i.e., a point of land with a small hook or angle in it), Primehook ("plum-point," from the occurrence of wild plum trees), and Sandy Hook: the name occurs on a Dutch map (1656) as Sant Punt, "Sand Point," but *hoek* was commonly used instead of *punt*, with the same general meaning; the English form is an adaptation.

1670 A Plantation with proporcon of meadow ground for Hay for their cattle on Verdrietiges or Trinity Hook at Delaware.
1781 I am just informed that the British Fleet have again sailed from the hook.
1848 *Hook*. (Dutch, *hoek*, a corner.) This name is given in New York to several angular points in the North and East rivers; as, *Corlear's Hook*, *Sandy Hook*, *Powles's Hook*. (Bartlett)
1872 It was in the same way that the Dutch *hoek*, a corner, though generally modified into English-looking *hook*, is still found as part of the name of certain corners or angular points in the Hudson and the East Rivers, such as *Sandy Hook*, the first land sighted by the traveller from abroad, and *Kinderhook*, high up the river, made famous by the name of its owner, Martin Van Buren. (Schele de Vere)

The most widely known Hook name is Kinderhook, New York, which literally means "children's point"; dating from the early seventeenth century, it may record some incident involving Indian children. This Kinderhook plays a key role in what Quinion calls "the best-known and widest travelled Americanism, used and recognized everywhere even by people who hardly know another word of English," namely the interjection ***OK***.

Over 33 explanations have been suggested for *OK*, but Allen Walker Read eventually demonstrated that it stands for *Oll Korrect*, a deliberate misspelling of *all correct*. In 1838 and 1839, making up abbreviations and acronyms was a popular game in Boston and New York City, and this was one of them. The oldest quote comes from the *Boston Morning Post*:

1839 He ... would have the "contribution box," et ceteras, *o.k.* – all correct – and cause the corks to fly, like *sparks*, upward.

OK is the only one of many abbreviations to have survived, which is due in part to Kinderhook, which is where Martin van Buren, the eighth president of the US, was born and where he died. His ancestors came from the Netherlands and they spoke Dutch at home. When Van Buren was campaigning to be reelected in 1840, his opponents called him "the Dutchman of Kinderhook" and "Old Kinderhook." The Democrats adopted the latter as a complimentary nickname and founded *The Democratic O.K. Club* to help get Van Buren elected for a second term of office. They used *O.K.* or *OK* as a slogan. As a consequence, *OK* became commonly known in the meaning of "all right," even though Van Buren was beaten in the elections. While it is not based on a Dutch name, the term *OK* would never have become so widespread and commonly known if it had not been for a Dutch-speaking president from a town with a Dutch name.

kill, channel, creek, stream (Craigie, DARE, Webster).
- From Dutch *kil*, meaning "stream, creek, channel"; adopted in the seventeenth century and still known. See also **binnacle**.
* The first Dutch immigrants in the US had to give new types of land a name, showing a predilection for the word *kil* when naming small streams and towns on their banks. The entry in Stewart's dictionary of place names reads: "*Kill*. From the Dutch *kil*, properly 'channel,' as in Arthur Kill and Kill van Kull, but more commonly in American usage 'small stream,' e.g. Kil Brook, NY. It is usually preserved as a second element, e.g. Wallkill, Catskill, and without recognition of its meaning, so that an

English generic is supplied, e.g. Wallkill River, Catskill Mountains." Incidentally, *kil* also exists in Dutch as a proper name for various streams and waters, such as *Dordtsche Kil* near the city of Dordrecht, the Netherlands.

1639 The Kil which runs behind the Island of Manhattan, mostly east and west.

1669 some Familyes from Maryland may haue liberty to come and settle upon ye Kill below Apoquenimi ...

1890 *Kill*... a Dutch word denoting any tidal channel or backset water. Haarlem river is a *kill.*

1937 Nearly every body of running water smaller than a river is called a "kill."

1955 The limitation of the term *kill* to the Hudson Valley, Catskills, and upper Delaware Valley ... can be accounted for quite readily. This Dutch equivalent of *brook* or *run* is almost exactly coterminous with the region of significant, or even transient, Dutch settlement.

1981 In the vicinity of Schenectady, New York, where such streams abound, it is common to speak of "a kill" or "the kill." In fact ... I have never heard another generic term used for these small streams.

Craigie also refers to the local use of this name as the name of a strait, especially for the straits separating Staten Island, New York, from New Jersey, often in plural with a singular meaning, for example:

1828 We took the right hand passage round Staten Island, called the Kills.

The word *kill* is still used around New York in the original Dutch settlement areas, as confirmed by DARE.

overslaugh, a sand bar or succession of islands which obstructs navigation in the Hudson River below Albany (Craigie).
- From Dutch *overslag*; adopted in the seventeenth or eighteenth century and still known as a specific name.
* Dutch sailors sometimes referred to sandbanks as *overslag*, possibly because this was where they frequently had to transship goods from one ship into another (in Dutch called *overslaan*) as the water was not deep enough to navigate. *Overslag* is a derivative of *overslaan*. Dutch colonists gave a special, shallow place in the Hudson River the name *Overslag*, which came to be pronounced as *Overslaugh* in English. This is the only incidence of the Dutch word in the US. However, see also **overslaugh** in 2.4.

1776 Having passed the overslaugh, had a distinct view of Albany.

1848 *Overslaugh.* (Dutch, *overslag.)* A bar, in the marine language of the Dutch. The *overslaugh* in the Hudson river near Albany, is, I believe, the only locality to which this term is now applied among us. (Bartlett)

1872 To these names may be added the Dutch term *overslaan*, to skip, to pretermit, which still survives in a few local names, where sandbars suddenly interrupt the free navigation of rivers, as in the *Overslaugh* in the Hudson below Albany, the dread of all *skippers.* (Schele de Vere)

1901 The "overslough" or bar formed in the Hudson ... prevented the steamers of greater draught from getting up to the wharf at Albany.

2.6 Human traits and characterizations

American English borrowed four adjectives from Dutch, two in the seventeenth or eighteenth century (**feest**, **logy**) and two in the nineteenth or twentieth century (**benaut**, **mauger**). Only **logy** is fairly widespread. Three characterizations were borrowed, all three in the nineteenth or twentieth century: **astamagootis**, **dumbhead**, and **rip van winkle**. The final two are still used on a regular basis, but like knickerbockers (in 2.13), **rip van winkle** is a literary rather than a genuinely Dutch borrowing.

Finally, two verbs were borrowed in the nineteenth century: **to ass around**, which is frequently used, and **to have long fingers**, which is only known regionally.

Virtually all words in this category were borrowed in the nineteenth or twentieth century, and four of the nine words are fairly to very common.

to ass around, to fool around (DARE).
- From Dutch *aarzelen*, meaning "to hesitate," previously also "to move backward"; borrowed in the nineteenth century, commonly used in the new meaning and still used regionally in its original meaning.
* Although this may not seem so obvious, the verb *to ass around* has Dutch roots, more specifically in the Dutch verb *aarzelen*, meaning "to hesitate," previously also "to move backward." This verb was adopted into American English in the nineteenth century as *arsle* or *azzle*, in the meaning of "to back out (of a place or situation)." Some decades later the word was found in the meaning "to move when in a sitting position; to fidget." Both meanings still exist in regional American English. When the word made the final step, both its form and meaning changed, unquestionably under the folk-etymological influence of *ass*: the form became *assle*, *assing*, *assen*, its meaning shifted to "to loaf, to idle about restlessly," and the preposition *around* was added, under the influence of the synonymous expression *to fool around*, which is how the current colloquial forms of *to ass around* ("Quit assing around!") and *ass about* originated in the meaning of "fool around."

The fact that the American English verb was influenced by *ass* is remarkable, seeing that the Dutch verb *aarzelen* is derived from Dutch *aars*, meaning "anus" (following the example of the French *reculer* ("to retreat, to move back"), which is derived from *cul* ("backside"). This folk etymology means more than appears at first sight. In any event, the word *aarzelen* underwent its own special development in American English in terms of both meaning (the word exclusively means "to hesitate" in Dutch) and form.

1899 To arsle, to move backwards; to back out.
1930 *Arsle* – To sit unquietly.
1954 *Ass around*: To wander aimlessly.
ca. 1960 *Assle*... Fool around, be obviously idle or in the way of those who are trying to work. *Assing around* is apparently the more common local variant.
1966 Loafing and assening around.
1970 He doesn't have anything to do so he's just assling around – [used by] the old folks; also: assin' around. (DARE)

2004 If you tell him to "ass around," he gives you the wagging finger or the "shame on you" gesture (weblog)
2009 All it needs is for me to quit half-assing around working the problem instead of the solution. (weblog)

astamagootis, a restless person; worrywart (DARE).
- From Dutch *als het maar goed is*, meaning "as long as everything is all right"; borrowed in the nineteenth or twentieth century and still used regionally.
* In Dutch, the phrase *als het maar goed is* is not used to characterize a person. In American English, on the other hand, it has become an evocative expression to refer to a nervous person who is hoping audibly that there are no problems. DARE provides wonderfully illustrative quotes containing the word; see below. Given that the quotes come from Michigan and Iowa, it was probably introduced by Dutch immigrants in the nineteenth or twentieth century, but it does not seem to be very common.
1980 A restless astamagootis? Of course!.. The term no doubt stems from the Dutch clause "Als het maar goed is," literally translated "If it only good is," or – more freely, "If only everything is all right."
1980 A few years ago I was in the midst of an X-raying process when the technician said, "Don't be a restless astamagootis." .. "What did you say?" .. "Don't be a restless astamagootis," she repeated. "The only person I ever heard use that expression was my mother, from Iowa." – "I have it from *my* mother, in Connecticut."

benaut, 1. of the atmosphere: close; oppressive; 2. uncomfortable, especially as the result of anxiety; hard pressed (DARE).
- From Dutch *benauwd*, meaning "having difficulty breathing, oppressive, heavy"; adopted in the nineteenth or twentieth century and still used regionally in Dutch communities.
* The word is used literally and figuratively in both Dutch and American English and is known only in very limited circles. The quotes come from DARE.
1982 The weather is benaut – not threatening, but overcast, dulling; it's lowering, and you know something's coming, though you're not sure what.
1982 A person can be benaut from anything that produces a panicky feeling, including heat, but central is a feeling of anxiety and pain.

dumbhead, a blockhead (Craigie, DARE, Webster).
- After Dutch *domkop* and German *Dummkopf*, meaning "stupid person," literally "dumb head"; probably borrowed in the nineteenth century and still commonly used.
* This term of abuse probably entered American English in three steps, the first being the regional adoption of the words *dom cop*, *dummkup*, also *dum(m)kopf*, meaning "blockhead." According to DARE, this word is predominantly found in the north today. In certain areas, particularly those where the Pennsylvania Dutch settled, it was borrowed from German *Dummkopf*, which also appears from the spelling *dum(m)kopf*. In other areas, especially those that attracted Dutch immigrants and where they say *dom cop* or *dummkup*, it was adopted from Dutch. And, of course, in the oldest

quote, taken from *A History of New York* by Knickerbocker (Irving), it also involves a Dutch derivation.

> **1809** We may picture to ourselves this mighty man of Rhodes like a second Ajax, strong in arms, great in the field, but in other respects (meaning no disparagement) as great a dom cop, as if he had been educated among that learned people of Thrace, who Aristotle most slanderously assures us, could not count beyond the number four.
>
> **1967-69** (*A dull and stupid person*) dumkop. (DARE)

The second step is a change that the English *dumb* underwent in the nineteenth century. *Dumb* is related to Dutch *dom* and German *dumm*. Originally, the word probably meant "not understanding" in Germanic; this was interpreted in English as "destitute of the faculty of speech," whereas in Dutch and German it meant more something to the effect of "foolish, stupid." American English *dumb* also acquired the meaning of "stupid" in the nineteenth century, presumably under the influence of the language used by German and Dutch immigrants. This meaning was recorded in American English for the first time in 1825, and in British English already somewhat earlier, from 1756 onwards, but especially from the nineteenth century. Given the nineteenth-century German and Dutch exodus to the US, it is assumed that the meaning in American English was adopted independently of British English.

> **1825** Do you think the Boston people so dumb as not to know the law?
>
> **1825** The dumb creature believes it.

At the end of the nineteenth century, there were regional forms *dom cop*, *dummkup*, etc. and the word *dumb* acquired the new meaning of "stupid." Now everything was ready for the third and final step: the regional forms *dom cop* etc., with their non-English spelling, could now easily be translated literally into *dumbhead* – a word that caught on immediately and is still one of the most frequently used mild terms of abuse ("Hey, you dumbhead!").

> **1887** We wouldn't elect such a dumbhead to be a hog-reeve.
>
> **1895** What a dumbhead I was, to bide with an empty belly in a place where at least there must be plenty of fish near at hand.
>
> **2008** People are usually referred to as dumbheads when they are drunk or do not agree with you. (*Urban Dictionary* on the Internet)

feest, also **feast**, **fees**, 1. usually with *of*: disgusted with; sated by; made nauseous by; nauseated; 2. untidy, unkempt; filthy (DARE).

- From Dutch *vies*, meaning "dirty, filthy"; (regional) "particular, fastidious"; probably borrowed in the seventeenth or eighteenth century and again in the twentieth century, and still known regionally.

* The Dutch word was probably adopted twice into American English. In the nineteenth century, it was used particularly in New York, where it is likely to have been a relic of the language spoken by the first immigrants. In 1872, Schele de Vere remarked that the word had virtually vanished. This was confirmed in 1904, but in 1908-1909 Carpenter claimed that it was "widely distributed," citing the variants *afease*, *afeese*; while Carpenter does not account for it, it was perhaps contaminated by *averse*: *I am averse from it*, which is very similar to *I am fease of it*. In his first Supplement, Mencken mentions the form *feaselick* in the meaning of "undesirable," which an informant had encountered in

Kingston, NY, in 1937, clearly an American English derivative of the Dutch loanword.

Whereas some sources claim that the word had almost vanished from the area around New York in the nineteenth century, DARE lists various occurrences in the twentieth century, also outside New York State, which suggests that the word was imported again by Dutch immigrants. According to DARE, it is now found chiefly in Dutch settlement areas, particularly in New York and in the north central states.

1859 *Feast.* A corruption of the Dutch *vies*, nice, fastidious. "I'm feast of it," is a literal translation of the Dutch *Ik ben er vies van*, i.e. I am disgusted with, I loathe it. A New York phrase, mostly confined to the descendants of the Dutch. (Bartlett)
1872 The word *feast*, a corruption of the original *vies*, and meaning "fastidious," can hardly be said to exist any longer. (Schele de Vere)
1903 *Feest...* Used in Iowa, s.e., in the expression, "I am feest of it." Also, "It makes me feest," the word *feest* in this latter sentence being the equiva lent of *sick* or *ad nauseam.*
1904 *Feest, adj.* Sated. "I was feest of it," referring to maple sugar, of which the speaker had eaten a large quantity. The word or expression was formerly common in central N.Y., but is now almost obsolete.
1966 "I'm feest of that" means I'm revolted by that. (DARE)
1985 "That room is fees!" means that it is absolutely filthy. (DARE)

finger: to have long fingers, to be thievish, to filch (DARE).
- From Dutch *lange vingers hebben* or German *lange Finger machen, haben*, meaning "to steal, be thievish"; adopted in the nineteenth century and still used regionally.
* The English expression *to have long fingers*, which was not encountered until the twentieth century and, therefore, introduced relatively late, is probably derived from Dutch or German, depending on the location in the US where it is found. It is a nice, euphemistic expression, which was probably the reason why it was adopted, albeit in a translated form. American English also has the term *long-fingered*, which is based on German *langfingerig*, meaning "thievish," for which there is no equivalent in Dutch.

1950 We say: "He has long fingers."
1967-69 *(To take something of small value that doesn't belong to you – for example, a child taking cookies)* He has long fingers; *(if somebody has dishonest intentions, or is up to no good ... "I think he's got –")* Long fingers – for stealing; Long or sticky fingers. (DARE)

logy, also **loggy**, dull, heavy, sluggish, slow (Craigie, DARE, Webster).
- From Dutch *log*, "fat and plump, slow"; adopted in the seventeenth or eighteenth century, and perhaps again in the twentieth century (possibly via English) and still in use.
* The Dutch word *log* was adopted into American English as *logy*, which is included in various nineteenth-century dictionaries of Americanisms. This indicates that the word was adopted as early as the seventeenth or eighteenth century. In Dutch, it is usually used in conjunction with people in the form of *logge*: *een logge man*, and so on. This conjugated form *logge* probably sounded like *logy* to Americans.

The word *logy, loggy* is also included in DARE, in which it is defined as "heavy, slow, lethargic; dull, stupid;

waterlogged"; hence *loginess*. According to information in DARE, the word is commonly used in regional American English, most frequently in the north, north Midland and west (see illustration 2.45), which does not tally with the original settlement of the Dutch on the East Coast. Perhaps the Dutch word was widely distributed at a very early stage, but it is also conceivable that it was reintroduced by later Dutch immigrants and/or that the British imported an English dialectal word that resembled it phonetically and semantically, thus promoting the distribution of the original Dutch loanword. For example, *louggy* or *loogy* exists in Cornish in the sense of "tired, slow"; *loggy* is found in Hampshire and the Isle of Wight, where it means "heavy, slow-moving." In any event, it is likely that American English *logy* was informed in part by Dutch *log*.

> **1848** *Logy*. (Dutch, *log*, heavy, slow, unwieldy.) We have received this word from the Dutch, and apply it generally to men. He's a *logy* man, i.e. a slow-moving, heavy man. "He is a *logy* preacher," i.e. dull. The Dutch say, *Een log verstand*, a dull wit. (Bartlett)
>
> **1863** He huddled down in one corner of the cage, ... like a logy, lumpy, country bumpkin as he was.
>
> **1872** Very much in the same manner Americans are still occasionally heard to speak of a *logy* preacher or a *logy* talker in society, when they wish gently to insinuate that such persons are not peculiarly interesting, but approaching the character of "bores." The term is derived from the Dutch *log*, which means prosy, slow, or dull, and being by its very sound suggestive of its meaning, has maintained its hold on our language. (Schele de Vere)
>
> **1889** *Logy*. – Dull; slow; prosy. Applied mainly to persons of Dutch descent, from *log*, with much the same meaning.
>
> **1902** *Logy* (Dutch *log*, prosy, dull). Heavy, slow, stupid. A term especially applied to men, and which comes very near the meaning of a "bore." A *logy* preacher, a *logy* talker, etc. (Clapin)
>
> **1950** *Logy* ... Dull, inert, slow. Used to describe a person's feelings. "After a heavy meal I feel logy."
>
> **1965-70** It seems to me that when I was a child, people had a wider variety of words that described their physical and mental condition. I never hear now of anyone's feeling logy, but I ride the bus every morning with many who *are* logy. (DARE)

mauger, 1. lean; peaked; sickly; 2. lazy (DARE, Webster).
- From Dutch *mager*, meaning "lean"; adopted in the nineteenth or twentieth century and still used regionally.
* According to DARE, the word *mauger*, which is considered to be archaic, occurs in the northeast of the US. The OED defines the word for regional English (now chiefly Caribbean) as "of a person: thin, lean, skinny" and for regional American English as "weak, feeble, sickly," adding that these are probably independent borrowings in Jamaican and US regional English. According to DARE, other Germanic languages such as German may have been the source of the American English word in certain areas. It was probably borrowed in the nineteenth or twentieth century, for none of the dictionaries of Americanisms from the nineteenth century refer to it. Strikingly, however, the three oldest quotes come from New York, but given

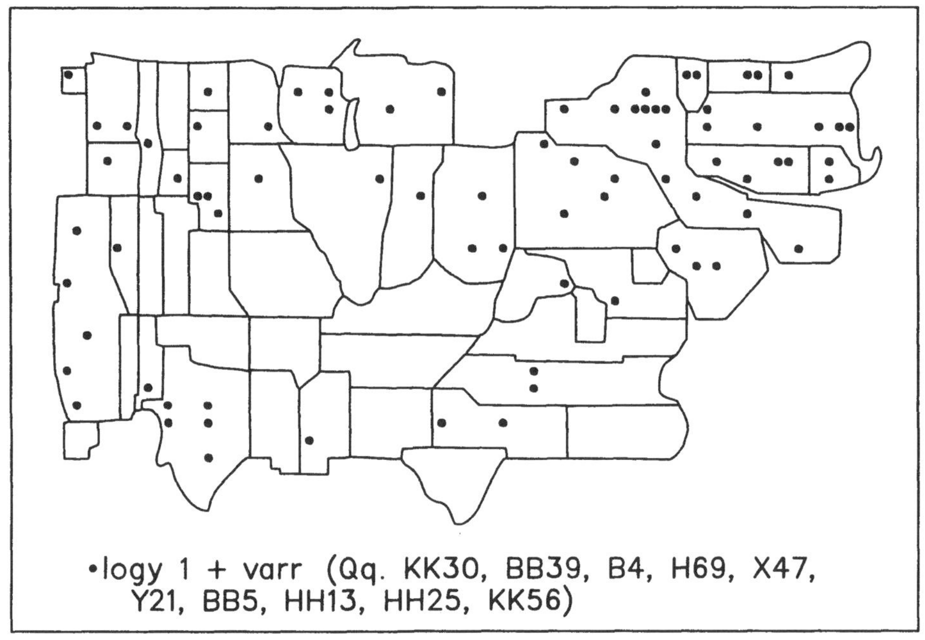

Illustration 2.45 – Map showing the distribution of logy *(heavy, slow) (source: DARE 3: 408)*

that Dutch settled there in the nineteenth century too, this does not necessarily indicate that it is an old loanword dating from the first Dutch settlement. The 1983 quote including "mauger as a spook" is amusing: **spook** (see 2.14) was also borrowed from Dutch, which may have been the donor language of the entire phrase.

> **1890** And though Jenette wuzn't the one to say anything, she began to look kinder pale and mauger.
> **1901** *Mauger*... Sickly, weak in appearance.
> **1903** *Mauger*... Lean, thin ... Common.
> **1932** *Mauger.* Poor, thin, peaked. The grown-up word for *puling*.
> **1983** [An elderly man] described someone as being "mauger as a spook."

rip van winkle, someone not alert to current conditions (Craigie, Webster).
- After the Dutch name of a character in a short story by Washington Irving; adopted in the nineteenth century and still in use.
* Under **knickerbockers** (2.13), it appeared that Washington Irving wrote a number of significant works under the pseudonym Diedrich Knickerbocker, which were set in Dutch communities in the US, including the book *A History of New York* as well as two short stories, *Rip van Winkle* from 1819 and *The Legend of Sleepy Hollow* from 1820, which were published in *The Sketch Book of Geoffrey Crayon.*

The story of *Rip van Winkle* is set in a town situated at the foot of the Catskill Mountains, which is the home town of Rip van Winkle, who is of Dutch descent. He is a well-liked yet lazy man, who is constantly being told off by his wife. One day, he goes into the mountains to escape her nagging. After a number of peculiar events, he falls asleep underneath a tree and wakes up twenty years later. He goes back to his town to discover that his wife and many friends have died and finds himself in trouble for pledging allegiance to King George III, not knowing that the American Revolution has in the meantime taken place.

The story of Rip was a huge success and the name *rip van winkle* came to signify someone who is not alert to current circumstances. Although the story is not of Dutch origin, it exudes a Dutch atmosphere. Rip van Winkle is, moreover, a Dutch name: Rip is, in fact, a Frisian first name, and Van Winkel an existing Dutch surname. The fact that the story was written about the Dutch in the US in the nineteenth century and became so popular that the name of the protagonist acquired a metaphorical meaning used to this day also says something about the Dutch influence in this period. *To be a Rip van Winkle* is to awake suddenly to profound changes in one's surroundings. The name was a source of all kinds of derivatives, such as *Rip Van Winkleish*, meaning "characteristic of or resembling Rip Van Winkle, ignorant of present conditions"; hence *Rip Van Winkleism*, "an outmoded custom or opinion." Hibernating animals were even compared to

Illustration 2.46 – The young Rip Van Winkle, 19th century US actor Joseph Jefferson, in his celebrated character of Rip Van Winkle. Original in New York Public Library (source: Wikimedia Commons)

Rip van Winkle: "By mid-October, most of the Rip Van Winkles among our brute creatures have lain down for their winter nap," someone wrote in 1875.

> **1833** Wm. C. Preston, of South Carolina, in one of his furious tirades, applied to the State of North Carolina, the somewhat degrading epithet of "the Rip Van Winkle of the South."
> **1856** Why, Col. Murray, you are the veriest old "Rip Van Winkle." Have you also been asleep twenty years?
> **2009** Living in a Rip van Winkle world (headline in www.thestar.com)

Illustration 2.47 – The Return of Rip Van Winkle, painting by John Quidor, 1849. Andrew W. Mellon Collection, National Gallery of Art, Washington D.C. (source: Wikimedia Commons)

2.7 Religion and religious festivals

Most of the Dutch who emigrated to the US were members of the *Gereformeerde Kerk* (Reformed Church); the *Nederlandse Hervormde Kerk* (Dutch Reformed Church) was not founded until the nineteenth century. The *Gereformeerde Kerk* had a privileged position in the Dutch Republic in the seventeenth century. While there was considerable freedom of religion and no one was persecuted on account of their religion, civil servants and administrators were expected to be members of the *Gereformeerde Kerk*. This freedom of religion was more restricted in other European countries. Given the central position of the *dominee* (minister) in Protestant churches, it is not surprising that **domine** was adopted into American English, but it was only used regionally and exclusively in reference to a preacher of the *Nederlands Hervormde Kerk*.

As there was no central government in seventeenth-century North America, where, moreover, land abounded, the continent attracted all sorts of Protestant groupings, who could safely found communities and start a new life. Members from various Protestant movements in the Low Countries also moved to the US. Most of the names attributed to members of these groups are international, but three names were introduced into American English from Dutch, namely **dumpler**, **labadist**, and **mennist**. The terms, of which only **mennist** is still used, were borrowed in the seventeenth or eighteenth century.

Four Dutch names for festivals were borrowed: **paas** and **pinkster** in the seventeenth or eighteenth century, and **kermis(s)** and **second Christmas (Day)** in the nineteenth century, none of which are widely known. Accordingly, Dutch did not exert any permanent influence on American English in the realm of religion.

domine, **dominie**, a pastor or minister of a Dutch church, especially the Dutch Reformed Church (Craigie, DARE, Webster).
- From Dutch *dominee*, meaning "clergyman, minister"; borrowed in the seventeenth century and still used regionally.
* Most of the Dutch immigrants who moved to the American continent were members of the Dutch Reformed Church, which was led by a *dominee* – a person who commanded great respect in the community. It is therefore obvious that the name and title of *dominee* were adopted into American English at a very early stage. Nineteenth-century Dutch immigrants, too, brought the word. However, *minister* remained the regular American English word and *domine* was and is used exclusively to refer to a leader of the Dutch community, meaning that it never really became part of American English. According to DARE, it is regionally known chiefly in Dutch settlement areas, especially those around New York, where it is also becoming ever more antiquated.

1669 I perceiue the Little Domine hath played ye Trumpeter to this disorder.

1896 This raised a small Dutch tempest, and the new domine soon left that parish.

1986 I grew up hearing "dominie" in the '50s and '60s, but I know of few

> people who use it today except for special effect (though it's still widely recognized). But Grandma Shirley says that the "older generation" at the nursing home still will say things like "The dominie was here today." (DARE)

An interesting aspect is the second sense of the word given in Craigie, namely that of "a variety of apple," an abridged form of *dominie apple*. This is a large apple variety that was grown in the US in the nineteenth century (even though the oldest quote from 1817 states: "The Domine was imported from England."). Why the apple was called that is not entirely clear, as the name does not exist in Dutch as far as is known. However, since it was a tasty variety, it may have been given the name by way of honor, in the same way as the name *mandarin (orange)*. However, the name of this apple variety has now passed into oblivion.

dumpler, a member of a body of Baptists, who administer baptism only to adults (Craigie, Webster).
- From Dutch *dompelaar*, old name for a Baptist, derived from *dompelen*, meaning "to submerge"; adopted in the seventeenth or eighteenth century and still known as a historical term.
* Baptism arose as a Protestant movement among English refugees in Amsterdam in 1609 and subsequently spread to many European countries. Since Baptists were frequently persecuted, many left the Netherlands, Germany, and other European countries for the US, where baptism is still a major Christian movement. German Baptists were dubbed *Dunker* or *Tunker* in American English, after the German names, derived from *tunken* (*dunken*), meaning "to baptize." A Dutch name for Baptists was *dompelaar*, which was adopted into American English in the form of *dumpler*. *Baptist* is now the internationally recognized word, in consequence of which the other words have become historical term

> **1778** Among the numerous sects of religion with which this province abounds, ... there is a sect ... called the Dumplers.
> **1789** The Tunkers ... are also called Tumblers, from the manner in which they perform baptism ... The Germans sound the letter *t* and *b* like *d* and *p;* hence the words Tunkers and Tumblers have been corruptly written Dunkers and Dumplers.
> **1801** Among the sects which abound in this country, a very distinguished one is that of the Dumplers.

kermis(s), also **kermes**, **kirmes(s)**, an entertainment and fair (Craigie, DARE, Webster).
- From Dutch *kermis*, meaning "a fair"; adopted in the nineteenth or twentieth century and still known regionally.
* Dutch *kermis* is, in fact, a compound of *kerk* ("church") and *mis* ("mass"), and originally referred to a solemn mass held to celebrate the annual Feast of the Dedication, as part of which a fair was held. This fair would soon eclipse the religious festival, causing the meaning of the word *kermis* to shift from "feast of dedication of the church" to "annual fair." Various languages came to know the word from Dutch, one of which was American English. The oldest form, dating from the nineteenth century, is *kirmess*, which was used to refer to "an indoor entertainment and carnival." This is interesting, because in Dutch the word always refers to an *outdoor* festival. The Dutch word also exists in British English, about which Craigie writes: "An independent borrowing

from the Dutch; the usual English form is *kermis*."

> **1885** The kirmess which opened yesterday in New York is a festival which originated in the Netherlands many years ago.
>
> **1888** Salem Mechanic Light Infantry Kirmess ... is destined to prove a brilliant success.

At a later stage, the meaning of the American English words *kermis* and *kirmess* changed to refer to an outdoor festivity, as it did in the Netherlands, possibly under the influence of new Dutch and Belgian immigrants, although German immigrants may also have contributed (the German word is *Kirmes*). The publication of the book *Hans Brinker or The Silver Skates* by Mary Mapes Dodge in 1865 may also have been a contributing factor. Generations of children in the US grew up with it – the book has been on the market ever since 1865 – and they are bound to remember the descriptions of the Dutch fair and the Dutch way of life, as in the following passage:

> Men, women, and children go clattering about in wooden shoes with loose heels; peasant girls who cannot get beaux for love, hire them for money to escort them to the kermis*, and husbands and wives lovingly harness themselves side by side on the bank of the canal and drag their pakschuyts to market."

In this book, the word *kermis* was explained in the margin as meaning "fair."

Illustration 2.48 – Kermis (source: Het vrolijke prentenboek voor kinderen, Amsterdam n.d. [ca. 1850])

In the US, *kermis*, *kirmess*, *kermiss* now means "an entertainment and fair, usually for the purpose of raising money," according to Webster, and is still used regionally in the meaning of "a community festival usually held in the fall and sponsored by a local church." DARE localizes its use especially to east-central Wisconsin. It is often associated with Belgian immigrants, a number of whom may have spoken French. The French term is *kermesse*, which is also derived from Dutch.

1931 There is no current holiday so distinctly Belgian as the "kirmess".. In our neighborhood these harvest festivals are a tradition. They begin in late August at Grandlez now Lincoln and spread from community to community – Brussels, Walhain, Rosière, Thiry Daems, Duvall, Sansouver, Tonet, Dyckesville, Namur.
1949 Near [New] Holstein, which was a Protestant '48er community, there was a small Catholic village St. Anna. Every summer, a festival known as "Kermes" was regularly held there in connection with the church.
1950 Kermiss and Schut – popular in Holland communities. Kermiss was a two-day dance, now obsolete.
1989 Each of the Catholic churches had kermis. Kermis was held on that church's saint's feast day ... First there'd be mass, then a potluck – a big dinner – and then people played cards and danced. We haven't had kermis here for awhile though; it kind of petered out. (DARE)

labadist, member of a communistic sect of radical pietists (Craigie, Webster).
- From Dutch *labadist*, a follower of Jean de Labadie (1610-74); adopted in the seventeenth century and still known as a historical term.
* The followers of French sect leader Jean de Labadie are called *labadists*, a name undoubtedly rooted in French. Labadie had a conflict with the authorities and fled to the Netherlands in 1666, where he surrounded himself with followers and, thereafter, was forced once again to take off due to problems with the authorities. Ultimately, there were small labadist communities at various locations in the Netherlands, the largest being located in the province of Friesland. When Labadie died, labadist communities attempted to found communities outside Europe, including an unsuccessful attempt in Suriname. In 1679, two prominent labadists, Jasper Danckaerts and Pieter Sluyter, went to North America to buy a suitable tract of land, ending up in what is currently called Cecil County, Maryland. In 1683, a group of labadists moved there, but only between 100 and 200 people were living in what was called "Labadie Tract" (De Jong, 1975: 44-46). In the early eighteenth century, most members gradually left the area but they had added the word *labadist* to the American English vocabulary by then. In addition, Danckaerts wrote a journal of his travels in North America in 1679 and 1680, which is still regarded as an important document because it is one of the first records of seventeenth-century life on the East Coast of the US.

1756 After we had dined, we took our Leave, and a Friend, my Guide, went with me, and brought me to a People call'd *Labadies*, where we were civilly entertained in their Way.
1881 Bohemia Manor, in Cecil County, Maryland, where the Labadists under Peter Schluter had formed a settlement.

1884 The Labadist travelers complained in 1680 that the garden vegetables in one part of Maryland were "few and coarse."

mennist, mennonite (Craigie, Webster).
- From Dutch *menist*, previously also *mennist*, a follower of Menno Simonsz; adopted in the seventeenth century and still in use.
* The followers of the Frisian Mennonite church reformer Menno Simonsz (1496-1561) called themselves *mennonieten* or *menisten*. Simonsz founded congregations in Holland and northwestern Germany, and congregations were founded in many other European countries after his death. In the US, the first congregation was founded in 1683 at Germantown, Pennsylvania, at the instigation of the English Quaker, William Penn, founder of the English colony "Provincie Pennsylvania" in North America, which was to become the American state Pennsylvania (Pennsylvania literally means "Penn's woods"). Penn's mother was Dutch and he visited the Netherlands several times to recruit followers.

Thirteen families moved to Germantown, and contrary to what the name of the town seems to suggest, a number of them came from the Netherlands. Initially, the Dutch even dominated in number: most names of the first inhabitants were Dutch, and, in 1690, all but eight or ten of the 175 residents came from the Netherlands or a northern German town immediately across the Dutch border. Until 1710, Germantown remained predominantlyDutch, after which the number of German immigrants grew rapidly (De Jong 1975: 40-44). One of the words that these Dutch Mennonites added to American English is the word *mennist*, which is only used in Dutch alongside the international name *mennoniet* or *mennonite*.

1759 The Nine Waggoners ... where [i.e. were] chiefly Menists.
1771 In the City of Philadelphia you see Churchmen, Quakers, Lutherans, Calvinists, Moravians, Catholics, Menists, ...
1869 The Mennists in many outward circumstances very much resemble the Society of Friends.

paas, the festival of Easter (Craigie).
- From Dutch *Pasen*, also abridged to *Paas*, meaning "Easter"; adopted in the seventeenth or eighteenth century but now only known in the regional plant names *pass blummies* and *poss flower* (see **Easter flower** in 2.2).
* Nineteenth-century dictionaries of Americanisms still include the words *paas* (also *paus*) and *paas-egg*, which are derived from Dutch *Pasen* and *paasei*. The regular English words are *Easter* and *Easter egg*. All these words were used in and around New York but, in contrast to **pinkster**, have since disappeared entirely. Dutch *Pasen* has only been preserved in the regional plant names *pass blummies* and *poss flower*, but the original Dutch word has changed morphologically and semantically beyond recognition.

1830 Thou canst lighten thy heart in the Paus merry-makings.
1859 *Paas Eggs*. Hard-boiled eggs cracked together by New York boys at the Easter season. They are often dyed of various colors in boiling. (Bartlett)
1872 This attachment to old words and old customs causes also the word *Paas* (Paasch) still to be used for Easter in many families of New York, and children especially are fond of calling their bright-colored Easter

eggs by their venerable name of *Paas-eggs*, when merrily cracking them against each other in Russian fashion, trying to break their neighbor's and not their own. (Schele de Vere)
1908-09 *Paas*, n., Easter [Du., *Paasch* same meaning]. ... The word also occurs in: *Paas-day*, Easter; *Paas-flower*, the yellow daffodil. (Carpenter)

pinkster, **pinxter**, the festival of Pentecost or Whitsuntide (Craigie, DARE, Webster).
- From Dutch *Pinkster(en)*, meaning "Whitsuntide"; adopted in the seventeenth or eighteenth century and still known.
* Whereas the Dutch name for Easter – *Paas* or *Pasen* – has disappeared from American English, *pinkster* is still listed in the dictionaries, albeit as a regional word that was particularly prevalent around New York and is now used only in talking about times past. Variants are *pinxter*, *pinckster* en *pinkster day*, and the word *pinkster* has also been preserved in the flower name **pinkster flower** (see 2.2).

1797 The settlements along the river are dutch, it is the holiday they call pinkster & every public house is crowded with merry makers.
1821 Upon my word you'd pass well at a pinkster frolic.
1902 *Pinxter* (Dutch *Pinkster*). A familiar name for Whitsuntide in the States of New York and New Jersey, where *Pinxter Monday* is specially well known as a day of great rejoicings. (Clapin)
1945 Pinkster ... I believe the celebration was on "Pink Monday." Traces of it survived into the early twentieth century; at least my great-aunt, born about 1860, used to mention the festival as late, say, as 1910. She made, I think, a special kind of cake for the day, and gave me, a small boy, some slight present. The Biblical descriptions of Pentecost suggest that the feast was modeled on stories from the Bible ... I cannot recall ever hearing it mentioned by anyone else.

Perhaps one of the reasons why the Dutch words *Pasen*, *Pinksteren* and *Tweede Kerstdag* (see **second Christmas (Day)**) were adopted into American English is that contrary to the British, Americans, and most other nations, the Dutch and Germans have a *second* day off after these holidays. In the nineteenth century, that second day was called *Pinkster Monday*, a public festival of African Americans, who celebrated a kind of carnival on that day.

ca. 1831 The first Monday in June, or as the Dutch call it, *Pinckster*, was formerly considerable of a festival among the Dutch inhabitants of Long Island ... But now poor *Pinckster* has lost its rank among the festivals, and is only kept by the negroes; with them, however, especially on the west end of this island, it is still much of a holiday.
1848 On Pinxter Monday, the Dutch negroes of New York and New Jersey consider themselves especially priviliged to get as drunk as they can. (Bartlett)
1872 [T]he Dutch were faithful to ancient customs in celebrating after Easter their *Pinxter* (German Pfingsten), the Pentecost of our churches, the Whitsuntide of civil life. Nor do their descendants forget the habit of their fathers of extending the festival over the next day, and *Pinxter Monday* is a great day with their families and servants.

1881 The Pinkster festivities commenced on the Monday after Whitsunday, and now began the fun for the negroes, for Pinkster was the carnival of the African race. The venerable "King of the Blacks" ... originally came from Africa ... [He was] the purchased slave of one of the most ... respectable merchant princes of the olden time ... During Pinkster-day the negroes made merry with games and feasting, all paying homage to the king, who was held in awe and reverence as an African prince.

second Christmas (Day), the day following Christmas Day (DARE).
- Translation of Dutch *tweede kerstdag* or German *zweiter Weihnachtstag*; adopted in the nineteenth century and still known regionally.
* As became clear under **pinkster**, it is typical of both the Low Countries and Germany that the principal religious festivals are celebrated in pairs. The official day is followed by a second day off, and the two days are distinguished from one another by the additions of *eerste* ("first") and *tweede* ("second"): accordingly, there are a First and Second Christmas Day, a First and Second Easter Day, and a First and Second Whitsun Day. The custom and name were introduced in the US by the Dutch and Germans, where the terms were regionally translated into *second Christmas (Day)* and *second Easter*. However, second Whitsun Day was called *Pinkster Monday* in the nineteenth century.

ca. 1860 The day preceding Christmas, preparations were made ... by baking cakes, boiling doughnuts, &c, on which to feast, especially the second Christmas day, when neighbors visited each other and partook of the good victuals ... The first Christmas was kept holy and reverential as Sunday, and the second as mentioned, on the evening of which the young people generally had a dance.
1940 The Day After Christmas ... What we used to call Second Christmas Day.
2002 When I was a very young child, we often had Christmas Eve with one set of grandparents, Christmas Day with the other set, and then "Second Christmas" at home. ... My own children, born in the 1970s, also experienced "Second Christmas." (DARE)

2.8 In and around the house

American English borrowed eight words that refer to a building, structure, or part of a house. **Block** and **bowery** refer to a complex of buildings or quarter, **best room**, **caboose**, and **clothes room** refer to special indoor rooms (with **caboose** having undergone a radical change of meaning), **crawl** and **hay barrack** are separate structures, and, finally, **stoop** is an extension to a house. All words were borrowed in the seventeenth or eighteenth century, and all of them are still used, although they are not equally widespread, **stoop** being by far the most well-known.

A word that only appears in Bartlett 1848 and Farmer 1889 is ***portaal***. Bartlett writes: "A portal, lobby. Used by people of Dutch descent, in New Jersey and New York, for a small passage or entry of a house, and pronounced *pit-till*. The principal entrance they call the *gang*; also Dutch." Apparently, ***gang*** was also borrowed at one time or another.

DARE mentions two other loanwords in this category, which are only scarcely known, namely ***klop door*** and ***louk***, from Dutch *klapdeur* ("swing door") and *luik* ("trapdoor"), respectively. These words were mentioned by a number of informants of Dutch descent in 1967-68 and were exclusive to the small Dutch community.

best room, the parlor (of a house) (Craigie, DARE).

- After Dutch *bestekamer*, literally "best room," used for the parlor of a house; borrowed in the seventeenth or eighteenth century and still used regionally.

* The compound *best room* was coined in American English and it is what the British call a *parlour*. According to Craigie, the *best room* is "the best finished and furnished room in a house, frequently reserved for Sundays and special occasions." Why did the Americans invent a new word for this concept? They probably did this following the example of Dutch *bestekamer*, which means exactly the same thing and is one of many words in this category adopted from Dutch. Schele de Vere was the only one to consider it a Dutch loanword in 1872 and I suspect he hit the nail on the head. In the olden days, *best parlor* was also used in American English by, for example, Knickerbocker (Irving) in his *History of New York*: "All visits of form and state were received with something of court ceremony in the best parlor."

As prosperity increased, the term became obsolete in both the Netherlands and the US. It still exists in regional American English as an old-fashioned word. The entries in DARE all stem from places that attracted Dutch immigrants in the nineteenth and twentieth century. Accordingly, it may have been brought to the US by both the first and second wave of Dutch immigrants.

1719 Moodey and I ... were married ... in the best room below stairs. ... Had a very good Dinner ... in the best room.

1771 I should like to have one window in the best Parlour.

1833 The room in which they were incarcerated was the parlor, or "best room," of his paternal home.

1841 The main part of the house, containing the "best parlor," and other rooms which were not in constant use, was shut up.

> **1872** The custom, also, to keep one room in the house as the *best room*, and to call it so, which still prevails in most of the Northern States, has been bequeathed to this generation by the first Dutch settlers of New York. The same name and usage may still be found in all the old towns of Holland, where these rooms are kept as dark as here, to preserve the furniture, and only opened on great occasions, when company is expected. (Schele de Vere)
> **1907** *Best room* ... Old-fashioned front parlor, used only on formal occasions, such as the visit of the minister.
> **1941** Most New England houses built more than a generation ago have one "best" room set aside for use on special occasions only.
> **1973** Three informants in Minnesota and Iowa, of Ohio and Connecticut background, reported the use of *best room*, a minor variant in New England.

block, a connected or compacted group of houses or other buildings (Craigie, DARE, Webster).
- Probably from Dutch *blok*, previously spelled *block*; borrowed in the seventeenth or eighteenth century and still commonly use.
* Thanks to the boy band "New Kids on the Block" founded in 1984, the whole world is familiar with the American phrase *new kid on the block* in the sense of "a new arrival." And the name *blockbuster* for a very popular play or movie has also been adopted into many other languages. This compound dates from World War II, when it had a much more unpleasant meaning, namely "an aerial bomb capable of destroying a whole block of buildings." In *new kid on the block* and *blockbuster*, *block* means "a connected or compacted group of houses." *Blok* or *block* is a word that exists in various languages in the general sense of "solid piece." The word originated in Dutch and Dutch *blok* was adopted into French, after which British English borrowed it from French in the fourteenth century. Both the English and the Dutch introduced the word on the new American continent. In the seventeenth century, the word *block* acquired a new meaning in Dutch, namely "a connected or compacted group of houses," which was used by, among others, the famous mathematician Simon Stevin. DARE suspects that American English adopted this meaning from Dutch, which, if true, must have occurred as early as the seventeenth or eighteenth century. What the Dutch call *een blok huizen*, *huizenblok*, or *woonblok* is called *block of buildings* and *block of houses* in American English.

In Dutch, *blok* can only be used to refer to a group of several houses, whereas its meaning in American English was expanded to include "a large single building" and chiefly in New England, according to DARE, "an apartment building."

> **1796** A fire broke out ... and raged with such fury as to baffle all human exertion, till it had laid in ashes the whole block of buildings.
> **1801** The buildings [in Washington] are brick, and erected in what are called large blocks, that is, from two to five or six houses joined together, and appear like one long building.
> **1881** In the case of Milwaukee ... solid blocks of houses flush with the side-walk are very few.
> **1967** Block houses – a row of houses that fill the block. (DARE)

bowery, part of a city notorious for low life (Craigie, DARE, Webster).
- From Dutch *bouwerij*, meaning "husbandry, farm"; borrowed in the seventeenth century and still in use.
* The word *bouwerij* underwent an exciting development in the US, where it initially meant "a farm in the early Dutch settlements in New York State."

> **1654** But before we weighed anchor, their boweries were in flames; Dutch and English were slain.

This is an instance of Dutch *bouwerij*, derived from *bouwen*, meaning "to farm" and in the olden days the regular word for "farm." In modern Dutch, the word has been replaced by *boerderij*, derived from *boer* meaning "farmer." The word *boerderij* originated precisely in the period when the Dutch settled in New Netherland. As governor of New Netherland, a position he held from 1647 to 1664, Peter Stuyvesant was allocated the largest farm. In 1651, he bought a second farm with land in the vicinity, which he referred to in its entirety as *The Great Bouwerij* – rather than using the neologism *boerderij*. Incidentally, this land remained in the hands of Stuyvesant's descendants until 1970! What the Dutch called the road leading to the farms is unknown, as the only terms found in documents are *the way*, *the street* and suchlike. However, in an American English document from 1690, this road is "commonly called the Bowry Lane or Highway." In the eighteenth century, this was abridged to The Bowery, which became the official name in 1813 and is the name by which it is still known.

> **1787** I ... left the city by way of the Bowery.

In the course of the eighteenth century, the Bowery became an upmarket street with expensive homes and fashionable shops. A century on, the street had deteriorated considerably, as a result of which *bowery* acquired the meaning of "a city street or district notorious for cheap saloons and homeless derelicts." The urchins roaming these streets, united in gangs, were called *Bowery boys*. They disappeared around 1900 but their life was romanticized half a century later in a series of films by a group of actors who called themselves the Bowery Boys.

> **1840** The Bowery boys of New York have, in our opinion, eclipsed the nice young men in Baltimore.
>
> **1872** But that crowded thoroughfare of New York, the *Bowery*, which for years reproduced all the fierce violence and reckless crime of ancient Alsatia, has little to remind us of the pleasant *Bouvery*, the garden-bower of old Dutch governors, who here enjoyed their fragrant flowers and luscious fruits in quiet rural retreats. (Schele de Vere)

In 1906, it was still acceptable to use *bowery* in the general sense of "part of a city notorious for low life." The *New York Times*, for example wrote: "Decatur Street, which in a way is Atlanta's Bowery." And in 1967-1969, informants of DARE from Pennsylvania and Texas referred to a notorious district in their city as *the bowery*. However, since the Manhattan street The Bowery has risen in prestige and prices, this usage is becoming obsolete: present-day Americans do not understand the connection between the expensive Bowery and a slum. Thanks to this street name, every American is familiar with the Dutch word *bouwerij*, whereas most Dutchmen will not understand it without an explanation.

caboose, a railroad car usually attached behind a freight train, where members of the crew may cook, eat, and sleep

(Craigie, DARE, Webster).
- From Dutch *kombuis*, previously also *kabuis*, meaning "cook's galley on a vessel"; borrowed in the seventeenth or eighteenth century and still in use.
* The meaning of "railroad car attached behind a freight train" is one that *caboose* acquired in the United States. The history of the word begins with the Dutch shipping term *kombuis*, also *kabuis*, meaning a kitchen on a ship. Given that the Dutch shipbuilders were leaders in their field throughout Europe and beyond in the seventeenth and eighteenth century, a great deal of Dutch nautical terminology was adopted into other languages.
This applied to the word *kombuis*. Dutch sailors started using this word in overseas areas to refer to a kitchen on shore as well, which landlubbers in the Low Countries called a *keuken* ("kitchen"), as a consequence of which *kombuis* became the regular word for kitchen in Afrikaans.

Dutch *kombuis* was also borrowed on the American continent, initially in the sense of "cook's galley on a vessel," which was encountered in mid-eighteenth century; British English followed this example, although not until twenty years later.

> **1747** They shipp'd a Sea which carried overboard ... their Boat and Carpouse.
> **1848** *Caboose*. The common pronunciation for *camboose* (Dutch *kombuis*), a ship's cooking-range or kitchen. (Bartlett)

In the US, the word soon came to be used to refer to "a cooking oven used on land":

> **1786** For sale, One elegant patent caboose.

While both meanings have become outdated in American English, the word started leading a life entirely of its own. Since kitchens ashore were usually housed in separate structures, the meaning could easily shift to "a hut" in general.

> **1839** We have a postmaster in our own little village ... and in his little caboose of a post office I have found electioneering interferences.

The normal present-day sense of *caboose* originated during the large western migration in the nineteenth century. The pioneers who moved westwards in wagon trains transported the foodstuffs in the rear wagon, which they called the *caboose wagon* or *caboose* for short. When the wagon trains were replaced by railway trains in the course of the nineteenth century, the name was transposed to the new means of transport, together with the crew's custom to cook and eat in the rear carriage, the *caboose* or *caboose car*.

> **1861** Another midnight ride in the "Caboose" of a freight train.
> **1862** No. of Caboose Cars [on Central Railroad of New-Jersey], 6.

According to DARE, *caboose* acquired even more new, figurative meanings in American English, such as "any small cramped building or place within a building," "a cowhide stretched under a wagon as a carrying dcvicc" and "anything that follows behind or comes last in a sequence, as: a. the buttocks (1932), b. the lastborn child in a family (1950), c. one who follows or imitates others; one who allows himself to be duped (1969)."

While the word *kombuis* is used exclusively as a nautical term in the Low Countries, its use expanded considerably in the US.

clothes room, a clothes closet, a room in which clothes are kept (Craigie, DARE).
- Probably after Dutch *kleedkamer*, *kleerkamer*, meaning "dressing room, room for hanging clothes"; borrowed in seventeenth or eighteenth century and still used regionally.

* *Clothes room* is used in the north (especially the northeast) of the US instead of the normal *closet*, and is probably a literal translation of Dutch *kleedkamer, kleerkamer*. Like the **best room**, the word may have been adopted from the first wave of immigrants as early as the seventeenth and eighteenth century, given that it was still mentioned by various New York informants in 1967.

1857 In the attic.. a space for lumber is marked on the plan; but this might be used as a clothes-room.
1865 She vanished up the end staircase, and hid herself away in the old clothes-room.
1967-70 (*A built-in space in a room for hanging clothes*) Clothes room. (DARE)

crawl, an enclosure for keeping various sea creatures alive in shallow water (Craigie, DARE, Webster).
- Alteration of Dutch *kraal*, also *koraal*, meaning "enclosure for keeping cattle and other animals"; borrowed in the seventeenth century and still used regionally.
* The Dutch borrowed the word *kraal* in Indonesia and South Africa from the Portuguese. A *kraal* denoted an enclosed area in which livestock or other mammals were kept. The word was adopted into American English, but in a special meaning, for there was already an American English word for a cattle enclosure, namely *pen*, which had been in use since the early seventeenth century (*corral* was adopted from Spanish as late as the nineteenth century). The Americans started using the Dutch loanword in the sense of "an enclosure for keeping sea creatures, such as turtles or terrapins." According to DARE, this is now used regionally, mostly in the southern states along the Atlantic Coast.

1682 They bring them [turtles] in Sloops alive, and afterwards keep them in Crauls, which is a particular place of Salt Water of Depth and Room for them to swim in, pallisado'd or staked, in round above the Water's surface.
1881 *Crawl*... A pen or *corral* made of upright stakes wattled together, intended to hold sponges while being cleaned; or turtle awaiting a market.
1966 And then they had what they called crawls, that was places fixed where they could come in with their sponge and put 'em in them places. And then they'd clean 'em. (DARE)
1981 The word *crawl* is in current use as a noun in Key West, Florida. I saw sea turtles in crawls there in 1979. Perhaps other sea creatures are also kept in crawls. (DARE)

hay barrack, a barrack or other structure for storing or protecting hay (Craigie, DARE, Webster).
- From Dutch *hooiberg*, meaning "haystack," literally "hay mountain, heap of hay"; adopted in the seventeenth or eighteenth century and still in use.
* Dutch farmers keep hay in large piles in rickstands made with four poles and covered with a roof. The name for such a haystack was adopted into American English, where the unrecognizable second part *berg* was folk-etymologically changed into *barrack*: the rickstand does, in fact, look somewhat like a hut or small house. Information from DARE shows that the word occurs regionally, particularly in the northeast and towards the south along the Atlantic Coast.

1797 Thomas Shoemaker and I measured at the hay barrack, below the house, where the water left a mark, and found it had been five feet four inches.

1848 *Hay barrack.* (Dutch, *Hooi-berg*, a hay-rick.) A straw-thatched roof, supported by four posts, capable of being raised or lowered at pleasure, under which hay is kept. A term peculiar to New York State. (Bartlett)

1872 *hay-barrack*, a somewhat ludicrous corruption of *hooiberg* (hay-mountain), is in like manner locally applied to a thatched roof supported on four posts, under which hay is protected against the weather. (Schele de Vere)

1965-70 Hay barrack – four corner poles, pole sides added, roof raised as needed on pegs. (DARE)

stoop, a porch, platform, entrance stairway, or small veranda at a house door (Craigie, DARE, Webster).

- From Dutch *stoep*, now "trottoir," previously "stone steps at the entrance of a house"; adopted in the seventeenth century and still in use.

* The commonplace image of a Dutch *burgher* is a chubby man wearing a jacket, vest and *knickerbockers*, smoking a pipe on a bench on a *stoop*. This image is largely due to Washington Irvings' brainchild, Diedrich Knickerbocker, who, in *History of New York*, portrays Stuyvesant several times on a *stoop*, for example, in Chapters 41 and 54:

1809 They found him [Stuyvesant], according to custom, smoking his afternoon pipe on the "stoop," or bench at the porch of his house.

1809 Justice he often dispensed in the primitive patriarchal way, seated on the "stoep" before the door, under the shade of a great button-wood tree.

The illustrations in the book in particular are likely to have made the word *stoop* widely known, but it already existed previously in American English, for example, in:

1755 Houses of one Story & a Stoop to each.

1789 Several persons were in a stoop and at windows within fifteen or twenty feet from the tree.

Today, most Dutch houses no longer have a doorstep and where they do they are called *veranda* or *bordes*. In the olden days, however, Dutch *stoep* was also used in the meaning of "a small porch with seats or benches," which is precisely what Craigie gives as the original meaning of *stoop*. On account of the pleasant climate, the Dutch built stoops in front of their houses on which they could sit outside in the evening, a custom that was adopted by the Yankees and spread beyond New England. The meaning of the word *stoop* was expanded in American English and now includes "any small porch, veranda, or entrance stairway at a house door." Since the original meaning of the word has disappeared in Dutch, *stoep* and *stoop* now refer to two completely different things. The following quotes are illustrative of the distribution of the word *stoop* in the US.

1848 *Stoop.* (Dutch, *stoep.)* The steps at the entrance of a house; door-steps. It is also applied to a porch with seats, a piazza, or balustrade. This, unlike most of the words received from the Dutch, has extended, in consequence of the uniform style of building that prevails throughout the country, beyond the bounds of New York State, as far as the backwoods of Canada. ... "Nearly all the houses [in Albany] were built with their gables to the streets, and each had heavy wooden Dutch *stoops*, with seats at the door." ... (Bartlett)

Illustration 2.49 – Stoop before the Rip Van Winkle House in Poughkeepsie (source: private collection)

1872 [T]he *stoop* of our houses is ... a genuine addition which we owe to New Netherlands. The good burghers loved to sit on their *stoeps* (seats) smoking their pipes in peace and "lordly silence," and having wife and children on the *stoep bancke* by their side. The custom was pleasant and well adapted to our climate, and hence soon spread all over the country; with it the *stoop* became the common name for any covered or open porch with seats, in front of a house. ... In Canada the word is often written *stowp* and in the West occasionally *stowp*, but probably more from inattention than any purpose to naturalize it by a change of form. (Schele de Vere)

2.9 Trade

This category includes general commercial terms rather than commodities, which are listed elsewhere, such as *duffle* under clothing in 2.13. **Vendue** was borrowed from Dutch in the seventeenth century, **beer-cellar** in the seventeenth or eighteenth century and **beer-hall** in the nineteenth century, but the last two words may be attributable in part to German immigrants.

The key innovation that Dutch introduced into the world of commerce is the suffix *-ery*, which is used to coin words denoting a "place where the activity referred by the verb is performed professionally." This was modeled on the loanwords **bakery**, **brewery**, **(book)bindery**, and **printery**. **(Book)bindery** was probably adopted in the nineteenth century, the other words in the seventeenth or eighteenth century. Once these words had been adopted, they were used in American English with the suffix *-ery* having the same meaning to create new words, words that did not exist in Dutch. Words ending in *-ery* also exist in British English but more rarely, and they were introduced at a later date than in American English. For example, Neumann stated in 1945: "The word *bakery* was regarded as an Americanism by British visitors to the US about a hundred years ago."

On pages 348-350 of his Supplement from 1945, Mencken provides a large number of examples of neologisms:

> "*Printery*, traced by the DAE [Craigie] to 1638 in America and not found in England until 1657, seems to have stood alone for a century and a half, but after *grocery* came in 1791 it was quickly followed by other forms in *-ery*, and their coinage continues briskly to this day. The DAE traces *bindery* to 1810, *groggery* to 1822, *bakery* to

> 1827, *creamery* to 1858, and *cannery* to 1870, and marks them all Americanisms. It suggests that Dutch forms in *-ij*, *e.g.*, *bakkerij* and *binderij*, may have produced the earlier examples, and a correspondent suggests that the later ones may owe something to German forms in *-ei*, e.g., *backerei* and *konditorei*, but the suffix *-ery* and its attendant *-ory* are really old in English, and *buttery*, never in general use in the US, goes back to the Fourteenth Century. It is, however, on this side of the water that they have been hardest worked, and that hard working has been frequently noted by both English travelers and native students of language. In the US, reported one of the former in 1833, 'shops are termed *stores*, and these again figure under the respective designations of John Tomkins's *grocery*, *bakery*, *bindery* or even *wiggery*, as the case may be.' ... Since 1900 many additions to the ever-growing list have been reported by lexicographical explorers, *e.g.*, *cobblery*, *renewry* (a hat-cleaning shop), *shoe-renewry* or *shu-renury*, *shoe-fixery*, *juicery* (apparently a stand for the sale of fruit juices), *cattery*, *rabbitry*, *cyclery*, *condensery* (a milk condensing plant), *chickery*, *bowlery*, *sweetery*, *beanery*, *eggery*, *refreshery*, *henry*, *eatery*, *cakery*, *car-washery*, *doughnutery*, *lunchery*, *mendery*, *stitchery*, *nuttery*, *chowmeinery*, *drinkery*, *dancery*, *hattery*, *cleanery*, *drillery* (a civil-service cramming school), *squabery*, *snackery*, *breakfastry*, *smeltery* and *skunkery* (a place where skunks are bred for their fur). Some of these, of course, show an effort to be waggish ..."

bakery, a place where baked products are made and sold, a bake-house or baker's shop (Craigie, Webster).
- In this sense probably after Dutch *bakkerij*, meaning "baker's shop"; borrowed in the seventeenth or eighteenth century and still in general use.
* *Bakery* is probably derived from Dutch *bakkerij*, which was used as early as the seventeenth century and which the first Dutch settlers must therefore have taken with them. The British English counterpart is *baker's shop*.

According to a number of sources, American English *bakery* is derived from the verb *to bake* to which *-ery* was suffixed. While this is not inconceivable, it is hard to rule out Dutch influence given its specific meaning. The word *bakery* also occurs regionally in the sense of "baked goods." This meaning, which is listed in DARE, is indeed an American English derivative of *to bake* and has nothing to do with Dutch *bakkerij*.

> **1827** For the year 1826 ... ten bakeries [employed] 28 hands.
> **1923** I bought my luncheon at a different bakery every day.

beer-cellar, a beershop located in a cellar or basement (Craigie, Webster).
- From Dutch *bierkelder*, meaning "cellar where beer is stored or served"; borrowed in the seventeenth or eighteenth century and still in use.
* The word may have been derived from both German *Bierkeller* and Dutch *bierkelder*. American English probably adopted it in certain regions from German and in others from Dutch. It dates from as early as the first wave of colonization, which started in the seventeenth century and in which the Dutch played a more prominent role than the Germans.

> **1732** At the Beer Cellar, over against Mr. Elliot's Bridge on the Bay.
> **1817** Diving into Stews and beer-cellars to acquire views of vice.

beer-hall, a beer-house (Craigie, Webster).
- From Dutch *bierhal*, meaning "large bar serving beer in particular"; borrowed in the nineteenth century and still in use.
* As with *beer-cellar*, *beer-hall* may have been derived from both German *Bierhalle* and Dutch *bierhal*. American English probably adopted it in certain regions from German and in others from Dutch. The Dutch word is, in fact, a German loanword. *Beer-hall* is likely to have been borrowed later than *beer-cellar*, because large drinking halls typically appeared in the nineteenth century, in Germany as well as the Netherlands and the US.

1896 Bicyclists who are making the concert gardens and beer halls in the suburbs flourish.

bindery, an establishment where books are bound; a book-bindery (Craigie, Webster).
- Probably after Dutch *binderij*, meaning "place were books are bound"; probably adopted in the nineteenth century and still commonly used.* *Bindery* is likely to have been derived from Dutch *binderij*, a word that became increasingly common in the nineteenth century, given that before this books were sold as loose sheets of paper and then bound at the

Illustration 2.50 – Bakery (source: Menu Designs, Amsterdam 1999)

Illustration 2.51 – (Book)bindery (source: Het boek in onze dagen, R. van der Meulen, Leiden 1892)

book collector's behest. Publishers did not sell industrially bound books until the nineteenth century, which is when the term *(book)bindery* began to be used.

> **1810** At Worcester, he ... set up a bindery.
> **1885** Flavilla ... took her death sloppin' to and from the bindery.

bookbindery, an establishment where books are bound (Craigie, Webster).
- Probably after Dutch *boekbinderij*, meaning "place were books are bound"; borrowed in the nineteenth century and still commonly used.
* The word is synonymous with **bindery**, but combined with *book*; it is likely to have been coined after Dutch *boekbinderij*, as *bindery* was coined after Dutch *binderij*. The word became known in the nineteenth century (probably on account of Dutch immigrants from those days), as evidenced by the fact that it is placed between quotation marks in the quote from 1846, which suggests that it was still relatively unknown.

> **1815** There are [in Pittsburg] ... 5 printing offices; 4 book binderies.
> **1846** [Harpers] manufacture their own types and paper, and have a "bookbindery" under the same roof.
> **1887** It is a sad thing that some of the most beautiful book-bindery and some of the finest rhetoric have been brought to make sin attractive.

brewery, an establishment where brewing is carried on as a business (Craigie, Webster).
- Probably after Dutch *brouwerij*, meaning "place where beer is manufactured"; borrowed in the seventeenth or eighteenth

century and still commonly used.
* *Brewery* is derived from Dutch *brouwerij* and also exists in British English; the oldest entry of the word is in Hexham's Dutch-English dictionary from 1658: "Een Brouwerye, a Brewerie, or a brewing-house." Accordingly, the word may – also – have been introduced into American English via British English.

1780 She ... is to be met with at the Brewery.
1794 In the city of New York there are at present a number of very large and respectable breweries established.

printery, a printing office (Craigie, Webster).
- Derived from the previously common Dutch *prenterij* or *printerij*, meaning "printing office," or translated from Dutch *drukkerij*, which has the same meaning; adopted in the seventeenth century and still in use.
* In seventeenth-century Dutch, a business engaged in printing was referred to as both *drukkerij* and *prenterij* or *printerij*, usually spelled *printerye*. In Dutch, the verbs *drukken* and *prenten* were both used to refer to the transfer of letters to paper. Only *drukken* and *drukkerij* survived. American English may have translated Dutch *drukkerij* literally, but considering the age of the word, American English *printery* is more likely to have been derived from *prenterij*.

1638 Wee haue a printery here.
1848 *Bakery*, *bindery*, have long been in use amongst us, and in New York even *paintery* and *printery*. (Bartlett, *printery*)
1906 The bindery division of the public printery.

vendue, a public sale or auction (Craigie, DARE, Webster).
- From Dutch *vendu*, previously also *vendue*, meaning "public auction"; adopted in the seventeenth century and still in use.
* Dutch *vendu* is derived from French – now obsolete – *vendue*, a derivative of the verb *vendre*, meaning "to sell." In Dutch, this became the common word for a public auction and was soon adopted into American English, where *at (a) vendue* and *by vendue* became standard collocations. The British English equivalent was *auction*. The former spellings *vandue*, *vandew*, and *vandoo* also existed in American English, as did the pleonastic collocation *public vendue*. While the word was considered peculiar to the East Coast in the early twentieth century, it is widely distributed today.

1678 The Purchazers were obliged to pay all the vendu Charges etc.
1680 [The] lot was formerly in the teniur or ocopation of trustam hoges and sould to the above sd. finch at a vandue.
1686 Which said lotts of grounde ye common councill will dispose of at a publike vendu or out cry.
1908 One of the treasured resources of the country banker has been the public auction – or "vendue," the Easterner might call it.

2.10 Money and units of measure

In the seventeenth century, four units of measure were adopted from Dutch, all four of which have become historical terms, also in Dutch, namely: **anker**, **morgen**, **muche**, and **schepel**. In the same century, three monetary names were borrowed: **dollar**, **gulden**, and **stiver**, of which **dollar** is still in use, having even become the currency of the US and other countries. The other two words are merely historical terms.

anker, a liquid measure usually reckoned at ten gallons; a cask or keg holding this quantity (Craigie, Webster).
- From Dutch *anker*, a liquid measure; borrowed in the seventeenth century and now a historical term (in Dutch, too).
* This word was frequently used in the oldest colonial period. In 1960, Krapp wrote (I, 160): "The liquid measure *anker*, *ancker* is mentioned frequently in early American records, for example, *Hempstead Records*, I, 59 (1658). It is of Dutch origin, but was in use in England also in the Elizabethan period, as the citations in the *New English Dictionary* show." Interestingly, the oldest quote given in the OED comes from the *Pennsylvanian Archives* from 1673: "one halfe Ankor of Drinke." As the quotes that follow date from the mid-eighteenth century, it is highly plausible that the English became acquainted with the name in the US. Craigie provides various quotes from 1654 onwards, as well as many different spellings, such as *ancker*, *ankor*, *ancher* and *anchor*. The spelling *anchor* seems to suggest that the author knew Dutch, as the word *anker* is a Dutch homonym with different meanings, namely, "appliance for holding a ship fixed in a particular place" and "liquid measure." Both words are derived from Latin, but from different forms. American English *anchor* is similarly ambiguous. With the introduction of the metric system, *anker* disappeared as a unit of measure in the Netherlands and in the US and has become a historical term in both countries.

> **1654** It is ... ordered, that every ancor of liquors that is landed in any place ... shall pay to the publique treasury 10 ss.
>
> **1654** That we brought eighteen ankers of liquers the first voyage.
>
> **1723** 2/2 Five quarter-casks and an anchor of French brandy, two hogsheads of clarret.
>
> **1855** 534 An anchor of Geneva, and a box of cocoa, and a bag of coffee.

dollar, 1. a coin; 2. basic monetary unit of the US (Craigie, Webster).
- From Dutch *daler*; adopted in the seventeenth century and still extremely common.
* The Dutch coin *daalder* (formerly *daler*) is derived from the Low German name *Daler*, which in turn is derived from High German *Thaler*, a shortened form of *Joachimst(h)aler*. *Joachimst(h)aler* is, in fact, a coin minted from silver from the mine in Joachimsthal (present-day Jáchymov in north Bohemia in the Czech Republic). These coins were produced from 1519 onwards. In the Low Countries, the name *daler* was also used to refer to coins that were minted in Dutch provinces from as early as 1538.

The name *daler* was adopted into British English and spelled in a variety of ways, including *daler*, *dallor* and *dolor*, and in the early seventeenth century occasionally *dollar*. The monetary units made for payments in England, however, were pounds, shillings, and pence, although *dollars* also circulated in the English colonies in the seventeenth and eighteenth century.

From the early seventeenth century, the history of the word *daler* transferred to the American continent. Its oldest monetary history is wonderfully described in Flexner (1984: 181-202). The Dutch brought their *daalders* to New Netherland. The first coins that they brought were what were known as *leeuwendaalders*, *daalders* which were minted in the Low Countries from 1575 onwards and featured a lion. This name was adopted into American English as ***lion dollar***, while the name *doller* was used simultaneously. That name continued to be used, even after the assumption of power by the English. Another name was *dog dollar*. Since the equivalent *hondendaalder* was not encountered in Dutch, it is possible that the image of the lion was so worn down and consequently bore so little resemblance to the animal that the Yankees, perhaps mockingly, coined the variant *dog dollar*.

> **1697** Dollers, commonly called Lyon or Dog Dollers, have no vallue ascertained whereby they may pass currantly amongst the inhabitants of this Country.
> **1708** The said Species of forreigne Coyne being rated as in the said Proclamation saving the Dog Dollars or Dollars of the Low Countreys.
> **1720** An Act appointing the Value Lyon Dollars shall pass current for.
> **1720** Gave to Saml's three children ... each 8s, and to Nat's two ... 1 dog doillar, both valued now at about 15s.
> **1723** The Current Cash being wholly in the Paper Bills of this Province and a few Lyon Dollars.

The transformation from *daler* into *doller* may have taken place via British English, but it would still be a long time before *o* was standardized in British English, whereas many examples show that Dutch *a* was often pronounced *o* in American English (for example, *boss* from *baas*). This means that the transformation may well have occurred in American English, and that Dutch *daler* was adopted into both British and American English, independently of one another.

Similarly, Dutch *rijksdaalder* as the name for a particular silver coin was adopted into American English in the seventeenth century in the form of ***rix-dollar***. However, this was used only rarely.

> **1643** Good Rialls of 8/8 and Reix Dollers shall passe betwixt man & man att hue shillings a peece.

In addition to *daalders*, the Yankees also paid in Spanish pesos, which have been called *Spanish dollars* or just *dollars* since 1684, a name that they did not have in Spanish, which shows the extent to which the name *dollar* had been vernacularized. The following quote refers to this coin.

> **1683** There was an act passed ... that pieces of eight royals of Spain, or dollars of Seville ... shall pass in payment.

From around 1750 onwards, every peso, whether it came from Spain or Spanish America, was called *Spanish dollar* or *dollar* for short.

In 1652, the British colony of New England started minting coins of its own in order to be independent of the scarce and inadequate supply from Europe –

a practice other colonies on the American continent would soon follow. The new coins had many names and values, which caused some confusion. In 1775, a year before the outbreak of the American War of Independence, the second Continental Congress decided the time had come for a single monetary unit, and provisionally issued *Continental money*, the value of which was expressed in dollars. During the War of Independence, the introduction of a national monetary system was contemplated. Senator Gouverneur Morris drafted a report in which he proposed a decimal system based on *dollars* and *cents*. Although the bankers would have preferred to continue calculating in British pounds, his proposal was adopted and defended by Thomas Jefferson, which earned him the nickname "the father of the American dollar." In 1785, Thomas Jefferson wrote a memorandum for Congress, in which he claimed the following:

> **1785** The unit or dollar is a known coin, and the most familiar of all to the minds of people. It is already adopted from south to north; has identified our currency, and therefore happily offers itself as an unit already introduced.

After Congress had adopted Jefferson's proposal in 1785, the *dollar* was statutorily introduced as the US currency in 1792. Today, the dollar is also the currency of a number of other countries, including Canada, Australia, New Zealand, and Suriname, thus far surpassing its parent, the *daalder*: when the decimal system was officially introduced in the Netherlands in 1816, the *daalder* disappeared as a separate coin and, gradually, from the language as well; it only lives on in the saying *de eerste klap is een daalder waard* (the first blow is half the battle) and in advertising slogan *op de markt is uw gulden een daalder waard* (your money goes farther at the market). Soon, the latter expression will not mean much anymore, now that after the disappearance of the daalder, the guilder has made way for the euro.

gulden, **guilder**, a gold coin (Craigie, Webster).
- From Dutch *gulden*, the name of a coin; adopted in the seventeenth century and still known as a historical term.
* The Dutch word *gulden* was also adopted into British English, where it was already corrupted into *guilder* and *gilder*, forms also found in American English.
A number of quotes show that despite the dollar being the standard currency, the Dutch guilder was used as legal tender on the East Coast for a period in the seventeenth century, albeit a very brief one. The guilder was used in the Netherlands until the introduction of the euro in 2002, which explains why *gulden* and *guilder* are still included in Webster's dictionary.

> **1649** For his bond at the Dutch being 400 Gilders.
> **1659** In ye case the sayd William setle not upon it [land] ye ensuing spring hee doth by these presents engage to pay fforty guldens to this Town of Rustdorp.
> **1675** His debt 521 guilders.
> **1677** The Pl[ain]t[iff] ... sayes that hee can proove the article of twenty fyve gilders about the Cano.
> **1704** Allowing Two Shillings for each Gilder, ten Gilders making one pound.
> **1741** Three gilder pieces of Holland twenty penny weight and seven grains, five shillings and two pence one farthing.

The *carolusgulden*, which was introduced in the Low Countries in the sixteenth century, is also sporadically encountered in American English as ***carol guilder***.

1657 Whosoever shall refues to gather aney towne rate or rates being ordered by the townesmen shall pay for his refusing it six Carrot [*sic*] guilder for the first refuesall thereof.
1659 I ... doe hereby ... sell and delliver vnto William Smith of Hemsteede aforesaid, ... the meadow-land w'th the appurtenances there vnto belongeing for and in concideration of six hundred carol guilders.

morgen, old Dutch unit of land area (Craigie, Webster).
- From Dutch *morgen*; adopted in the seventeenth century and now a historical term (also in Dutch).
* Although Dutch *morgen* is no longer widely known as a measure of area, it does mark the beginning of the European history of Manhattan. When the Dutchman Peter Minuit "bought" the island of Manhattan, this was reported to the States General in The Hague as follows: "Have bought the island *Manhattes* from the natives at the value of 60 guilders; is 11.000 *morgens* large" (see also 1.1). The value in 1891 was calculated in the *Financial World*: "The assessed value of the real estate on this island of eleven thousand morgen [was] ... set down officially for 1890 at $1,353,893,473." (Mathews)

The Yankees also expressed the size of land in *morgens* for some time. In official deeds, the word was used in American English as early as 1658. *Morgen* survived until 1869, and was used in the Federal Commissioner of Agriculture's annual report for that year (Mencken 1937, 109-110, note 2). In Dutch, *morgen* actually means: the amount of land that one can till in one morning.

1681 Rod in all amounting to abouth 450 morgen. (Mathews)
1688 Granted him two flatts or plains upon both sides of ye Maquase river ... containing about eleven morgen.
1744 We met several Dutchmen on the island [near Albany, N.Y.], who had rented morgans of land upon it.

muche, a liquid measure (Craigie).
- From Dutch *muts*, a liquid measure; borrowed in the seventeenth century and no longer extant.
* In the olden days, Dutch *muts* was not only used to refer to headgear (see **mutch** in 2.13), but also as a liquid measure, often in the diminutive form *mutsje*. Originally, this was probably the amount measured in a hat. This meaning of Dutch *muts* was once used in the US, as was the liquid measure *anker*. The word was never widely known and is now totally obsolete. The word also existed in Scottish and northern English, in the diminutive form *mutchkin*.

1673 If any man shall Refuse to: go: ... he shall pay six muches of Rume to them that gose [i.e., to run the bounds of the town]
1937 Krapp in The English Language in America, adds a few Long Island obsoletisms, e.g., *scule*, from *fiskaal*, meaning a public prosecutor ... and *much*, from *mutsje*, a liquid measure (ditto 1673). (Mencken 1937 109-110, note 2)

schepel, **skipple**, an old unit of dry measure of about three-fourths of a bushel (Craigie, Webster).
- From Dutch *schepel* "a dry measure"; borrowed in the seventeenth century and now a historical term (also in Dutch).
* The first meaning of the Dutch word *schepel* is "spade used to scoop grain, potatoes, etc."; the word is derived from the verb *scheppen*, meaning "to shovel."

The word was adopted into American English at an early date, in both the Dutch form and the anglicized form *schipple* or *skipple*. It is now a historical term.

> **1658** Our tithe may be paid unto the Governor according to our agreement, being one hundred schepells of wheate.
> **1677** 20 schipple of wheat to bee delivered att New Yorke.
> **1702** S. V. Cortland ... [has] said summe in hand, L2: 18: 6, and 4 schepels somer Tarwe, or wheat.

stiver, **stuiver**, a coin worth one-twentieth of a guilder (Craigie, Webster).
- From Dutch *stuiver*, the name of a coin; adopted in the seventeenth century and still known as a historical term.
* The Dutch diphthong *-ui-* does not exist in English, causing the word *stuiver*, formerly also spelled *stuyver*, to be adopted in various ways, including *stiver*, *styver*, and *stuyver*. The word also exists in British English but was independently adopted into American English. The coin was used in the Netherlands until the introduction of the euro in 2002, which probably explains why the word *stiver* is still included in Webster's dictionary, seeing that the Yankees were quick to exchange this coin for pennies. Dutch settlers stuck to the stuiver for a longer period of time, for Bartlett still included the expression "He's not worth a *stiver*" in 1848, which is doubtless derived from *hij heeft*, *bezit geen stuiver*, meaning "he does not own so much as a stuiver."

> **1676** A horse and man to pay for passage [on the ferryboat] 2 gilders a man with out a horse 10 styvers.
> **1680** One Thousand Eight hund[re]d forty eight Gilders tenn Stivers Sewant.
> **1701** The assessment ... [is] approved off, and laid 4$ stuyver upon ye pound.
> **1701** Upon which assessment... is laid three stuyvers wampum upon the pound.
> **1789** Four white grains and three black ones, should pass for the value of a stiver or penny.
> **1848** *Stiver*. A Dutch coin about the value of a cent. A common expression in New York is, "He's not worth a *stiver*," i.e. he's very poor. (Bartlett)

2.11 Children's language

The words **hoople**, **hunk**, and **knicker** were adopted as names for children's games as early as the seventeenth century, when many other names were borrowed, almost all of which had practically vanished by the nineteenth century. Bartlett mentions the use of ***pile*** in 1848, from Dutch *pijl*, meaning "an arrow," noting that boys in New York still used the word. According to him, the same applies to ***snore***, meaning "a string with a button on one end to spin a top with," from Dutch *snoer*, meaning "string, rope," and to ***scup***, meaning "a swing" and ***to scup***, meaning "to swing," from Dutch *schop* ("swing") and *schoppen* ("to swing"), two words that have lost these meanings in Dutch too. As late as 1984, ***sliding pond***, meaning "slide," was still deemed a typical word in New York children's language, as evidenced by research conducted by David Gold. Initially, the term probably referred to a shallow frozen pond across which children could slide – the Dutch *glijbaan*, which literally means "slide-path," was initially also a thing on ice. American English *sliding pond* is likely to be a partial translation of this Dutch term, the first part being the translation, the second (*pond*) being a folk-etymologization of Dutch *baan*.

Pinkie is a word typically found in children's language that was also borrowed in the seventeenth or eighteenth century. **Bakkes** and **rolle bolle** followed in the nineteenth or twentieth century, but not many people know these words.

The only significant word that Dutch children's language donated to American English is **Santa Claus** – a word that is indispensable to both children and adults, Santa being the personification of the most important feast of the year.

bakkes (also **bakkie**, **baks**, **bax**, **bah**, **akkes**, **akkie**, and **akkes bakkes**), is characterized by foulness or filth; repulsive; dirty! filthy!; often used as a warning to children (DARE).
- From Dutch *bah*, *akkie bakkie*, etc.; borrowed in the nineteenth or twentieth century and still used regionally.
* There are several Standard Dutch exclamations expressing disgust, such as *bah!*, *jakkes!*, *jakkie!*, *ajakkes!*, *ajakkie!*, *ajakkert!*, *ajasses!*,and *ajesses!* Although not listed in any Dutch dictionary, *akkiebakkie* and *jakkiebakkie* are frequently heard in children's language. *Bah* may also be used as a noun, particularly in relation to children, in *een bah doen*, meaning"to take a dump," *kijk uit voor die bah*, meaning "watch out for that filth." Not all variants reported in American English are listed in Dutch dictionaries, although that does not mean very much because dictionaries are notorious for omitting colloquialisms, which lend themselves perfectly to endless associations. Accordingly, certain variants in American English may have originated from Dutch forms, such as *bah*, *jakkes*, and so on, but it is also quite conceivable that they existed or still exist in colloquial European Dutch. They probably come from nineteenth- and twentieth-century Dutch immigrants in the US; see the instructive quotes from DARE.

> **1982** My students confirm that *bakkes*, *bah* and *akkes* are all used to describe filth. The forms *akkie* and *bakkie* are also very common, as is the combination *akkes bakkes*. The students who know and use these words

Illustration 2.52 – Sliding pond (source: Voor 't Jonge Volkje, compiled by I. and L. de Vries, Utrecht 1980, illustration from 1880-1900)

Illustration 2.53 – Hoople (source: Kroniek van de Kempen, Frans Hoppenbrouwers et al., Kempen Pers, Hapert, 1991)

are from Dutch backgrounds in Lynden, WA; Bellflower, CA; Denver, CO; Sioux Co., IA; Pella, IA; Grand Rapids, MI; Whitinsville, MA; and Paterson, NJ.

1982 *Bakkes* is used as an adjective or as an expression of disgust or revulsion. I use *bakkie* in the same way – so do my kids. Not too long ago, Joel came into the house and said, "I just stepped in something bakkie." A shorter form, *baks* or *bax*, is used only as an exclamation. My German grandfather always used it, but I assumed that it was a form of our Dutch word. He'd say "Baks!" to warn a child away from something the kid was messing in, but he'd also use it to warn his dog.

1982 I recently caught myself warning my daughter that something was "bakkie." Since then I've talked to a lot of Dutch people back in Holland and Grand Rapids about it; most of them know "bakkie" as an adjective and "bakkes" as an exclamation for something unpleasantly dirty or repulsive. The words are used most often in referring to food or excrement, and usually they're spoken to children.

And under the noun *bakkie*:

1982 When the first vowel in *bakkie* is long, the word is specifically a noun meaning excrement: "I want to take a bakkie." When the vowel is shorter, the word is an adjective. Then it doesn't necessarily refer to biological elimination but can refer to anything filthy or distasteful, including spoiled soup or rancid butter.

hoople, a hoop rolled by children (Craigie, DARE, Webster).

- From Dutch *hoepel*, meaning "hoop"; adopted in the seventeenth or eighteenth century and still used regionally.

* *Hoepelen* (playing with a *hoepel*) is a well-known Dutch children's game that is referred to in British English as *(play with a) hoop*. American English adopted the Dutch word, also as *hoople wheel* or *hoopel*. According to DARE, the word is now old-fashioned.

1848 *Hoople*. (Dutch, *hoepel.)* The boys in the city of New York still retain the Dutch name *hoople* for a hoop. (Bartlett)

1872 Boys ... were ... ignorant of ... [the] meaning ... of the word *hoople*, by which they called their trundling hoops, and which they little suspected they owed to the *hoeple* of Dutch ancestors. (Schele de Vere)

1902 *Hoople* (Dutch *hoepel*). A common term, amongst New York boys, for a trundling hoop. (Clapin)

1907 Master Aldrich in his "hoople" days.

1957 A hoop of iron prodded on with a stick [is called] "hoople wheels" in Iowa.

hunk, goal, base, home (Craigie, DARE, Webster).

- Derived from Dutch *honk*, meaning "home base"; adopted in the seventeenth century and still known.

* *Honk*, in dialects and in Frisian also *hunk*, is a word Dutch children shout when they mean "goal, base, home" when playing. The word is listed in various sources of Americanisms. As a regional English word, it is still known in New York, but is old-fashioned, according to DARE.

1848 *Hunk*. (Dutch, *honk.)* A goal, or place of refuge. A word much used by New York boys in their play.

1889 *Hunk* ... In *tag* and other games,

> the goal; home: as, to reach hunk. On hunk; at the goal. [Local, New York.]
> **1968** *(The place where the player who is "it" has to wait and count)* Honk. (DARE)

The word *hunk* underwent a unique development in the US, where the noun *hunk* served as the model for the adjectives *hunk* and *hunky*, known since 1843 in the meaning of "fine, all-right," and derived from the phrase *to be hunk*, literally meaning "to have reached the goal without being intercepted by one of the opposite party," in other words, "to be safe, all-right." Clapin cites the following examples:

> **1902** *Hunk* (Dutch *honk*, place, post, home). The goal, or home, in a child's game. Especially used by New York boys ... also *hunky*, *hunkey*, meaning very fine, tip-top, good, jolly, and *to be hunky*, or *all hunky*, to be all right.

As derivative of *hunk*, Farmer mentions:

> **1889** *Hunkers* or *Old Hunkers* – Also derived from the Dutch *honk*. A local political term, originating in New York in 1844, to designate the Conservative Democrats as opposed to the Young democracy or Barn Burners ... The *Hunkers* themselves clung to the homestead or old principles, but unkind critics insisted that it rather meant a clinging to a large *hunk* of the spoils of office.

The origin of this *hunker* is not entirely certain. While Mathews concurs with Farmer, the *New World Encyclopedia* and other sources claim that *hunker* "was derived from someone who 'hunkers' (hankers) after a political office." The name *Barnburners* that Farmer mentions also appears to have Dutch roots, not only because the party was led by the first president of Dutch-American descent, Martin van Buren (see **OK** under **hook** in 2.5), but also on account of the following explanation that Farmer gives for the name:

> **1889** *Barnburner* – A nickname given to certain progressive New York Democrats, about 1835, who were opposed to the conservative *Hunkers* ... The name is derived from the legend of the Dutchman, who set his barn afire in order to kill rats which infested it, the inference being that the democrats in question would fain destroy all existing institutions in order to correct their abuses.

In slang the expression *to get hunk on* or *with someone* is used, which Webster's Third defines as "to get even with someone." Although the above is not common knowledge, it is thanks to the compound **hunky-dory** (see 2.14) that *hunk* was adopted into common usage.

knicker, **nicker**, a playing marble (Craigie, DARE).
- From Dutch *knikker*, meaning "marble," derived from the onomatopoeic verb *knikken*, meaning "knock against one another, producing a clicking sound"; adopted in the seventeenth or eighteenth century and possibly again in the twentieth century; still known regionally.
* The Dutch word *knikker* ("marble") is one of the names of children's games adopted into American English. The word was adopted early and therefore adapted to the English pronunciation, in which the letter *k* in words beginning with *kn-* is silent. Archaic *nicker* also exists in British English, into which it was also adopted from Dutch. However, it seems likely that American and British English adopted the word independently. DARE provides some twentieth-century incidences with

Illustration 2.54 – Knicker, litho after a watercolor by the Belgian artist F. Charlet, titled "Spring in Holland" (source: The Printing Art, vol. 1, March-August 1903, Cambridge University Press)

the spellings *kinick* and *canick* – certain instances of which may have been influenced by German *Knicker* – and the shortened form *nick*, particularly in the sense of a small or cheap marble, whose use is reported several times in Delaware. The corruption of these words from children's language is self-evident.

1843 "Hit black alley! – knock his nicker! – 'tan't fair!"
1859 Knicker or Nicker, ... a boy's clay marble; a common term in New York.
1890 *Nicker*: the marble to be knocked out of the ring.
1957 *Kinick* – a five cent shooter for playing marbles.

1958 *Canick* ... "real agate marble, 30 c tot $1.50 apiece."
1967 Kinicks – made out of colored stone, agate. (DARE *kinick*)
1968-70 Nicks or commies – made out of clay. (DARE *nick*)
1970 *Marbles – nicks* (small marbles) put in *faddy* (a row) and shot out with shooter. Whoever hit the most out won. (DARE *nick*)

pinkie, also **pinky**, the little finger (Craigie, DARE, Webster).
- From Dutch *pink*, diminutive form *pinkje* or *pinkie*, meaning "the little finger"; adopted in the seventeenth or eighteenth century and still in use.
* The origin of the Dutch word *pink* or *pinkje* is unknown, but it probably originated in children's language. In the nineteenth century, *pinkie* was generally regarded as being children's language in American English too. The Dutch word was adopted not only in American English but also into Scottish as *pinkie*, which makes it likely that it was brought to the American continent by Scots as well as Netherlanders. In any event, the word is common in traditional Dutch settlement areas and still frequently used. The *Urban Dictionary* lists many examples, compounds and phrases with the word, including *pinky swear*, meaning "an eternally binding act of hooking pinky fingers together in an attempt to seal the deal of a promise that has been made," a custom Dutch children are also familiar with, called *pinkie zweren* in Dutch.
1848 *Pinky*. (Dutch, *pink*.) The little finger. A very common term in New York, especially among small children, who, when making a bargain with each other, are accustomed to confirm it by interlocking the little finger of each other's right hands and repeating the following doggerel: *Pinky, pinky*, bow-bell,/ Whoever tells a lie/ Will sink down to the bad place/ And never rise up again. (Bartlett, appendix)
1934 Ever since I left Mona I had worn the ring on my pinkie.
1941 [Cartoon caption:] Pinkey Straight Up, That's The Class Way To Drink Tea, Pal!
1955 The assumption of these users of the word in the New York area seems to be that *pinkie* is known the length and breadth of the land ... My own investigations, however – so far as they have gone – reveal vast stretches of the continent in which *pinkie* "little finger" is known to very few. It has a considerable degree of currency in Connecticut and Massachusetts, and it seems to be known in some parts of upper New York State as well as in the Hudson River region; but to the west and south of New York State there are few areas, with the exception of central and northern Michigan, where it passes current.
1962 When two people say the same thing at the same time, they should say nothing, link their pinkies, i.e., their little fingers, and make a wish ... Variant: they should link their pinky fingers.
2000 "Pinkie swear?" Spoken in reply to a promise; an affirmative response is followed by the discourse participants linking their pinkies with the rest of the fingers in a fist. (DARE)

rolle bolle, also **rol(l)y-bol(l)y**, a game similar to lawn bowling or boccie, but using heavy disks instead of balls (DARE).
- From Dutch *rollebol*, being the name

of several games that involve rolling a marble or other round object over the ground; adopted in the nineteenth or twentieth century and still used regionally.
* Dutch *rollebol* is a compound of *rollen* ("to roll") and *bol* ("ball"). *Rollebol* and the cognate verb *rollebollen* are especially prevalent in the southern part of the Netherlands and Belgium. The noun was brought to the US by both Flemish and Dutch immigrants. According to DARE, it is predominantly known in the Upper Mississippi Valley and is only used in Dutch and Belgian settlement areas, where the game is still played on the annual Rolle Bolle Day or Roly-Boly Day. In other areas, the word became known through Eddy Leonard's famous song *Roll them Roly Boly Eyes* from 1928.

> **1939** In the portion of Henry County near Annawan, Atkinson, and Kewanee, Belgian settlers play a game called *rolle bolle*. The game, which is played with heavy discs of wood, combines certain features of bowling and horseshoe pitching. So popular is thc gamc in thc region that the Henry County Fair, held annually at Cambridge, features a Rolle Bolle Day.
> **1945** The Hollanders say there are no young men this year to play rolly-bolly, a Dutch game of horseshoe.
> **1947** Garretson, South Dakota, was originally settled by Belgians and there still exist some of the manners, customs, and games of that country. Once a year, in the summer, there is "Roly-Boly Day," but such good times are had that it usually lasts two or three. "Roly-Boly" is a bit like horseshoes.
> **2000** My grandparents were Belgian and lived in Moline, Illinois. The East End Club in Moline was one of the centers of rolle bolle (We said "roily bolly.") I remember watching the old guys play roily bolly in the '50s and '60s but I think the game is still played there. The disks were rolled not tossed as you would toss a horseshoe. They were rolled toward a mark or an area at the other end of the lane. I think the lanes were clay, not dirt.

Santa Claus, the religious and holiday spirit of Christmas personified (Craigie, Webster).
- From Dutch *Sante klaas*, a dialectal variant of *Sinterklaas*, which is a corruption of *Sint Nicolaas*; adopted in the seventeenth century and very widespread.
* Every year, the Dutch Sinterklaas sails from Spain to the Netherlands on his steamship, surrounded by Black Petes, his attendants, who throw *pepernoten* (spice nuts) to the children. On the evening of 5 December, the eve of his birthday, Sinterklaas lands on the roofs of houses on a horse, throwing presents, such as chocolate letters, down the chimney and into children's shoes. Naughty children get no presents but the *roe*, a bunch of branches used for spanking, and are threatened that they will be put in a gunny sack and taken to Spain by Sinterklaas. Sinterklaas has a long beard, wears a red-and-white gown and a miter, and carries a staff.

What a contrast with Santa Claus, who comes from the North Pole flying through the sky on his reindeer-drawn sleigh with jingling bells (see **sleigh** in 2.12). He, too, distributes presents but does so on Christmas Eve, 24 December, for which the children hang stockings from the chimney. Santa Claus is a chubby man shouting "ho ho ho" and is dressed in a red and white suit, aided by elves, who make the presents for him.

So how did Sinterklaas become Santa Claus? It is important to note that most paraphernalia surrounding Sinterklaas did not become part of the holiday in the Low Countries until the nineteenth century. The Sinterklaas holiday that the Dutch settlers introduced on the East Coast of the US in the seventeenth century was different from its present-day version. It has been customary since the sixteenth century at least for children in the Low Countries to put their shoe in front of or hang stockings on the hearth on 5 December, the day before the name day of Saint Nicholas (which is contracted into *Sinterklaas*), to find a present in it the next morning. In the course of the sixteenth century, the Reformation increasingly gained a foothold in the Low Countries, and the Catholic saints were renounced. In the seventeenth century, certain municipal authorities even went so far as to prohibit the celebration of Saint Nicholas. To no avail, however, as the holiday was very popular among young and old. There is no doubt that the New Netherlanders definitely brought this popular custom to the US. From a baker's receipt from 1675 it appears that Miss Van Rensselaer had bought *sinterklaesgoet* and, in 1773, Sinterklaas suddenly appeared in New York, never to depart. By then, he was already called *Santa Claus*, after the Dutch dialectal form *Sante Klaas*.

> **1773** Remember there will be a visit from Santa-Claus to-night. (Mathews)
>
> **1773** Last Monday the Anniversary of St. Nicholas, otherwise called St. A Claus, was celebrated at Protestant-Hall. (Mathews)

At that time, the Sinterklaas holiday was still a local New York event, about which the following was reported in the ensuing years:

> **1808** The noted St. Nicholas, vulgarly called Santaclaus – of all the saints in the kalendar the most venerated by true hollanders, and their unsophisticated descendants. (OED)

John Pintard, who had founded the New York Historical Society in 1804, promoted *Sancte Claus* as a patron saint of the society and of the city of New York. He was a friend of Washington Irving, and it is therefore no coincidence that Irving's *History of New York*, published under the pseudonym Diedrich Knickerbocker, appeared on Saint Nicholas Day in 1809. In the book, Irving regularly puts the saintly man on the stage, painting an idiosyncratic picture of him, a picture that captivated the whole of the United States. Irving portrays the children's friend as a chubby Dutch *burgher* who is smoking the ubiquitous pipe. In chapter 7 he describes him as "St. Nicholas, equipped with a low, broad-brimmed hat, a huge pair of Flemish trunk hose, and a pipe." And in chapter 16 he writes:

> **1809** [I]n the sylvan days of New Amsterdam, the good St. Nicholas would often make his appearance in his beloved city, of a holiday afternoon, riding jollily among the treetops, or over the roofs of houses, now and then drawing forth magnificent presents from his breeches pockets, and dropping them down the chimneys of his favorites. Whereas, in these degenerate days of iron and brass he never shows us the light of his countenance, nor ever visits us, save one night in the year; when he rattles down the chimneys of the descendants of the patriarchs, confining his presents merely to the children, in token of the degeneracy of the parents.

In chapter 55, he writes about Peter Stuyvesant:

> So far from indulging in unreasonable austerity, he delighted to see the poor and the laboring man rejoice; and for this purpose he was a great promoter of holidays. Under his reign there was a great cracking of eggs at Paas or Easter; Whitsuntide or Pinxter also flourished in all its bloom; and never were stockings better filled on the eve of the blessed St. Nicholas.

It is funny to see how Irving manages to blend myth and reality in chapter 64, in which he talks about the agreements made between Stuyvesant and the English on the transfer of the colony (see 2.4), providing the following summary:

> Finally, that he [Stuyvesant] should have all the benefits of free trade, and should not be required to acknowledge any other saint in the calendar than St. Nicholas, who should thenceforward, as before, be considered the tutelar saint of the city.

Thanks to Irving, Sinterklaas would be a reality to all Americans from 1809 onwards. John Pintard also contributed his share to the saint's renown. In 1810, he published an illustration with a bilingual poem:

> Sancte Claus goed heylig man!
> Trek uwe beste Tabaert aen,
> Reiz daer mee na Amsterdam,
> Van Amsterdam na Spanje,
> Waer Appelen van Oranje,
> Waer Appelen van granaten,
> Wie rollen door de Straaten.
> SANCTE CLAUS, myn goede Vriend!
> Ik heb U allen tyd gedient,
> Wille U my nu wat geven,
> Ik zal U dienen alle myn Leven.
>
> Saint Nicholas, good holy man!
> Put on the Tabard, best you can,
> Go, clad therewith, to Amsterdam,
> From Amsterdam to Hispanje,
> Where apples *bright* of Oranje,
> And likewise those *granate* surnam'd,
> Roll through the streets, all free unclaim'd,
> Saint Nicholas, my dear good friend!
> To serve you ever was my end,
> If you will, now, me something give,
> I'll serve you ever while I live.

Tabard is explained in the margin as meaning a kind of jacket, *apples bright of Oranje* as "oranges," and *granate* as "pomegranate." Remarkably, this poem marks the first time that *Spain* is referred to as the country of origin of Sinterklaas. The informant who had submitted the poem was around 80 years old. Already in the first half of the eighteenth century, then, Dutch children were led to believe that Sinterklaas came to the Netherlands from Spain. It is astonishing that we should obtain this information from an American source, because the first reports in the Low Countries that Sinterklaas hailed from Spain began to circulate in the nineteenth century!

In the course of the nineteenth century, *Sinterklaas* was increasingly transformed into the modern Santy. In 1819, he was associated with *cookies*, another Dutch import product of which people generally partook in the nineteenth century on holidays such as New Year's Day. The consumption of *klaaskoek* and *speculaas* during the Sinterklaas holiday is also an old tradition in the Netherlands.

> **1819** In old times ... St. Class used to cross the Atlantic and brought immense supplies of cookies etc. from Amsterdam. (Funk 2005: 143)

The most important step towards the metamorphosis was taken on 23 December 1823, when a poem by Clement Clarke Moore, who was also on friendly terms with Pintard, was published, entitled

Illustration 2.55 – Sinterklaas (source: Sinterklaaslexicon p. 268, reproduced from C. Singer, Santa Claus comes to America (1942))

"A Visit from St. Nicholas," but commonly known under the title "'Twas the Night Before Christmas." This is the poem in which Santa collects most of his attributes. Moreover, the feast moved from 5 December to 24 December, as evidenced by the poem's title. The sleigh and the reindeer are also presented, the latter even with their names. Santa is depicted with a red nose, a pot belly, a beard and – a trace left by Irving – a pipe in his mouth.

> **1823** 'Twas the night before Christmas, when all through the house
> Not a creature was stirring, not even a mouse;
> The stockings were hung by the chimney with care,
> In hopes that St. Nicholas soon would be there;
> ...
> When, what to my wondering eyes should appear,
> But a miniature sleigh, and eight tiny reindeer,
> With a little old driver, so lively and quick,
> I knew in a moment it must be St. Nick.
> More rapid than eagles his coursers they came,
> And he whistled, and shouted, and called them by name;
> "Now, Dasher! now, Dancer! now, Prancer and Vixen!
> On, Comet! on Cupid! on, Donder and Blitzen!
> ...
> So up to the house-top the coursers they flew,
> With the sleigh full of toys, and St. Nicholas too.
> And then, in a twinkling, I heard on the roof
> The prancing and pawing of each little hoof.
> As I drew in my hand, and was turning around,
> Down the chimney St. Nicholas came with a bound.
> ...
> His eyes - how they twinkled! his dimples how merry!
> His cheeks were like roses, his nose like a cherry!
> His droll little mouth was drawn up like a bow,
> And the beard of his chin was as white as the snow;
> The stump of a pipe he held tight in his teeth,
> And the smoke it encircled his head like a wreath;
> He had a broad face and a little round belly,
> That shook, when he laughed like a bowlful of jelly.
> He was chubby and plump, a right jolly old elf,
> And I laughed when I saw him, in spite of myself; ...

In the same period, German immigrants introduced the Christmas tree in the US, the first mention of both Christmas and Santa is as early as 1856:

> **1856** Who can think ... of the anxious children gathered round the Christmas tree – the fabulous visits of Santa Claus ... without feeling that man has other ends than those that characterize every day life? (Mathews)

In 1863, Thomas Nast drew an illustration of Santa for *Harper's Weekly* that would greatly influence his image: a very chubby man with a white beard, wearing a red and white suit. This suit was adopted for the Coca Cola advertisements in the 1930s, thereafter becoming an inseparable part of his outfit. Chapter 9 of Mary Mapes Dodge's famous *Hans Brinker or the Silver Skates* published in 1865 is devoted entirely to the holiday of Sinterklaas and the similarities and differences between him and Santa Claus ("It was said that he originally came from Holland. Doubtless he did, but, if so, he certainly, like many other foreigners, changed his ways very much after landing upon our shores").

In the Netherlands, too, the myth of Sinterklaas was elaborated to what it is today in the nineteenth century. Even though the Sinterklaas holiday had been celebrated for centuries, the living figure of Sinterklaas did not appear until the mid-nineteenth century when the songs sung for him were also recorded for the first time. In his 1843 collection *Kinderliederen* (*Children's Songs*), Jan Pieter Heije published one of the oldest and most famous Sinterklaas songs, which begins with the lines: "'t Heerlijk avondje is gekomen, / 't Avondje van Sint Niklaas" (The wonderful evening has come, the evening of Saint Nicholas). The modern image of Sinterklaas is largely attributable to Jan Schenkman, who published the frequently reprinted picture book *Sint Nikolaas en zijn knecht* (*Saint Nicholas and his servant*) around 1850, featuring the opening lines "Zie, ginds komt de stoomboot/ Uit Spanje weer aan!" (Lo, yonder comes the steamboat from Spain, which will soon be here). Sinterklaas's arrival on a steamboat is an invention of Schenkman's. This was also the first song in which Sinterklaas's black servant appeared, who would not be called "Piet" (Pete) until 1911, in S. Abramsz's song "Op de hoge, hoge daken" (On the high, high roofs). From 1927 onwards, he was called "Zwarte Piet" (Black Pete). The Sinterklaas holiday was not celebrated during the Second World War, but the Canadians helped reinstitute the holiday after the liberation in 1945 and, to add to the fun, they surrounded Sinterklaas with a crowd of Black Petes, a custom that was to stay. Since 1990, Sinterklaas's gray horse has had a name, which, curiously, refers to America, namely *Amerigo*. During Sinterklaas's arrival in Elburg in 1990, the role of Sinterklaas's horse was played by a police horse named Amerigo, after the explorer who gave the American continent its name, Amerigo Vespucci. Amerigo has remained Sinterklaas's horse's name ever since. After Santa conquered the entire US in the twentieth century – helped, according to some cynics, by the retail trade – he also appeared in a large number of other countries. In the second half of the twentieth century, Sinterklaas even reemerged in the Netherlands in the form of Santa Claus, where he is called *Kerstman* to avoid confusion with his relative. The Low Countries are now blessed with two successive holidays, celebrated on 5 and 24 or 25 December, at which presents are handed out by what was once one and the same saint.

Illustration 2.56 – Santa Claus in his American appearance (source: Vignettes, Paris 2001)

2.12 Transport by sea and land

American English adopted four names for types of ships. All four were adopted in the seventeenth or eighteenth century and are still known to a greater or lesser degree: **hooker**, **keel(boat)**, **pinkie**, and **scow**. Besides maritime transport, the Dutch were specialized in transport over frozen land, for which they brought the words **skate** and **sleigh** to the American continent; both words were adopted in the seventeenth century and are still widely used.

hooker, a work boat, especially one used for fishing; an old or clumsy boat (DARE). - From Dutch *hoeker*, meaning "fishing vessel"; adopted in the seventeenth or eighteenth century and still in use.
* The Dutch name *hoeker* is derived from *hoek* (see **hook** in 2.5), which has various meanings, including "fishhook," which is now obsolete. A *hoeker* was originally a fishing vessel used to catch fish with a *hoek*. The name *hooker* was also adopted into British English, but American English probably borrowed it independently, for two reasons. Firstly, the word acquired a specific meaning – "work boat" and "old, clumsy boat" – in American English that it does not have in British English. And secondly, DARE shows that the word is particularly prevalent in New England, where, it should be said, it sounds somewhat old-fashioned.

> **1830** My *debut* as a blue jacket took place in 1815, on board an "old barn of a hooker," that was built during the war, down east.
> **1910** "He wrote me that he came up the river on a brig." "Yes, I commanded the old hooker."
> **1918** *Hooker* ... A boat, especially of an inferior sort. "It was pretty rugged out there for his old hooker."
> **1969** They had two ... they always called them hookers, boats ... They'd load the day's fish and then go that night [from Washington Island] to Green Bay. (DARE)
> **1975** *Hooker* – Originally a Dutch fishing boat with sturdy lines; hence any good workboat.

The word *hooker* is less likely to be associated with a boat than with the "Happy Hooker," Xaviera Hollander, a pseudonym of Vera de Vries, whose candid autobiography published under this title in 1971 sold over 16 million copies worldwide. Does *hooker* ("whore") come from Dutch? Is *hooker* in this sense derived from the name of a boat, as *tramp* is derived from *tramp steamer*, because the first tramps traveled by boat?

Bartlett provides a more plausible explanation in the second edition of his *Dictionary of Americanisms* (1859), in which he suggests that the word *hooker* is derived from the name Corlear's Hook, Hook for short, a point of land on the East River with several sailors' brothels.

> **1859** *Hooker.* A resident of the Hook, i.e. a strumpet, a sailor's trull. So called from the number of houses of ill-fame frequented by sailors at the Hook (i.e., Corlear's Hook) in the city of New York.

Corlear's Hook was previously named Corlaers Hook, after Jacobus van Corlaer, who settled there prior to 1640 and was a relative of Arendt van Corlaer, who founded the Schenectady colony on the banks of the Mohawk River in 1662, and

Illustration 2.57 – Hooker (source: private collection)

whose name came to be used in Iroquoian as a title for high-ranking people.

The etymology suggested by Bartlett is disputed, however, because the word had already been encountered in 1845 in North Carolina, far from Corlear's Hook. However, a new incidence has since emerged, namely in the *New York Transcript* dating from 25 September 1835, which contains a report of an examination in a police court, in which a woman is referred to as a *hooker* because she "hangs around the hook," which, again, appears to be Corlear's Hook. In spite of this, certain etymologists, including Quinion and Wilton, still allow for the option that *hooker* is not derived from *hook*, as borrowed from Dutch, but from indigenous English *hook* in the sense of a fastener, and that the name implies that a hooker "hooks or snares clients." A compromise, on the other hand, cannot be ruled out either: the hookers from the Corlear's Hook area were possibly named after this district whereas in other places the name may have been associated with *(fish)hook*.

In any event, there is one etymology of the word *hooker* which, although frequently recurring, is definitely incorrect: *hooker* is not named after Joseph "Fighting Joe" Hooker, major general in the Northern Army during the American Civil War and notorious for his conduct. Although his headquarters were half bar, half brothel, it is unlikely that his name was the source of *hooker*, for the simple chronological reason that Fighting Joe was commander in 1863, when *hookers* had already been around for nearly 30 years.

keel, **keelboat**, a shallow, covered riverboat (Craigie, Webster).
- From Dutch *kiel*, *kielboot*, used to refer to a flat-bottomed vessel; adopted in the seventeenth or eighteenth century and now a specialist and historical term (also in the Netherlands).
* Like English *keel*, Dutch *kiel* means "bottom of a ship." The word exists in the compound *kielboot* to refer to a vessel with a flat bottom, and *kiel* acquired the same meaning, either as short for *kielboot* or because *kiel* came to be used figuratively to refer to the entire vessel. Keelboats were suitable for navigating the Hudson River, a practice pioneered by the Dutch and copied by the Yankees, who adopted the boats and their names *keel* and *keelboat*. The boats were also used to navigate the Ohio and Mississippi rivers.

> **1785** Our fleet now consists of twelve small keels and batteaux.
> **1786** Great numbers of Kentucke and keel boats passing every day; some to the Falls, others to Post Vincent – Illinois Country &c.

1837 Before the introduction of steam-boats on the western waters, its immense commerce was carried on by means of keel-boats and barges. The former is much in the shape of a canal boat, long, slim-built, sharp at each end, and propelled by setting-poles and the cordelle, or long rope.
1883 Some hundreds [of rivers subordinate to the Mississippi] ... are navigable by flats and keels.

Illustration 2.58 – Keel, detail of a painting by Kees Terlouw (source: The Printing Art, vol. 4 #5, Jan. 1905)

pinkie, also **pinky**, a small sailing vessel with a sharp stern (Craigie, DARE, Webster).
- From Dutch *pinkje*, *pinkie*, a diminutive of *pink*, being the name of a particular type of vessel; adopted in the seventeenth century and still known.
* The origin of the Dutch word *pink* as the name of a certain vessel is unknown. The word was adopted into British English at an early time, but *pinkie* occurred first and almost exclusively in North America, including such variants as *pink (stern)*, *pink(ey)-stern schooner*. The word is particularly prevalent in New England but has also become known elsewhere. The vessel is used in the cod and coast fisheries.

1636 When the pinckes comes downe I hope the will bringe hay.
1840 Chebacco boats and small schooners are known to him as "*pinkies*," "*pogies*," and "*jiggers*."
1903 On another occasion the Houghton ran into a pinkey-stern schooner.
1932 True smacks were often sharp-sterned craft called pinkys, with rail rising aft to a high peak, ending in a crotch for holding the main boom when sail was lowered. Pinkys, often known as "pinks," were noted for their seagoing qualities and were, above all others, of purely New England origin.
1975 *Pinky* – A distinctive small schooner with sharp or "pinked" stem. Designed in Massachusetts, they had a vogue in Nova Scotia and were common along the Maine coast in short-haul trading. An occasional *pinky* is seen today in the summer fleet, preserved by someone who cares.

scow, a large, flat-bottomed boat, usually serving to transport sand, gravel or refuse (Craigie, Webster).
- From Dutch *schouw*, being a flat-bottomed type of vessel; adopted in the seventeenth century and still in use.
* The Dutch took their flat-bottomed scows to New Netherland, and because these boats were eminently suited to carrying goods across the numerous rivers, the Yankees were quick to adopt both the vessel and its name. The boats

were also used as ferries and occasionally referred to as *scow-boat* or *scow schooner*. Dutch *schouw* was also adopted into Scottish and Irish but independently of American English and later, in the nineteenth century.

1669 The Governor hath given me Orders ... to provyde a scow to help ye souldiers in their provision of fire wood.
1828 The ferry flat is a scow-boat.
1835 The Scows, used exclusively for grain, flour, lumber, &c, ... are employed by the farmers to carry their own produce to market.
1913 At the foot of Castro street ... the scow schooners, laden with sand and gravel, lay hauled to the shore in a long row.

The crew on the boats were called *scow-gang* or *scowmen*:

1891 The oyster next falls into the hands of the "scow-gang," men whose specialty it is to remove them from the floats.
1906 12 Scowmen and bargemen along the North and East River fronts.

In the twentieth century, the *scow* was developed further in the US into a small flat-bottomed racing yacht, after it had been equipped with sails in the nineteenth century. The *scow* had since become known in a large part of the US and, for some time now, is no longer confined to the East Coast:

1848 *Scow*. (Dutch, *schouw*.) A large flat-bottomed boat, generally used as a ferry boat, or as a lighter for loading and unloading vessels when they cannot approach the wharf. On Lake Ontario they are sometimes rigged like a schooner or sloop, with a lee-board or sliding keel, when they make tolerably fast sailers. (Bartlett)
1929 The result of these changes was that ten years after the Britannia was built the type of racing yacht had developed into a scow with a fin keel. (OED)

There also used to be a specialized scow in the US, the Dutch *modderschouw*, anglicized to ***mud-scow***, which was a barge or flatboat used for dredging:

1766 To Be Sold, a new Mud-Scow, 24 Foot long, and can carry 12 or 14 Tons Weight.
1848 A *mudscow* (Dutch, *modderschouw*) is a vessel of this description, used in New York for cleaning out the docks. (Bartlett, *scow*)
1894 Charlie Thayer ... could manage any kind of a boat from a crack yacht to a mudscow.

skate, one of a pair of devices worn on the feet for skating on ice (Craigie, Webster).
- From Dutch *schaats*, meaning "a (metallic) runner that may be clamped or fitted to a shoe, used to glide over ice"; adopted in the seventeenth century and still in use.
* As the Low Countries were known for their skating tradition and ice sports, many fifteenth- and sixteenth-century paintings depict skating scenes, as a result of which the word *schaats* was introduced in other languages, including British English. There are various records of *Dutchmen on* or *with scates* in the seventeenth century, which invariably describe a foreign phenomenon, which was to continue into the eighteenth century in British English. In American English, the word *skates* was encountered somewhat later, in the early eighteenth century, but this related directly to a New York phenomenon, which proves that British and American English adopted the word from Dutch independently. The final *-s* is part of the Dutch word, the plural being

Illustration 2.59 – "Roller-skating for the first time" (source: Voor 't Jonge Volkje, compiled by I. and L. de Vries, Utrecht 1980, illustration from 1880-1900)

schaatsen. In English, however, the form *skates* was interpreted as being plural, leading to the singular back formation *skate* in the nineteenth century.

> **1701** Upon the Ice its admirable to see Men and Women as it were flying upon their Skates.
> **1756** We proceeded down the lake, on the ice, upon skaits.
> **1790** Frederick W. Starman ... has just received ... from Amsterdam ... Skates.
> **1911** The runner of this skate is made of the very best cold rolled cast steel.

Thanks to Mary Mapes Dodge's famous children's book *Hans Brinker or the Silver Skates* from 1865, speed-skating became commonly known in the Unites States.

The affinity that the Dutch had with skating is clear from Farmer's comment in 1889 that a specific type of skates are called *dutchers*:

> **1889** *High Dutchers*. – Skates, the blades of which are ornamentally curled in front ... The Dutch are well known as the best skaters in the world – hence the name as given to a superior kind of skate.

In the eighteenth and nineteenth century, there were experiments with shoes with wheels fitted to the sole, a technique that was innovated in the US in the nineteenth century, culminating in the 1863 patent application for what was called a *roller skate*.

> **1863** A roller skate provided with two rows of tubular adjustable rollers, and the whole constructed and operating as shown and described.
> **1881** Children glide peacefully along the asphalt on roller-skates.

The innovated product led to a roller skate mania in the US and Western Europe, including the Netherlands, where the product was called *rolschaatsen*, probably translated from American English *roller skates*.

In the late twentieth century, all kinds of new, faster, and better versions of the roller skate were invented in the US, such as the *inline skate* with four wheels fixed in a single line. These roller skates often used to be called *skates*, as short for *roller skates*, *inline skates*, and so on. To distinguish them from these new skates, the earlier skates for use on ice have since been called *ice skates*. These innovations in skates, that is, both the product and the word, were adopted from the US in both the Netherlands and Belgium, and so the original Dutch *schaats* made its comeback in Dutch in the form of *skate* in the late twentieth century.

Illustration 2.60 – Skating couple (source: Schaatsenrijden, J. van Buttingha Wichers, The Hague 1888)

However, this was not a question of one-way traffic. In the Netherlands, there were also innovations with regard to the "real" skate – the one used to move on ice: in 1983, staff at the faculty of Human Movement Sciences at the VU University Amsterdam developed the *klapschaats*. The name reflects the fact that the skate allows skaters to give themselves an extra push to generate more thrust and speed. When the Dutch convincingly demonstrated the superiority of the skate in 1996, other countries were quick to adopt it, including its Dutch name. Initially, the skate was called *slapskate*, which was replaced by *clapskate* but, on account of the association with "the clap" (slang for gonorrhea) and possibly influenced by the Dutch word, it was eventually named ***klapskate***. While this name has acquired an official status in that the International Skating Union uses it in its documents and publications, the variants *clapskate* and *slapskate* are sometimes used as well. Thanks to the invention of the klapskate, the Dutch word *schaats* was adopted into American English twice.

sleigh, a vehicle on runners used for transporting persons or goods on snow or ice; dialect: a child's sled (Craigie, DARE, Webster).

- From Dutch *slede*, also contracted into *slee*, meaning "child's sledge," formerly "sledge employed for the transport of goods or people over ice or snow"; adopted in the seventeenth century and still in use.

* The leading role of the Dutch in the field of transport by ice is evident from the fact that English not only adopted **skate** from Dutch but also from the Dutch origin of all three English words for "vehicle, that is pulled sliding over ice and snow", – *sled*, *sledge*, and *sleigh*. *Sledge* has existed in British English since 1617; *sled* has even been known in English from as early as the fourteenth century, but is nowadays only used in dialects and American English. *Sleigh* is the only word that American English adopted directly from Dutch settlers, and is found in a variety of spellings, including *sley*, *slay*, and *slae*. The Dutch spelling was even preserved in the first quote.

> **1696** It is resolved ... to Present ... Two good and sufficient horses, & a Slee. (Mathews)
> **1703** Corps is brought to Town in the Governours Slay.
> **1708** Deleware River so froze that Loaden Slaes goes from hence upon it to Philadelphia.
> **1721** They went to church in a sley.
> **1759** [I] send you twenty-two sleys to transport your sick.
> **1832** Americans ... draw a distinction between a sled, or sledge, and a sleigh; the sleigh being shod with metal. (Craigie *sled*)

In the nineteenth century, *sleigh* evolved, as did *slee* in the Low Countries, from a means of transport into a children's toy, possibly as a shortened form of the older compounds *hand sleigh* and *handslee*, respectively.

> **1841** They prepared a rude hand sleigh ... The flat and wide side was the bottom of the runner, and it was bent up forward.
> **1869** Wheelbarrows and Childrens' Sleighs.

In the same century, the sleigh, whose function as a means of transport over snow and ice was gradually being taken over by the train and other means of transport, began to be associated with the Christmas season in the United States. The famous song "One-horse open sleigh," perhaps better known under the name "Jingle bells," was written in 1857. Recorded for the first time in 1790, *Sleigh bells* – the bells attached to a harness or the sleigh – would play a prominent role in many Christmas carols, including Irving Berlin's very popular "White Christmas" from 1940. And before that, "Winter Wonderland," written in 1934, started with "Sleigh bells ring, are you listening." The sleigh became **Santa Claus**'s sole means of transport (see 2.11). It is interesting to see how two Dutch export products became related in the US, whereas they had or have no relation whatsoever with one another in their country of origin.

Illustration 2.61 – Sleigh (source: Schaatsenrijden, J. van Buttingha Wichers, The Hague 1888)

2.13 Clothing

The words **duffle**, **mutch**, and **wamus** were borrowed in the seventeenth century. While the latter two are by now used only occasionally, **duffle** is still used frequently, albeit with a new meaning. **Knickerbockers** is derived from a Dutch name, probably a nickname, and underwent a unique semantic development in the nineteenth century.

Bartlett is the only source to list the word ***winkle-hawk*** in this category in 1848, stating: "(Dutch *winkel-haak.)* A rent in the shape of the letter L, frequently made in cloth. It is also called a *winkel-hole*. A New York term." DARE labels *winklehawk* "chiefly Hudson River Valley" and "old-fashioned."

duffle, 1. coarse woolen cloth used chiefly for blankets, coats, etc.; 2. articles of dress and personal use, carried on a camping or hunting trip (Craigie, Webster).
- From Dutch *duffel*, meaning "thick woolen fabric, heavy (winter) coat made of that fabric"; borrowed in the seventeenth century and still in use.
* The name *duffel* comes from the town of Duffel in the Belgian province of Antwerp, where the fabric was originally manufactured. While *duffle* was already found in American English as the name of a material as early as 1649, it was not encountered in British English until 1677. This means that the word was adopted into American English independently of British English, and the fabric immediately became a frequently traded commodity. The *duffelse jas*, called *duffle coat* in American English, soon emerged. The fabric was not only traded by the Dutch, but by others as well, as evidenced by the following quote from 1674: "[Indians] buy of them [English, Dutch, and French] for clothing a kind of cloth, called duffils, or trucking cloth, ... made of coarse wool." And 150 years later, the Indians still appeared to wear duffles, as evidenced by this 1832 record: "[The Indians] lodge in the woods, about a great fire, with the mantle of duffils they wear by day wrapt about them."

> **1649** An Inventory: ... 25 yards greene tammy ... 13 peeces of duffles.
> **1671** He shall have a coat of Duffils, or fifteen shillings.

In American English, the word acquired in the second half of the nineteenth century a meaning that it does not have in Dutch, namely "camping gear"; a *duffle bag* is used in the sense of "kit bag."

> **1884** Every one has gone to his chosen ground with too much impedimenta, too much duffle.
> **1925** Camp duffle and placer tools lay scattered on the ground.

knickerbockers, short, loosely fitting trousers gathered at the knee (Craigie, Webster).
- Named after Diedrich Knickerbocker, the fictional author of *A History of New York*, published in 1809 and written by Washington Irving. The name Knickerbocker is probably a corruption of the Dutch nickname *Kinnebak* ("jawbone"). The word *knickerbockers* is still in use.
* In 1809, after a well-thought-out marketing campaign with enticing preliminary announcements in the newspaper, the two-volume *A History of New York from the Beginning of the World to the*

End of the Dutch Dynasty, by Diedrich Knickerbocker was published. In the New York literary scene, it was soon a public secret that the book was written by Washington Irving. Irving's initial intention was to write a parody on *A Picture of New York*, a travel guide written by Samuel Latham Mitchill in 1807, but it soon turned into a history of the seventeenth-century Dutch colony of New Amsterdam. The book's satirical nature is obvious, as apparent from the subtitle: "containing, among many surprising and curious matters, the unutterable ponderings of Walter the Doubter, the disastrous projects of William the Testy, and the chivalric achievements of Peter the Headstrong – the three Dutch governors of New Amsterdam: being the only authentic history of the times that ever hath or ever will be published."

Irving, who could read Dutch and German fluently, was not so fastidious about the historical facts, but his book was the first to focus on the Dutch history of New York, casting a critical eye over the past ("What right had the first discoverers of America to land, and take possession of a country, without asking the consent of its inhabitants, or yielding them an adequate compensation for their territory?") and thus holding up a mirror to his contemporaries.

The book was an instant blockbuster, both in the US and in Europe. Irving made generations of Americans, to this day, aware of the Dutch roots of New York and of the history of the Knickerbockers – as the descendants of the original Dutch settlers were soon positively nicknamed. The nickname even came to be used for New Yorkers in general.

> **1841** We Knickerbockers, I fear, do not sufficiently appreciate the leaven of Eastern scholarship.
>
> **1857** I am an Albany Knickerbocker – a Dutchman of purest Belgic blood – and I justly claim to be heard.
>
> **1881** It has become common to speak of the *élite* of Albany as Knickerbockers – a name derived from Knik-ker-bak-ker (pronounced as spelled), a baker of knickers [marbles].

As in the 1881 quote above, most sources claim that the name Knickerbocker is derived from Knickerbakker, the name of an occupation that is assumed to be called *knikkerbakker* in Dutch; that is, a "baker of knickers" (see also **knicker** in 2.11), which is derived from a seventeenth-century Dutch settler who allegedly had this occupation.

The book itself shows, however, that the name was inspired by an existing contemporary, Herman Knickerbacker, a lawyer who became a US Congressman from the Albany, New York, area in 1808. The beginning of the book, which provides information about its author, states that Diedrich Knickerbocker is "cousin-german to the congress-man of that name." Herman's cousin was called Derrick, which may have been Irving's inspiration for Diedrich.

Herman Knickerbacker (currently known mostly as Herman Knickerbocker) was the son of Johannes Knickerbacker (1749-1827), a descendant of Hermen Jansen Knickerbacker, one of the earliest Dutch settlers in New York State. All Knickerbackers or Knickerbockers in the US are thought to be descendants of this once ancestor, who was probably born around 1648 and moved to the US in 1674. But where does the ancestor's name come from? Irving's own explanation (in Chapter 49) has never been taken seriously: "... the Knickerbockers ... derive their name, as some say, from *Knicker*, to shake, and *Beker*, a goblet, indicating thereby that they were sturdy toss-pots of yore; but, in truth, it was derived from *Knicker*, to nod, and *Boeken*, books; plainly meaning that they were great nodders or dozers over books; from them did descend the writer of this history."

As stated before, modern sources stick to the explanation of the name of the occupation of Knickerbacker ("baker of knickers"), but this is highly unlikely, because it is doubtful that someone with such a specialized occupation could make a living in the seventeenth century. What is certain, however, is that *knikkerbakker*, howsoever spelled, exists in Dutch neither as the name of an occupation nor as a family name.

The Knickerbacker or Knickerbocker family went to great lengths to trace the origin of their name (see www.knic.com/Kn_Hist.htm). They attempted to find out what name Hermen Jansen used when signing official documents, often being Hermen Jansen van Bommel – his family hailed from Bommel (now Zaltbommel) in the province of Gelderland. He was a native of Wijhe in the Dutch province of Overijssel, and therefore was also named Herman van Wye. In 1682, Hermen Jansen signed a document with "Hermen Jansen van Wyekycback(e)," which the family interpreted as Hermen Jansen van Wye-Kijk-back. Kijk was then believed to refer to the small town of Kijk or Kijc where the Dutch fleet fought under the command of M.A. de Ruyter, and *back* allegedly referred to the Dutch word for "jaw." It is now assumed that Hermen Jansen took part in the battle in 1673 (although there is no further evidence for this) and that he was wounded in the jaw, hence the nickname Kijk-back: "Kijk cheek," or "cheek marked at Kijk." In the effort to read the name, the "Wye," which might easily be mistaken for 'Nye' (it has been read in both ways by different clerks), was so interpreted and the name became Niekicbacker-Niekerbacker, from which the transition was easy to the final form of Knickerbacker.

Unfortunately, however, the construction Kijk-back is impossible in Dutch. In spite of this, it may be helpful to think of the possibility of a corrupted nickname in an attempt to explain the name. *Kinnebak* is used in present-day Dutch to refer to someone with a large mouth or jaw, *kinnebak* being a compound of *kin* ("chin") and *bak* ("jaw"). In the fourteenth century, there was a resident of Huizingen (Flemish Brabant) called *Kennebac*. The name Knickerbacker may well have been a corruption of Kinneback. It appears that Hermen's name was spelled in many different ways in official documents, as happened frequently at the time. Below is a list drawn up by the family (only the relevant information is provided):

1682 (Dec.11) Hermen Jansen van Wyekycback(e); Harme Jansz Kinnekerbacker
1683 Harmen Jansz Knickelbacker
1684 (May 6) Harmen Jansen Kinnekerbacker
1695 (July 21) Harmen Knickelbacker
1696-7 (Feb. 26) Harmen Jansen Knickerbacker Van Wyye
1702 (April 19) Harme Knickelbacker
1704 (May 1) Harmen Jansen Kinckerbacker
1706-7 (March 15) Harmen Janssen Nyckbacker.
1707 (Feb. 26) Heermen Jansen Kynckbacker

Among the many spellings we also observe that of Knickerbacker, but this definitely does not seem to have been the original spelling and is obviously a corruption of an older variant, and I put my money on *Kinneback*.

Being oblivious to all of this, Irving simply based the name on that of his contemporary Herman Knickerbacker or Herman Knickerbocker. Which raises a new question: when did the Knickerbacker family change its name to Knickerbocker? As far as can be verified, this happened after the publication of Irving's book, possibly even as a consequence of it. And the ancestors who had called themselves Knickerbacker were likewise retroactively rechristened Knickerbocker, which makes it difficult for outsiders to ascertain exactly when the name was changed.

Enough about the origin of the name of Knickerbocker. Let's move on to the question of why and when *knickerbockers* became the name for a certain type of knee breeches. This comes from the picture that Irving painted of the original Knickerbockers: chubby men with their ubiquitous pipes, dressed in a vest, coat and...baggy knee breeches. Irving describes this in chapter 7: "The dress of the original settlers is handed down inviolate from father to son – the identical broad-brimmed hat, broad-skirted coat, and broad-bottomed breeches continue from generation to generation; and several gigantic knee-buckles of massy silver are still in wear." More importantly, however, it was depicted in illustrations. In the second edition of the book from 1812, William Strickland depicted Diedrich Knickerbocker wearing knee breeches, and even more impressive were the illustrations that the famous British illustrator George Cruikshank made for the book in 1834. This special and comfortable garment would soon be named *knickerbockers*, and became popular as casual or sportswear.

> **1864** Imagine a South-Western Robin Hood, with a tawny beard, homespun knickerbockers, and a Rip-Rap hat.
> **1883** We donned our knickerbockers, ... and bicycled to the wharf.
> **1893** [She] darned the great holes which the boys' knees wore in stockings and knickerbockers.

In the 1880s, English women and children started wearing underwear that reached down to just below the knees, which resembled knickerbockers and were called *knickers* for short. This is now the general term in Great Britain (not in the US) for women's underpants. The name *knickerbockers* was adopted in many languages, including Dutch (as singular *knickerbocker*). While the name is still known, the garment is now out of fashion.

Thanks to Irving, New York was nicknamed *Knickerbocker land*. Many institutions, streets, and so on have been named after Knickerbocker (Diedrich or his ancestors, the original Dutch settlers), such as the basketball team the New York Knicks, Knickerbocker Avenue, as well as a hotel, a theater and a village, all of which can be found in various places.

A History of New York was not the end of Diedrich Knickerbocker's writing career. Irving published two other works under this pseudonym: *Rip van Winkle* in 1819 and *The Legend of Sleepy Hollow* in 1920, which are considered to be the first American short stories. And like its author Knickerbocker, **Rip van Winkle** (see 2.6) became a household term, thanks to their creator Washington Irving.

mutch, a woman's cap (Craigie, Webster). - Derived directly and indirectly from Dutch *muts*, "headgear"; adopted in the seventeenth century and still known.
* The Dutch word *muts*, which was used to refer to the typical headgear worn by Dutch women, was adopted into American English, as well as in Scottish and Irish. It has since become a historical term in all three. The word is listed in Webster, based on the assumed survival of the Scottish rather than the Dutch word. Since the same word is involved, it may have ended up in modern American English via both sources.

> **1680** His wyfe had stole a mutch or Capp.
> **1704** The Dutch ... women, in their habitt go loose, were French muches wch are like a Capp and a head band in one, leaving their ears bare.

Illustration 2.62 - Seventeenth-century mutch (source: Kleding en het AaBe ervan, Tilburg 1953)

Obsolete and no longer listed in Webster is a Dutch compound with *muts*, which must have been adopted into American English in the old days and is cited much more frequently than the simplex *muts*, namely ***clockmutch***, also ***clapmatch***. These words are also used to refer to a woman's cap, specifically one consisting of loose parts that could be folded up - hence the Dutch name *klapmuts*, from *(op)klappen* ("to fold up"). This was a typical, conspicuous type of headgear worn by Dutch women. When it was adopted into American English, Dutch *a* was transformed into *o* (as in *boss*, etc.). The word was then probably transformed through folk etymology into *clock*. It is included in a number of dictionaries of Americanisms from the nineteenth century and the early twentieth century, but was already archaic by then - the garment and its name were also going out of fashion in the Netherlands. In Dutch, *klapmuts* is still the common name for the *hooded seal*. The males have a conspicuous bulge on their head, which they blow up so that it appears as if they are wearing a hat, as the English name *hooded* also suggests. Apparently, *klapmuts* was also adopted into American English at one time or another as the name of a seal, given that the quote from 1902 states that *clapmatch* "is applied moreover to the designation of a certain kind of sealskin."

> **1848** *Clockmutch*. (Dutch, *klapmuts*, a night-cap.) A woman's cap composed of three pieces, - a straight centre one, from the forehead to the neck, with two side pieces. A New York term. (Bartlett)
> **1889** *Clockmutch, clapmatch*.
> - Literally a night-cap, from the Dutch *clapmuts*. A form of head-dress which, though still worn in Holland, is as rarely seen, in America, even in

Illustration 2.63 – Wamus. Hugo de Groot wore this when he escaped in disguise in a book chest from Castle Loevestein in 1621. It is the typical attire of a bricklayer in those days (source: Photo of the Historical Museum Rotterdam)

> the most remote parts of the Dutch settlement, as is the old, curtained, coal-scuttle bonnet in England. This cap has been made familiar to English eyes through painters of the old Dutch School. (Farmer)
> **1902** *Clockmutch* (Dutch *klap-muts*, a night cap). A New-York provincialism designing a quaint, though not unbecoming woman's cap, composed of three pieces, a straight centre one, from the forehead to the neck, with two side-pieces. The *clockmutch* is still worn by some old-fashioned ladies, and a fair representation of it is often seen in Gerard Dow's paintings. Also *clapmatch*, which besides being used in the above sense, is applied moreover to the designation of a certain kind of sealskin.

wamus, wammus, warmus, a warm work jacket (Craigie, DARE, Webster).
- From Dutch *wambuis*, *wammes*, meaning "a piece of men's clothing, a kind of vest"; adopted in the seventeenth or eighteenth century and still known.
* In the Middle Ages, both rich and poor people in the Low Countries wore a *wambuis*, a word derived from French, colloquially called *wammes*. This garment was a kind of vest, which was worn over a shirt and under an over-garment or coat of mail. It was thick and warm, covering the body from neck to waist. Through the ages, rich people replaced the garment with other pieces of clothing that came into fashion. In the nineteenth century, servants and workers often still wore a *wambuis*.

The colloquial name of the garment *wammes* was adopted into American English in the forms *wamus*, *wammus*, *waumus*, *warmus*. The form *warmus*, spelled *warm-us* in 1841, was undoubtedly transformed through folk etymology under the influence of *warm*. The *wamus* was worn mostly by workers. At present, the word is particularly prevalent in the south and west of the US. Although German *Wams* may have contributed to its proliferation, the original source of the loanword must be Dutch given the forms with two syllables.

> **1805** I got up, and found that my waumus was bloody, which I had not observed before.
> **1841** His long, matted locks overhung the back of a red flannel *warm-us*.

1847 The "*warmus*" is a working garment, similar in appearance to a "roundabout," but more full, and being usually made of *red* flannel, is elastic and easy to the wearer.
1872 Instead of a coat he wore that unique garment of linsey-woolsey known in the West as wa'mus (warm us?), a sort of over-shirt.
1912 *Wammus*, a coat-like jacket worn by men in such work as threshing wheat. (Western Indiana).

2.14 Miscellaneous

This category comprises a small number of words that do not fit into the previous categories, namely **bazoo**, **dingus**, **hunky-dory**, **poppycock**, and **spook**. Dating from the nineteenth century, all these words are colloquial, with the exception of **spook**, which probably became known through literature and was probably introduced by the earliest settlers.

It is interesting to consider a number of constructions that are used regionally in American English and that are based on Dutch and/or German. According to DARE, the preposition ***under through*** is used instead of the normal *under* in Dutch or German settlement areas, modeled on Dutch *onderdoor* or German *untendurch*. Furthermore, half hours in indications of time are sometimes expressed as *half* followed by the hour in the meaning of "thirty minutes before the hour named." Standard English *half past one* is then regionally referred to as ***half-two***, after Dutch *half twee* (or German *halb zwei* in certain areas). Compare the 1832 quote "Waggons set off at half-two o'clock" and the 1987 quote "Half two means 1:30, it was commonly heard in the Pennsylvania Dutch country as recently as ten years ago, and is still heard in parts of Wisconsin." Kurath (1949: 24) supplements the list with the constructions ***right good, right smart***, which are probably literal translations of Dutch *recht goed*, *recht slim*.

bazoo, mouth (Craigie, DARE, Webster).
- Corruption of Dutch *bazuin* "trumpet"; borrowed in the nineteenth century and still commonly used as a slang word.
* The senses listed by Craigie demonstrate its changes in meaning. The word was initially adopted in the Dutch sense of "(toy) trumpet"; hence as a newspaper title *The Bazoo*. From this evolved the meaning of "assertive or boastful talk", that is "to blow one's own horn"; *he blows his own bazoo* is said of someone who is boastful and obtrusive. The next step is to the instrument used to boast: the mouth. The chronological development of the meaning is evident from the following quotes in Craigie:

1877 *Blowin' his bazoo*, gasconade.
1884 People ... listen to the silvery tinkle of his bazoo.
1888 Among the far-west newspapers, have been, or are, ... *The Bazoo*, of Missouri.
1902 You are jest my sort of a Christian – better'n me, a sight, fer you don't shoot off yore bazoo on one side or t'other.
1906 We've had enough of your bazoo.

1906 Shut up your bazoo.

Bazoo ("mouth") and the expression *shooting off one's bazoo* are still used in American English slang in the sense of "to talk exaggeratedly and boastfully." These developments are truly peculiar to American English, because in Dutch the word only means "trumpet."

DARE states that these meanings also exist in regional American English, with that of "boastful talk" now being used predominantly in the West. Another, interesting meaning that is only known regionally is that of "buttocks," which has been listed as a jocular word, and is sometimes pronounced *bazoon* or *bazookas*. The origin of this meaning is not immediately apparent.

DARE also lists the regional name *bazoo wagon*, with a quote from 1977, meaning: "a caboose, the rear wagon of a freight train." *Bazoo wagon* stems from *bazoo* ("mouth") and *wagon*; probably also influenced by *zoo*, and phonetically by *caboose* (see ***caboose*** in 2.8).

In American English, *bazoo* is the source from which **bazooka** is derived as a name for a trombone-like instrument, which became commonly known around 1935 thanks to the American comedian, Bob Burns. In 1942, the meaning shifted to "a tubular gun for firing small rockets." This is the meaning in which many languages, including Dutch, adopted the word *bazooka* from American English.

dingus, a thing the proper name for which is unknown or does not come readily to mind; a "gadget" or "jigger" (Craigie, DARE, Webster).
- From Dutch *dinges*, meaning "what's his name"; borrowed in the nineteenth century and still in use.
* The Dutch word *dinges* is derived from *ding* ("thing") under the influence of German *Dings*. It is a typical colloquialism, just like American English *dingus*. It is therefore no surprise that various spellings exist in American English; DARE, for example, lists the forms *dangus*, *dinkus*, *dingass*, and *dingis*. In American English, it is also used in the euphemistic and vulgar sense of "penis." Thanks to a contamination of *dingus* in this sense and the synonymous *dick*, the form *dink* also arose in the sense of "penis," while it was later also used as a derogatory term for a person or animal.

1876 The latest thing in the way of a soul-warmer that the youths of Pioche have got up is a dingis made thusly.

1882 Taking a plug out of the end of it, they pull out a dingus and three

Illustration 2.64 – Bazoo, advertisement for Bell Company Telephones (source: The Printing Art, vol. 5, #4, June 1905)

joints of fish-pole come out.
1955 At the top of the plant was a queer-looking, half-formed cluster of pale berries. "What kind of a dingus do you call that?" Reno asked.
1982 I have secretly recorded some of the unusual phrases ... in my mother's conversation ... Dinkus = penis.
2009 The word "dingus" came about through the popular movie, *The Maltese Falcon* where the star, Humphrey Bogart, refers to the Maltese falcon as "The Dingus." So, the definition of the word "dingus" is a way of referring to any noun (including people) in an offhand manner. - Who did you go to the movies with? Eh, some dingus. - Could you please pass the dingus? (*Urban Dictionary* on the Internet)
2009 A complete moron, usually used in a joking manner to a friend. "Dude, stop being such a dingus." (*Urban Dictionary* on the Internet)

hunky-dory, all right, satisfactory, fine (Craigie, DARE, Webster).
- Derived in the nineteenth century from *hunk*, which is derived from Dutch *honk*, meaning "home base"; *hunky-dory* is a commonly used slang word.
* The oldest quote in which *hunky-dory* is used, which dates from 1866, addresses the question of where the evocative word comes from:

> **1866** "I cannot conceive on any theory of etymology that I ever studied why anything that is 'hunkee doree', or 'hefty' or 'kindy dusty' should be so admirable." (*The Galaxy*, October 1866)

The author has no idea but, fortunately, scholarly insights have progressed.
The word has been proven to be rooted in the Dutch children's game that was adopted into American English as *hunk*, a noun meaning "goal, base, home" (see **hunk** in 2.11) from which, in turn, the adjective *hunky* was formed, which has been known since 1843 in the meaning of "fine, all-right." *Dory* was added at a later date, probably as a humorous, expanded colloquial form. Before that, in 1842, the reduplication *hunkum-bunkum* had been found ("Everything was hunkum-bunkum for immediate flight"), and *hunky-dory* (or *honkey-dorey*) was probably a variation on this.
Words meaning "fine, all-right" have often been the object of variation, compare, for example, *okey-dokey* alongside *OK*, *okay*.

> **1868** [Even Samuel Slater admitted that Tostee, when and if she sang, was] hunky-dory.
> **1875** He was all "hunky-dory," in certain quarters.
> **1894** "Oh, *we're* hunkidori in a box!" declared the bridegroom.
> **2009** I checked the situation; everything is hunky dory, we have nothing to worry about. (*Urban Dictionary* on the Internet)

In 1877, Bartlett provided another explanation for the origin of *hunky-dory*, which is regularly repeated to this day, namely: "*Hunkidori*. Superlatively good. Said to be a word introduced by Japanese Tommy and to be (or to be derived from) the name of a street, or bazaar, in Yeddo [Tokyo]."

Japanese Tommy was the stage name of the variety performer Thomas Dilward, popular in the USA in the 1860s. He was a black dwarf, who was not familiar with Japanese and had probably never been to Japan. He was called *Japanese* to hide his real ethnic background from the white public. It is possible that Tommy popularized or even invented the expression *hunky-dory*, probably using the existing words *hunky* and *hunkum-bunkum* and adding *dori*. It is conceivable that he was inspired from sailors who had been to Japan and had picked up the Japanese term *honcho-dori*, meaning "main street." On coming home, the sailors may have told enthusiastic stories about the Japanese *hunky-dori* street that offered all manner of entertainment. However, the Japanese connection is not necessary: *hunky-dori* may just have been an ear-pleasing variant of *hunky*. The name of the Christy Minstrels is also mentioned in this connection. According to the *Morris Dictionary of Word and Phrase Origins*, this singing group sang a hugely popular song during the American Civil War (1861-1865), entitled "Josephus Orange Blossom," including the line *red-hot hunky-dory contraband*. Apparently, the popularity of the expression *hunky-dory* was enhanced via various channels.

poppycock, nonsense, foolish talk (Craigie, Webster).
- From Dutch *poppekak*, which literally means "doll's excrement"; adopted in the nineteenth century and still in use.
* In American English, the informal *poppycock* sounds rather corny and has been superseded by more powerful synonyms, such as *crap*, *bull* or *bullshit*. Although the word is now mostly used by civilized speakers of British English, the word was initially adopted in the US. Most dictionaries suggest that the word is derived from Dutch *pappekak*, which literally means "excrement as soft as porridge, soft dung," a compound of *pap* ("porridge") and *kak* ("excrement"). However, the word has never been encountered in Dutch.

Therefore, the word is now assumed to be derived from Dutch *poppekak*, literally "doll's excrement," from *pop* ("doll") and *kak* ("excrement"). There is a Dutch expression *zo fijn als gemalen poppestront* (literally "as fine as powdered doll's excrement") that is used to refer to a deeply religious person. The Frisian equivalent is *hy is sa fyn as poppestront*, "he is devout as shit, ultra-orthodox and a bit of hypocrite." *Stront* and *kak* are synonyms, and although the saying *zo fijn als gemalen poppekak* has not been found in written sources, it is likely to have existed alongside the version with *poppestront* – as the expression is regarded as vulgar, it is not readily recorded in writing. *Poppestront* exists in Dutch dialects also in the meaning of "big fuss, overdone kindness," being the meaning of *póppesjtróntj* in the dialect of Limburg. Similarly, *wat een poppestront!* means "what a fuss!," which may easily have become "what nonsense!"

It is unclear when American English borrowed the word, but most likely in the nineteenth century, as an expression such as *zo fijn als gemalen poppestront* is more typical of the critical nineteenth century than the seventeenth, when religion played such a prominent role in society that deeply religious people were unlikely to be targets of scorn. While the Dutch word *poppestront* or *poppekak* was certainly regarded as vulgar in the nineteenth century, English speakers did not grasp the literal meaning, allowing the expression to spread much more widely in American English than in Dutch. The fact that this meaning was not immediately apparent is clear from the fact that the Lincoln Snacks Company marketed a well-known glazed popcorn variety under the trademark *Poppycock*. According to the company's legend, the snack was invented by Howard Vair in the 1950s.

The word *poppycock* underwent the normal phonetic change in American

English, with *a* in *kak* being changed into *o* (as in *boss*) and *-y-* becoming the linking phoneme (compare *pannicake*). The word spread from American English to Great Britain in the 1910s.

> **1852** "Justice," said the policeman, ... "I'm blamed if this will do." "Poppycock," answered the Justice, "it's all right; sit down and mingle."
> **1865** You won't be able to find such another pack of poppycock gabblers as the present Congress of the US.
> **1890** All their alleged wealth and respectability is poppycock.
> **1904** "Bosh!" cried the lawyers. "Poppycock," the cynics sneered, and the courts rule out the cases.

spook, a ghost or specter (Craigie, Webster).
- From Dutch *spook* "ghost"; probably adopted in the seventeenth or eighteenth century and still in use, with new meanings.
* Virtually all Dutch loanwords that were adopted into American English have become known through verbal contact between English and Dutch speakers, but this does not seem to be true for *spook*. The word was mentioned for the first time as late as 1801, which is late for a word that came with the first wave of Dutch settlers. Apparently, it was only used in Dutch circles for a long period of time, possibly because ghost stories were only told in family circles. The word was probably introduced into American English via literature, seeing that the two oldest quotes are both literary quotes. The first mention is in a poem published in the *Massachusetts Spy* of 15 July 1801, written by a certain Hans, featuring words and spellings that look Dutch and German (quoted in Thornton):

> **1801** If any wun you heart shool plunder,
> Mine horses I'll to Vaggon yoke,
> Und chase him quickly; – by mine dunder
> I fly so swift as any spook

The following quote is also from a literary work:

> **1840** Be't you for sartain, or only your spook?

After that, the word apparently became commonly known, given its use in a newspaper:

> **1884** He was really run out of a fine position by spooks.

A quote from 1896 goes "You look just 's if you'd seen a spook!" which is a literal translation of Dutch *je ziet eruit alsof je een spook hebt gezien!* As Schele de Vere rightly states, German *Spuk* may also have influenced American English:

> **1872** ... *spook*, which may be the Dutch *spook*, a spirit or a ghost, or the German *Spuek*, a phantom or a vision. The manner of writing it speaks for the former presumption, and so does the fact that the word is not only used in the British colonies, but even by classic writers like Lord Lytton. But, on the other hand, *spooks* prevail most in regions where Germans abound, as in the great Valley of Virginia and in the Northwest.

The reason for the word's success in American English is unclear: why did the words *ghost*, *phantom*, etc. not suffice?

The cognate adjective *spooky* was coined as early as 1854 and the verb *to spook* appeared for the first time in 1867, also in a poem: "Yet still the New World spooked it in his veins, / A ghost who could not lay with all his pains." And in 1942, when the Second World War was in full swing, Americans called their spies *spooks*. British English borrowed the word *spook* and its derivatives from American English.

Illustration 2.65 – Spook; drawn by Howard Chandler Christie; from: James Whitcomb Riley, "An olde sweetheart of mine", 1903 (source: The Printing Art, vol. 3, #4, June 1904)

2.15 Dutch loanwords that did not originate from immigrants

The words mentioned above were all adopted from Dutch immigrants and reveal the linguistic influence these immigrants have had on the American continent. In the twentieth century, especially after the Second World War, Dutch loanwords ended up in American English via channels other than verbal contact between Dutch speakers and English speakers, such as scientific contacts, sport, journalism, or trade. The examples provided below merely serve as illustrations; they fall outside the scope of this book in that they are Dutch words that became known internationally and are not indicative of the specific influence that Dutch has had on American English, which is the subject of this book. Further, most of the words in question are known only in small specialist circles, and some are words that will probably soon disappear from the vocabulary as a result of new discoveries.

In the twentieth century, Dutch had the greatest impact on scientific language, often because a Dutch scientist managed to link his name to his theoretical or practical invention, as did the physicists Johannes van der Waals, Pieter Zeeman, H.B.G. Casimir, and H.A. Lorentz; the physicians Christiaan Eijkman and Willem Einthoven; the chemist J.H. van 't Hoff; the astronomers Jan Hendrik Oort and Gerard Kuiper; and the biologist/author Leo Vroman. In American English, scientists speak of ***van der Waals forces*** (from Dutch *vanderwaalskrachten*), ***Zeeman effect*** (from Dutch *Zeemaneffect*), ***Casimir effect*** (from Dutch *Casimireffect*), ***Lorentz transformation*** (from Dutch *Lorentztransformatie*), ***Eijkman('s) test*** (from Dutch *Eijkmans test*), ***Einthoven's law*** (from Dutch *wet van Einthoven*), ***van 't Hoff equation*** (from Dutch *vergelijking van Van 't Hoff*), ***Oort cloud*** (from Dutch *Oortwolk*), ***Kuiper belt*** (from Dutch *Kuipergordel*), and ***Vroman effect*** (from Dutch *Vromaneffect*). A scientific name that contains the name of a Belgian is ***bakelite***, which was named after the inventor Leo H. Baekeland, who was born in Ghent and emigrated to the US. While there are definitely more scientists after whom an invention has been named, the above examples suffice by way of illustration of the phenomenon.

Various Dutch scientists coined a name for a new invention. For example, the terms ***superconductor*** and ***superconducting*** are derived from the Dutch words *supergeleider* and *supergeleiding*. The phenomenon was discovered and named in 1911 by Leiden-based scientist Heike Kamerlingh Onnes, who was awarded the Nobel Prize for it in 1913. In his inaugural speech in 1932, Dutch Romanist Marius Valkhoff was the first to use the linguistic term ***adstratum*** to refer to "linguistic elements that induced changes in a language that is otherwise dominant." He coined the word after the linguistic terms *substratum* and *superstratum*.

Two Dutch car makers have made an impression on the world: ***Daf*** and ***Spyker***, each serving two entirely different market segments. On 26 October 2005, the *New York Times* wrote about Yahoo Autos Groups under the heading "Repairing Your Daf? Places to Get Some Tips." *Daf* was originally an acronym of *Van Doorne's Aanhangwagenfabriek*, later *Van Doorne's Automobielfabriek*. The name of Dutch airplane manufacturer ***Fokker*** ("he flew a Fokker") also made it into American English.

Koninklijke Philips Electronics N.V. – Philips for short – the electronics giant that was originally based in Eindhoven, churned out a multitude of adopted brand names.

Philips is a global supplier of electric razors that are marketed under the registered trademark ***Philishave***. The ***(compact) audio tape cassette***, called *audiocassette* or *compactcassette* in Dutch for short, was invented by Philips and launched in 1963 under the name that was coined in the Netherlands. Its successor, the ***compact disc***, also comes from this company. The *compact disc* was developed by Philips and Japan-based Sony in the 1980s, and its name was modeled on the older word *compactcassette*, likewise a Dutch development and adopted into American English as ***compact cassette***. For obvious marketing reasons, the names are composed of words or morphemes that already existed in English, as a result of which they do not look particularly Dutch. In 2002, Philips developed the hugely successful *Senseo coffee machine* in association with the Dutch firm Douwe Egberts. The name ***Senseo*** is used to refer to the product as well: "Can I make you a Senseo?"

In 1988, the Netherlands was the first country to introduce a quality label that is granted to products produced in developing countries at a fair price, called *Max Havelaar*. This was the titled of a novel published by Eduard Douwes Dekker in 1860 under the pseudonym Multatuli, in which he condemned the loathsome practices on coffee plantations in Indonesia. At present, Max Havelaar products are sold in fourteen European and thirteen non-European countries, including the US.

A number of Dutch inventions ended up in the US in the twentieth century under their Dutch name. An example is the ***rollator***, manufactured by the Dutch company Premis Medical under the name *Provo rollator* in 1986. On 28 July 2008, the *New York Times* dubbed this walker "The Cadillac of Walkers." In 1964, urban developer Niek de Boer built the first ***woonerf*** in the Dutch municipality of Emmen. The term was introduced in the US by Boudewijn Bach from the Delft University of Technology on a Fulbright lecture tour. The concept caught on and the nearly unpronounceable name was adopted, often accompanied by an explanation, such as "street for living," "living street," "living yard," "residential yard," "urban yard," "living environment" or "home zone." People even talk about *woonerf streets*.

A Dutch invention in an entirely different area is *snoezelen*: a therapy designed for people with a mental handicap and demented elderly people, who are placed in a room – the *snoezelkamer* or *snoezelruimte* – with objects, images, colors, smells, and sounds that pleasantly stimulate the senses. On 23 December 2003, the *New York Times* wrote about the phenomenon of ***snoezelen***: "An import from Europe, Snoezelen, or multisensory stimulation for the elderly and for disabled children and adults, is being discovered in the US. About 500 to 600 Snoezelen rooms have opened here."

In the area of sport, the term ***klapskate*** was already discussed above under **skate** (see 2.12). An older invention is that of *korfbal*, called ***korfball*** in American English. The name was made up by Dutch teacher Nico Broekhuijsen, who founded the *Nederlandsche Korfbal Bond* (Dutch Korfball Association) in 1903. The sport became international in the 1970s and has been regulated and supervised by the International Korfball Federation since 1993.

In his *Word Watch* (1995) Soukhanov defined ***mudwalking*** as "the sport of trekking for miles through muddy tidal flats on the North Sea coast of the Netherlands." The activity is explained in more detail in the *Washington Post* dated 23 August 1992: "Over the past 25 years, *mudwalking* – *wadlopen* – has become a popular pastime in the northern province of Friesland. While the Swiss scale the Alps and the Norwegians crisscross their mountain ranges on skis, the Dutch are busy walking in the *wad. Wad* is Dutch for tidal flat."

Dutch has also made a contribution to American musical terminology, albeit a small one: ***gabber*** or *gabba* is a style of house music that originated in Rotterdam in the early 1990s under the name *gabberhouse*, and has since become known all around the world. The 1997 edition of *The Oxford Dictionary of New Words* defines it as "a harsh, aggressive type of house music with a rapid beat. A direct borrowing from Dutch *gabber*, meaning 'mate, fellow, lad'." In the US, gabba is made by, among others, the Chicago-based hardcore techno DJ and producer Dave Rodgers, better known as Delta 9. In *Dictionary of New English 1963-1972* by Barnhart et al. the music style is called *Dutch house*.

In the twentieth century, the Dutch have little to be proud of in terms of literary influence, judging from the list of the hundred most influential books after the Second World War published by the *Times Literary Supplement* in 2005; not a single Dutch work was included. The compilers added, however, that the list would have looked different if it had included books dating from before the Second World War, in which case ***The Waning of the Middle Ages***, the pioneering study written by Dutch historian Johan Huizinga in 1919 about the culture of nobility in the Late Middle Ages would have definitely featured on the list. The title of this work is so well known that it is sometimes used outside the context of Huizinga's book as well and it inspired variations ("The Waning of the Renaissance").

American English also adopted a number of Dutch words in the fields of politics and economics. In 1940, Dutch educationalist and educational reformer Kees Boeke gave a new meaning to the word *sociocratie* (sociocracy), which French philosopher August Comte had used previously, in 1851, in a different sense. Boeke used it as a name for a system of administration based on the principle of equality of all individuals and on consensus. He founded a school according to his principles, which was attended by such pupils as the current Dutch queen, Beatrix. Another student was Gerard Endenburg, who later became a professor at Maastricht University, where his teaching focused on the "learning organization, specifically sociocratic circle organization." Thanks to Endenburg, who spent some time in the US and authored a number of publications on sociocracy, the term *sociocracy* was introduced in the US in its modern sense.

In the 1980s and 1990s, the Dutch political system adopted a consensus model similar to that outlined by Boeke; at the time this was called the *poldermodel*. This term was known in the US as the ***polder model*** as well, but more frequently it was also called the *Dutch miracle*, the *Dutch model*, or the *third way*. On 16 June 1997, the *New York Times* wrote: "As Europeans wring their hands over what is usually presented as a choice between heartless American-style modernizing of their economies and preserving the old European social safety nets, many people say the Dutch have found a 'third way' combining an open, vigorous market with generous social benefits and a measure of social justice," and on 1 October 2004: "Under the Polder model, the Netherlands was described as an economic miracle in Europe."

In the 1960s, the image of the ***Provos*** or *the Dutch Provo movement* prevailed abroad. The word is included in Ayto's dictionary of neologisms. Jonathon Green's dictionary of new words has listed ***Kabouter*** since 1960 to mean: "a member of a Dutch group of political activists who promoted pacifism and anarchism; the kabouters – literally the 'dwarves' – were best known outside Holland for their 'white bicycles' scheme of the mid-1960s: white bicycles were left all over Amsterdam, free for anyone to use." Later, around 1980, the Dutch recalcitrance over the deployment of American nuclear missiles in Western Europe spawned the contemptuous term ***Hollanditis*** or *Dutch disease*. The word *Hollanditis* was coined by the well-known commentator Walter Laqueur in his 1981 article "Hollanditis: A New Stage in European Neutralism."

The terms *Polder model*, *Provos*, *Kabouter*, and *Hollanditis* describe Dutch phenomena that do not exist in the US. The same goes for the word ***coffeeshop***, which, interestingly, is an American English word that acquired a new meaning in Dutch. While a *coffeeshop* in the US is an innocent establishment serving coffee, light meals, and snacks, a Dutch ***coffeeshop*** is an establishment that sells soft drugs, attracting large numbers of tourists, including Americans, to major cities such as Amsterdam.

The last word that merits mentioning is ***LAT-relation*** or ***LAT-relationship*** – where *LAT* stands for *living apart together*. While this will seem like perfect English to everyone, everything is not what it seems. The term did not originate in English but is derived from the film *Frank and Eva, Living Apart Together*, made by Surinamese/ Dutch film director Pim de la Parra in 1973, as a result of which *lat-relatie* became a common term in the Netherlands and was adopted by sociologists around 1980. From the Netherlands, it spread to other countries, including the US. On 4 May 2006, the *New York Times* reported: "[R]esearchers are seeing a surge in long-term, two-home relationships. They have even identified a new demographic category to describe such arrangements: the "living apart together," or L.A.T., relationship. These couples are committed to sharing their lives, but only to a point."

2.16 Conclusion

Of the words that American English adopted from Dutch immigrants, as listed in sections 2.1 to 2.14, over 70 percent came from the first wave of settlers; only 30 percent was introduced by the second wave (for the reasons for this, see the section 1.5, "What remains of the nineteenth- and twentieth-century Dutch"). In the category of foodstuffs, the influence of the first and second waves is almost equal; in the category of human traits and characterizations, the nineteenth and twentieth centuries were more influential than the seventeenth and eighteenth. In all the other eleven categories, however, the loanwords from seventeenth and eighteenth centuries have the upper hand, with the terms relating to landscape and in and around the house dating exclusively from these two periods. Most Dutch loanwords are still known in American English, although some only regionally. Most of the words from the first wave, in particular, are still listed in dictionaries, although some have now become historical terms. This means that the earliest Dutch settlers have left their mark on the American English language up to the present day.

The Dutch laid the foundation for the American political system, based as it is on democratic values, freedom of religion and conduct, and the concept that everyone is equal and therefore has the same chances of climbing the social ladder; everyone can become *boss*. All these values were reflected in Dutch words that referred to the various citizens and form of government and which were adopted into American English for a period of time, such as *burgher*, *scout*, and so on, but were eventually replaced by English words. Their meaning, however, was transferred to the English words, thus preserving the Dutch influence. As stated previously, it is notable that the name for northerners, or even Americans in general, *Yankee*, is derived from a Dutch word. As for religion, while the Dutch introduced the notion of freedom of religion on the East Coast, Dutch religious loanwords never gained a foothold.

Other Dutch influences were generally very concrete. The Dutch language furnished no abstract terms, no high-minded words about cultural phenomena, no literary or philosophical terms nor words in the areas of art and sciences. American English did, however, adopt names for dishes, calls for farm animals, agricultural utensils, children's games, and suchlike. On the other hand, every menu in American bars or restaurants is likely to include some names that are of Dutch origin. The important international term *dope* is derived from Dutch, as is the US currency *dollar* and, notably, *Santa Claus*, who arrives by *sleigh* – also Dutch! Linguistically, American flora and fauna and the American landscape would have looked different had it not been for Dutch input. In the world of commerce, the Dutch even introduced a suffix that has become significantly more productive in American English than it ever has been in Dutch, namely *-ery* to refer to "a place where a certain activity is conducted professionally." And American colloquial speech cannot dispense with Dutch terms, such as *assing around*, *dingus*, *dumbhead*, *hunky-dory*, *poppycock*, *the whole boodle*, *the whole caboodle* and *shooting off one's bazoo*.

In conclusion, it is interesting to note a number of general phonetic changes that Dutch loanwords underwent in American English. Dutch *a* frequently became *o*, which may be a result of the Dutch (*Holland* dialect) of seventeenth-century pronunciation (see 1.2) but may just as well be attributable to English influence. The change affected such words as *bockey*, *boss*, *canol* (besides *canal*), *clockmutch*, *dollar*, *mossbunker*, *poppycock* and *woffle iron* (besides *waffle iron*). In American English, Dutch long *-a-* sometimes became *-aw-* or *-au-*; compare *canawl* (besides *canal*), *crawl* and *(Santa) Claus*.

The Dutch linking *-e-* became *-i-* or *-y-*, compare *killifish*, *pannicake* and *poppyock*, or ***potty-baker*** ("a potter"), included only in Bartlett in 1848 and derived from Dutch *pottenbakker*.

A strikingly large number of Dutch words were adopted into American English in their diminutive form. This seems to confirm a prejudice about the national character of the Dutch that can be inferred from their frequent use of diminutives to express (either false or sincere) modesty – such as the author who referred to his latest 1,100-page novel as "boekje" ("little book"), or are used euphemistically – "hij heeft een buikje" (he has a little pot belly), or "het is me het weertje wel" ("nice weather, isn't it?").

In Standard Dutch, the diminutive suffix is *-je* (plus variants), colloquially pronounced as *-ie*, which form was adopted into American English (spelled *-y*, *-ie* and *-ey*). Americans do not find these suffixes odd, as they also exist in English. Moreover, the suffixes *-ie* and *-y* are also used to form diminutives in English (cf. *dearie*, *auntie*, *Billy*, *pussy*). A series of Dutch words were borrowed with the diminutive form *-ie* after *k*: *blickey*, *bockey*, *cookie*, *kliekies*, *pinkie*. In addition to these, a number of words that had the diminutive form *-etje* in Dutch also were adopted into American English in plural, yielding the forms *applejees*, *blumachies*, *noodlejees*, and *rollichies*.

Finally, in a limited number of Dutch loanwords, the diminutive form *-tje* became *-chie*, as in *frowchey*. This suffix is also found in two wholly archaic Dutch loanwords which have not been discussed before, namely ***prawchey*** and ***terawchey***. *Prawchey* is derived from Dutch *praatje*, about which Clapin wrote in 1902: "A painful corruption of the original, and designating a gossip, in the sense of a pleasant neighborly talk. This word now retains only an antiquarian interest, being at present almost entirely extinct." Farmer also included it in 1889.

Much less easy to recognize is the source of *terawchey*, about which Clapin wrote: "*Terawchey* (Dutch *te-ratje*). A familiar word still lingering in New York nurseries, and the equivalent for the 'creep-mouse.' This word, as will be seen, is made up exactly like *prawchey*, from *praatje*." This explanation does, however, require some clarification. Creep-mouse is a game that parents play with their children by walking their fingers over their child, saying "Here... comes... the creep-mouse... from... the barn... into... the house..." In Dutch, they say something like: "Er komt een muisje aangelopen / Trippel trippel trip / Stiekem in jouw nekje gekropen / Trippel trippel trip." In Dutch and English, the animal is a mouse, but in certain Dutch dialects it is a small rat. Apparently, the Dutch took the word *ratje* to the US, where the word became completely corrupted in children's language: in speech, people said *'t ratje*, with the Dutch article *'t*; which sounded like *teratje* and thus became *terawchey* in American English. Unfortunately, this nice Dutch word has now disappeared from American English completely but provides an apt conclusion to this glossary.

CHAPTER 3.

Dutch influence on North American Indian languages

3.0 Introduction

The Dutch loanwords in Amerindian languages have been collected from the works of Peter Bakker, Ives Goddard, Jay Miller, and J. Dyneley Prince (see bibliography at the back of this book). There must have been other Dutch loanwords in Amerindian languages: much information is sure to have been lost since the seventeenth century. In his book from 1999, Cecil Brown says that Dutch loanwords have been found in Onondonga and Oneida, but he does not give concrete examples. (On inquiry, it appeared that the data from the original study were no longer available.)

3.1 Delaware Jargon

In chapter 1.1 we already mentioned that almost immediately on arrival, the Dutch settlers made contacts with Native Americans. They carried on a brisk trade with each other; in the course of time there were some conflicts, too. In order to be able to trade and negotiate with each other, the European colonists and the Native Americans developed a simple colloquial language, a pidgin. Perhaps there were more pidgins, but we only have details about one of them, which was based on the Amerindian language Unami Delaware (see 3.2). This pidgin is nowadays called "Delaware Jargon." The grammatical structure of this language was extremely simple, and the vocabulary, which contained only a few hundred words, was a mixture of Amerindian words and a limited number of loanwords from other languages, especially Dutch, English, and Swedish. The American linguist Buccini claims that Delaware Jargon was developed when, for practical reasons, both Native Americans and Dutchmen used simplified versions of their mother languages in their communications with each other. The point is that the Amerindian languages possess an extremely rich variety of forms and are difficult to learn for others. Realizing this, the Native Americans used a simplified form of Unami Delaware in their contacts with the Dutch; this simplified language forms the basis of Delaware Jargon. The Dutch settlers probably used a simplified form of Dutch as well, which can be inferred from the names for some animals (see 3.4 and 3.5).

Delaware Jargon was an important language in the seventeenth century, used by English, Dutch, and Swedish colonists. The earliest data about Delaware Jargon are to be found in the Dutchman Johannes de Laet's *Novus Orbis* from 1633. De Laet, author of various works on geography and ethnology, was governor of the West Indian Company, founded in 1621, and later became co-director with Rensselaerswijck – although he

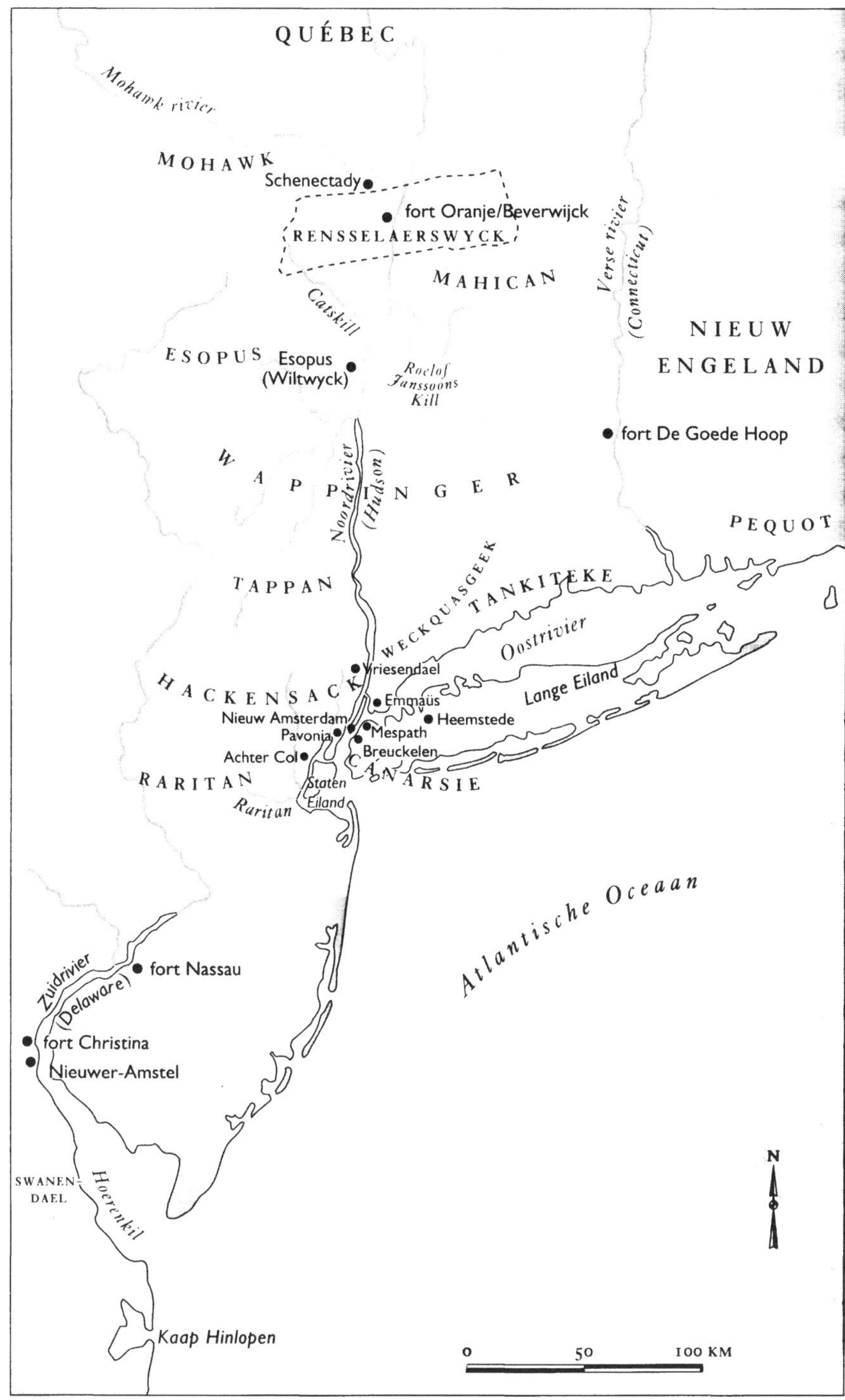

Illustration 3.1 – New Netherland with the most important Native American tribes and European settlements around 1650 (source: Frijhoff 1995: 716)

has never been in America. In his *Novus Orbis*, there are only a few words in Delaware Jargon. Most of what we know about the language comes from a handwritten list containing 261 words and phrases in English followed by a translation in Delaware Jargon, with the title "The Indian Interpreter." This list was found in a document from 1684 and probably dates from around that year.

There were Dutch settlers who learned one or more Amerindian languages and Native Americans who learned Dutch and acted as interpreters for the settlers. How well they spoke each other's language remains, of course, guesswork. In 1628, dominie Jonas Michaëlius, at any rate, wrote that communication was effected "almost as often by pointing with fingers and thumb as by speaking." It is certain that in the eighteenth century, there were groups of Native Americans for whom Dutch was the only European language they knew, for in 1750, English officials had to invoke the help of Dutch settlers to act as interpreters in their contacts with Native Americans.

3.2 Amerindian languages that were spoken on the East Coast in the seventeenth century

The Dutch had contacts with different groups of Native Americans speaking different languages, a fact of which they were well aware. In his *Beschryvinge van Nieuw-Nederlant* ("Description of New Netherland," 1655), Adriaen van der Donck divided the Amerindian languages into four groups: "Manhattan, Minquas, Savanoos and Wappanoos." Among the "Minquas" he includes the "Senecas," "Maquaas," and other tribes in the interior. The "Savanoos" lived, he said, in the south, and the "Wappanoos" in the east.

These days, we use different names for the various tribes and languages. Along the upper reaches of the Hudson River, we find the Mahican Indians, along the Delaware the (Munsee and Unami) Delaware. The Mohawks or Iroquois were settled around Lake Mohawk. The biggest Iroquois tribe was formed by the Seneca, who lived around what is now called Seneca Lake. Finally, on a narrow strip on the coast of present-day Connecticut we find Pequot Indians.

Through their contacts with the Dutch colonists, the Native Americans got to know a number of Dutch notions which they adopted as loanwords into their languages. Such loanwords have been found in Mahican, Munsee Delaware, Unami Delaware or Lenape, Western Abnaki, Mohegan-Pequot, Loup and Mohawk or Iroquois. All these languages except Mohawk are interrelated and belong to the Algonquian language family. This does not apply to Mohawk, which is a member of the Iroquois language family. The earliest information about Mohawk can be found in the diary kept by Harmen Meyndertsz van den Bogaert during a journey through the Mohawk Valley in 1634-1635. In it, he included a list of Mohawk words. A number of words from the list were first published by Johannes de Laet in his *Notae ad dissertationem Hugonis Grotii. De origine gentium Americanarium* from 1643. A year later, in 1644, a letter of dominie Megapolensis was published with the title *Een kort ontwerp van de Mahakvase Indiaenen, haer Landt, Tale, Statuere, Dracht, Godes-Dienst ende Magistrature*

("A Short Account of the Mohawk Indians, their Country, Language, Figure, Costume, Religion, and Government"). Megapolensis, who was a missionary among the Native Americans, states that the language of the "Mahakuaas" (Mohawk) is very difficult and that he was trying to learn the language and was composing a vocabulary by asking the Native Americans what they called certain things.

It is possible, and even probable, that Dutch also supplied loanwords to other Amerindian languages than the ones mentioned, but that, unfortunately, is difficult to establish, because some of the Amerindian languages spoken along the East Coast in the seventeenth century were not or only inadequately described and have since become extinct. Thus, of the Loup language, which must at one time have been spoken in the North West of New England by the "Loups" (a French name literally meaning "wolves"), only an eighteenth-century manuscript has survived (the Algonquian word *Mahigan*, *Mohican*, incidentally, also means "wolf").

The Amerindian languages that still exist are now usually spoken in other places than they were in the seventeenth century, and most of them count only a handful of speakers. Already in the Dutch period, many Native Americans moved to new territories in search of beavers and martens, which were overhunted in New England, or because they were crowded out by European colonists or by other tribes of Native Americans. In the course of time, moreover, Native Americans moved to special reserves, of their own free will or otherwise. Thus, most of the Mohawks have, since the American War of Independence at the end of the eighteenth century, lived in

Illustration 3.2 – Mohawk Indians (source: engraving from David Pietersz. de Vries, Korte historiael, 1655: 156)

Illustration 3.3 – Ritual dance of the Native Americans (source: engraving from David Pietersz. de Vries, Korte historiael, 1655: 177)

Canada, together with the Western Abnaki – whose language has by now become practically extinct. Of Unami Delaware, too, no native speakers are left, whereas the closely related Munsee Delaware is nowadays spoken by only a few elderly people in Wisconsin and Ontario.

The Pequot, who had practically been annihilated in the so-called Pequot War with the English in 1637, were absorbed by the tribe of the Mohegan. The language of the Mohegan and the Pequots has become extinct, but in or around 1903, an American linguist recorded a few Dutch loanwords from the mouth of a Native American woman, Fidelia A.H. Fielding, who was living in Mohegan near Norwich, Connecticut.

The fate of the Mahican, finally, is well-known. In the eighteenth century they got caught up in the struggle for colonial supremacy in the US between the English and the French. The book James Fenimore Cooper devoted to this struggle in 1826 immortalized the name of this tribe because of its title: *The Last of the Mohicans*. In many languages the book title became a popular expression for "the last of a particular group or party." This is somewhat ironic, for Cooper had mistaken the name of the tribe: the main character was not a member of the tribe of the Mahicans or Mohicans, but of that of the Mohegans. Mahican, like Mohegan, has by now died out, but in 1755, Schmidt, a missionary of the Herrnhut community doing mission work among the Mahicans, compiled a dictionary of the language, and translated religious songs into Mahican.

From the *Kort ontwerp* by dominie Megapolensis (1644), the *Beschryvinge van Nieuw-Nederlant* by Van der Donck (1655), and *Korte historiael* by David de Vries (also 1655), we can learn something, not only about the language of the Native Americans, but also about their way of life – the Dutch historian Jaap Jacobs in 2005 lined up the facts in his *New Netherland: A Dutch Colony in Seventeenth-Century America*. The physique of the Native Americans was comparable to that of the Dutch; they had a yellowish skin, black-brown eyes and jet-black hair. The women wore their hair in long braids, but the men shaved off their hair, leaving only a central front-to-back mohican. The men painted their faces in various colors. To the disgust of the Dutchmen, the Native Americans never washed themselves. In winter the Native Americans wore animal skins and pelts, in summer, Van der Donck tells us, the men wore only loincloths. They lived in villages, in big wooden huts that housed several families. The chiefs, called *sachem*, *sackimas* or *sackemackers* by the Dutch with an Amerindian loanword, saw to it that no quarrels could arise, by exchanges of gifts. The Native Americans did not worship any god, but they did ascribe certain powers to the sun, the moon and the planets. They poured libations and by means of rituals they cast out evil spirits from their sick brothers. The first dominies, Jonas Michaëlius, Everardus Bogardus (Evert Willemsz.) and Johannes Megapolensis all tried to convert the Native Americans, but without success. For their livelihood the men occupied themselves with hunting and fishing, and the women worked on the land. The main crop was corn, of which a sort of mush was made that was called by the Dutch *sappaen* (a loanword, see **sup(p)awn** in 2.1). In addition, the Native Americans ate beans that were cooked with fresh meat; fish was either cooked or dried.

3.3 Thematic overview of Dutch loanwords

What kinds of words did the North-American Indians borrow from the Dutch? We are dealing with clearly defined semantic fields (the notions have been put in bold and in between double quotation marks). Many of the Dutch loanwords, moreover, appear in more than one Amerindian language. For an exact list of the borrowed words, and for more detailed information, see the alphabetical overview in 3.4.

Foodstuffs

The majority of the words borrowed are names of foodstuffs that were unknown on the new continent and were introduced by the Dutch – fifteen words in all. Six plant names were borrowed in Amerindian languages: the Dutch words for "**apple**" (borrowed by Loup, Mahican, Mohegan-Pequot, Munsee, and Unami Delaware), "**cucumber**" (borrowed by Loup, Mahican, Munsee, and Unami Delaware), "**cole, cabbage**" (borrowed by Mahican), "**peach**" (borrowed by Mahican, Munsee, and Unami Delaware), "**lettuce**" (borrowed by Munsee Delaware), "**flax**" (borrowed by Mahican), and "**watermelon**" (borrowed by Loup and Munsee Delaware). The Native Americans began to grow a number of these plants themselves, such as cucumbers, cabbages, and watermelons. American English, incidentally, borrowed *coleslaw* from Dutch (see 2.1).

Dairy products, too, were new, which is not surprising, since cows and the keeping of domesticated cattle were introduced by Europeans to North America. The Dutch word for "**butter**" was borrowed by Loup, Mahican, Munsee, and Unami Delaware, and that for "**milk**" by Munsee Delaware. Traditional Dutch "**pancakes**," made with, among other things, milk, eggs, and butter, were new to the Native Americans; the name was borrowed by Loup, Munsee Delaware, and Western Abnaki. The word is also

Illustration 3.4 – A pipe-smoking Native American. In the ninetheenth century advertisements for tobacco often, especially in Great Britain, portrayed Native Americans (source: Graphic ornaments, Amsterdam 2007)

known in American English (see 2.1).

The Dutch seasoned their food with spices, sugar, and salt, and traded these products with the Native Americans. The Dutch word for "**pepper**" was borrowed by Munsee and Unami Delaware; the word for "**sugar**" was borrowed by Munsee and Unami Delaware, and that for "**salt**" by Loup and Mahican.

The final two words in this category are not really terms for foodstuffs, but rather stimulants. The Dutch introduced liquor as a means of payment and as a means to let negotiations go more smoothly. This "fire water" was unknown to the Native Americans. The Dutch authorities and the chiefs of the Native Americans had made an agreement that no liquor should be sold to Native Americans, but not everyone lived by that agreement. Delaware Jargon and Mahican borrowed the Dutch word for "**brandy.**" The English word *brandy*, incidentally, was also borrowed from Dutch *brandewijn* in this period. English *brand-wine* occurs in 1622 and was shortened to *brandy* in 1657 (see also 2.1). Finally, the Dutch word for "**snuff**" ("powdered, stimulating tobacco for inhaling") was borrowed by Mahican. This loanword is remarkable, for tobacco was unknown in Europe, and had only recently been introduced from America. For the Mahican, the practice of inhaling powdered tobacco was new apparently.

Household utensils and tools

In second place, with thirteen loanwords, we find names for household utensils and tools. It is noteworthy that American English, too, took over many of this kind of words, as we have seen in chapter 2, be it different words than the Amerindian languages borrowed. In the Amerindian languages we find the Dutch words for "**bed**" (borrowed by Mohegan-Pequot), "**flask**" (borrowed by Loup and Mahican), "**jar**" (borrowed by Mahican), "**chest**" (borrowed by Munsee Delaware), "**basket**" (borrowed by Mohegan-Pequot), "**pan**" (borrowed by Munsee Delaware), "**pin**" (borrowed by Munsee Delaware), and "**sack**" (borrowed by Munsee Delaware). Five names for tools were borrowed: the Dutch words for "**hammer**" (borrowed by Munsee Delaware), "**knife**" (borrowed by Loup in the meaning "iron"), "**mallet**" (borrowed by Munsee and Unami Delaware), "**spade**" (borrowed by Munsee Delaware), and "**whip**" (borrowed by Munsee Delaware).

Animals

In third place, with seven loanwords, we find names for cattle and domestic animals introduced by the Dutch, namely the Dutch words for "**turkey**" (borrowed by Mohegan-Pequot), "**chicken**" (borrowed by Loup, Mahican, Mohawk, and Munsee Delaware), "**pig**" (borrowed by Munsee Delaware), "**cow**" (borrowed by Loup, Mahican, and Munsee Delaware), "**sheep**" (borrowed by Mahican and Munsee Delaware), "**peacock**" (borrowed by Munsee Delaware), and "**cat**" (borrowed by Loup, Mahican, Mohawk, Mohegan-Pequot, Munsee, and Unami Delaware). As a result of the introduction of cattle and domestic animals, the Native Americans changed their lifestyle – they began to keep pigs and chickens. However, Dutch cattle frequently led to conflicts as well: cows wandered into the Native Americans' fields of grain and caused great damage. The Native Americans would sometimes kill the cattle, which in turn led to Dutch farmers demanding compensation.

Money and units of measure

Words for money and units of measure are in fourth place. As means of payment, the Native Americans used *wampum* (a string of white shells) or *sewant* (a string of dark shells), or they exchanged articles. From the colonists, they got to know European coins and measures, sometimes borrowing the Dutch names, namely the Dutch words for "**guilder**" (borrowed by Delaware Jargon), "**half-anker**" (the name of an old standard measure for liquor; borrowed by Munsee Delaware), "**pound**" (borrowed by Munsee and Unami Delaware in the meaning "to weigh"), "**nickle**" (the name of a coin; borrowed by Delaware Jargon), and "**silver**" (borrowed by Loup, Mahican, and Munsee Delaware, used for both "silver" and "money"). American English has borrowed some words in this category too, such as *anker*, *gulden*, and *stiver* (see 2.10).

Clothes

In fifth place we find words for articles of clothing or parts of them. The Dutch way of dressing was new to the Native Americans – both the materials (wool, cotton, etc.) and the articles of clothing themselves. Before long, the Native Americans started wearing shirts. The following notions for articles of clothing have been borrowed from Dutch: "**trousers**" (borrowed by Munsee Delaware), "**shirt**" (borrowed by Mahican, Munsee, and Unami Delaware), "**cotton**" (borrowed by Munsee Delaware), "**button**" (borrowed by Munsee and Unami Delaware), and "**mitten**" (borrowed by Munsee Delaware).
In 2.13, we also saw that Dutch *duffel*, borrowed in American English as *duffle*, was a popular trading product, but as yet, the name has not been found in any Amerindian language.

Illustration 3.5 – Jew's harp (source: detail from an engraving after the painting "Het zottenfeest" by Pieter Breughel the older)

Miscellany

The remaining categories are small ones. Two names for musical instruments were borrowed: the Dutch words for "**Jew's harp**" (borrowed by Munsee Delaware), and "**violin**" (borrowed by Mahican and Munsee Delaware).

In the days before television or radio, people spent their leisure time playing card games, often for money. The Native Americans took over this habit, together with the terms used: "**spades**" was borrowed by Loup, and Munsee and Unami Delaware – in those languages usually with the meaning "playing cards" in general; in Unami Delaware a verb was derived from this word, meaning "to gamble." As late as 1970 and 1976, reseachers in northeast Oklahoma asked Unami Delaware speakers the names of their playing cards, and it turned out that, in addition to the word for "spades," they also knew the terms "**hearts**," "**diamonds**," and "**clubs**" from Dutch.

The division of a week into seven days was typically European. In Mohegan-Pequot, all the names of the days of the week ("**Monday**," "**Tuesday**," etc.) were borrowed from Dutch. The way in which the Dutch celebrated the beginning of the year was also new to the Native Americans, hence the Dutch word for "**New Year**" was borrowed by Munsee Delaware.

Finally, the Amerindian languages borrowed a small number of terms from Dutch that somehow reflect Dutch society and culture. The impressive fortification Fort Amsterdam caused the Dutch word for "**castle**" to be borrowed by Mahican in the meaning "the Dutch fortress." A number of professional names or personal names for certain (groups of) people were borrowed: the Dutch words for "**smith**" (borrowed by Munsee and Unami Delaware), "**Frenchman**" (borrowed by Munsee and Unami Delaware), "**bishop**" (borrowed by Mahican), and "**congregation**" ("parish"; borrowed by Mahican) – these last two referred to the religious organization that was unknown to the Native Americans. The word for "**king**" (Dutch *koning*) may have been borrowed by Mohegan-Pequot, where *kunnung* means "head" – the meaning will have been transferred via that of king as "head" of the people. Reading and writing were new to the Native Americans and that is why they borrowed the Dutch notions of "**reading**" (borrowed by Mahican), and "**paper**" (borrowed by Munsee and Unami Delaware).

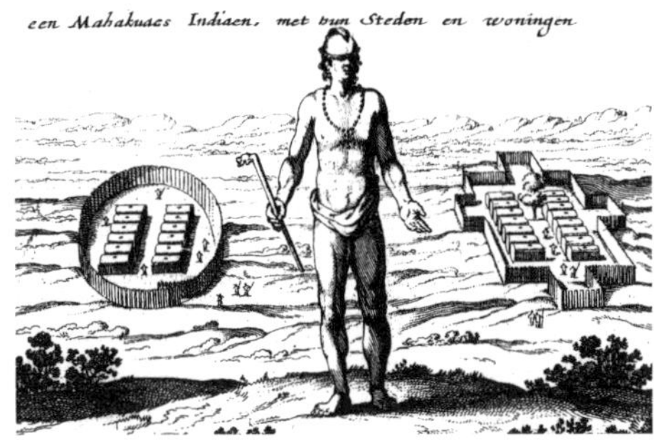

Illustration 3.6 – A Mohawk, with villages in the background (source: Johannes Megapolensis, Kort ontwerp, 1644: 15)

It has been suggested that Mohegan-Pequot *piskut* comes from Dutch "**penis**," but if only because this does not fit in with the kind of words borrowed by Native Americans, this does not seem likely. The sounds of the word, too, would have to have been very much altered. What is certain is that the name of Arendt van **Corlaer** still lives on in the modern Iroquois spoken in Canada. Van Corlaer founded the colony of Schenectady on the banks of the Mohawk River in 1662. His name has been corrupted to *Kora* in Iroquois, a word used as the title of the governor-general or of the king of England.

3.4 Alphabetical survey of Dutch loanwords

Here follows an alphabetical list of the Dutch loanwords in Amerindian languages. To facilitate the looking up of items, the English entry will be given first, followed by the Dutch word that was borrowed. After that comes information about the Amerindian language(s) containing the Dutch word. For easier readability, the spelling of Amerindian words has been simplified: *š* appears as *sh*, *č* as *ch*, and *shwa* as *e*; there are no length marks on vowels or consonants. Accents (*á*) indicate stress.

Dutch loanwords have been adapted to the sound system of the Amerindian languages. Thus, Delaware does not distinguish between *p*, *b*, *f*, and *v* – all these consonants have become *p* in Delaware. Many Amerindian languages do not differentiate between *r* and *l*. If an Amerindian word has acquired a different meaning from that of its Dutch origin, this has been indicated.

apple, Dutch *appel*, borrowed as: Loup *abel*; Mahican *ápenes* "apples"; Mohegan-Pequot *appece* (perhaps from English); Munsee Delaware *ápelesh*; Unami Delaware *ápelesh*.
bag, Dutch *zak*, borrowed as: Munsee Delaware *shakinótay*, with Delaware suffix meaning "bag."
basket, Dutch *mand*, borrowed as: Mohegan-Pequot *manodah*.
bed, Dutch *bed*, borrowed as: Mohegan-Pequot *beed* (perhaps from English).
bishop, Dutch *bisschop*, borrowed as: Mohegan *bishop* (perhaps borrowed in the eighteenth century from Hernhutter German).
brandy, Dutch *brandewijn*, borrowed as: Delaware Jargon *brandywyne;* Mahican *p'natt'weñ*.
butter, Dutch *boter*, borrowed as: Loup *boutel*; Mahican *póten*; Munsee Delaware *pótel*; Unami Delaware *pótel*.
button, Dutch *knoop*, borrowed as: Munsee Delaware *kenóp*; Unami Delaware *kenóp*.
castle, Dutch *kasteel*, borrowed as: Mahican *gasténik*, with Mahican ending, indicating "Fort Albany, the Dutch fort."
cat, Dutch *poes*, call-name also *poesje*, *poessie*, *poespoes*, borrowed as: Loup *puspus*; Mahican *póschees*, *poschesh*; Mohawk *takús* with prefix *ta-*; Mohegan-Pequot *bopoose*; Munsee Delaware *póshish*; Unami Delaware *póshis*.
chest, Dutch *kist*, borrowed as: Munsee Delaware *kesht*.
chicken, Dutch *kip*, call-name *kipkip*, borrowed as: Loup *kipkip*; Mahican

kikipus (plural *keképsak*); Mohawk *kitkit*; Munsee Delaware *kikípesh* (with Delaware diminutive suffix).
clubs ("figure on playing cards"), Dutch *klaver(en)*, borrowed as: Unami Delaware *kwales*.
cole ("cabbage"), Dutch *kool*, borrowed as: Mahican *gónan* (with plural ending).
congregation, Dutch *gemeente*, borrowed as: Mahican *geménde*.
Corlaer, Dutch (Arendt van) *Corlaer*, founder of the colony of Schenectady on the banks of the Mohawk River in 1662; in Iroquois *Kora* is the title of the governor-general or of the king of England.
cotton, Dutch *katoen*, borrowed as: Munsee Delaware *káton*.
cow, Dutch *koe*, popular *koei*, borrowed as: Loup *kui*; Mahican *kójak* "cows" with plural suffix; Munsee Delaware *kówey*, *koj*.
cucumber, Dutch *komkommer*, borrowed as: Loup *kemegom*; Mahican *kumkumsch*; Munsee Delaware *komkómesh*; Unami Delaware *kúkumes*.
diamonds ("figure on playing cards"), Dutch *ruiten*, borrowed as: Unami Delaware *lish*.
flask, Dutch *fles*, borrowed as: Loup *plas*; Mahican *pnásch*.
flax, Dutch *vlas*, borrowed as: Mahican *pnax* (perhaps from English).
Frenchman, Dutch *Fransman*, borrowed as: Munsee Delaware *pelánsheman*; Unami Delaware *pelánsheman*.
Friday, Dutch *vrijdag*, borrowed as: Mohegan-Pequot *beitar*.
guilder, Dutch *gulden*, borrowed as: Delaware Jargon *gull* "coin."
half-anker, Dutch *halfanker* (an old liquid measure), borrowed as: Munsee Delaware *halpánkel*.
hammer, Dutch *hamer*, borrowed as: Munsee Delaware *hámel*.
hearts ("figure on playing cards"), Dutch *harten*, borrowed as: Unami Delaware *halet*.
jar, Dutch *kan*, borrowed as: Mahican *kánnisch*, with Mahican diminutive ending.
Jew's harp, Dutch *tromp* "wind instrument," borrowed as: Munsee Delaware *telémp*.
king, Dutch *koning*, perhaps borrowed as: Mohegan-Pequot *kunnung* "head."
knife, Dutch *mesje*, borrowed as: Loup *meschu* "iron."
lettuce, Dutch *sla*, borrowed as: Munsee Delaware *sheläsh*.
milk, Dutch *melk*, borrowed as: Munsee Delaware *melek*.
mitten, Dutch *want*, borrowed as: Munsee Delaware *wañt*.
Monday, Dutch *maandag*, borrowed as: Mohegan-Pequot *mundetar*.
New Year, Dutch *nieuwjaar*, borrowed as: Munsee Delaware *níwejal* "New Year's Day"
nickel, Dutch *stuiver*, borrowed as: Delaware Jargon *steepa*.
pan, Dutch *pan*, borrowed as: Munsee Delaware *pán*.
pancake, Dutch *pannenkoek*, borrowed as: Loup *panegug*; Munsee Delaware *pán'kok*; Western Abnaki *pongoksak* "pancakes."
paper, seventeenth-century Dutch *pampier*, borrowed as: Munsee Delaware *pámpil* "(sheet of) paper, newspaper, book"; Unami Delaware *pámpil*.
peach, Dutch dialect form *pierk* (Standard Dutch *perzik*), borrowed as: Mahican *pénegesak* "peaches"; Munsee Delaware *pilkesh*; Unami Delaware *pílkesh*.
peacock, Dutch *pauw*, borrowed as: Munsee Delaware *páw*.
penis, Dutch *penis*, perhaps borrowed as: Mohegan-Pequot *piskut*.
pepper, Dutch *peper*, borrowed as: Munsee Delaware *pipel*, *pépel*; Unami Delaware *pépel*.
pig, Dutch *keus*, *koes*, *keuskeus*, call-names for "pig", borrowed as: Munsee

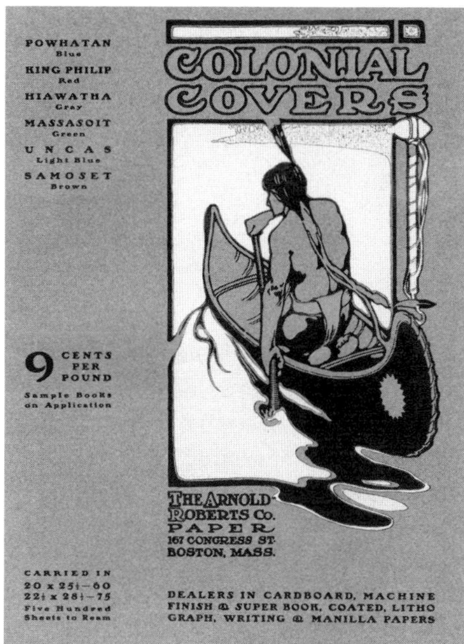

Illustration 3.7 – The word paper is borrowed in two Amerindian languages. At the end of the nineteenth and the beginning of the twentieth century some American paper manufacturers gave their products names referring to the history of the Native Americans (source: The Printing Art, vol. 2 #3, Nov. 1903; advertisement for products of The Arnold Roberts Company)

Delaware *kóshkosh*. This word also occurs in other Algonquian languages, such as Cree and Ojibwe, and probably originated partially from Munsee Delaware.

pin, Dutch *pinnetje*, borrowed as: Munsee Delaware *pinch*.

pound, Dutch *pond*, borrowed as: Munsee Delaware *ponthe* "weigh" (with Delaware ending); Unami Delaware *púntahkat* "it weighs."

read, Dutch *lezen*, borrowed as: Mahican *lesówu* "he/she is reading" – perhaps borrowed from Hernhutter German.

salt, Dutch *zout*, borrowed as: Loup *sat*; Mahican *saschuak*, perhaps from Hernhutter German.

Saturday, Dutch *zaterdag*, borrowed as: Mohegan-Pequot *zotortar*.

sheep, Dutch *mek*, *mekkie*, *mekketje*, call-names for sheep, derived from the verb *mekkeren* ("to bleat"), borrowed as: Mahican *mamaksimsák* "sheep" (plural); Munsee Delaware *memekis* "sheep" (singular).

shirt, Dutch *hemd*, borrowed as: Mahican *hámed*, *hamet* "linen material"; Munsee Delaware *hémpet*; Unami Delaware *hémpes* "shirt, clothing, fabric."

silver, Dutch *zilver*, borrowed as: Loup *sinibat*, *chinebat*, *chinibat* "silver, money"; Mahican *sehnpatt*, *senpett* "silver"; Munsee Delaware *shelpel* "money."

sledgehammer, Dutch *moker*, borrowed as: Munsee Delaware *mókel*; Unami Delaware *mókel*.

smith, Dutch *smid*, borrowed as: Munsee Delaware *shemét*, Unami Delaware *shemit*.

snuff, Dutch *snuif* "powdered tobacco for inhaling," borrowed as: Mahican *snup*.

spade ("shovel"), Dutch *schop*, *schup*, *schep*, borrowed as: Munsee Delaware *shkep*.

spades ("figure on playing cards"), Dutch *schoppen*, borrowed as: Loup *skebai* "playing cards"; Munsee Delaware *shkep* "spades" and "playing card," and *shephamaaw* "he is playing cards" (with Delaware ending); Unami Delaware *shkupháma* "he gambles" and *shkepa* "spades."

sugar, Dutch *suiker*, borrowed as: Munsee Delaware *shókel*; Unami Delaware *shókel*.

Sunday, Dutch *zondag*, borrowed as: Mohegan-Pequot *zunatar*.

Thursday, Dutch *donderdag*, borrowed as: Mohegan-Pequot *dozortar*.

trousers, Dutch *broek*, borrowed as: Munsee Delaware *pelók*.

Tuesday, Dutch *dinsdag*, borrowed as: Mohegan-Pequot *doosetar*.

turkey, Dutch *kalkoen*, borrowed as: Mohegan Pequot *goongeyox*.

violin, Dutch *viool*, borrowed as: Mahican *pion*; Munsee Delaware *peyól*.
watermelon, Dutch *waterlimoen* (later *watermeloen*), borrowed as: Loup *watelamu*; Munsee Delaware *watelamókan*.
Wednesday, Dutch *woensdag*, borrowed as: Mohegan-Pequot *wonsartar*.
whip, Dutch *zweep*, borrowed as: Munsee Delaware *shewíp*.

3.5 Conclusion

Fom the above it appears that the majority of Dutch loanwords were borrowed in Munsee and Unami Delaware. Since the pidgin language used between colonists and Native Americans was based on (Unami) Delaware, too, it looks as if the Dutch had contacts especially with the Native Americans around the Delaware River, who spoke the closely related Munsee or Unami Delaware. But we must sound a note of warning here: so much information about seventeenth-century Amerindian languages has remained unknown or has been lost, that this may be coincidental. What may be said here is that the number of known Dutch loanwords in Amerindian languages – 3.4 gives a list of 69 words found in at least one Amerindian language – can without doubt be called substantial, if we consider the brevity of the Dutch colonists' regime on the American East Coast.

The words that the Native Americans took over from the Dutch language illustrate the "innovations" that the Dutch introduced in North America. For the greater part, they are common words for daily things: simple foodstuffs, household utensils, tools, domestic animals, clothes, and so on. Most of the Dutch who went to America were of simple origin, it seems – they did not go there to spread culture, or to propagate prominent Dutch science, literature, painting, and the like, but to improve their financial situation on the new continent. There were indications of this in the case of the loanwords in American English, but we find confirmation of this in the loanwords in Amerindian languages. The colonists' humble origins can also be inferred from the fact that, for the names of pig, chicken, sheep and cat, it was not the usual names for these animals that were borrowed, but their call-names instead. Did the Native Americans hear these words when they went to visit the Dutch colonists? Or do we get some insight here into the ways in which Dutch settlers and Native Americans communicated in a pidgin? The American linguist Buccini believes that the Dutch used onomatopoeias or call-names because they are easier to understand and remember for the Native Americans than the normal Dutch animal names.

It is also interesting to note which words were *not* borrowed. Thus, not a single word was borrowed for "firearm," whereas it is known that the Native Americans were acquainted with firearms through the colonists and bought firearms from them, at first to be able to kill more beavers – traditionally, the Native Americans set traps – later to use both against rival gangs of Native Americans and against Dutch colonists. But there is not a trace of this to be found in the Amerindian vocabulary.

From comparative studies of the influence of European languages on Amerindian languages, it appears that other European languages supplied loanwords in the same

or comparable fields; colonists heading for the new continent obviously had similar backgrounds. This investigation also showed that the greatest influence on Amerindian languages in general came from Spanish, followed by English.
Other languages, such as Dutch, French, and Portuguese, were much less influential.

Finally, there was, of course, no such thing as one-way traffic: the European colonists on the North American continent discovered numerous objects, animals, and plants that were theretofore unknown to them; as a rule, they adopted the Amerindian names for them. The contact with the New World had a lasting influence on the ways of life of the inhabitants of both North America and Europe. Both continents came to know new, useful plants, animals, and foodstuffs. Thus, from North and South America the potato, pineapple, cocoa, chocolate, corn, and tomato were introduced in Europe, causing in due course the dietary systems of the European population to be drastically changed. There was an exchange of stimulants, too – tobacco came to Europe and liquor flowed back to America.

For the names of the new American products, Dutch often used loanwords from an Amerindian language, but these usually date from after the New Netherlands period – most of them were borrowed through other European languages, usually Spanish or English. Dutch contacts with Amerindian languages were short-lived, lasting just over half a century, so they did not leave permanent traces in Dutch. A remarkable fact is that in their settlements the Dutch borrowed one word – the name of a gnat – from Munsee Delaware, which subsequently, through Dutch, found its way to American English, where it still exists; see **punkie** in 2.2. The Native American tribe **Seneca** (see 2.4), and the dish **sup(p)awn** (see 2.1) owe their name in American English to Dutch. Finally, mention deserves to be made of the fact that in 1910, J. Dyneley Prince identified at least two loanwords from Munsee Delaware that occurred in the Jersey Dutch dialect: *häspân* "raccoon" and *tahääim* "strawberries." The Jersey Dutch dialect was at that moment still being spoken by descendants from the original Dutch colonists in Bergen County, New Jersey. These must be very old loanwords indeed, for Munsee Delaware speakers had long since left Bergen County by then.

Bibliography

Algeo, John (ed.) (1991), *Fifty Years Among the New Words. A Dictionary of Neologisms, 1941-1991*, Cambridge.
Algra, B.C., et al. (1952), *Friesland. Toen, nu, straks*, Leeuwarden.
Anema, T., T. de Graaf & H.F. Schatz (1988), "The Frisian Language in America", in: *Nowele* 12, 91-108.
Ayto, John (1999), *Twentieth Century Words. The Story of the New Words in English over the Last Hundred Years*, Oxford.

Bachman, Van Cleaf (ca. 1980), *Introduction to Low Dutch Dictionary*, unpubl. ms.
Bachman, Van Cleaf (1982), "The Story of the Low Dutch Language", in: *De Halve Maen* 56: 3, 1-3, 21; 57: 1, 10-13.
Bachman, Van Cleaf (1983), "What is Low Dutch?", in: *De Halve Maen* 57: 3, 14-17, 23-24.
Bachman, Van Cleaf, Alice P. Kenney & Lawrence G. van Loon (1980), "'Het Poelmeisie'. An Introduction to the Hudson Valley Dutch Dialect", in: *New York History* 61, 161-185.
Bakel, Jan van (1996), *Lokwoorden voor huisdieren in Nederland*, Amsterdam.
Bakker, D.M. & G.R.W. Dibbets (1977), *Geschiedenis van de Nederlandse taalkunde*, 's-Hertogenbosch.
Bakker, Peter (1995), "Nederlandse leenwoorden in Noordamerikaanse Indianentalen", in: *Yumtzilob* 7.1, 5-16.
Bakker, Peter (forthcoming), "Nederlandse leenwoorden in de talen van Ghana (met een noot over Nederlandse woorden in een Amerikaanse Indianentaal)", in *Trefwoord*, http://www.fryske-akademy.nl/fa/uitgaven/trefwoord.
Barnhart, Clarence L., Sol Steinmetz & Robert K. Barnhart (1973), *A Dictionary of New English 1963-1972*, London.
Barnhart, David K. & Allan A. Metcalf (1997), *America in So Many Words. Words That Have Shaped America*, Boston/New York.
Barnhart, Robert K. (ed.) (1988), *The Barnhart Dictionary of Etymology*, n.p.
Bartlett, John (1848), *The Dictionary of Americanisms*, New York. Various editions. See also Keijzer.
Berrey, Lester V. & Melvin van den Bark (1953), *The American Thesaurus of Slang*, New York.
Brinks, Herbert J. (1978), *Schrijf spoedig terug. Brieven van immigranten in Amerika 1847-1920*, The Hague.
Brown, Cecil H. (1999), *Lexical Acculturation in Native American Languages*, New York.
Bryson, Bill (1994), *Made in America*, London.
Buccini, Anthony F. (1995), "The Dialectical Origins of New Netherland Dutch", in: *Dutch Linguistics in a Changing Europe. The Berkeley Conference on Dutch Linguistics 1993*, ed. by Thomas Shannon & Johan P. Snapper, Lanham, MD, etc., 211-263.
Buccini, Anthony F. (1996), "New Netherlands Dutch, Cape Dutch, Afrikaans", in: *Taal en Tongval*, special issue 9, 35-51.
Buccini, Anthony F. (2000), "*Swannekens Ende Wilden*: Linguistic Attitudes and Communication Strategies Among the Dutch and Indians in New Netherland",

in: *The Low Countries and the New World(s): Travel, Discovery, Early Relations*, ed. by Johanna Prins et al., Lanham, MD, etc., 11-28.

Carpenter, Wm. H. (1908-1909), “Dutch Contributions to the Vocabulary of English in America. Dutch Remainders in New York State”, in: *Modern Philology* 6, 53-68.
Carver, Craig M. (1987), *American Regional Dialects. A Word Geography*, Ann Arbor.
Cassidy, Frederic G. & Joan Houston Hall (eds. in chief) (1985-), *Dictionary of American Regional English*, Harvard University Press.
Clapin, Sylva (n.d [1902]), *A New Dictionary of Americanisms, Being a Glossary of Words Supposed to Be Peculiar to the United States and the Dominion of Canada*, New York.
Cohen, David Steven (1974), *Ramapo Mountain People*, New Brunswick, NJ.
Craigie, William A. & James R. Hulbert (1938-1944), *A Dictionary of American English on Historical Principles*, Chicago.

Daan, Jo (1970), “Trouw aan het Fries in de U.S.A.”, in: *Flecht op 'e koai*, Groningen, 177-188.
Daan, Jo (1971), “Verschuiven van isoglossen”, in: *Taal en Tongval* 23, 77-80.
Daan, Jo (1987), *Ik was te bissie... Nederlanders en hun taal in de Verenigde Staten*, Zutphen. Translation by W.H. Fletcher (1995), *Dutchmen and Their Language in the United States*, Ann Arbor, MI.
Daan, Jo (1988), “Problems of Code-switching: Dialect Loss of Immigrants of Dutch Descent”, in: *Papers from the Third Interdisciplinary Conference on Netherlandic Studies*, held at the University of Michigan, Ann Arbor, 12-14 June 1986, ed. by Ton J. Broos, Lanham, MD, etc., 149-155.
Daan, Jo (1989), Review of Philip E. Webber (1988), *Pella Dutch. The Portrait of a Language and Its Use in One of Iowa's Ethnic Communities*, in: *Taal en Tongval* 41, 179-180.
Daan, Jo (1997a), Review of Caroline Smits (1996), *Disintegration of Inflection: The Case of Iowa Dutch*, in: *Nederlandse Taalkunde* 2, 70-75.
Daan, Jo (1997b), “Dutch in the United States of America”, in: *Dutch Overseas. Studies in Maintenance and Loss of Dutch as an Immigrant Language*, ed. by J. Klatter-Folmer & S. Kroon, Tilburg, 237-253.
DARE = *Dictionary of American Regional English*. See entry for Cassidy.
Davis, Daniel R. (ed.) (2003), *Glossaries of Americanisms*, vol. 2, London/New York.
Dodge, Mary Mapes (1865), *Hans Brinker or The Silver Skates*, New York. http://onlinebooks.library.upenn.edu/webbin/gutbook/lookup?num=764
Dosker, Nicholas H. (1880), “De Nederlandsche taal in de Vereenigde Staten van Noord-Amerika”, in: *Noord en Zuid* 3, 45-48, 226-231.
Dunkling, Leslie (1993), *The Guinness Book of Curious Phrases*, Enfield.

Elsevier (2009), *Ons Amerika. 400 jaar Nederlandse sporen in de Verenigde Staten*. Special issue, March 2009.
Elwyn, A.L. (1859), *Glossary of Supposed Americanisms*, Philadelphia.

Farmer, John S. (1889), *Americanisms - Old and New. A Dictionary of Words, Phrases and Colloquialisms Peculiar to the United States, British America, the West Indies, etc., etc., Their Derivation, Meaning and Application, Together with Numerous Anecdotal, Historical, Explanatory, and Folk-lore Notes*, London.
Feister, Lois M. (1973), “Linguistic Communication Between the Dutch and

Indians in New Netherland 1609-1664", in: *Ethnohistory* 20, 1, 25-38.
Fishman, Joshua A. et al. (1966), *Language Loyalty in the United States. The Maintenance and Perpetuation of Non-English Mother Tongues by American Ethnic and Religious Groups*, London etc.
Flavell, Linda & Roger Flavell (1999), *The Chronology of Words and Phrases. A Thousand Years in the History of English*, London.
Flexner, Stuart Berg (1976), *I Hear America Talking. An Illustrated History of American Words and Phrases*, New York.
Flexner, Stuart Berg (1982), *Listening to America. An Illustrated History of Words and Phrases from Our Lively and Splendid Past*, New York.
Friederici, Georg (1926), *Hilfswörterbuch für den Amerikanisten. Lehnwörter aus Indianer-Sprachen und Erklärungen altertümlicher Ausdrücke*, Halle.
Frijhoff, Willem (1995), *Wegen van Evert Willemsz. Een Hollands weeskind op zoek naar zichzelf 1607-1647*, Nijmegen.
Funk, Elisabeth Paling (1987), "Netherlands' Popular Culture in the Knickerbocker Works of Washington Irving", in: *New World Dutch Studies. Dutch Arts and Culture in Colonial America 1609-1776*, ed. by R.H. Blackburn & N.A. Kelley, 83-93.
Funk, Elisabeth Paling (1992), "De literatuur van Nieuw-Nederland", in: *De Nieuwe Taalgids* 85, 383-395.
Funk, Elisabeth Paling (2005), "Knickerbocker's New Netherland: Washington Irving's Representation of Dutch Life on the Hudson", in: *Amsterdam-New York: Transatlantic Relations and Urban Identities since 1653*, ed. by George Harinck, 135-147.

Gehring, Charles T. (1973), *The Dutch Language in Colonial New York. An Investigation of a Language in Decline and Its Relationship to Social Change*, Ann Arbor, MI.
Gehring, Charles T. (1984), "The Survival of the Dutch Language in New York and New Jersey", in: *De Halve Maen* 58, no. 3, 7-9, 24,
Gehring, Charles T. & William A. Starna (1985), "A Case of Fraud: The Dela Croix Letter and Map of 1634", in: *New York History* 66, July, 249-261.
Gehring, Charles T., William A. Starna & William N. Fenton (1987), "The Tawagonshi Treaty of 1613: The Final Chapter", in: *New York History* 68, October, 373-393.
Ginneken, Jac. van (1913-1914), *Handboek der Nederlandsche taal. De sociologische structuur*, 's-Hertogenbosch.
Goddard, Ives (1974), "Dutch Loanwords in Delaware", in: *A Delaware Indian Symposium*, ed. by H.C. Kraft, 153-160.
Goddard, Ives (1982), "The Historical Phonology of Munsee", in: *International Journal of American Linguistics* 48, 16-48.
Gold, David L. (1981), "Three New-York-cityisms: *Sliding Pond, Potsy*, and *Akey*", in: *American Speech* 56, 17-32.
Gold, David L. (1984), "More on a Dutch-origin Word in New York City English: *Sliding Pon(d)*", in: *Leuvense Bijdragen* 73, 171-175.
Goode, G. Brown (1888), *American Fishes. A Popular Treatise upon the Game and Food Fishes of North America with Especial Reference to Habits and Methods of Capture*, Boston.http://www.archive.org/details/americanfishespooogood.
Gove, Philip Babcock (ed. in chief) (1961), *Webster's Third New International Dictionary of the English Language*, unabridged, Springfield; 1st edition of *Webster's Dictionary* (1828) online at: http://1828.mshaffer.com, 2nd edition (1913): http://1913.mshaffer.com.

Green, Jonathon (1991), *Neologisms. New Words Since 1960*, London.
Green, Jonathon (2005), *Cassell's Dictionary of Slang*, London.
Griffis, William Elliot (1909), *The Story of New Netherland. The Dutch in America*, Boston/New York.

Harrison, F. (1730), *The English and Low-Dutch School-master*, New York. (Reprint 1976.)
Heyden, Ulrich van der (1992), *Indianer-Lexikon. Zur Geschichte und Gegenwart der Ureinwohner Nordamerikas*, Berlin.
Hinte, Jacob van (1985), *Netherlanders in America. A Study of Emigration and Settlement in the 19th and 20th Centuries in the United States of America*, Grand Rapids (translation of: *Nederlanders in Amerika. Een studie over landverhuizers en volksplanters in de 19e en 20ste eeuw in de Verenigde Staten van Amerika*, 1928, Groningen).
Hodge, Frederick Webb (ed.) (1959), *Handbook of American Indians North of Mexico*, part 1, "Dutch influence", Washington.

Irving, Washington (1809), *A History of New York from the Beginning of the World to the End of the Dutch Dynasty, by Diedrich Knickerbocker*, London. http://www.online-literature.com/irving/knickerbockers.

Jacobs, Jaap (2005), *New Netherland: A Dutch Colony in Seventeenth-Century America*, Leiden (based on *Een zegenrijk gewest. Nieuw-Nederland in de zeventiende eeuw*, 1999, Amsterdam).
Jong, Gerald F. de (1975), *The Dutch in America, 1609-1974*, Boston.
Jong, Gerald F. de (1978), *The Dutch Reformed Church in the American Colonies*, Grand Rapids, MI.

Keijzer, M. (1854), *John Russell Bartlett's Woordenboek van Americanismen, bewerkt door M. Keijzer*, Gorinchem.
Kenney, Alice P. (1975), *Stubborn for Liberty. The Dutch in New York*, Syracuse, NY.
Klein, Ernest (1971), *A Comprehensive Etymological Dictionary of the English Language*, Amsterdam/Oxford/New York.
Knowles, Elizabeth & Julia Elliott (eds.) (1997), *The Oxford Dictionary of New Words*, Oxford/New York.
Krabbendam, Hans (2006), *Vrijheid in het verschiet. Nederlandse emigratie naar Amerika 1840-1940*, Hilversum.
Krapp, George Philip (1960), *The English Language in America*, New York.
Kurath, Hans (1949), *A Word Geography of the Eastern United States*, Ann Arbor, MI.

Lagerwey, W. (1982), *Neen Nederland, 'k vergeet u niet*, Baarn.
Laird, Charlton (1972), *Language in America*, Englewood Cliffs.
Lammers, A. (1989), *Uncle Sam en Jan Salie. Hoe Nederland Amerika ontdekte*, Amsterdam.
Liberman, Anatoly (2005), *Word origins ... and How We Know Them*, Oxford.
Liberman, Anatoly (2008), *An Analytic Dictionary of English Etymology. An Introduction*, London.
Lighter, J.E. (1994-), *Random House Historical Dictionary of American Slang*, New York.
Ligtenberg, Lucas (1999), *De Nieuwe Wereld van Peter Stuyvesant. Nederlandse voetsporen in de Verenigde Staten*, Amsterdam.
Logeman, Henri (1929), "The Etymology of 'Yankee'", in: *Studies in English Philology: A Miscellany in Honor of Frederick Klaeber*, ed. by Kemp Malone, 403-413.
Lokotsch, Karl (1926), *Etymologisches Wörterbuch der amerikanischen*

(indianischen) Wörter im Deutschen, Heidelberg.
Loon, L.G. van (1938), *Crumbs from an Old Dutch Closet. The Dutch Dialect of Old New York*, The Hague.
Loon, L.G. van (1939a), "Ave atque vale. Jersey Lag Duits verdwijnt", in: *Onze Taaltuin* 8, 91-95, 107-119.
Loon, L.G. van (1939b), "Hedendaagsche Nederduitsche cultuursporen uit de XVIIe eeuw in New York en New Jersey", in: *Eigen Volk*, 337-344.
Loon, L.G. van (1939-1940), "Letter from Jeronimus de la Croix to the Commissary at Fort Orange and a Hitherto Unknown Map Relating to Surgeon Van den Bogaert's Journey into the Mohawk Country", in: *The Dutch Settlers Society of Albany Yearbook* 15, 1-9.
Loon, L.G. van (1968), "Tawagonshi, the Beginning of the Treaty Era", in: *Indian Historian* 1, 22-26. (Reprinted in Rupert Costo (ed.) (1974), *The American Indian Reader*. Vol. 4. *History*, San Francisco, 38-44).
Lucas, Henry S. (1955), *Netherlanders in America. Dutch Immigration to the United States and Canada, 1789-1950*, Ann Arbor, MI/London.
Lucas, Henry S. (1997), *Dutch Immigrant Memoirs and Related Writings*, Grand Rapids, MI/Cambridge.

Marckwardt, Albert H. (1980), *American English*, New York/Oxford, 2nd edition revised by J.L. Dillard.
Marle, Jaap van (1997), "Waarom er geen Amerikaans Zeeuws bestaat", in: *Nehelennia* 114, 47-56.
Marle, Jaap van (2000), "Het Fries in Amerika", in: *Philologia Frisica Anno 1999. Lêzingen fan it fyftjinde Frysk filologekongres 8, 9 en 10 desimber 1999* (Papers from the 15th Frisian Philological Congress), ed. by P. Boersma, Ph. H. Breuker, L.G. Jansma & J. van der Vaart, Leeuwarden, 165-179.
Marle, Jaap van (2001), "American 'Leeg Duits' ('Low Dutch') – a Neglected Language", in: *Global Eurolinguistics: European Languages in North America: Migration, Maintenance and Death*, ed. by P. Sture Ureland, Tübingen, 79-101.
Marle, Jaap van (2003), "Toen cowboys en Indianen Nederlands spraken". Interview in: *Taalschrift. Tijdschrift over taal en taalbeleid* 14-11-2003. (taalschrift.org/reportage/000303.html)
Marle, Jaap van (2006), "Preservation of the Language and Perseverance of the Saints: Critical Comments on Religious Orthodoxy and the Loss of the Native Tongue", in: *Morsels in the Melting Pot. The Persistence of Dutch Immigrant Communities in North America*, ed. by George Harinck & Hans Krabbendam, Amsterdam, 125-130.
Marle, Jaap van (2008a), "Myths and Forgeries Relating to American 'Low Dutch', with Special Reference to Walter Hill's Notebook", in: *From* De Halve Maen *to KLM. 400 Years of Dutch American Exchange*, ed. by Margriet Bruyn Lacy, Charles Gehring & Jenneke Oosterhoff, Münster, 321-329.
Marle, Jaap van (2008b), "Yankee Dutch" Literature as a Marker of Acculturation', in: *Dutch-American Arts and Letters in Historical Perspective*, ed. by Robert P. Swierenga, Jacob E. Nyenhuis & Nella Kennedy, Holland MI, 61-67.
Marle, Jaap van & Caroline Smits (1989), "Morphological Erosion in American Dutch", in: *Vielfalt der Kontakte*, ed. by Werner Enninger, Bochum, 37-65.
Marle, Jaap van & Caroline Smits (1993), "The Inflectional Systems of Overseas Dutch", in: *Historical Linguistics 1989*. Papers from the 9th International Conference on Historical Linguistics,

Rutgers University, 14-18 August 1989, ed. by Henk Aertsen & Robert J. Jeffers, Amsterdam/Philadelphia, 313-328.
Marle, Jaap van & Caroline Smits (1995), "On the Impact of Language Contact on Inflectional Systems: The Reduction of Verb Inflection in American Dutch and American Frisian", in: *Linguistic Change under Contact Conditions*, ed. by Jacek Fisiak, Berlin/New York, 179-206.
Marle, Jaap van & Caroline Smits (1996), "American Dutch: General Trends in Its Development", in: *Language Contact Across the North Atlantic*, ed. by P. Sture Ureland, 427-442.
Marle, Jaap van & Caroline Smits (1997), "Deviant Patterns of Lexical Transfer: English-origin Words in American Dutch", in: *Dutch Overseas. Studies in Maintenance and Loss of Dutch As an Immigrant Language*, ed. by J. Klatter-Folmer & S. Kroon, Tilburg, 255-272.
Marle, Jaap van & Caroline Smits (2000), "De ontwikkeling van het Amerikaans-Nederlands: een schets", in: *Overzees Nederlands*, ed. by J. Berns & J. van Marle, Amsterdam, 63-83.
Marle, Jaap van & Caroline Smits (2002), "On the (Non-)Persistence of Dialect Features in American Dutch (1): General Aspects", in: *Present-day Dialectology. Problems and Findings*, ed. by Jan Berns & Jaap van Marle, Berlin/NewYork 231-242.
Mathews, M.M. (1956), *A Dictionary of Americanisms on Historical Principles*, Chicago.
M[encken], H.L. (1926), "Americanism", in: *The Encyclopaedia Britannica*, 13th edition.
Mencken, H.L. (1937-1948), *The American Language. An Inquiry into the Development of English in the United States*, 4th edition, 1937, New York; *Supplement I*, 1945, New York; *Supplement II*, 1948, New York.
Metcalf, Allan (1999), *The World in So Many Words. A Country-by-country Tour of Words That Have Shaped Our Language*, Boston/New York.
Miller, Jay (1978), "Delaware Terms for Playing Cards", in: *International Journal of American Linguistics* 44, 2, 145-146.
Morris, William & Mary Morris (1988), *Morris Dictionary of Word and Phrase Origins*, New York.
Mulder, Arnold (1947), *Americans from Holland*. Philadelphia/New York.

Naborn, Robert A. (2002), "NT2 in New Jersey in 1730. Francis Harrisons *De Engelsche en Nederduytsche School-Meester* nader bekeken", in: *Voortgang, Jaarboek voor de Neerlandistiek* 21, 113-142.
Neumann, J.H. (1945), "The Dutch Element in the Vocabulary of American English", in: *Journal of English and Germanic Philology* XLIV, 274-280.
Nieland, Dirk (1919), *Yankee Dutch*, Grand Rapids, MI.
Nieland, Dirk (1929), *'n Fonnie Bisnis*, preface by Frederick ten Hoor, vocabulary by Annie Nieland-de Boer, pen drawings D. Lam, Grand Rapids, MI.
Noordegraaf, Jan (2008), "Nederlands in Noord-Amerika. Over de studie van het *Leeg Duits* (Low Dutch)", December 2008, 1-29, in: *Trefwoord*: http://www.fryske-akademy.nl/fa/uitgaven/trefwoord.
Noordegraaf, Jan (2009a), "Vreemde woorden, valse vrienden. Over het woordenboek van het Leeg Duits (Low Dutch)", in: *Fons verborum, Feestbundel voor prof. dr. A.M.F.J. (Fons) Moerdijk*, ed. by Egbert Beijk et al., Leiden, 73-83.
Noordegraaf, Jan (2009b), "The Dutch Language and Literature in the United States, 1624-1782", in: *History of Dutch-American Relations, 1609-2009*, ed. by Hans Krabbendam, Cornelis A. Van Minnen & Giles Scott-Smith, Amsterdam/New York.

OED = *Oxford English Dictionary*. See entry for Simpson.
Onions, C.T. (ed. in chief) (1983), *The Oxford Dictionary of English Etymology*, Oxford.
Ostyn, Paul (1972), *American Flemish: A Study in Language Loss and Linguistic Interference*, Rochester, NY.

Philippa, Marlies, Frans Debrabandere, Arend Quak, Tanneke Schoonheim & Nicoline van der Sijs (2003-2009), *Etymologisch Woordenboek van het Nederlands*, Amsterdam.
Prince, J. Dyneley (1910), "The Jersey Dutch Dialect", in: *Dialect Notes* 3, 459-484.
Prince, J. Dyneley (1912), "An Ancient New Jersey Indian Jargon", in: *The American Anthropologist* 14, 508-524.
Prince, J. Dyneley (1913), "A Text in Jersey Dutch", in: *Tijdschrift voor Nederlandsche Taal- en Letterkunde* 32, 306-312.
Prince, J. Dyneley & Frank G. Speck (1999), *A Vocabulary of Mohegan-Pequot*, Southampton.
Pyles, Thomas (1954), *Words and Ways of American English*, London.

Quinion, Michael (2004), *Port Out, Starboard Home: and Other Language Myths*, London.

Read, Allen Walker (1963-1964), "O.K.", in: *American Speech* 38, 1, 2; 39, 1, 2, 4.
Reenen, Pieter van (1999), *The Hollandish Roots of Pella Dutch in Iowa* (Vrije Universiteit Working Papers in Linguistics 46), Amsterdam.
Reenen, Pieter van (2000), "De Zuidhollands-Gelderse herkomst van het Pella Dutch in Iowa", in: *Nederlandse Taalkunde* 5, 301-324.
Reenen, Pieter van (2007), "The Hollandish Roots of Pella Dutch in Iowa", in: *Historical Linguistics 2005*, Selected Papers from the 17th International Conference on Historical Linguistics, Madison, WI, 31 July-5 August 2005, ed. by Joseph C. Salmons & Shannon Dubenion-Smith, Amsterdam, 385-401.
Room, Adrian (1986), *Dictionary of True Etymologies*, London/New York.

Sanders, Ewoud (1993), *Eponiemen-woordenboek*, Amsterdam.
Sanders, Ewoud (1995), *Geoniemen-woordenboek*, Amsterdam.
Schele de Vere, M. (1872), *Americanisms. The English of the New World*, New York.
Schulte Nordholt, J.W. & Robert P. Swierenga (eds.) (1992), *A Bilateral Bicentennial. A History of Dutch-American Relations 1782-1982*, Amsterdam.
Shetter, William Z. (1957), "Brabants dialekt in Wisconsin", in: *Taal en Tongval* 9, 183-189.
Shetter, William Z. (1958), "A Final Word on Jersey Dutch", in: *American Speech* 33, 243-251.
Shorto, Russell (2004), *The Island at the Center of the World. The Epic Story of Dutch Manhattan and the Forgotten Colony That Shaped America*, New York. (Dutch translation: *Nieuw-Amsterdam. Eiland in het hart van de wereld*, Amsterdam 2004).
Sijs, Nicoline van der (1996), *Leenwoordenboek. De invloed van andere talen op het Nederlands*, Sdu, The Hague (2nd edition 2005).
Sijs, Nicoline van der (1998), *Geleend en uitgeleend. Nederlandse woorden in andere talen & andersom*, Amsterdam.
Sijs, Nicoline van der (2001), *Chronologisch woordenboek van het Nederlands. De ouderdom en herkomst van onze woorden en betekenissen*, Amsterdam.
Sijs, Nicoline van der (2006), *Klein uitleenwoordenboek*, The Hague.
Sijs, Nicoline van der & Roland Willemyns (2009), *Verhaal van het Nederlands.*

Twaalf eeuwen Nederlandse taal, Amsterdam.
Simpson, J.A. & E.S.C. Weiner (eds. in chief) (1989), *Oxford English Dictionary* 2nd edition, Oxford; 3rd edition online: http://dictionary.oed.com.
Smits, Caroline (1996), *Disintegration of Inflection: The Case of Iowa Dutch*, Amsterdam.
Smits, Caroline (2001), "Iowa Dutch Inflection: Translations versus Conversations", in: *Sociolinguistic and Psycholinguistic Perspectives on Maintenance and Loss of Minority Languages*, ed. by Tom Ammerlaan et al., 299-318.
Smits, Caroline (2002), "On the (Non-) Persistence of Dialect Features in American Dutch (2): The Case of Iowa Dutch", in: *Present-day Dialectology. Problems and Findings*, ed. by Jan Berns & Jaap van Marle, Berlin/NewYork 243-268.
Sonneck, O.G.T. (1909), *Report on "The Star-Spangled Banner","Hail Columbia" "America","Yankee Doodle"*, Washington.
Soukhanov, Anne (1995), *Word Watch: The Stories Behind the Words of Our Lives*, New York.
Stellingwerff, J. (1975), *Amsterdamse emigranten. Onbekende brieven uit de prairie* van Iowa 1846-1873, Amsterdam.
Stewart, George R. (1970), *A Concise Dictionary of American Place-Names*, Oxford.
Storms, James B.H. (1964), *A Jersey Dutch Vocabulary*, with illustrations by Joel Altshuler, Park Ridge, NJ.
Stott, Annette (1998), *Holland Mania: The Unknown Dutch Period in American Art and Culture*, New York. (Dutch translation: *Hollandgekte. De onbekende Nederlandse periode in de Amerikaanse kunst en cultuur*, 1998, Amsterdam.)
Stoutenburgh, John L. jr. (1960), *Dictionary of the American Indian*, New York.
Swierenga, Robert P. (1976), "Netherlanders in America", in: *The American and the Dutch*, The Hague, 24-28.
Swierenga, Robert P. (1992), "Exodus Netherlands, Promised Land America: Dutch Immigration and Settlement in the United States", in: Schulte Nordholt, J.W. & Robert P. Swierenga (eds.) (1992), 127-147.
Swierenga, Robert P. (2000), *Faith and Family. Dutch Immigration and Settlement in the United States, 1820-1920*, New York/ London.

Tauber, Gilbert (compiler), *Old Streets of New York. A Guide to Former Street Names in Manhattan*. http://www.oldstreets.com.
Thornton, R.H. (1912), *An American Glossary Being an Attempt to Illustrate Certain Americanisms upon Historical Principles*, Philadelphia/London.
Trigger, Bruce G. (ed.) (1978), *Handbook of North American Indians. Vol.15: Northeast*, Washington, D.C.
Tulloch, Sara (1992), *The Oxford Dictionary of New Words. A Popular Guide to Words in the News*, Oxford/New York.

Urban Dictionary, http://www.urbandictionary.com. (selections published in books compiled by Aaron Peckham)

Vande Kopple, William J. (1982), "Hendrik and Jipke Den Hollander and American English: 'De Dutch Most Furgit Us'", in: *Papers in Linguistics* 15, 139-162.
Van der Werf, Dorothy De Lano (1958), "Evidence of Old Holland in the Speech of Grand Rapids", in: *American Speech* 33, 301-304.
Veen, P.A.F. van & Nicoline van der Sijs (1997), *Etymologisch woordenboek. De herkomst van onze woorden*, Utrecht/ Antwerp.

Veltman, Peter (1940), "Dutch Survivals in Holland, Michigan", in: *American Speech* 15, 80-83.
Vermeule, C.C. (1928), "Raritan Valley, Its Discovery and Settlement", in: *Proceedings of the New Jersey Historical Society* 13, 3, 282-298.
Voort, J.H. van der (1894), *Hedendaagsche amerikanismen*, Gouda.
Vries, Jan W. de (1991), "Dutch Influence on American English and Indonesian", in: *The Berkeley Conference on Dutch Linguistics 1989. Issues and Controversies, Old and New*, ed. by Thomas F. Shannon & Johan P. Snapper, 85-96.

Walker, Jessica (2006), "Thomas Jefferson and the New American Language", in: *Trans, Internet journal for cultural sciences*, No. 16/2005. http://www.inst.at/trans/16Nr/03_2/walker16.htm.
Webber, Philip E. (1979), "'Pella Dutch': Mogelijkheden voor sociolinguïstisch onderzoek", in: *Taal en Tongval* 31, 83-84.
Webber, Philip E. (1980), "Nederlanders en Vlamingen in Iowa", in: *Ons Erfdeel* 23, 458-460.
Webber, Philip E. (1988), *Pella Dutch. The Portrait of a Language and Its Use in One of Iowa's Ethnic Communities*, Ames, Iowa.
Webster = *Webster's Third New International Dictionary of the English Language*. See entry for Gove.
Wentworth, Harold (1944), *American Dialect Dictionary*, New York.
Wentworth, Harold & Stuart Berg Flexner (1960), *Dictionary of American Slang*, London, etc.
White, Robert J. (1994), *An Avalanche of Anoraks*, New York.
Wilton, David (2004), *Word Myths. Debunking Linguistic Urban Legends*, New York.
Winkel, J. te (1896), "Het Nederlandsch in Noord-Amerika en Zuid-Afrika", in: *Vragen van den dag*, 337-362, 418-442, 483-505.
Woordenboek der Nederlandsche Taal (1882-2001), online: http://wnt.inl.nl.

List of illustrations

Preface

Chapter 1

Chapter 2

2.52 Sliding pond (source: *Voor 't Jonge Volkje*, compiled by I. and L. de Vries, Utrecht 1980, illustration from 1880-1900)
2.53 Hoople (source: *Kroniek van de Kempen*, Frans Hoppenbrouwers et al., Kempen Pers, Hapert, 1991)
2.54 Knicker, litho after a water color by the Belgian artist F. Charlet, titled "Spring in Holland" (source: *The Printing Art*, vol. 1, March-August 1903, Cambridge University Press)
2.55 Sinterklaas (source: *Sinterklaaslexicon* p. 268, reproduced from C. Singer, Santa Claus comes to America (1942))
2.56 Santa Claus in his American appearance (source: *Vignettes*, Parijs 2001)
2.57 Hooker (source: private collection)
2.58 Keel, detail of a painting by Kees Terlouw (source: *The Printing Art*, vol. 4 #5, Jan. 1905)
2.59 "Roller-skating for the first time" (source: *Voor 't Jonge Volkje*, compiled by I. and L. de Vries, Utrecht 1980, illustration from 1880-1900)
2.60 Skating couple (source: *Schaatsenrijden*, J. van Buttingha Wichers, The Hague 1888)
2.61 Sleigh (source: *Schaatsenrijden*, J. van Buttingha Wichers, The Hague 1888)
2.62 Seventeenth-century mutch (source: *Kleding en het AaBe ervan*, Tilburg 1953)
2.63 Wamus. Hugo de Groot wore this when he escaped in disguise in a book chest from Castle Loevestein in 1621. It is the typical attire of a bricklayer in those days (source: Atlas van Stolk, Rotterdam)
2.64 Bazoo, advertisement for Bell Company Telephones (source: *The Printing Art*, vol. 5, #4, June 1905)
2.65 Spook; drawn by Howard Chandler Christie; from: James Whitcomb Riley, "An olde sweetheart of mine", 1903 (source: *The Printing Art*, vol. 3, #4, June 1904)

Chapter 3

3.1 New Netherland with the most important Native American tribes and European settlements around 1650 (source: Frijhoff 1995: 716)
3.2 Mohawk Indians (source: engraving from David Pietersz. de Vries, *Korte historiael*, 1655: 156)
3.3 Ritual dance of the Native Americans (source: engraving from David Pietersz. de Vries, *Korte historiael*, 1655: 177)
3.4 A pipe-smoking Native American. In the ninetheenth century advertisements for tobacco often, especially in Great Britain, portrayed Native Americans (source: *Graphic ornaments*, Amsterdam 2007)
3.5 Jew's harp (source: detail from an engraving after the painting "Het zottenfeest" by Pieter Breughel the older)
3.6 A Mohawk, with villages in the background (source: Johannes Megapolensis, *Kort ontwerp*, 1644: 15)
3.7 The word *paper* is borrowed in two Amerindian languages. At the end of the nineteenth and the beginning of the twentieth century some American paper manufacturers gave their products names referring to the history of the Native Americans (source: *The Printing Art*, vol. 2 #3, Nov. 1903; advertisement for products of The Arnold Roberts Company)

Index to the American English words in chapter 2

Spelling variants are not included.